BRANDING LAW

A GUIDE TO THE LEGAL ISSUES IN BRAND MANAGEMENT

Ross D. Petty
PROFESSOR OF MARKETING LAW
BABSON COLLEGE

WEST ACADEMIC PUBLISHING

444 Cedar Street, Suite 700
St. Paul, MN 55101
1-877-888-1330

Printed in the United States of America

ISBN: 978-1-63460-477-2

Acknowledgments

Thanks to journals and, in some cases, co-authors listed below who have published earlier versions of material that now appears in this book:

After the Dot: Marketing Policy Issues with the New Generic Top Level Domain Names Program, 2015 Marketing and Public Policy Conference Proceedings (Stacey Menzel Baker and Marlys Mason, eds.) 38–42 (2015).

"Natural" Claims in Food Advertising: Policy Implications of Filling the Regulatory Void with Consumer Class Action Lawsuits, 34(1) *Journal of Public Policy & Marketing* 131–141 (Spring 2015).

International Advertising Law and Regulation: A Research Review and Agenda—The Devil Is in the Details in HANDBOOK OF INTERNATIONAL ADVERTISING RESEARCH, Hong Cheng ed. Chapter 20, 395–413 (Wiley-Blackwell 2014).

Coca-Cola Brand Protection Before WWII—It's the Real Thing, 4(2) *Journal of Historical Research in Marketing*, 224–244 (2012).

From Label to Trademark: The Legal Origins of the Concept of Brand Identity in 19th Century America, 4(1) *Journal of Historical Research in Marketing* 129–153 (2012).

The Evolution of Trademark Law and the Co-development of the Concept of Brand Marketing in the U.S. before 1946, 31(1) *Journal of Macromarketing* 85–99 (2011).

Marketing Tactics Discouraging Price Search: Deception and Competition (with Joan Lindsey-Mullikin), 64(1) *Journal of Business Research* 67–73 (2011).

Slogans that Both Promote and Identify the Brand—Using U.S. and E.U. Trademark Law to Protect Slogans from Imitation (with Susanna H.S. Leong and May O. Lwin), 29(3) *International Journal of Advertising* 473–500 (2010).

The Strategic Use of Legal Margins: How to Introduce an Extension of Someone Else's Brand in LEGAL STRATEGIES: HOW CORPORATIONS USE LAW TO IMPROVE PERFORMANCE, Antoine Masson and Mary J Shariff, eds. Chapter 15, 317–334 (Springer Publishing 2010).

Naming Names: Part Three—Safeguarding brand equity in the U.S. by developing a family of trademarks, 17(8) *Journal of Brand Management Special Issue on Brand Governance—Managing and Safeguarding Brand Equity* 561–567 (2010).

The Use of Dead Celebrities in Advertising and Marketing: Balancing Interests in the Right of Publicity (with Denver D'Rozario), 38(4) *Journal of Advertising* 39–51 (2009).

Covert Marketing Unmasked: A Legal and Regulatory Guide for Practices that Mask Marketing Messages, (with J. Craig Andrews), 27(1) *Journal of Public Policy & Marketing*, 7–18 (Spring 2008).

Naming Names: Trademark Strategy and Beyond: Part Two—Dealing with Rival Brand Names, 15(4) *Journal of Brand Management* 232–238 (March 2008).

Naming Names: Trademark Strategy and Beyond: Part One—Selecting a Brand Name, 15(3) *Journal of Brand Management*, 190–97 (Jan. 2008).

The Regulation of Practices that Promote Brand Interest: A 3 Cs Guide for Brand Managers, (with Joan Lindsey-Mullikin), 15(1) *Journal of Product & Brand Management* 23–36 (2006).

Marketing Law: Hit or Mislead—Secondary Brand Associations, 15(5) *Marketing Management* 44–48 (2006).

Advertising Law in the U.S. and E.U. 16(1) *Journal of Public Policy & Marketing* 2–13 (Spring 1997).

Advertising Challenges: A Strategic Framework and Current Review (with R. J. Kopp) 35(2) *Journal of Advertising Research* 41–55 (1995).

Introduction

The Inexorable Intertwining of Law and Brand Marketing

Even today, the American Marketing Association still defines a brand as:

> A name, term, design, symbol, or any other feature that identifies one seller's good or service as distinct from those of other sellers. The legal term for brand is trademark.

No brand manager today would limit the definition of brand to just being a trademark. Similarly, while most brand managers probably have some familiarity with trademark law, no one would argue that is the only law that brand managers need to know. The only insight offered by this simplistic definition of brand is that it correctly suggests that brand marketing is inexorably intertwined with the law and in fact enabled by the law.

For this reason, I developed an experimental MBA elective at Babson College entitled Branding Law and started work on this book that examines the legal issues crucial to brand management in ways I hope will be interesting and useful to brand managers. I try to focus on common tactics employed by brand marketers and offer sufficient examples that readers will get a sense of when their brand marketing tactics approach the line between legal and illegal. While I necessarily must include technical information, I prefer factual examples and conceptual models over quotes from judicial opinions. For example, instead of a legally technical discussion of trademark fair use, this book examines the strategic concept I call Judo Brand Diversion. While other books on trademark law for lay people have been published, this book goes beyond trademark law to cover other legal areas important for brand management such as advertising, consumer protection and even some antitrust and international trade law.

A Legally-Based Conceptualization of Brand Management

Today "brand" means much more than just one or more trademarks. Modern brands no longer necessarily identify the producer of goods or services, but rather they seek to establish a marketing identity or "brand personality" to serve as a platform for building customer relationships (Dawar 2004). The brand identity no longer is necessarily tied to the maker of the product (Drescher 1992). Strong brands have been shown to attract consumer attention, lead to favorable consumer evaluations, and engender consumer loyalty (Hoeffler and Keller 2003).

Despite this current emphasis on relationships, between brands and customers, branding is essentially a differentiation of a product or service offering—"Buy my brand not someone else's." Differentiation may occur based on product design, innovative attributes, superior performance, safety, reliability or durability. Differentiation may also occur based on the selling environment such as delivery, service warranty or other terms of sale. For the brand manager, differentiation may occur based on brand image or personality. Brand marketing accomplishes all these types of differentiation by creating a legally protect-able and customer-appealing identity for the product and brand's unique bundle of attributes.

In order to develop and sustain strong brands, the modern brand manager must be prepared to perform five tasks as illustrated by the figure on the opposite page in order to cultivate the brand identity/personality at the center of the diagram. Most brand management experts recognize that this often includes both a rational appeal based on product performance and attributes as well as an emotional attachment or liking of the brand. The first task (as numbered in the diagram) is the development of brand identifiers or elements that can both identify and to some degree position the brand in the minds of consumers. These elements need to be legally protectable against imitation by competitors as explained in the first part of this book. A related second task is often connecting the brand to various secondary associations. These elements include geographic indicators, component brands, certification marks and the use of celebrities. Each of these types of secondary brand associations has particular legal rules that are explained in part two of the book. Every brand manager must develop a program for communicating brand benefits both product-related and brand personality-related. Finally, the brand manager must promote trial and continued use and loyalty. One way to develop trial is to take advantage of trademark fair use, which as mentioned above is examined under the strategic concept of Judo Brand Diversion—taking advantage of the strength of some other brand. Finally, the book concludes with a chapter on particular legal issues of interest to large successful brands.

Five Phase Brand Management

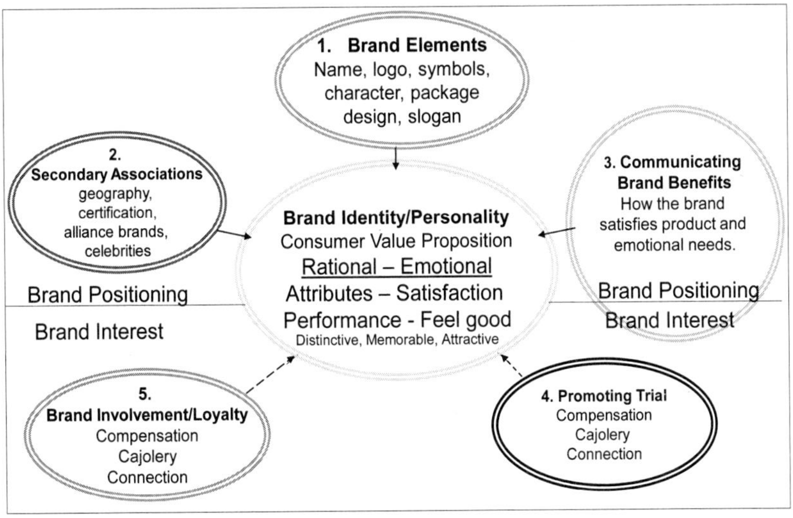

It should be noted that most brand experts suggest a complex model of brand equity that would substitute for the center figure of Brand Identity/Personality in this model. For example, Kevin Lane

Keller (2007) proposes a four-stage pyramid model of brand equity that starts at the base with developing a salient brand identity and rises up through two levels of increasing equity that involves both rational judgments and emotional feelings toward the brand. The top point of the brand pyramid is labeled resonance and occurs when brands obtain an intensely loyal relationship with their consumers. These complex models of strengthening brand equity over time are useful to brand managers who must decide what tactics are most appropriate for reaching the next level of the pyramid. However, the legal issues involved with the use of these tactics depend generally on the how the tactics are used, not the level of equity enjoyed by the brand. The simple model above is sufficient for purposes of examining legal issues.

Summary of Contents

Table of Contents

BRANDING LAW

A GUIDE TO THE LEGAL ISSUES IN BRAND MANAGEMENT

PART 1

The Foundations of Brand Protection—Trademark Law and Beyond

After discussing the historical development of brand marketing and trademark law, this part examines how trademark law can be used to protect various types of brand identifiers such as names and logos. It also analyzes various alternative forms of possible brand identifiers such as product configuration including color, sounds, scents and even slogans that might identify brands in the minds of consumers. Finally, it looks at other forms of law, including domain name assignment, that may protect the exclusive use of specific brand identifiers and in some cases product category labels.

CHAPTER 1

A History of Brand Marketing from the Legal Perspective

"You have to know the past to understand the present."

—Carl Sagan

This chapter examines the historical evolution of brand marketing in the U.S. and its connection to an evolving trademark law in order to provide context for modern legal developments and applications. Duguid (2009, pp. 3–4) states: "The history of modern brands is to a significant degree dependent on the history of trademarks" so let's look at both.

The use of marks or brands in trade dates back to ancient times. These marks were used administratively to keep track of what goods came from which merchants. By the middle ages, guild marks were used for that purpose as well as quality control and the use of counterfeit marks was illegal. Some ancient marks even may have been symbolic (e.g., white rabbit sewing needles in China), but there is no evidence that these products were promoted based on the brand. So while branding or marking goods is an ancient practice, brand marketing—the use of a brand identity to develop and promote a brand personality in order to sell branded goods appears to be a modern practice (Petty 2016).

It is difficult to tell exactly when brand marketing may have begun. As countries industrialized, large firms developed but often were named simply for the firm founders. If the firm name is then used to promote products, is this brand marketing or business celebrities attempting to promote what we today would call their personal brand? For example, McKendrick et al. (1982, p. 124) note that in England Wedgwood wrote to his then partner Thomas Bentley in 1773 that it was "absolutely necessary" that they mark their goods and that they "advertise the mark." He already had developed some business fame, so was he merely seeking to extend that fame through self-promotion? If subsequent advertising (and other promotion) focused on the brand identity evidenced by the Wedgwood & Bentley circular mark, this would appear to be brand marketing even though the brand identifier consists merely of personal names written within a circle. Alternatively, Wedgwood could have been insisting that the mark be advertised only to educate consumers to avoid counterfeits. This still would be promotion of the brand identifier but not brand marketing focused on an abstract brand personality at least beyond genuineness.

While today many brands are still based on founder names, these brands often develop their own personalities and equity distinct from that of the founders. Henry Ford founded the Ford Motor Company and enjoyed a fair degree of business celebrity during his lifetime, but today the Ford brand contains multiple meanings and connections beyond merely being Henry Ford's company. So one question worth exploring within the history of brand marketing is when did brand names shift from founders' names to words that related to the product or even words that had no prior connection or meaning with the product beyond what marketing and promotion would provide?

To examine U.S. brand marketing history, we shall examine four historical eras: (1) the early 18th century when marketers first sought brand identity protection; (2) the post-Civil War era where patent medicines and tobacco products led the way into brand marketing, federal trademark registration was established, and technical trademarks were distinguished from trade names leading to brand identity; (3) 1905–1945 when the concept of trademark advertising developed the modern concepts of brand equity and brand marketing and (4) 1946 to the present when expansions in trademark protection led to expansions in brand marketing including trademark protection for multiple brand identifiers, brand extensions and eventual explicit recognition of brand management and strategy in the marketing literature.

A. PRE-CIVIL WAR BRAND IDENTITY PROTECTION EFFORTS

By the founding of the United States, the use of small administrative marks in trade had become common. George Washington registered his mark "G. Washington" for flour with a Fairfax, Virginia court in 1772. Nearly 50 years later a New York court decided the first trade name lawsuit. It held that the name "The New York National Advocate" was not confusingly similar to "The National Advocate" for newspapers both located in New York (Trademark Timeline 1992). The first U.S. case to condemn the false "passing off" of one product for another involved a medicine made by an unknown pharmacist but sold as a "Thomsonian Medicine." This was held to be improperly fraudulent so long as the latter name had not become a generic indicator of a type of medicine (*Thomson v. Winchester* 1837). The law condemned such fraudulent diversions of trade which typically were deliberate (McKenna 2007) but there are only a handful of reported cases before 1850.

Laird (1998, p. 17) suggests that in the early 1800s, U.S. consumers selected items for purchase based on inspection and merchant reputations rather than by brand name. Nevertheless as this began to change, marketers found value in product identities (brand) and began to seek ways to prevent unauthorized imitation. The first effort seems to be registering product labels as copyrights in local federal courts that started at least by the late 1830s (Petty 2012a, pp. 132–135). Attempts to register product labels as books, engravings or prints suggest that marketers sought exclusivity for their product labels. Many of these labels contained a pictorial element either of the product or person or other sign. However, there appear to be few court cases accusing competitor labels of copyright infringement. Perhaps, the filing itself was sufficient to provide notice not to copy.

In 1848 when courts began denying copyright protection to merely descriptive product labels, marketers became worried. They next turned to design patents first authorized in 1842 to protect ornamental (rather functional) aspects of product design. Marketers continued to seek copyright registrations but starting in 1855, they also sought to register labels and bottle designs as design patents Petty (2012a, p. 139). Such "Trade Mark Designs" could include a bottle or other unique packaging as well as labels so long as the product name was not in "ordinary type." Unlike copyrights that were registered in local federal courts, design patents were registered with the federal Patent Office, so that when trademark registration was authorized in 1870, the office stopped accepting trademark design patent registrations. Petty (2012a, p. 140) notes that from 1861 through 1870, trademark design patent registrations consistently exceeded federal trademark/passing off court cases.

Thus, during this time marketers wanted some ability to invest in developing their own particular products without fear of being "ripped off" (as we would say today) by counterfeiters seeking to free ride on their efforts. While it is clear they were attempting to cultivate protectable brand identities, it is less clear the degree to which they promoted the brand identity itself (brand marketing) as opposed to simply protecting the brand identity as a source of the genuine product.

B. THE LATE 1800S—EXPANDING BRAND IDENTITY PROTECTION WITH TRADEMARK REGISTRATION

Despite this evidence of early interest in brand identity protection through copyright and design patent registrations and occasional court actions, business historians tend to argue that brand marketing did not develop in the U.S. until the post-Civil War industrialization. Jones (1986) suggests that brands evolved as further protection for patent holders. Process patents that improved the consistency and quality of manufactured items needed brands to assure consumers that they could consistently identify these high quality items. Product patents provided a short term monopoly in new products such as the safety razor, but forward thinking marketers knew they need to develop the brand before the patent expiration and subsequent competition.

Strasser (1989) generally agrees with this analysis but adds that patented products and methods of factory production were aided in the development of modern national brands by national consumer product distribution systems based on railroads such as parcel post in 1912, color printing techniques, and the development of the "new media"—magazines that allowed brands to be connected with particular lifestyles and personalities. Furthermore, the country was becoming increasingly urban and urban factory workers purchased more goods rather than self-produce them as farmers tended to do.

Goodrum & Dalrymple (1990) attribute the start of modern branding to patent medicines in the 1800s that accounted for roughly half of all advertising after the Civil War. In fact, such medicines were routinely distributed to union soldiers during the war which added to their fame. Laird (1998) notes that patent medicines were the largest group of advertisers by 1870. Patent medicines were sold under a trade name, typically with a logo or slogan and with distinctive packaging. Patent medicines often used symbols of re-assurance such as angels, doctors and grandmothers, symbols of power or symbols of exotic origin (Laird 1998, pp. 16–18). This approach gradually expanded to other goods outside of patent medicines including some brands that are still well known today: Borden's Eagle Brand Condensed Milk—1866, Campbell's Soup—1869, Stetson hats—1866, Vaseline—1870, Pillsbury—1873, Levi Strauss overalls—1873.

Before federal trademark registration was finally established in 1870, the states were active in attempting to meet marketer demands for legal protection from imitation. The first efforts were by anti-counterfeiting statutes (for stamps, labels, wrappers and eventually trademarks) beginning with New York in 1845 and other eastern states in the next five years (Petty 2012a, pp. 137–138). It is not clear how much enforcement occurred under these laws. This effort was followed by state trademark registration schemes starting with California in 1863. Contrary to the story that national industrialization stimulated the demand for trademark registration in the U.S., California and other early registration states were primarily agricultural. Of the 151 marks registered in California during the first decade of registration. 83% were from small companies in the medicine, food, drink, alcohol, tobacco and cosmetic industries (Duguid 2013, pp. 588–590).

By the end of 1870, 121 marks were federally registered and medicines were only the third most common category: 21 registrations were for tobacco or snuff; 10 for whisky or liquor; 9 for medicines; 6 for soaps and other cleaners; 5 for fertilizers; 4 for brooms, dry and other types of goods, and white lead; 3 for metal and metal tubing, bitters, burning fluids, various foods, and various powders. Even items like steam governors, sewing machines, wagon axles and wheels and watches received trademarks in this first year (Commissioner of Patents 1870, pp. 260–261). Thus the interest in trademarks seemed to span across industries including consumer products but also some durable goods.

The federal trademark registration statute and its 1876 amendment were declared unconstitutional in 1879 for being improperly based on the patent and copyright clause of the Constitution (*Trade-Mark Cases* 1879). At this point some 8000 marks had been registered (Wilkins 1992). As more companies set up national brands, pressure continued on the government to enact trademark laws. In 1881, a new federal statute was enacted that authorized registration only for trademarks used in foreign commerce (or in commerce with Indian tribes). In 1883, the Paris Convention for the Protection of Industrial Property (including trademarks) was signed by 11 countries. However, the 1881 statute did not address interstate commerce. Indeed in 1903, the U.S. Supreme Court held that federal courts lacked jurisdiction to enjoin the use of a trademark unless it was used in foreign commerce (*Warner v. Searle & Hereth Co.* 1903).

Marketers and courts also worked on the development of trademark doctrine during this period. Courts began to distinguish technical trademarks from trade names. Trade names identified the source of products, but did so with descriptive (e.g., company founder or location) names. Such names were only protected when intentional imitation by competitors caused consumers to be confused about product source. Such lawsuits were based in fraud and typically required proof of the intent of the second user to confuse consumers (*Amoskeag Mfg. Co. v. Spear* 1837; *Lawrence Mfg. Co. v. Tennessee Mfg. Co.* 1891). Some court decisions allowed an innocent second adopter to use the same descriptive name as long as the source of the product was clearly identified and distinguished from the competitor who had first used that descriptive name (Handler and Pickett 1930).

Room (1998) looks at brand names of leading American advertisers in the 1890s and develops the following categories: personal names, place names, descriptive names (e.g., Shredded Wheat or 57 for Heinz's variety of products)—these would clearly be trade names, but not technical trademarks, good association names (e.g., Sunlight soap), status names (e.g., Monarch bicycles), invented scientific names (e.g., Cuticura Soap), and artificial names (e.g., Kodak). These latter categories would be eligible for technical trademark registration and protection. They were protected from trademark infringement by primarily focusing on the similarity of the imitation mark with that of the original mark when used on products in the same industry rather than on the imitator's intent and whether consumers were diverted from purchasing the brand they intended to buy (McKenna 2007). As the Supreme Court noted: "If a plaintiff has the absolute right to the use of a particular word or words as a trade-mark, then, if an infringement is shown, the wrongful or fraudulent intent is presumed . . ." (*Elgin National Watch Co. v. Illinois Watch Case Co.* 1901, 674). Despite the apparent breadth of this statement, it is important to remember that at that time infringement was limited only to other uses in the same industry.

The Supreme Court also recognized that technical trademarks were a form of property based on use in commerce (*Trade-Mark Cases* 1879). This theory was consistent with the natural rights theory of law that was popular at the time and courts sought to grant property rights to those who created property through their own efforts (McKenna 2007). So for example, in a well-publicized court decision, Nabisco was recognized as having a valid trademark, Uneeda Biscuit, and it received an injunction against use of the trademark and similar packaging by a competitor selling Iwanta Biscuit (*National Biscuit Co. v. Baker* 1899). Thus, technical trademarks, by creating what modern brand strategists would call a brand identity, established a platform for developing relationships with consumers (Dawar 2004).

C. 1905–1945: TRADEMARK LAW ENABLES THE PROMOTION OF BRAND IDENTITY TO CREATE BRAND EQUITY

The 1903 *Warner* decision led to enactment of a new trademark statute in 1905. It provided for federal registration of (technical) trademarks that had been used in interstate commerce for more than ten years. A special provision also allowed the registration of any mark used exclusively in commerce for ten years prior to the enactment of the act, even if descriptive, but descriptive marks could not otherwise be registered.

Once registered federally, these marks were presumed valid throughout the country so the courts no longer allowed innocent second users in distinct geographic markets to use the same trademarked name. This change recognized the growing importance of national brands and brands that wanted to be national in scope. Instead of lasting only 30 years, trademarks would now last 20 years but could be renewed indefinitely (Petty 2011). Strasser (1989, p. 45) states that pent up demand led to over 10,000 applications for trademark registrations to be filed during the first year. It also seems likely that many of these applicants also realized that this would be the only time that descriptive trade names in use for more than ten years could be registered as trademarks. The new law also eliminated intent to prove infringement but infringement was limited to use of an identical or confusingly similar mark on "merchandise of the same descriptive qualities" as those for which the original mark was registered.

The legal development of technical trademark protection as distinct from, and more easily proven than, passing off is important for the history of brand marketing because it encouraged businesses to switch from the traditional practice of identifying products solely by company name. Companies often took the name of their location or the personal name(s) of the company founder(s). Since other companies in the same location or with founders of the same name also were entitled to use such trade names, brands marketed under such names were less likely to be distinctly identified in the minds of consumers. Geographic names could only be registered if they had proven secondary meaning and were arbitrary for the product, e.g., Vienna bread (*Fleischman v. Shuckmann*, 1881). Secondary meaning had developed as a judicial concept that would allow brand marketers to earn the right through extensive advertising and promotion of exclusive use of a particular descriptive name in the sale of their particular type of goods. This right was limited to allow others to use that same description so long as consumers are not confused about the source of the other products (Lane 1909).

However, there were clear limitations on the registration of other types of trademarks. Names or slogans that merely described product attributes could not be registered. Slogans could not be registered because they were considered advertisements rather than trademarks that had to be affixed to the product. Similarly, products themselves, packages and particular colors were not considered trademarks because they were not marks affixed to products (Thompson 1911).

Marketers and others recognized the additional value of technical trademarks over descriptive trade names during this second period of trademark law and brand marketing development. At some point in the early 1900s J. Walter Thompson published an advertisement explaining the value of "trademark advertising." The point of the ad was straightforward: advertise your trademark directly to consumers and they will request your product by name from retailers. The advertiser will no longer be dependent on jobbers or retailers for brand promotion. Direct-to-consumer advertising was not a new concept, but by tying advertising to the trademark, J. Walter Thompson was explicitly promoting brand advertising.

This one page trade advertisement was soon followed by books about the use of trademarks to promote and advertise products. For example, Acheson (1917, p. 25) took this simple message one step further claiming that "continuous and properly pitched advertising made it [the trademark] such a part of the average purchaser's consciousness that it has become habitual to demand it . . . " At this point advertising agencies, attorneys and other sorts of marketing experts began offering their services to businesses. Consistent with the legal distinction, the message of these experts was clear—develop a technical trademark for your product. In other words, develop an identifier of the brand for consumers to rely upon rather than having them rely on the company name as certifying the source (and quality) of the product.

Indeed Buck (1916) extensively discusses the importance of having both a name and a unique symbol mark to concisely and distinctively identify the brand for consumers. Such trademarks readily cause consumers to recall brand impressions and allow the marketer to communicate "the one all-important point concerning his product" (Buck 1916, p. 61). Thus the legal recognition of property rights in technical trademarks led to those marks being used to communicate the brand identity rather than the source of the product. Modern brand strategists have recognized the importance of this distinction (Drescher 1992).

Trademarks as identifiers of brand identity were recognized as intangible assets whose value could be increased over time through advertising and promotion. Acheson (1917, p. 9) asserts "There is no more valuable and permanent property—if insured by continued publicity—than the trade mark of a staple commodity which has been well standardized by years of consistent advertising." Royal brand baking powder's goodwill in 1905 was valued at $5 million—a million dollars per letter. Three years later another advertising man estimated that "At least fifty percent of advertising being done today is for the purpose of creating property in trademarks" (Pope 1983, pp. 68–69). In less than a decade Coca-Cola and Nabisco for its Uneeda brand were claiming similar valuations for their trademarks (Strasser 1989, p. 47). Thus the concept of what today would be called brand equity became recognized during this period.

Behavioral research conducted during this time period also helped establish the intrinsic value of well-known brands. The very first volume of the *Journal of Applied Psychology* included an article on consumer brand associations with common products (Geissler 1917). A book examining the relative consumer familiarity with various brands was published six years later (Hotchkiss and Franken 1923).

Trademark litigation to ensure exclusive rights to brand identifiers was commonplace in this era. By 1915, Nabisco could report that in the wake of its 1899 court victory against Iwanta Biscuit, it had successfully stopped 13 imitative products with lawsuits and caused another 882 imitative marks to be abandoned (Strasser 1989, pp. 45, 49).

Some of those imitations and they year they were enjoined are illustrated below.

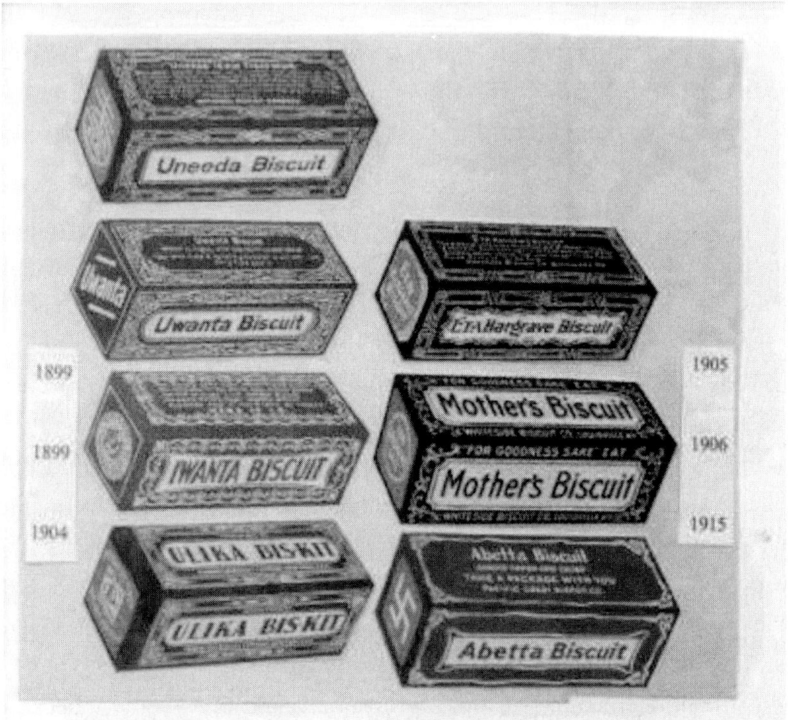

Similarly by 1926, Coca-Cola was bragging that it had driven 7000 imitators into the "copy cat's graveyard" (Johnson 1926, cited in Tedlow 1990, p. 391). The company's first volume of legal decisions (all but one in its favor) issued in 1923 contain about 70 opinions against bottlers, about 45 decrees against retailers for substituting another beverage when Coca-Cola was ordered and over 20 successful oppositions before the U.S. Patent and Trademark Office. The vast majority of these cases were unopposed or settled, sometimes by injunction in order to avoid paying any damages. Several of the decrees against retailers involved a substitution beverage (e.g., Gayola Cola) where the bottler of the beverage also was sued (Coca-Cola Co. 1923). Therefore, it is difficult to tell how much hyperbole was built into the 7000 number of copycats. There is little doubt that attorneys for Coca-

Cola were quite busy during this period (Petty, 2012b). Because of their widespread use and growing trademark law enforcement, the period of 1915–1929 has been called the "Golden Age" of manufacturer brands on consumer products (Low and Fullerton 1994, p. 177).

Finally as Low and Fullerton (1994) discuss, this period of proliferating brands within both the marketplace and single companies saw the management of those brands change hands from top level managers before the turn of the century to functional managers in charge of advertising, sales etc. These professional marketing managers and the companies that employed them were not satisfied with the legal status quo. They sought protection of descriptive names as trademarks and the expansion of trademark protection to cover uses that were not directly competitive.

In 1914, the Supreme Court carefully reviewed the legislative history of the 1905 Act and affirmed that descriptive trade names could be registered as trademarks if they had been used exclusively in interstate commerce for at least ten years before the passage of the Act (*Thaddeus Davids Co. v. Davids Man. Co.* 1914). Statutory amendments in 1920 extended this policy further by allowing registration of any descriptive name that could be proved to have secondary meaning. In addition, registration that previously could be perpetual by renewal was now perpetual unless cancelled.

With this expansion of trademark law to cover descriptive names that had acquired secondary meaning, trademark law appeared reasonably content to simply let marketers promote their brands through the use of trademarks that were protected from close imitation by competitors. When innovative companies attempted to claim trademark protection for the names of products whose patents had expired, courts were not sympathetic because the alleged trademarks were actually generic descriptions of the product category (e.g., shredded wheat and cellophane: *Kellogg Co. v. National Biscuit Co.* 1938; *Dupont Cellophane Co. v. Waxed Products Co.* 1936). So even though marketers recognized the value of trademarks in identifying brands, the courts still looked to traditional source identification—secondary meaning—to determine whether a name qualified as a trademark or merely described a type of product.

However, Frank Schecter (1927) in a still famous Harvard Law Review article argued that the old legal source identification standard was obsolete. Rather he argued that while the use of the same mark would indicate products from the same source, consumers may not know and may not even care the specific identity of the source. They only know they like the brand. He further stated:

> . . . today the trademark is not merely the symbol of good will but often the most effective agent for the creation of good will . . . The mark actually *sells* the goods. And, self-evidently, the more distinctive the mark, the more effective is its selling power (Schecter 1927, p. 819) (emphasis in the original).

Schecter (1927, p. 825) argued that in cases of trademark use on non-competing products, while there is no trade diversion from the trademark owner, there would be "a gradual whittling away or dispersion of the identity and hold upon the public mind of the mark." He argued that protection against such trademark dilution should be provided for truly unique (arbitrary, coined or fanciful) marks, but not for descriptive marks.

Schecter's proposal had only limited support from past cases. For example, Schecter cited the 1917 Second Circuit decision finding infringement of the Aunt Jemima mark for self-rising flour when another firm started using the identical mark for the complementary product of pancake syrup (*Aunt Jemima Mills Co. v. Rigney & Co.* 1917). The court justified its decision by using the language of the 1905 statute that permitted protection against use by others on goods with the "same descriptive properties." In that case both were food products. By 1925, another decision found infringement between Rolls Royce cars and airplanes and Rolls Royce radio tubes both having the descriptive property of electricity (*Wall v. Rolls Royce of America, Inc.* 1925). Similarly, in 1919, the USPTO denied trademark registration for Coca-Cola gum when the gum company failed to answer Coca-Cola's objection (Coca-Cola Co. 1923, pp. 560–61). In 1927, Coca-Cola also settled with a company using the name Coca-Cola for a bar written in the same script type as the Coca-Cola trademark (Coca-Cola Co. 1939, pp. 780–783).

After Schecter's article appeared, a couple of courts found liability for the use of Tiffany by a motion picture company rather than the original jewelry company and Yale as a trademark for flashlights as opposed to the original lock and key brand (*Tiffany & Co. v. Tiffany Productions, Inc.* 1933; *Yale Electric Corp. v. Robertson* 1928). However, Schecter's proposals were only followed in a small number of cases and only a few states adopted trademark statutes prohibiting dilution.

Another effort to expand trademark law at this time involved licensing. Under traditional trademark law, licensing another firm to use your trademark was prohibited because consumers associated the mark with the original source of the goods. They would be misled when a second source starting selling goods using the same trademark. Trademark owners found this prohibition to be too constraining and so beginning in the 1930s, some courts attempted to allow licensing with assurances of quality control (e.g., *Finchley, Inc. v. George Hess Co., Inc.* 1938).

D. 1946–PRESENT: THE EXPANSION OF TRADEMARK LAW'S PROTECTION OF BRAND IDENTITY

In 1946, the modern U.S. Trademark statute, the Lanham Act, was enacted. By this point some 300,000 marks had been federally registered under the prior statutes (Wilkins 1992, p. 77). The 1946 Lanham Act adopted the policy of judicial decisions that allowed trademark licensing with quality control, but rejected Schecter's proposal to prohibit trademark dilution by non-competing goods. The act also generally expanded trademark law rejecting arguments by Chamberlin (1933) that trademarks led to monopolistic competition. His work had influenced some courts to narrow trademark protection for non-competing goods and hold more marks descriptive or generic (McClure 1979, p. 331).

The Lanham Act also continued to allow, but not require, federal registration for marks already being used in interstate commerce. Common law protection against passing off would still apply to unregistered marks. Under this act, trademark registration may still last for perpetuity, but the system returned to one of periodic renewal, this time every ten years. The renewal requirement not only creates an ongoing revenue stream for the USPTO, but allows abandoned marks to be identified, since few who abandon marks actually notify the USPTO and request cancellation.

As Low and Fullerton (1994) document, the concept of product or brand managers originated in 1930 but did not take off until after World War II. They report that by 1967 most large consumer packaged goods companies had brand managers. Also during this time, most advertising agencies gave up their role as "counselors and almost-equal partners in brand management" to focus on media and creative work

(Low and Fullerton 1994, p.182). With a proliferation of brands at many companies, the brand manager could focus on the needs of a particular brand in ways that a functional manager such as an advertising manager could not. There were simply too many brands in many firms for functional managers to cover. The focus of brand managers on the needs of protecting their particular brands appears related to the three areas of trademark law expansion: obtaining trademark protection for additional brand attributes that identify the brand, protecting those brand identifiers against encroachments even by non-competing products and licensing those brand identifiers in some cases to non-competing products in order to increase total brand revenue and enhance brand equity. Each of these three areas will be discussed in turn.

I. Expanding the Types of Legally Protectable Brand Identifiers

The 1946 Lanham Act allowed the registration of service marks expanding trademark protection beyond products and further reducing the traditional requirement that marks be affixed on goods in order to be protected. The 1905 Act arguably slightly weakened the affixation requirement by defining infringement to include affixation to signs and prints in addition to goods and packaging, but courts only reluctantly expanded affixation to advertising. The Lanham Act defined infringement to cover in use in commerce of an imitation of a registered mark in connection with the sale, offering for sale, distribution or advertising for any goods or services (Barrett 2006, pp. 380–383). This broader language eventually allowed for trademark protection to other brand identifiers beyond names, logos, and characters.

In 1950, the U.S. Patent and Trademark Office (USPTO) registered its first sensory trademark—the NBC three chime sound mark. This was followed in 1952 by registration of the first slogan, "The Fate of a Fabric Hangs by a Thread," for a particular brand of rayon thread. This slogan was registered because it was found to be arbitrary rather than descriptive. After that, slogans that had double meanings, one of which was not descriptive were routinely registered. It was not until 1970 that a court upheld the trademark registration of Clairol's descriptive but famous slogan: "Hair Color So Natural Only Her Hairdresser Knows for Sure" because evidence demonstrated that consumers identified the slogan with the Clairol brand (Grover 1991). Copywriter Rosser Reeves gained fame at this time for several advertising campaigns that used slogans to capture a brand's unique selling proposition (Reeves 1961).

The U.S. registered its first motion mark in 1957—a spinning coin. Since then other motion marks have included the famous MGM lion that both moves and roars. Both of these marks include sound and motion (Matty 2006). This early expansion continued in 1958 when the USPTO finally allowed packaging to be registered on the Principal Register to receive full trademark protection. In fact, the famous "contour" Coca-Cola bottle was registered in 1960 (U.S. Reg. No. 696,147). The reluctance to register packaging for full protection is somewhat ironic since many early passing off decisions focused on imitation of both the product name and package.

A second period of expansion of types of permissible trademarks started in 1974 when a court of appeals approved registration of a non-functional product design. In 1981, the Fifth Circuit Court of Appeals held that some trade dress, like other trademarks, could be inherently distinctive so for the first time proof of secondary meaning was not required (*Chevron Chemical Co. Inc. v. Voluntary Purchasing Groups Inc.* 1981). Some firms also sought trademark protection for the product or package color aspect of trade dress. In 1985, a court of appeals affirmed the registration of pink for insulation by Owens Corning (*In re Owens Corning Fiberglass Corp.* 1985). Owens Corning colored its home insulation pink and promoted it using the Pink Panther cartoon character. However, other appellate courts disagreed as to whether registration was proper. The Supreme Court settled this issue in favor of registration for non-functional distinctive colors if they identify a particular brand in the minds of consumers in 1995 (*Qualitex Co. v. Jacobson Products Co., Inc.* 1995).

Traditionally, most courts agreed that trade dress could not be inherently distinctive and must be proven to identify a particular brand in the minds of consumers in order to be protected. In 1992, the U.S. Supreme Court agreed with the Fifth Circuit that trade dress could be inherently distinctive and therefore protected the décor of a Mexican restaurant under trademark law without a showing of secondary meaning in the minds of consumers (*Two Pesos, Inc. v. Taco Cabana, Inc.* 1992). It noted that the protections of the Lanham Act apply with equal force to trademark and unregistered trade dress infringement through section 43. Later, the Court retreated somewhat from this expansive position and clarified that product configuration trade dress, such as the product shape or color, may not be inherently distinctive under law and must be proven to have secondary meaning in the minds of consumers. Only packaging trade dress may be inherently distinctive (*Wal-Mart Stores, Inc. v. Samara Brothers Inc.* 2000).

At least one commentator has decried the "explosion" of product configuration trademark cases that started in the 1980s (Lemley 1999). It remains to be seen whether the Supreme Court's decision in *TrafFix Devices, Inc. v. Marketing Displays, Inc.* (2004), will reign in efforts of brand owners to claim that their product configuration identifies the brand in the minds of consumers. In *TrafFix*, the Court held that expired utility patents on product configuration created a strong presumption that the product configuration was functional and could not be protected under trademark law. This means that brand managers must now consider carefully whether they should apply for a patent to product design features that have limited functionality or whether they should promote those features as brand identifiers and hope they are protected under trademark law.

During the debate on trade dress including packaging and non-functional product design, the USPTO quietly allowed registration of an olfactory sensory mark. Products such as perfumes or laundry detergents that have a scent as part of their function could not register the scents. But registration was allowed for a brand of embroidery thread, once the brand owner proved that the fragrance, reminiscent of plumeria blossoms, identified the source of the product for embroidery thread purchasers (*In re Clarke* 1990).

The most recent expansion of coverage to a new type of mark occurred with the advent of electronically-assisted commerce and the use of vanity telephone numbers and internet domain names. Domain names, as such, are registered with companies that are completely independent of the USPTO, just as phone numbers are assigned by a telephone company. Vanity phone numbers and domain names, unless generic or purely descriptive (e.g., patents.com), also may be registered or protected as trademarks, e.g., "1–800–SLEEPY'S" (U.S. Reg. No. 1,946,855). The U.S. also has condemned cybersquatting, the bad faith registration or selling of a domain name that is identical or confusingly similar to a registered trademark or dilutive of a famous trademark. Early case law held that the mere registration of a trademarked word or phrase as a domain name did not constitute commercial use of the mark, so that Federal trademark law did not apply (*Academy of Motion Picture Arts & Sciences v. Network Solutions, Inc.* 1997). However, later trademark decisions (*Panavision Int'l v. Toeppen*, 1998; *1–800 Contacts, Inc. v. WhenU.com* 2003) and the 1999 amendments to the Lanham Act condemn this practice for trademarks, but not for generic terms. Domain names and cybersquatting are discussed in Chapter Six.

II. Restricting Trademark Use by Non-Competitors

The courts did not develop a consistent method of analysis for cross-product infringement until the Second Circuit adopted the so called *Polaroid* factors that were first proposed in the 1938 Restatement of Torts (*Polaroid Corp. v. Polaraid Electronics, Corp.* 1961):

- **Strength of the first (senior) user's mark**—including both inherent and acquired strength. As discussed under brand names below, stronger marks are entitled to broader protection.
- **Similarity of the marks**—marks may look or sound similar or have similar meanings or connotations.
- **Proximity of goods & likelihood of brand extension**—confusion is more likely if the goods are similar or competing or related in such a way to suggest a brand extension. Courts also look at whether the goods are sold in similar channels.
- **Junior user's intent**—was the mark adopted in good faith after a careful search by the second (junior) user?
- **Evidence of actual confusion**—although not required, evidence that consumers were actually confused about source or sponsorship is relevant.
- **Care of buyers**—expert buyers may be less likely to be confused than casual consumers.
- **Quality of junior user's goods**—courts disagree on whether a significant disparity in quality between the senior and junior user's goods make harm from confusion more likely or make the probability of confusion less likely.

By explicitly examining the proximity of goods and often similarity of channels of distribution, courts acknowledge that trademark use on non-competing goods, particularly if somewhat related to the type of goods that originally used the trademark, could be challenged. But courts tempered this expansion by also examining the sophistication of consumers and looking for evidence of actual confusion or intent to confuse. The Second Circuit's *Polaroid* factors would soon imitated with some variation by the other Circuits. They allowed courts to condemn some uses of trademarks on non-competing goods, but not all such uses.

In 1995, Congress finally amended the Lanham Act to cover dilution for famous trademarks. By that time only 16 court decisions had granted dilution relief under state statutes enacted after Schecter's 1927 article. However federal courts also were not sympathetic to the concept in most cases. In the first year of judicial enforcement of the new provision, relief was granted in a respectable half of all decided dilution cases. This level of dilution protection slipped to less than twenty percent by 2003 when the Supreme Court ruled on its first trademark dilution case (Long 2006).

The Court in *Moseley v. V. Secret Catalogue, Inc.* (2003) followed the language of the statute to hold that actual dilution must be proven rather than the easier likelihood of dilution standard specified in most state statutes. The Court did not indicate how to prove actual dilution but made it clear that proving the existence of a mere association between the newer trademark and its famous predecessor mark was not sufficient. Dissatisfaction with this ruling by brand owners led to the passage of the Trademark Dilution Revision Act of 2006 that changed the statute so that plaintiffs only had to prove a likelihood of dilution by blurring or tarnishment rather than actual dilution.

III. Trademark Licensing to Third Parties

This expansion of protection to cover dissimilar goods combined with the 1946 Lanham Act's allowance of licensing with quality control combined to stimulate growth of the merchandise licensing industry allowing greater revenue from a brand's equity. Licensing started in the 1930s with Shirley Temple dolls and Mickey Mouse merchandise. Mickey was protected by copyright law, but its licensing did not take off until the 1950s, after the change in trademark law. Two major areas of development started the current licensing boom. Between 1977 and 1982, the retail sales of STAR WARS merchandise based on the first two movies are estimated to exceed $1.5 billion. This stimulated the growth of other merchandising efforts in the toy and children's goods industries (Battersby and Grimes 1986). Two court decisions in 1975 started the trend toward protection of sports team merchandise. Despite some initial controversy, by 1982 most courts had decided trademark owners needed some evidence to prove likely confusion of source, sponsorship or endorsement (*National Football League Properties, Inc. v. Wichita Falls Sportswear, Inc.* 1982; *University of Pittsburgh v. Champion Products, Inc.* 1982). Such evidence was not difficult to obtain from appropriate consumer surveys (Dogan and Lemley 2005).

In 1988, the trademark statute was amended to give further protection to the practice of licensing. Instead of merely condemning confusion as to the source or origin of a product, the new language condemned confusion as to the affiliation, connection of association of product sources as well as confusion concerning the origin, sponsorship or approval of a product. According to the Licensing Industry Merchandisers' Association total licensing revenue in 2004 was about $5.8 billion. Professional sports and collegiate licensing revenue amounted to $1 billion and entertainment licensing revenue was another $2.5 billion.

These changes also helped McDonald's to extent its family of trademarks into licensing including such areas as formerly unlicensed uses of McClass, McJobs and McShuttle. By 1995, it also licensed McClip" for hair-cutting services; "McCash" for financial services; "McD" for cleaning products; "McBucks" for redeemable certificates; "McBunny" for toys; "McMatch" for games; "McShirt" for clothing; "McGift Shop" for retail store services; "McHat" for hats; "McLots of Fun" for stage productions; "McMasters" for recruiting elderly employees; and "McBear" for stuffed toys. "McKids" was licensed for children's clothing sold at Sears's retail stores (*McDonald's Corp. v. John L. McClain* 1995).

Allowing trademark licensing with quality control also provided the legal basis for modern business method franchising as used by McDonald's and many other firms. The franchisor develops both its trademarked brand identity and a business format that provides for quality control and licenses both to franchisees. This saves the franchisor from the expense of opening all of its own retail outlets and allows franchisees to reduce risk by investing in a proven brand and business format rather than trying to develop their own brand and format.

Fast food and other road side services were stimulated to franchise with the growth of the inter-state highway system in the 1950s. In 1950, only about 100 companies offered business format franchises. That number grew to about 900 in 1960 with an estimated 200,000 outlets. According to a survey conducted for the International Franchise Association's Educational Foundation, as of 2001, there were more than 767,483 franchise-related businesses (including franchisor owned), generating over 9 million jobs (equivalent employment of all manufacturers of durable goods, such as computers, cars, trucks, planes, communications equipment, primary metals, wood products, and instruments), meeting a $229.1 billion payroll, and producing $624.6 billion of output. The same survey found that franchised businesses in 2001 accounted for 7.4 percent of all private-sector jobs, 5.0 percent of all private sector payrolls, and 3.9 percent of all private sector output (Herman 2003).

For the outright sale (assignment) of the trademark, courts up until 1962 required the sale of assets needed to manufacture the goods as well. This practice allowed (but did not require) manufacturing to continue at the same level of quality that consumers come to associate with the mark. A 1962 court decision held that merely reciting in the assignment that the goodwill related to the trademark also was being sold was sufficient (*Hy-Cross Hatchery, Inc. v. Osborne* 1962). However, this approach was rejected by other courts for being too lax. Now courts simply seek to determine whether sufficient continuity exists between the post-sale goods associated with the trademark and the pre-sale goods (*Pepsico, Inc. v. Grapette Co.* 1969). Assignments, but not licenses, must be registered with the USPTO. In the late 1980s, the boom in the importance of brands was further demonstrated by several acquisitions where the primary goal appeared to be to acquire profitable brands and their trademarks. For example Philip Morris bought Kraft for four times the value of Kraft's tangible assets apparently paying a premium for the value of Kraft's brands (Economist 1998).

IV. Other Expansions

The Lanham Act also added the concept of trademark incontestability for marks that have enjoyed five years of continuous use in commerce since the date of registration. This concept extends the presumption of trademark validity based on registration to limit the defenses that can be used to challenge a trademark that has been registered for five years. The mark owner must file a declaration of incontestability, but once achieved, an incontestable mark only can be challenged based on: becoming generic, abandonment or procurement by fraud. It is important to note that descriptive marks, once ineligible for trademark protection or registration, now may be registered and if unchallenged for five years may not be challenged on the grounds of being merely descriptive (*Park 'N Fly, Inc. v. Dollar Park & Fly, Inc.* 1985). This adds greater certainty to brand marketers that if they invest in a brand, their trademark won't be declared descriptive and become available for competitors to use.

Infringement also was expanded by a 1962 statutory amendment that eliminated the need to prove likely confusion by purchasers. As a result some courts began to recognize post-purchase or onlooker confusion *Mastercrafters Clock & Radio Co. v. Vacheron & Constantin-LeCoultre Watches, Ltd.* (1955), and initial interest confusion even though it was corrected before purchase (*Grotrian, Helfferich, Schultz, Th. Steinweg Nachf. v. Steinway & Sons*, 1975; *Mobil Oil Corp. v. Pegasus Petroleum Corp.* 1987). Both types of confusion, although not yet widely adopted, provide further brand protection in cases where purchasers are not ultimately confused as to the brand identity.

E. TRADEMARK LAW AND MODERN BRAND MANAGEMENT

This expansion of brand protection by the 1946 Lanham Act added to duties to those who managed brands. Licensing, which led to franchising in some industries and renewal (as well as non-renewal) of trademarks became of immediate concern. As the second half of the twentieth century unfolded, brand marketers asserted and gained rights over new types of brand identifiers. By the 1970s and 1980s, acquiring existing brands to augment existing product lines became easier under the law and a popular marketing practice. By 1988, brand marketers could register proposed future trademarks without using them in commerce under new intent-to-use ruled discussed in the next chapter. It is little wonder that the practice of organizing marketing by brand managers proliferated during this time.

Of course with brand managers, the modern concept of brand marketing and strategy slowly developed during this time. Writing in 1975, Morein noted that the past 25 years had seen the development of sophisticated brand marketing for consumer products. The modern discussion of brand marketing appears to have begun in 1955 when Gardner and Levy echoed writings published forty years earlier by discussing the difference between the product and the brand. They recognized the "brand name" (rather than trademark) as a complex symbol representing a variety of ideas and attributes that build up in the minds of consumers over time. The net result was a brand personality that might be more important for sales than technical aspects of the product (Gardner and Levy 1955, p. 35).

An empirical study of the importance of brand in making continuing sales was presented the following year. Cunningham (1956) reported on the results of a three year consumer panel study of brand loyalty. He found that many purchasers were loyal to at least some brands with some being secondarily loyal to a second brand. However, brand loyalty varied across consumers and product categories. There did not seem to be any "loyalty-prone" consumers who were loyal to a brand in every category of low-priced frequently purchased products in the study.

In 1960, Theodore Levitt cautioned marketers not to define their business too narrowly as the railroads had done. Instead, he urged that a company not think of itself as producing products, but rather as "buying customers, as doing the things that will make people want to do business with it" (Levitt 1960, p. 12). By the mid-1960s, studies were showing that customers often preferred family brands—brands that were used for two or more similar products such as fruits and vegetables or various paper products (Fry 1967).

Edward Tauber (1981) later built upon Levitt by suggesting that existing brand names could be used not only for line extensions of similar products but also for new product categories. Both Tauber (1981, p. 39) and Ries and Trout (1981) recognized the risks of such strategies and the fact that the new opportunity had to be appropriate for the brand. This concept of brand extensions (extensions to a new product category) became popularized in Aaker and Keller's (1990) *Journal of Marketing* article. Recent estimates suggest that as many as 80% of new product introductions are brand extensions (Kim and Mauborgne 2005, p. 7).

Thus, changes in trademark law led to a broadening of the practice of brand management to include the development of new brand identifiers, brand extensions, third-party licensing and franchising, and brand acquisitions. The expansion of trademark law has enabled the expansion of the scope (and therefore the revenues and value) of brands.

F. CONCLUSION

Modern brand management developed only after trademark law evolved to allow marketers to protect their brands. Early unfair competition and trademark law sought to prevent the unfair diversion of trade from the trademark owner to an imitator that confused consumers about the source of its goods known as passing off. Today, trademark law is recognized to have both the goal of providing accurate information to consumers and to provide sufficient protection of brand identity that businesses have the incentive to develop high quality brands. Registration allowed trademarks to be established with more certainty. Such marks now become incontestable after five years of registration. Marks can now be licensed to franchises, merchandise producers, and manufacturers. Trademarks can now be readily bought and sold.

The types of brand elements or brand identifiers that can be protected under trademark law has expanded from non-descriptive names and marks to all sorts of devices that now are used to identify brands. The types of activities that may now be challenged in enforcement lawsuits have expanded as have penalties for trademark violations including criminal sanctions for intentional counterfeiting. All of this and more suggests that the modern brand manager cannot be successful without a solid understanding of legal issues related to branding.

CHAPTER 2

Trademark Protection

A. INTRODUCTION

While some countries require registration before a trademark is protected, the U.S. and other common law countries traditionally required use in commerce before a trademark was protected. However, now U.S. applicants can file an Intent-to-Use trademark application as discussed below. The first use or filing date is crucial for determining which user of two very similar marks has priority. Once a trademark is federally registered in the U.S., affidavits of use and renewal applications must be filed every ten years. Of course, it is common for brand marketers to upgrade the look of their trademarks (called tacking). As long as the new slightly modified mark and the original are legal equivalents—create the same continuing commercial impression—the marketer enjoys priority from the original first use or filing. Otherwise, the new updated mark is protected only since its first use or filing date.

Before discussing use and registration of trademarks, we must first examine the concept of trademark strength. The concept is simple enough—some trademarks are stronger than others and stronger marks enjoy broader protection in terms of mark and industry similarity. This concept is particularly important for word trademarks discussed in the next chapter but also applies in a somewhat simplified form to other trademark forms as discussed in Chapter Four.

B. TRADEMARK STRENGTH

Traditionally, trademark strength is divided into two categories: acquired strength and inherent strength. A trademark acquires strength in the minds of consumers from promotion and sales of the branded product, the length of time the product has been sold, and its total revenue. Beebe (2006) argues that acquired strength is the most important factor in determining the success of a trademark lawsuit and that inherent trademark strength is one additional factor for determining overall trademark strength. For example, MCDONALDS is an extremely well-known brand, so its mark has great acquired strength even though the word is simply a family name making it an intrinsically weak mark. When starting out, brand managers may have little control over advertising budgets and sales, but do have control over the selection of the mark itself. They can choose trademarks from one of the four categories of inherent trademark strength as defined in U.S. case law.

The strongest of the inherent strength trademark categories is fanciful marks—made up words or numbers that have no prior meaning such as KODAK. These tend to be preferred by lawyers (Hemnes 1985). The next strongest are arbitrary marks—words that have meaning but no association with a particular use such as APPLE computers or CAMEL cigarettes. The third level of strength is suggestive marks—words that allude to product features or performance without actually describing them such as RAIN DANCE car wax or SURFVIVOR suntan lotion.

The fourth category is descriptive marks, including words that are primarily family names, descriptions of product performance, style or grade terms or attributes and descriptions of geographic origin. The Trademark Trial and Appeal Board recently refused Yosemite Beer as a trademark because Yosemite was primarily geographically descriptive. Numerical marks also may be descriptive if they describe product attributes or performance. Intel's switch to the PENTIUM brand name derives from a court decision that the x386 indication was generically descriptive of the third generation of x86 processors and the entire industry had copied Intel's previous designations of processors, e.g., 8086, 80186 or x186 80286 or x286 without objection from Intel (*Intel Corp. v. Advanced Micro Devices, Inc.*, 1991). This category of mark cannot be registered or enforced unless the user can prove the mark identifies a particular product source or brand in the minds of consumers which the law calls secondary meaning.

The line between suggestive marks and descriptive marks is not clear. For example TENDER VITTLES for cat food, SUDSY for ammonia, JOY for both perfume and detergent, IVY LEAGUE for clothing and SOLID STATE for printing ink have all been held to be descriptive. In contrast, the MONEY STORE for financial services, QUICK GREEN for grass seed, HANDI-WIPES for cleaning cloths, PIZZA ROLLS for snack food, ACTION SLACKS for pants, RAPID-SHAVE for shaving cream and both COPPERTONE and FLORIDA TAN for suntan lotion have been held to be suggestive. Similarly a trial court determined that POLY PITCHER was descriptive of polyethylene pitchers, but on appeal, the mark was found to be suggestive because most consumers did not associate poly with polyethylene (Stim 2000, pp.23–24). In deciding that SEXY LITTLE THINGS was suggestive rather than descriptive, the court noted that the purchaser must use some imagination to connect the mark to some characteristic of the product. In this case, the name suggested the young women who were the targeted consumers (*Menashe v. V. Secret Catalogue, Inc.* 2005). An earlier decision had a somewhat more elaborate discussion of the distinction:

> A term is suggestive if it requires imagination, thought or perception to reach a conclusion as to the nature of goods. A term is descriptive if it forthwith conveys an immediate idea of the ingredients, qualities or characteristics of the goods.

As noted above, Beebe (2006) found that acquired strength "almost invariably trumped" inherent strength in cases where one category of strength was found to be strong, but the other found to be weak. Even descriptive marks may develop acquired strength as they become well known. MICROSOFT (micro-computer software) and WINDOWS are two examples of descriptive marks that enjoy strong acquired secondary meaning. When Microsoft sued Lindows for infringing its Windows trademark the judge said he would instruct the jury to consider how the word "windows" was understood before the November 1985 release of the first Windows operating system. This reportedly caused Microsoft to settle by purchasing the rights to Lindows for $20 million (Peterson 2004). Despite the importance of acquired distinctiveness, Beebe (2006) also found that inherently stronger marks were more likely to win infringement cases than inherently weaker marks.

There is a fifth category of inherent strength, called generic, that is so weak it is denied trademark protection altogether with no chance of proving secondary meaning. Generic terms identify the product category (or genus) rather than a particular offering within that type of product. Some courts also have used the phrase "common descriptive terms" to apply to words commonly used to describe certain types of goods that also are never afforded trademark protection. For example, the Trademark Trial and Appeal Board (TTAB) recently ruled that "limited" was a common descriptive term in the sports trading cards industry and could not be registered as a trademark. Chapter Six examines the few ways in which marketers can exercise some control over category names.

Other courts distinguish "what we are" (generic) from "who we are." For example, the name "Surgicenter" for surgical centers that perform day surgery was so descriptive it was declared generic (*Surgicenters of America, Inc. v. Medical Dental Surgeries Co.* 1979). Similarly, "light" beer (*Miller Brewing Co. v. G. Heileman Brewing Co.* 1977), "light" cigarettes (*Phillip Morris, Inc. v. RJR Tobacco Co.* 1975), "chocolate fudge"

(*A.J.Canfield Co. v. Honickman* 1986), "Pilates Studio" (*Pilates, Inc. v. Georgetown Bodyworks Deep Muscle Message Ctrs., Inc.* 2001) and "first aid" for bandages and other medical items (*National Patent Dev. Corp.* 1986) all have been declared generic.

One ongoing dispute as this book is being written is the registration of PRETZEL CRISPS opposed by Frito-Lay for being generic. The TTAB ruled that PRETZEL is generic for pretzel snacks and CRISPS is generic for crackers so the phrase would be generic for pretzel cracker products. However, the Federal Circuit Court of Appeals sent the case back for the TTAB to consider the public's understanding of both words together (*Princeton Vanguard, LLC v. Frito Lay Inc.* 2015).

A similar case involved registration of THE SOFA & CHAIR COMPANY as a service mark for a custom furniture and upholstering firm. The court of appeals upheld the finding that the words were not generic for this type of firm (but presumably would have been generic for a furniture retailer) (*In re K-T Zoe Furniture, Inc.* 1994). Similarly, "safari" was found generic for hats, jackets and expeditions in Africa, but would be fanciful for grills and scarves (*Abercrombie & Fitch Co. v. Hunting World, Inc.,* 1976). Although LITTER BASKET arguably appears to be generic, it was found to be descriptive (*Sterling Prods. Co. v. Crest Mfg. Co.* 1970).

The addition of the word Company or Inc. or a top level domain name such as ".com" does not change the registration status of a mark. For example, the name "blindsanddraperies.com" was held to be generic for an internet store selling blinds and draperies and "buyautoparts.com" was found to be generic for an online retailer of auto parts (*In re Eddie Z's Blinds and Drapery, Inc.* 2005; *In re Meridian Rack & Pinion DBA buyautoparts.com* 2015). Typically, a trademark registrant must disclaim any rights over "-.com" or any other top level domain name just like it would disclaim any rights to "Inc." or "Co." The same seems to be true so far with the use of hashtag—"#"—it helps organize social media but adds no trademark distinctiveness to whatever else it is added to and should be disclaimed so that others also may use it.

Most countries have similar rules. For example, the European Union now registers Community Trademarks in addition to allowing trademark registration in member countries. The E.U. will not register marks that are "devoid of any distinctive character"—roughly the equivalent of a generic description of goods that does not allow end users to identify the particular source of the goods. For example, the Court of First Instance recently held that "Lite" was only descriptive and would not distinguish goods from one enterprise from those of another enterprise. Similarly, Trademark Board of Appeal recently held that "Optima" which means excellent or very good in Portuguese was descriptive and devoid of distinctiveness for medical instruments. However, the Board also allowed registration for "Maxima" meaning the largest, greatest or most intense holding it would not be perceived as descriptive for medical instruments (O'Reilly 2004).

The E.U. also prohibits purely descriptive marks from registration. Two more famous European cases involve DOUBLEMINT and BABY-DRY. The former was recently declared "merely descriptive" European Court of Justice as a trademark for chewing gum although it has been registered in the U.S. since 1915 (U.S. Reg. No. 0102001). In contrast, the ECJ had previously allowed BABY-DRY for disposable diapers because of the 'syntactically unusual juxtaposition' of the words baby and dry. In Europe, marks consisting of descriptive components are normally considered descriptive, but can develop a distinctive capacity if sufficiently unusual. This appears similar to suggestive marks. However, the E.U. appears to differ from the U.S. in that both marks devoid of any distinctive character and marks that are purely descriptive may be registered if proven to have acquired secondary meaning before registration.

Stronger marks generally are entitled to broader protection against infringement. For example, an old English case decided that use of the brand name Kodak to sell bicycles would confuse consumers into wondering if the camera maker had diversified into the bicycle business (*Kodak Case* 1898). In contrast as discussed in Chapter Fifteen, descriptive marks receive little protection even against competitors using similar terms. For example, a lipstick company did not infringe another's "Sealed with a Kiss" trademark when it distributed promotional cards for mailing with instructions to place a lipstick imprint on the cards and the statement "Seal it with a Kiss!" (*Cosmetically Sealed Industry, Inc. v. Chesebrough-Pond's USA Co.* 1997). Similarly, "fish fry" may be used descriptively by competitors despite registration of the trademark "Fish-Fri" (*Zatarain's Inc. v. Oak Grove Smokehouse, Inc.* 1983). Lastly, a VCR marketer registered the brand name VCR-2 for its double deck VCR, but because the name was descriptive, could not prevent other audio component marketers from labeling terminals on the back of their machines VCR-1 and VCR-2 (*Dual-Deck Video Cassette Recorder Antitrust Litigation* 1993). The expansive protection advantage of stronger marks over both similar marks and products in similar industries is illustrated by the figure below:

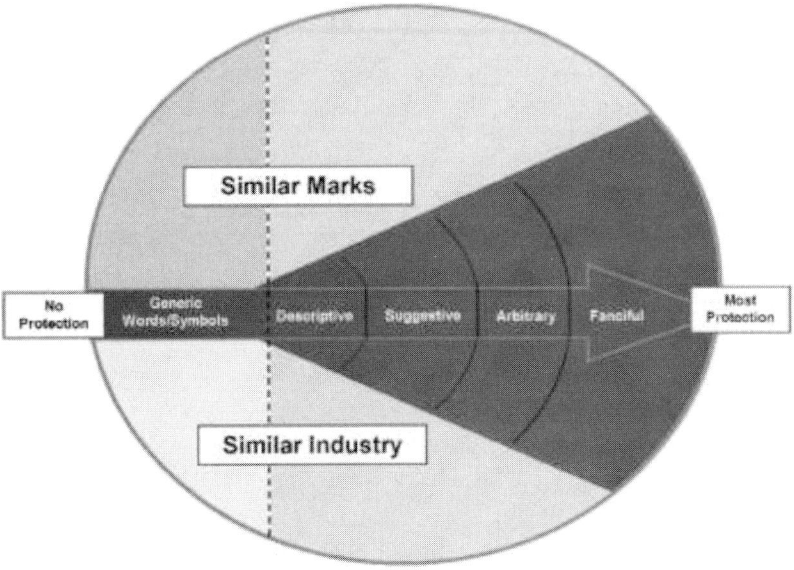

C. ESTABLISHING TRADEMARK RIGHTS

In the United States, trademark rights may be obtained in three ways: (1) acquisition or license of an existing trademark, (2) use in commerce of a new mark with possible enforcement by lawsuit to the extent of use in commerce and (3) registration (at the federal or state level) of a new mark in one or more industries. Apple is well known example of a firm purchased trademark rights such as APPLE for music services, IPHONE and IPAD. In the first two cases, it used the mark first and then purchased rights when accused of infringement (Brazilian courts upheld the validity of 2000 registration of IPHONE as having priority over Apple's more recent efforts to register that mark in Brazil). In the case of IPAD, Apple attempted to purchase worldwide rights from a Chinese firm by using a U.K. intermediary. While that initially worked, the Chinese firm later claimed it never sold the Chinese trademark rights.

Similarly, in the 1990s, there were several large consumer goods mergers that seemed primarily motivated by the acquisition of valuable trademarks and brands. Any change in actual ownership of a registered mark must be registered with the USPTO. Such assignments are only valid if accompanied by the assets necessary to produce the branded product or if the assignee already has that capability. Similarly, a trademark license where the new user obtains permission but not ownership from the trademark owner must include quality control provisions to be enforceable. An important goal of trademark law is to try and protect consumers who have come to associate a particular mark with a particular level of quality.

Small start-ups may simply adopt a trademark of their goods or services and use that mark in commerce. They should document both initial use and any expansion to other goods or locations and may document their intent to use the trademark by labeling it with ™. So long as they continue to use the mark (rather than abandon it), first use information establishes their priority in any subsequent state or federal lawsuit they might bring against a later user of the mark or any lawsuit they may face by another party claiming first use. Since most federal registrants use the mark in interstate commerce before registering it, they enjoy common law protection for the period of use before registration is granted.

However, the date of filing for federal registration (assuming registration eventually happens) takes priority over any new unregistered use after that date. Thus, the earliest unregistered trademark user enjoys priority over later users and applicants but only to the extent of actual use in geographic and product marketers. Newer unregistered users of the same trademark are free to use the mark in other geographic and product markets. Federal registrants have exclusive rights over the entire rest of the country in the product categories specified in the registration.

Trademark registration is the third way to gain U.S. trademark rights and many other countries and the European Union only grant trademark rights upon registration. Purely local businesses often may choose to register their trademark only in their state of business rather than federally. At a minimum this provides notice to others in the state of the owner's trademark rights. Some states follow the federal system of presuming trademark validity based on registration as explained below. However, small businesses should beware that state registration may not even provide exclusive rights throughout the entire state just in areas of use.

Federal law provides for registration of marks used in interstate commerce (sold across state or national borders) or intended to be used within the near future. Trademark law offers certain advantages to federal trademark registration with the U.S. Patent and Trademark Office (USPTO), costing a few hundred dollars for each category of goods and services for which the mark is registered (www.uspto.gov).

The USPTO offers the Principal Register for marks that are either inherently distinctive or have acquired distinctiveness (secondary meaning) through use. Applications to the Principal Register can be based on actual use of the mark in interstate commerce or intent to use the mark after it is declared eligible for registration.

Marks that are not inherently distinctive, such as descriptive marks and have not yet acquired secondary meaning, but are capable of distinguishing the source of goods or services from those of another, may be registered on the Supplemental Register after they have been used in interstate commerce for at least one year. However, generic product categories would not be allowed to be registered even on the Supplemental Register. Registration on the Supplemental Register yields four modest benefits:

- Right to use the ® symbol
- Right to sue in federal court
- Notice to others of ownership (and availability in trademark search databases) and the date of first use
- Basis for trademark filings in other countries

Five years of uncontested registration results in a presumption that the mark can then be registered on the Principal Register. When marks are registered on the Principal Register, they receive the benefits listed above plus the following:

- Presumption that the mark is valid and the registrant has the exclusive right to use it in commerce in connection with the specified goods and services.
- Nationwide priority over the use of the registered mark even in locations where the mark has not been used.
- Constructive notice of the prior use of the mark so that subsequent users may not argue they adopted the mark in good faith without knowledge that it had been previously registered.
- Criminal penalties and damages for counterfeiting cases

- Statutory damages and attorneys' fees for infringement cases where there is a presumption that infringement was willful after registration
- Right to stop importation of products with infringing marks
- Trademark incontestability after at least 5 years of continuous use

International brands or those who aspire to be international in scope must be registered in other countries to gain trademark rights in those countries. Most countries grant registration on a first-to-file basis rather than granting rights based on first use in commerce like the U.S., United Kingdom, Canada and Australia. However, most industrialized countries are members of the Paris Convention. This convention allows companies to register in their home country, obtain a filing date and then use that initial filing date for priority in other signatory countries as long as the company applies for registration in those countries within six months of its home country filing date.

Two recent innovations make international registration even easier. First, as noted, the European Union (E.U.) established in 1994 European Community Trademarks administered by the Office for Harmonization of the Internal Market (OHIM—now the E.U. Intellectual Property Office) in Spain. Like federal registration in the U.S., this system provides for a single trademark registration that may be used and enforced in all 25 member states.

The second innovation is the Madrid Agreement and Protocol recently agreed to by both the U.S. and E.U. The protocol provides for one stop registration. A company can file an international application with the USPTO and designate foreign signatory countries where registration is being sought. This application is then forwarded to the International Bureau of World Intellectual Property Organization that performs a cursory examination to see that requirements are satisfied and then issues an international registration for the trademark that is then examined by each designated country (including Community Marks for Europe). This international registration is not yet effective anywhere, each jurisdiction has up to 18 months to examine the registration and possibly reject it. Otherwise, the international registration takes effect in that country. Grounds for rejection are consistent with most countries' trademark laws: (1) conflict with an existing registration, (2) lack of distinctiveness, (3) contrary to morality or public order, and (4) likely to cause deception. Use of this system will be less expensive and probably faster than country-by-country registration, but if the home country registration is totally or partially cancelled within five years, the entire Madrid registration is cancelled to the same effect.

D. FEDERAL REGISTRATION PROCEDURE

This section discusses trademark registration procedures in the U.S. Other countries and the E.U. will have similar procedures but the Madrid Protocol makes it less likely that brand marketers will engage in the more expensive procedure of filing locally in each country where protection is sought. Registration can be thought of as a four-step process.

1. After selecting a proposed mark, the brand marketer should consider whether to perform a trademark search to see if the proposed mark is already being used before starting the registration process. A search is not required and applicants can conduct an internet search and use the USPTO trademark search function themselves. Alternatively, many firms offer a more thorough search option that could include state trademarks, company names, domain name registrations and even Madrid Protocol searches. Search firms exercise tricks of the trade that occasional registrants may not consider such as searching for plurals, alternative words with similar

meanings and alternative genders and ages (woman and boy in addition to "The Paint Man"). Finally, searches may be conducted for foreign language translations of a proposed word mark.

2. Deciding to proceed, a U.S. applicant can file a "use in commerce application" along with a specimen of the mark if the mark is currently being used or an "intent-to-use" application if the application has a good faith intent to use the mark in commerce. For word marks, applicants may file a standard character mark for the word itself regardless of font and appearance and/or a special character mark that protects only the particular rendition of the word mark but not the word itself. Marks are filed in one or more industry categories and applicants may have actual use in some categories but only intent-to-use in others. When the proposed mark is actually used in a particular line of commerce, the applicant must file a statement of use for that industry category. At the latest, this should occur within 6 months of mark approval, but this deadline can be extended for up to three years.

3. Typically five to six months after filing the application with the USPTO, the trademark examiner examines the mark. Roughly 40% of the time, the examiner approves the mark with no changes. Forty percent of the time, the examiner rejects the application based on technical issues that are typically easily corrected. Twenty percent of the time, the mark is rejected for substantive issues such as a prior similar registration. A response to the rejection can be filed, often with an amended application. Ultimately, if the examiner rejects all responses, the rejection can be appealed to the Trademark Trial and Appeal Board (TTAB).

4. About four months after the application is accepted, it is published for opposition in the USPTO's Official Gazette. In 2–3% of cases an opposition is filed by a third party. Otherwise, the mark is generally approved thirty days after publication and the official registration is issued in another two months. Now the applicant may use ® designation next to the mark.

Oppositions must be filed within thirty days (extendable to ninety days and another sixty days with the applicant's consent) of the publication of the proposed trademark. For this reason, it is important that brand owners have a method of systematically monitoring applications and oppositions. Oppositions are litigated before the TTAB and the losing party may appeal the result to the Court of Appeals for the Federal Circuit. A recent Supreme Court decision held that a finding by the examiner or TTAB of likelihood of confusion with a previously registered mark is final and can't be re-litigated in federal court under normal circumstances (*B&B Hardware, Inc. v. Hargis Industries, Inc.* 2015). In Europe, oppositions must be filed within three months of publication. Once the opposition is allowed, proceedings are delayed an additional two months to allow the parties to try and settle. Decisions may be appealed to the Board of Appeal and to the courts (O'Reilly 2004).

An "informal study" indicates that oppositions in the U.S. are relatively expensive averaging $150,000 to $500,000 compared to India at $3k, the E.U. and Japan at $5k to $25k, Australia at $15k to $30k and Canada at $20k to $50k. The U.S. system is more court-like and provides for discovery and motion practice. Ninety percent of U.S. oppositions are settled compared to the E.U. and Canada where more than 80% of the oppositions are settled. The E.U. was identified as the preferred jurisdiction by almost a two to one margin by study participants (Kilmer 2013).

In the U.S., cancellations proceedings may be brought before the TTAB any time after a mark's registration. Reasons of fraud, abandonment and genericness may be asserted at any time, but descriptiveness and likelihood of confusion or dilution may only be asserted within five years of registration.

Examiner rejections and sometimes oppositions may be based on the fact that certain proposed marks may not be registered under U.S. law. Immoral, scandalous or disparaging marks (such as "A-Hole Patrol", but the logo was allowed), the name or picture of living people or a deceased president without permission, marks that are deceptive or create a false connection and flags, coats of arms, and insignia of government entities (15 U.S.C. § 1052). (Marks incorporating the Capitol Building and the Statue of Liberty have been allowed because neither of these well-known landmarks is considered to be an insignia of the United States.) As this is being written, the Federal circuit court of appeals has struck down the ban on scandalous marks for unconstitutionally interfering with freedom of speech under the First Amendment. Because other appellate courts have disagreed arguing that denial of registration does not restrict speech because firms can continue to use the name they selected, this issue may go to the Supreme Court for a final ruling.

Finally, marks that are generic, functional or confusingly similar to registered marks or are misleading as to product quality, sponsorship, association or geographic source are not register-able. For example, "EMDrops" was rejected as a trademark for a nutrition supplement because it was misdescriptive of the product. The product did not contain "effective microorganisms." The examiner found that consumers of this sort of product would expect a product with such a name to contain "EMs." The E.U. has a similar list of unregister-able proposed marks: signs that do not satisfy the definition of a trademark: marks devoid of any distinctive character, descriptive marks, deceptive marks, generic terms or customary trade terms, immoral or illegal marks (E.U. Directive 2008/95/EC).

E. ENFORCEMENT

Since searching before applying to register a trademark is optional, it is not unusual for one party to use or attempt to register a trademark that is similar to a mark already in use by another party. Before jumping into litigation, parties should consider the degree of similarities of their marks and goods and whether they can peacefully co-exist. Perhaps one party licenses the other or perhaps the second user can negotiate some time to sell existing inventory and develop a modified mark. The parties may even negotiate and agree over modifications made to one of the marks or limits as to the use of the marks as part of a settlement of the dispute.

When a marketer deliberately passes off its product as coming from another source by using the other's (identical) registered trademark on the same type of goods, the brand counterfeiter can be punished in the U.S. by criminal sanctions of up to a $2 million fine and ten years in prison for the first offense (15 U.S.C. § 1117 and 19 U.S.C. § 1526(f)). Imported goods that are not authorized to carry a particular trademark in the U.S. also may be challenged under both trademark law and various sections of the Tariff Act. Tariff Act challenges are examined in Chapter Eighteen.

Otherwise, confusingly similar marks used by similar products can be subject to a variety of remedies under federal trademark infringement including injunction of the infringing use, cancellation of a confusingly similar mark, seizure and destruction of the infringing goods, and monetary damages (15 U.S.C. §§ 1116–1119). Some states limit remedies to an injunction of use of the trademark but others allow recovery of any proven damages as well as possible attorney fees.

Parties that intentionally induce others to commit trademark infringement may be held liable for contributory infringement. For example, a website might knowingly allow sellers of counterfeit goods to advertise on the website. The sellers would be liable for infringement (or distributing counterfeit goods) and the website would be liable for contributory infringement. In such cases, suing one website is easier than pursuing numerous sellers that post on that website, but the brand marketer must prove knowledge and intent by the website. This is typically done by submitting complaints about particular sellers/goods and waiting to see if they are removed from the website.

As noted in Chapter One, to determine whether one trademark is confusingly similar to another, U.S. courts developed a series of factors that differ somewhat from circuit to circuit. However four factors are common to all of the circuits and a fifth factor is common to all but one. Trial courts nearly always examine every factor in their judicial circuit in order to avoid being overturned upon appeal, but Beebe (2006) suggests, based on examination of all U.S. decisions from 2000–2004, that the first three factors are nearly always dispositive.

- **Similarity of the marks**—as discussed below, marks may look or sound similar or have similar meanings or connotations. Beebe (2006) demonstrates that if this factor alone is proven, plaintiffs win 90% of the time with little difference between marks found to be identical versus those found merely to be similar. For example, the fanciful trademark, POLAROID (for self-developing cameras and films), was protected against infringement by a similar suggestive mark, POLARAID, for a refrigeration services company (*Polaroid Corp. v. Polaraid, Inc.* 1963).
- **Second user's intent**—was the mark adopted in good faith after a careful search or was there intent to confuse consumers? Beebe (2006) shows that if the court finds the second user adopted its trademark with the intent to

confuse consumers, the second user nearly always was held liable for trademark infringement.

- **Proximity of goods and likelihood of brand extension**—confusion is more likely if the goods are identical (i.e., directly competitive), competitive substitutes even if not identical, or related in such a way to suggest a brand extension. Courts also look at whether the goods are sold in similar channels. Beebe (2006) found that plaintiffs always won in cases where both the goods were identical and the marks similar. In contrast, if this factor was found not to favor the plaintiff, then the plaintiff only won 3% of the cases. In cases where the goods were found to be similar but not identical, plaintiffs won just over 60% of the time.
- **Strength of the original mark**—as discussed at the beginning of this chapter, the acquired and inherent strength of the first trademark is considered an important factor in infringement analysis.
- **Evidence of actual confusion**—although not required, evidence that consumers were actually confused about source or sponsorship is relevant. While consumer testimony may be used, survey evidence is typically used to attempt to prove this factor. However of the cases examined by Beebe (2006), only 20% involved survey evidence and only half of those actually found the evidence to be credible with a mere 7% of all cases finding liability consistent with the results of the survey evidence.

U.S. courts also typically examine the number of third-party uses of a mark both within the registrant's industry and in other industries. Regardless of the mark's inherent strength, it is entitled to less protection if it is used widely by others. In contrast, if a mark is used in a market with little or no competition, it is likely to be considered strong. In fact, it may be so strong as to be declared generic. For this reason, firms also try to promote a generic term such as copier or tissue in order to avoid having XEROX or KLEENEX declared generic as were cellophane and shredded wheat once the patents on those products expired and competitors entered the market. If a trademark is broadly licensed across an array of industries, the distinctiveness of the mark for any particular product is lessened, but it also is less likely to be declared generic (Greene and Wilkerson 2013).

The E.U. follows a similar system of examining various factors to see if consumer confusion is likely, which it sometimes calls a link between the two products in the minds of consumers. In a recent case, the European General Court found that despite similarities between SWATCH, a well-known trademark for watches and "Swatchball" a proposed trademark for industrial movie equipment, other factors such as the differences in the goods, their channels of distribution and the differences in potential purchasers made confusion unlikely so that "Swatchball" should be registered (Baz 2015).

Trademarks are considered confusingly similar to each other in at least four ways. First, they may sound similar when spoken out loud such as CUP-A-COLA and COCA-COLA (*Coca-Cola Co. v. Clay* 1963), as COMSAT and COMCET (*Communications Satellite Corp. v. Comcet, Inc.* 1970) or HINT O'HONEY and HIDDEN HONEY (*Roux Labs, Inc. v. Clairol, Inc.* 1968). Second, the appearance of the words or other attributes may be visually similar such as PLATINUM PUFF and PLATINUM PLUS (*Clairol, Inc. v. Roux Labs, Inc.* 1971). Third, marks may be similar if they are conceptually similar, such as MOUNTAIN KING Christmas trees compared to ALPINE EMPEROR trees (*American Technical Industries, Inc. v. General Foam Plastics Corp.* 1978). Finally, marks may be confusing similar at a conceptual level even if they are opposite or mirror images of each other such as MR. CLEAN and MR. STAIN, IWANTA BISCUIT and YOUNEEDA BISCUIT or SHIPREADY and READYSHIP. Of course some marks are similar in multiple ways to earlier trademarks such as "Smog" and LONDON FOG that are similar in both sound and meaning. Courts also are careful to point out that marketing ideas are not protected so that a competing raincoat could use a name derived from weather such as Cloud or Hurricane. It could not use a weather-related name with similar meaning to fog (*Londontown Manufacturing Co. v Cable Raincoat Co.* 1974).

Marketing research, but not yet trademark law, recognizes that the likelihood of confusion may depend on consumer involvement with the purchase. In low involvement situations similarly sounding brand names (e.g., Hurricane and Hurri-Drane for drain cleaners) may elicit more confusion. In high involvement situations, consumers may find brand names with similar meanings (Hurricane and Cyclone) to be more confusing (Howard et al. 2000). This research also suggests that courts should consider likely degree of involvement when judging the likelihood of confusion. The closest analogy to this concept is the sophistication of the consumer factor used by some circuits who believe that sophisticated consumers would be more careful distinguishing trademarks than less sophisticated consumers.

Beebe (2006) also notes that different circuits appear to have significantly different trademark infringement success rates. On average plaintiffs are successful just over half the time in trademark infringement cases that involve the use of the multifactor test. However, in the Second Circuit, located in New York, plaintiffs won in only 41% of cases, but in the Ninth Circuit, located in California, plaintiffs won 59% of the time (Beebe 2006).

It is important to note that U.S. law offers a fair use defense against allegations of infringement. For example, a recent decision allowed WD-40 to (truthfully) describe one of its lubricating products as a "Long-Term Corrosion Inhibitor" despite the fact that a rival firm had registered the trademark THE INHIBITOR. While the latter mark is weak because it is descriptive, the court focus on the defense of descriptive fair use that allows firms to fairly describe their products as long as it does so in promotion without adopting a confusingly similar trademark (*Sorensen v. WD-40 Co.* 2015). Fair use defenses are discussed in Chapters Fifteen and Sixteen.

Most foreign countries protect marks that are famous in that country from infringement, typically because they are famous throughout the world, even if the mark is not yet registered in the country. However, U.S. courts do not consistently prohibit U.S. companies from adopting famous foreign trademarks that are neither used nor registered in the U.S. (Jackson 2009).

Owners of famous trademarks in the U.S. also may sue for dilution by a similar mark even if used in a completely different industry. Dilution has traditionally not been favored by federal courts. As noted in Chapter One, after the federal statute became effective, dilution was found in about half of all cases, but this declined to less than 20% in 2003 (Long 2006, p. 1042).

It remains to be seen whether the expansive Trademark Dilution Revision Act of 2006 will reverse this trend. The first dilution decision under the revised act by the TTAB found that GULPY as a mark for animal dishes did not dilute (or infringe) 7–Eleven's family of famous GULP marks (including BIG GULP, SUPER BIG GULP and DOUBLE GULP). The board found that the marks were not "essentially the same" and 7–Eleven failed to show any association between its marks and GULPY in the minds of potential customers (*7–Eleven, Inc. v. Wechsler* 2007).

The Revision Act clarifies that brand owners alleging dilution do not have to prove actual dilution as held by the Supreme Court in 2003 at least for non-identical marks. Rather the new act only requires mark owners to show that the challenged use is "likely to cause dilution by blurring or tarnishment." The Revision Act also clarifies that tarnishment is covered under the Act by defining dilution as "an association arising from the similarity" of a second trademark to the famous trademark that causes either blurring ("impairs the distinctiveness of the famous mark") or tarnishment ("harms the reputation of the famous mark").

The original Act condemned dilution "regardless of competition or likelihood of confusion," making it clear that a challenger did not have to prove competition or any likelihood of confusion between its goods and those of the alleged dilutor. The Revision Act further notes that the challenger does not have to prove "actual economic injury." Courts may interpret this language as requiring proof of likely economic injury as part of proving likelihood of dilution. This interpretation is consistent with the fact that dilution reduces the economic value of the trademark to its owner. Indeed, the Revision Act continues to allow for additional remedies to compensate for this economic loss such as damages or disgorgement of wrongfully obtained profits in cases of deliberate dilution.

The Revision Act also makes three other important clarifications:

1. The original 1927 law review article proposed that dilution should only apply to inherently distinctive trademarks such as made up words like Kodak. However, the Revision Act only requires that the mark be famous and distinctive the latter being either inherent or acquired by use. So any type of mark is potentially eligible for dilution protection once it is proven famous.

2. Trade dress is eligible for protection from dilution but the owner bears the burden of proving that it is non-functional and famous and that if the trade dress is unregistered, that it is famous apart from any registered marks that are normally included in the trade dress such as the brand name.

3. By defining fame as "widely recognized by the general consuming public," the Act appears to reject the concept of "niche" fame within a narrow subgroup of

consumers. Local brands with less well known trademarks should consider filing a state dilution claim in a state where only limited fame is required (keeping in mind that any injunction of the dilution may be limited to the single state).

There continues to be some concern that dilution should not restrict non-commercial use of famous trademarks such as use in news commentary and stories. The Revision Act expands the permitted areas of use to include parody, criticism and "any noncommercial use." It also continues to allow fair use in comparative advertising but now also specifically allows any fair use or facilitation of such fair use including both nominative and descriptive fair use. While the Act does not define these two types of fair use, nominative fair use simply identifies a product by name, often to compare to an advertised but distinctively identified second product. In contrast, descriptive fair use is the use of descriptive terms that also may be part of a trademark. Trademark fair use is discussed in Part Three of this book under the concept of Judo Brand Diversion.

The final interesting change in the Revision Act is its reallocation of the eight factors to be considered when deciding whether a mark is famous under the original statute. Half of these factors continue to be factors for determining fame under the Revision Act. These factors include: the duration and extent of use of the mark, the extent of advertising and publicity of the mark, the geographic extent of the trading area where the mark is used, and whether the mark is registered. It is important that while registration is a factor for determining fame, it is not required to bring a dilution lawsuit under the Act.

Three of the remaining factors previously considered when determining fame are now designated for determining whether dilution by blurring has occurred. These three factors are: the degree of inherent or acquired distinctiveness of the mark, the degree of recognition of the mark and the nature and extent of use of the same or similar marks by third parties (extent of substantially exclusive use of the mark). The Revision Act drops the eighth factor in the original statute—the channels of trade for the goods with which the mark is used. It adds three new factors to consider for blurring: (1) the degree of similarity between the two marks, (2) any actual association between them and (3) whether there was intent to create such an association by the owner of the allegedly diluting mark. Interestingly, the Revision Act offers no factors to consider when determining whether a famous mark has been diluted by tarnishment. It remains to be seen whether courts will place any significance on this shuffling of factors between the two statutes and what sorts of evidence courts will rule satisfy the lower burden of proving likely dilution by blurring or tarnishment.

The E.U. Trademark Directive and Regulation have similar prohibitions of the use of an identical or closely similar mark that "has a reputation" on dissimilar goods when the unauthorized use would take unfair advantage of the mark or be detrimental to the distinctive character or repute of the mark (Council Regulation 40/94/EEC, 1994 O.J. (L11)). To date there are no European decisions to clarify the meaning of this language. Canada and Japan also have trademark laws that could be interpreted to cover dilution situations, but courts have been reluctant to interpret the statutes too broadly (Whittaker 2006).

F. CONCLUSION

Brand managers have several options for obtaining trademark protection for their brand identifiers. Small firms and brands under test market may not want to register brand names and other identifiers, preferring to receive the limited protection provided by common law passing off protection based on actual usage. However, trademark registration is relatively inexpensive and offers several advantages for brand managers. Furthermore, registered trademarks can be protected against counterfeiting, infringement and dilution. Enjoining unauthorized use by another marketer is the primary remedy and often a preliminary injunction can be obtained within a few months.

Monetary damages are rare and must be proven with some degree of specify so most enforcement actions end with injunctive relief. However, is particular cases, damages may be provable or perhaps negotiate-able.

It is important to note that just because two trademarks are closely similar or even identical does not necessarily mean the senior user can prevail against the newer user. Identical trademarks, particularly of common words, often co-exist across two or more industries. For example, recently LAND O LAKES fishing tackle unsuccessfully sued LAND O LAKES dairy. The court of appeals affirmed finding no dilution or likelihood of confusion because the product categories were just too different (*Huguin v. Land O' Lakes, Inc.* (2016).

CHAPTER 3

Verbal Brand Identifiers—Names and Logos

A. INTRODUCTION

This chapter examines the application of trademark law to brand names and logos. Logos are defined here to be stylized designs or symbols that contain some verbal element such as initials, numbers or words. Verbal brand identifiers are just one type of identifier protected by trademark law. The next chapter discusses all other sensory identifiers including visual (but non-verbal) identifiers such as abstract symbols and designs and product trade dress including color. It also examines other forms of sensory marks such as sound, scent and touch identifiers.

The dichotomy between verbal and sensory brand identifiers is useful, but not airtight. Most verbal marks have some sensory components such as color and font. Logos, as defined here to include some verbal element, have a greater visual design element than the brand name itself. Verbal marks also may have a sound component such as Captain Crunch breakfast cereal or Sizzler restaurants whose names are reminiscent of the sound made when the cereal is eaten or streak is being grilled. Indeed, as noted in Chapter Two, marks may be considered confusingly similar to each other if they sound similar when spoken out loud such even if they have distinct meanings such as 'Hurricane' and 'Hurri-Drane.'

There are two types of verbal brand identifiers that are not discussed in this chapter. The first are slogans, which are considered primarily promotional, but if they become uniquely identified with a particular brand they may act as a brand identifier and receive trademark protection. They are examined in Chapter Seven. Advertising jingles also are verbal, typically longer than slogans, but with a strong sound-music component. However, jingles are typically thought (albeit it incorrectly) not to identify particular product sources. For this reason, they have traditionally been protected by copyright law rather than trademark law (e.g., *Dr. Pepper Co. v. Sambo's Restaurants, Inc.* 1981). Jingles are discussed in Chapters Five and Seven.

B. SELECTING A BRAND NAME

Since consumers discuss, describe and ask for a branded product or service by name, the name is arguably the most important brand element (Kohli, Suri and Thakor 2002). Roughly 60% of U.S. product and brand managers believe the name itself without advertising support can influence product sales. Approximately, half of those surveyed reported using an outside agency to help create a new brand name (Kohli and LaBahn 1997). Some brands use a company name as part of the company's brand name. It is important to remember that merely establishing a company or a website with a particular name or registering that company name with a particular state does not establish any trademark rights to use that name as a brand name or to prevent others from using that name as a brand name for a product or service (Hemnes 1985).

As noted in the preceding chapter, trademark law recognizes four categories of trademark strength: fanciful, arbitrary, suggestive and descriptive (with secondary meaning). The strongest trademarks tend to be preferred by lawyers (Hemnes 1985). However fanciful names initially communicate little if any meaning about the product to consumers. Arbitrary names suffer from the same limitation and also may be shared among different product categories (such as APPLE computers and APPLE records) as well as be a generic word for a category of products. Thus, it is not surprising the marketing literature tends to favor descriptive and suggestive names.

Descriptive names have the obvious disadvantage of being, well, descriptive. The brand owner must prove such names actually identify a particular brand rather than merely describe an attribute of the product. For example, at least two law firms have a name partner named Foley. When the Milwaukee law firm of Foley & Lardner decided to expand to Boston, the longtime home of Foley Hoag, F & L applied for a trademark on the descriptive name FOLEY. Not surprisingly, FH opposed registration. In October 2005, FH filed a trademark infringement lawsuit in federal district court. The case settled nearly a year later with F & L agreeing not to use a logo with the single word Foley without also stating Foley & Lardner in close proximity and prominence. Similar issues have been resolved with names like Ford (cars and modeling agency).

In general, most countries try to allow people to use their own names in the name of their business. The new E.U. Directive states that a European trademark does not entitle the registrant to prevent natural people from using their names in business so long as the use is consistent with "honest practices." Often the burden is placed on the newer user to take steps such as distinctive lettering, additional words or a disclaimer in order to avoid consumer confusion. In cases of bad faith such as where someone is invited to join a business because of that person's name, U.S. courts typically enjoin the use of the name altogether. For example when a younger Gallo brother decided to offer his name to a firm selling cheese, the court felt the cheese was a product closely related to wine and consumers would be confused with the GALLO trademark, so it prohibited use of the family name by the cheese marketer (*E. & J. Gallo Winery v. Gallo Cattle Co.* 1992).

Descriptive names also must not be misdescriptive or misleading. Most trademark authorities will refuse to register a descriptive trade name that is likely to mislead consumers about attributes of the associated product. However, except in some cases such as geographically misdescriptive words, discussed in Chapter Six, or names based on ingredients, it is unlikely that the trademark registration authority will know if the proposed name is misleading.

For this reason, misleading names are more likely to be condemned under deceptive advertising laws, discussed in Chapter Eight. For example, the Third Circuit Court of Appeals ordered the injunction of registered trademark names "Nighttime Strength Mylanta" and "Breathasure" because they would mislead consumers about product performance (*Novartis Consumer Health Inc. v. Johnson & Johnson-Merck Consumer Pharmaceuticals, Inc.* 2002; *Warner-Lambert Co. v. Breathasure, Inc.* 2000). Similarly, the National Advertising Division (NAD) of the Council of Better Business Bureaus recently recommended that a hair care marketer change the names of several products because the name such as Nourishing Coconut Milk communicated to consumers that the ingredient coconut milk made the shampoo nourishing to hair, but the marketer had no substantiation that the ingredient identified in the name actually had the benefit claimed. The NAD recommended that Nourishing Coconut Milk Shampoo be changed to Nourishing Shampoo with Coconut Milk (ASRC Press Release 2015). In contrast, early Supreme Court decisions discouraged the FTC from enjoining the use of misleading trademarks, preferring that a qualifying disclosure be used in conjunction with the name if the disclosure would be sufficient to prevent deception (*Jacob Siegel Co. v. FTC*, 1946; *FTC v. Royal Milling Co.* 1933).

Marketers while desiring distinctive brand names that may be legally protected also seek names that are memorable, likeable, and meaningful (Keller 2003; Kohli and Suri 2000; Robertson 1989). A survey of marketing managers found the top five brand name criteria in descending order of importance to be: relevance to the product category, connotations (meaning), overall liking, ease of recognition, distinctiveness and ease of recall (Kohli and LaBahn 1997). These criteria tend to be correlated with each other. A recent study found that meaningful names scored higher on an overall liking scale and had higher recall than non-meaningful names. However, when recalled, arbitrary names were always recalled correctly (Kohli and Suri 2000).

Although linguists argue that certain sounds (phonemes), while lacking a specific meaning, can suggest meaning (Robertson 1989, p. 68), fanciful marks are generally considered to be "blank slates" for consumers having neither meaning nor any likable associations with them. Consumers do tend to associate certain types of marks with certain products. For example, plural words are more consistent with breakfast cereals than singular words, but the reverse is true for home appliances (Peterson and Ross 1972). Similarly, alpha-numeric names such as WD-40 often enjoy a high technology connotation and are common in brands of chemical products and automobiles (Pavia & Costa 1983).

Fanciful marks also can be memorable if they are simple, readily pronounceable, and have repetitive sounds. Arbitrary marks can't have a meaning that is suggestive of the product, but they may still have favorable emotional connotations and be easy to remember. For example, consumers can form a mental image for the trademark for APPLE computers, but the trademark TEMPO does not suggest a similar memorable image.

Suggestive marks may satisfy all three marketing requirements, but some better than others. For example BAN and OFF describe the product's function with strong meaning and some likeability but they suggest a negative connotation. In contrast, Caress and Joy seem to have a stronger emotional-likeability content. Similarly, descriptive marks can satisfy the three marketing recommendations, but are only protected if they communicate a product source (e.g., brand) rather than category of products to consumers. Descriptive names also must not be deceptive or misdescriptive as noted above. Currently there are disagreements between the U.S. and E.U. over terms considered geographically descriptive such as some wine and food names. This issue is examined in Chapters Six and Twelve. Table One on the opposite page illustrates the combination of legal issues (trademark strength) with marketing issues.

Market research suggests that different types of names are effective in different ways. Kohli and Suri (2000) analyzed name effectiveness by collapsing the four types of legal strength into two categories: meaningful (descriptive and suggestive) and non-meaningful (arbitrary and fanciful). They further found that meaningful names were easier for consumers to recall and liked more than non-meaningful names.

A more recent study confirmed that consumer liking as well as quality evaluations of a brand were higher for brands with meaningful names than for brands with non-meaningful names. However, over time overall liking of a brand, regardless of its type of name, increased, but consumer evaluation of the attribute suggested by the meaningful name did not improve over time, whereas consumer evaluation of the same attribute for non-meaningful names did improve over time. Similarly, the evaluation of the non-meaningful brand, while initially lower than that of the meaningful brand name, seemed to improve at a higher rate over time (Kohli et al 2005).

Table One			
Legal and Marketing Recommended Brand Name Characteristics			
Distinctive	**Memorable**	**Emotionally Attractive**	**Meaningful**
Fanciful (made up word—no prior meaning)	Simple words, U2 music group; Repetitive sounds, e.g., Kodak, Xerox	To be developed	To be developed
Arbitrary (real word not associated with product type)	Mental image e.g., Apple (linked with actual image)	Favorable connotation from outside the category, e.g., White Diamonds perfume, Midas mufflers, Monarch bicycles, Regal shoes	To be developed
Suggestive (word(s) that allude to product performance or characteristics)	Sound e.g., Sizzle steak house, Capt'n Crunch cereal Compounds e.g., Powerbook, Surfvivor suntan lotion, Uneeda biscuit	Sounds also are emotionally attractive Emotional suggestions, e.g., Caress, Joy,	Performance or attribute allusions, e.g., Odor-Eaters, Ban, Off, 60 Minutes, Camel cigarettes (made from Turkish tobacco)
Descriptive (protected only with secondary meaning)	Simple words, e.g., Clue board game Compound words, e.g., Chap Stick, personal and place names	e.g., Playboy, Betty Crocker, Aunt Jemima	Performance or attribute allusions, e.g., Beef & Brew, Bufferin (buffered aspirin)

Keller et al (1998) also found that meaningful brand names can facilitate initial brand positioning and recall. However, if the brand is later repositioned to focus on attributes other than those suggested by its name, the name can interfere with the ability of advertising to link to the brand in the minds of consumers. Arbitrary and fanciful names are more flexible to better adapt to brand repositioning or brand extensions. These marketing benefits and drawbacks for each type of name are summarized in Table Two below.

Table Two		
Benefits and Drawbacks of Brand Name Types		
Name Type	**Benefits**	**Drawbacks**
Meaningful (Descriptive & Suggestive)	• Instant communication of product benefits • Initial positive consumer evaluation and liking.	• Lower level of trademark protection • Less flexible for future changes in brand positioning • Less ability to improve rating for attributes suggested by name
Non-Meaningful (Arbitrary & Fanciful)	• More adaptable to changing brand image • Allows more breadth in brand extensions • Stronger trademark protection	• No initial communication benefit • Positive consumer evaluation and liking must be built over time (but may build at a faster rate)

One final factor to consider when selecting a brand name is e-commerce compatibility as discussed in Chapter Six.

C. NUMERICAL NAMES

Numbers can be registered as trademarks such as Levi's famous "501" brand of jeans (U.S. Reg. No. 1552985). Numeric or alphanumeric marks can be arbitrary if they have no prior meaning and can be registered or protected without proof of secondary meaning. However, some marks, such as T-50 in the fastener industry, start out as model numbers and are often used by others in the industry. If the original user can prove secondary meaning, it can protect these designations from adoption by the industry as standardized model designations (*Arrow Fastener Co. v. Stanley Works* 1995). If the original user does not protect against this industry adoption, even a previously registered trademark (M4 for a type of rifle) can be declared generic (*Colt Defense LLC v. Bushmaster Firearms, Inc.* 2007). As noted in Chapter Two, it was the loss of control of the "x86" designation of computer chips that led the now famous "Intel Inside" advertising campaign to couple with each new generation of chip branded with an arbitrary but high-tech sounding name such as PENTIUM.

D. COMBINING BRAND NAMES AND BRAND ARCHITECTURE

Combining two components, whether verbal or numerical, into a single word such as MINITMIX may be protected as a trademark even if the two components must be disclaimed as generic words during registration. Such a disclaimer means the trademark owner is not claiming any rights to exclusive use of either the word "minute" or "mix." However, as noted in Chapter Two, the more usual result of combining two generic terms is that the resulting one or two words also will be considered generic, e.g., Surgicenter and Pilates Studio.

Many brands today enjoy both a trademarked company name as well as a trademarked product name. For example, the FORD EXPLORER has a related but distinct brand identity from the compact FORD ESCAPE. Both of these products share the common FORD brand and enjoy some benefits from the FORD brand identity. But each also has a distinct position as a certain type of vehicle. Brand managers refer to this a brand architecture or brand portfolios.

Some go to great effort to distinguish different types of relationships between the two names. For example, Aaker and Joachimsthaler (2000) describe four basic relationship strategies and nine sub-strategies. The basic strategies vary from using only a company brand such as VIRGIN and HEALTHY CHOICE, to using two brands with various types of relationships with each other (e.g., equal co-brands or one brand subordinate to the other) to using a single brand for the product with no mention of the company such as HEAD & SHOULDERS, PANTENE and PERT all of which are shampoo brands from P & G, although the P & G source is not mentioned, much less promoted.

Since brand extensions have become commonplace, they raise similar naming issues. TIDE with bleach, for example, is only protected from imitation by competitors for the trademark TIDE. "With bleach" is a descriptive phrase that would be available for all to use. Had a less descriptive phrase been selected such as ULTRAWHITE, the extension by itself may have been trademarked if it developed secondary meaning in addition to registering the combination of words.

Thus, from the legal perspective, if two names are used, brand marketers should carefully consider how important it is to protect both names independently of the other. While trademarks are not ordinarily dissected to analyze infringement or dilution questions, if one word is always used with another such as POLAROID ALPHA, it is less likely that consumers will be confused by a second ALPHA brand of camera from a different manufacturer (*Pignons S.A. de Mecanique de Precision v. Polaroid Corp.* 1981). Thus, the desire to avoid imitation by competitors may direct marketers to prefer some brand name portfolio strategies over others.

A two brand name strategy may allow marketers the opportunity to try to couple a descriptive name that might develop secondary meaning from use with a strongly distinctive brand name. For example, the Trademark Trial and Appeal Board allowed trademark registration of ULTRAMATIC as a designation of the top price line of well-known brand of stoves when it was convinced that the term also independently identified the source of the stoves in the minds of consumers (*Caloric Appliance Corp. v. Knapp-Monarch Co.* 1963). In contrast, the Second Circuit Court of Appeal upheld denial of a preliminary injunction of Gillette's registration of "Innocent Color" for hair dye. The court held that Clairol failed to prove that its use of "Innocent Ivory" and "Innocent Beige" for hair dye caused the use of "innocent" to indicate the source of products (Clairol) in the minds of consumers rather than simply the color (*Clairol Inc. v. Gillette Co.* 1968). Consumers would not be confused about the sources of these two products if the color names were perceived only as colors, not as brand identifiers.

In such situations where trademark protection is sought for words other than the brand name, the burden will be on the brand owner to prove the words identify the source of the product rather than simply describe it. Of course, marketers always have the option of registering the combined set of names as a single trademark such as Gillette Innocent Color and then disclaiming any exclusive rights to the words innocent or color by themselves. However, as noted above this approach still allows others to use the words innocent and color so they are not exclusive to a single brand.

E. NICKNAMES

The legal protection of nicknames, used by the public but not (at least initially) by the brand owner, started with a series of lawsuits by Coca-Cola over attempts by competitors to use some form of its well-known nickname COKE. The court decisions all found infringement of coke-like names such as Koke and Koke-Up and started what is now known as the Public Use Rule in trademark law. The rule simply provides that trademark owners have superior rights to trademark nicknames then third parties. However the legal basis for such a rule is much stronger if the trademark owner also made some use of the nickname. Coca-Cola eventually did start using COKE as a trade name in the early 1940s and sought registration for the name in 1944. It was initially reluctant because "coke" also was a common nickname for cocaine.

Other cases have involved the nickname "bug" for the Volkswagen Beetle and "hog" for Harley Davidson motorcycles. At least one court decision found "hog" generic for large motorcycles and "March Madness" was held to be generic for basketball tournaments held in March (Brody 2005). Because the legal rights to nicknames are much clearer and stronger once a brand owner adopts a nickname and uses it as a trademark, brand owners should consider promptly adopting any nickname started by the public. When London Fog sued the makers of Smog raincoats, it was able to show that the trade referred to the brand as "Fog" or "The Fog," but the court held this was not sufficient. It needed to prove that consumers used the nickname. However, the court found Smog to be confusingly similar to London Fog based both on meaning and sound (*Londontown Manufacturing Co. v Cable Raincoat Co.* 1974).

Celebrities commonly enjoy nicknames and the right of publicity in many states protects celebrities from unauthorized use of their nicknames as discussed in Chapter Twelve. More recently, celebrities also register their nicknames such as JOHNNY FOOTBALL to ensure they received protection regardless of state law. Celebrities and the right of publicity are discussed further in Chapter Thirteen.

F. FAMILIES OF TRADEMARKS AND BRANDS

Successful new brands often try to develop successful brand extensions—similar products with similar brand names. Searches for possible related names will alert marketers to small firms that have registered trademarks that might be sufficiently similar to be able to allege reverse confusion should the larger firm attempt to use the mark. Brand extensions may also result from the adoption of brand nicknames. It is not clear whether McDonald's started its family of names as its own marketing idea or whether publicly created nicknames such as McDonut and McPizza that inspired the tactic. In either case, McDonald's more than any other fast food restaurant has tied its product offerings to its overall brand by using the "Mc-" prefix in product names.

It also has enjoyed good success in U.S. courts preventing others from using brand names such as "McBagels" (*McDonald's Corp. v. McBagels, Inc.* 1986) as well as "McDugal McPretzel" and "McPretzel" (*J & J Snack Foods Corp. v. McDonald's Corp.* 1991). U.S., courts even have refused to allow the use of McSleep Inns as a trademark for a hotel chain (*Quality Inns International v. McDonald's Corp.* 1988) finding that restaurants and hotels were frequently co-marketed and McDental as a name for a dental practice (*McDonald's Corp. v. Druck & Gerner DDS, P.C.* 1993). The TTAB also refused to register McClaim's Legal Services with a slogan "Fast Food Justice" (*McDonald's Corp. v. John L. McClain* 1995).

The TTAB recently ruled in favor of McDonalds once again by affirming the denial of trademark registration for "McSweet" for pickled vegetables finding infringement and dilution by blurring were likely between the restaurant chain and this packaged food product (*McDonald's Corp v. McSweet LLC* 2014). David Bollier (2005, pp. 6, 212) reports that McDonald's also informally challenged McCoffee, McSushi and McDharma in California as well as McMunchies in England.

Part of McDonald's success is based on its licensing program of similar marks to industries quite different from food. These include "McClip" for hair-cutting services; "McClass" for computer services; "McCash" for financial services; "McD" for cleaning products; "McBucks" for redeemable certificates; "McBunny" for toys; "McMatch" for games; "McShirt" for clothing; "McGift Shop" for retail store services; "McHat" for hats; "McLots of Fun" for stage productions; "McMasters" for recruiting elderly employees; "McShuttle" for transportation services; "McBear" for stuffed toys; "McKids" for children's clothing sold at Sears retail stores; and "McJobs" for training handicapped people (*McDonald's Corp. v. John L. McClain* 1995). However as the table on the opposite page suggests, McDonald's has had only mixed success in other countries (Leong and Lwin 2005).

Another retailer also started using a family of trademarks approach in the 1980s, this time to develop different types of stores rather than specific product brands. TOYS "R" US successfully sued a retailer doing business as KIDS "R" US. The court enjoined use of this name finding both likelihood of confusion for infringement and dilution under the New York statute (*Toys "R" Us v. Canarsie Kiddie Shop, Inc.* 1983). TOYS "R" US then began using the mark for both children's apparel and retail stores that same year and sought registration for apparel in 1983 and stores in 1989.

Since then, it has registered numerous similar marks such as SPORTS "R" US, PETS "R" US, BABIES "R" US, and even GOODIES "R" US, the latter being used for toy vending machines in the TOYS "R" US stores. It also has successfully litigated against companies using Guns Are Us, Phones-R-Us and Adults "R" Us as trade names and opposed registration of similar marks Loans "R" Us and Flowers "R" Us before the Trademark Trial and Appeal Board. Many other "R" us marks that have been filed have been simply been abandoned including Beds, Pets, Dollars, Loans, Feets, and Homes "R" Us. Lastly, the company obtained a court order transferring the domain names Toysareus.com and Kidsareus.com (*Toys "R" Us, Inc. v. Eli Abir* 1999).

Table Three				
Legal Challenges by McDonald's of "Mc"Names				
Name	**Year**	**Location**	**Allowed**	**Comments**
McBagels	1986	U.S.	No	Food
McPretzel	1991	U.S.	No	Food
McTeddy (Bears)	1990	U.S.	No	McD's features toys in kid's meals
McSleep Inns	1988	U.S.	No	Hotels often related to restaurants
McDental	1993	U.S.	No	Likely consumer confusion (?)
McClaim's Legal Services	1995	U.S.	No	Likely consumer confusion (?)
It's not just big, Mac	1985	U.K.	No	Slogan used by rival Burger King
McIndians	1996	U.K.	No	Indian restaurant also sold fired chicken, burgers & fries
McChina Wok Away	2001	U.K.	Yes	McD's doesn't serve Chinese food and the name means "son of China"
MacChocolate, MacTea, MacNoodles	2004	Singapore	Yes	Sold through supermarkets using dissimilar mark design
McBeans	1994	Canada	Yes	Coffee sold in stores not restaurant
McHair	1995	Austria	Yes	Hairdressing services & products distinct from fast food
McAllan	1995	Denmark	No	Used by hot dog stand
McSalad, McFresh	1997	Australia	No	Deceptively similar
McMint and McVeg	1997	Australia	Yes	Confectionary business distinct; McVeg for a veggie hamburger confusion unlikely!!
McVeggie	2005	Argentina	No	
McCurry	2006	Malaysia	No	Colors also similar
McSweet	2014	U.S.	No	Sold in grocery stores with dissimilar packaging, but still likely to cause confusion

The family of trademarks strategy was first protected in the U.S. back in the 1960s when Motorola had a series of "Golden" trademarks for electronic equipment and parts. The Court of Customs and Patent Appeals affirmed the PTO's decision not to allow registration by a TV component supplier of "Golden Grid" for the electron gun used as part of the television picture tube. The court noted that "Golden" as used was not descriptive of color but suggestive of high quality (*Motorola Inc. v. Griffiths Electrons, Inc.* 1963).

Around the same time, Maidenform offered an entire line of "dream" bras—DAYDREAMS, DREAMLINES and DREAM-AIRE. When Bestform launched its TEEN-DREAM bra, Maidenform sued and won. The Trademark Trial and Appeal Board held that consumers would likely be confused concerning the source of TEEN-DREAM bras. The TTAB also based its decision on the well-known advertising slogan used by Maidenform at the time "I dreamed that . . . in my MAIDENFORM bra" (*Maidenform, Inc. v. Bestform Foundations, Inc.* 1969).

Alberto-Culver is another company that has successfully defended its TRESEME family of names. This family includes TRESPAC, TRESSPRAY, TRESGELEE, TRESWAVE and TRESHOLD, among others. A-C also had used one word slogans in advertising such as TRESchic and TRESprofessional. It successfully prevented registration of the name "Trevive" for hair care products arguing that the prefix TRES is pronounced "tray" just as it would be in "Trevive" because the latter also appears to have a French connotation (*Han Beauty, Inc. v. Alberto-Culver Co.* 2001).

In order to establish a family of names, brand marketers must show joint advertising and promotion of at least some of the names and that they have a common element that is distinctive and not merely descriptive of the products. For example, "jet" as a name suffix was found descriptive of spray nozzles, "aqua" was found not distinctive for water faucets and "servo" was too commonly used as an industry abbreviation for servomotors and servomechanisms to be distinctive. Indeed the suffix "-ettes" and similar suffixes are so commonly used in a wide variety of products that no one could have a family of names based on that common element (Mack, et al. 2004). Similarly, a court held that a generic term such as Aloe or its phonic equivalent "Alo" cannot serve as the basis for a family of brands. Any product using gel from the Aloe Vera plant should be able to use Aloe descriptively in its name (*American Aloe Corp. v. Aloe Crème Labs, Inc.* 1970).

However, five years later the Trademark Trial and Appeal Board upheld an opposition to a rival registration of an "Alo-" mark based on the long exclusive use of a family of marks by another company. The Board found that the original family of descriptive marks had developed distinctive secondary meaning in the minds of consumers and to allow another firm to register a similar mark would likely cause consumer confusion regarding the source of the goods (*Aloe Crème Labs, Inc. v. Aloe99, Inc.* 1975). This illustrates the difficulty in predicting where courts will draw the line between generic elements and those that are descriptive and might develop secondary meaning to become distinctive.

Just as the TTAB did not protect 7–Eleven's GULP family of trademarks against the registration of GULPY for animal water bowls (*7–Eleven, Inc. v. Wechsler* 2007), a court also allowed the co-existence of Citigroup's family of marks (CITIBANK, CITICORP, CITICARD, etc.) and City Holding's series of composite marks (CITY NATIONAL BANK, CITY FINANCIAL GROUP, etc.). Although the first part of each set of marks sounds the same, they had co-existed for a long time and were well differentiated in writing. The unusual spelling of the "CITI-" prefix caused the public to recognize all of these marks as identifying a common source or single brand, so the court found that Citigroup enjoyed a family of brands. However, according to the court, the public did not recognize that the various "CITY" trademarks all came from a single source and formed a common brand because "city" is a common word. City Holdings did not enjoy a family of brands (*Citigroup Inc. v. City Holding Co.* 2003). It is important to note that each name must be separately registered as a trademark whether it is part of a family of marks or simply a series of similar marks. The USPTO does not accept place-filler registrations such as Mc_______ in part because they may be difficult for others to search (*In re International Flavors & Fragrances, Inc.* 1999).

Today Apple has claimed trademark rights not just in iPod, but also iTunes, iPhoto, iSight, iWork and iWeb. It also is challenging other firms with similar trademarks starting with the lower case "i" or containing the word "Pod" (Branfman and Broberg 2006). However, with the advent of the internet, trademarks starting with "i" have become common and over one thousand applications and registrations exist for trademarks containing "pod." Apple may have a difficult time convincing trademark authorities that consumers associate all "i-" or "-pod" marks with it.

One case where there was no effort to enforce a family of names involved the licensee who has used PONDEROSA and BONANZA as names of steak house restaurants since 1965. The licensee failed to challenge the registration of the name HOSS'S STEAK AND SEA HOUSE, but of course this is only a family of names so long as consumers recognize Hoss was one of the Cartwright family members who lived on the ranch Ponderosa in the TV series Bonanza.

G. LOGOS

There is no single generally accepted definition of logos. As used here, logos denote a graphic or symbolic representation of the brand name or initials. Graphic symbols such as Apple's apple design with no lettering are discussed under symbols in the next chapter. To some degree, almost all brand names have a unique design and style (lettering style, color, etc.) and therefore could be considered logos. However, simple borders and nondescript type styles offer little additional distinctiveness to a name or set of initials. Many marketers believe it is important to select a typeface that is consistent with the brand message and refer to the font as the handwriting or DNA of the brand (Birkner 2015). As noted in Chapter Two, Google recently adjusted its typeface to be more visible on small cellphone screens. Fonts generally are not protected from imitation under copyright law in the United States, but the font as part of a trademarked logo can be important part of a visual similarity analysis between two trademarks.

Once a designed logo has been selected, it is typically registered as a stylized or special form trademark. If the letters contained within the logo design are distinctive, they also may be registered as a "standard character" (formerly "typed") drawing on the trademark application that would then cover the letter(s) or word(s). Often brand marketers apply for both types of protection when they can. The special form drawing alone would have to be used for a logo containing generic words since the words themselves would not be eligible for trademark protection. For example, as noted in Chapter Two, the term "lite" or "light" has been held to be generic description. However Miller beer has a registered trademark for its logo of "lite" used on beer and illustrated below on the original can next to the modern logo (*Miller Brewing Co.* 1985). A special form logo also may be rejected if it is merely descriptive with non-distinctive graphic components. This happened to the proposed state of Tennessee logo also illustrated on the next page.

It is common for stylized drawing applications to disclaim the word(s) or initials themselves indicating that no trademark protection is being sought for the word(s) or initials per se. For example, in the case of "the sofa & chair company," the Trademark Trial and Appeal Board found the words not generic, but descriptive and required proof of secondary meaning. The proof that was presented only showed secondary meaning for the stylized rendition of the words and the appellate court upheld the Board's requirement that the words themselves be disclaimed (*In re K-T Zoe Furniture, Inc.* 1994). The advantage of filing both a standard character and a special form application is that the applicant may be successful and register both for the broadest possible protection.

Henderson and Cote (1998) argue that in many cases logos are an important brand element. For example, Taco Bell spends 20 times more on its permanent in-store media, which contain its logo, than it spends on advertising. Logos are used not just on packaging and advertising, but business cards and letterhead, corporate giveaways and logo decorated clothing or other items may be a significant source of revenue. Because of the pictorial quality of many logos, they may be recognized more quickly than the words of the brand name and may help consumers remember the brand (Kohli et al. 2002). The various design elements of logos can influence consumer's ability to remember the brand, recognize it and start to develop either a positive or negative emotional affect (Kohli, et al. 2002; Keller 2003, pp. 193–5). A recent study found that people described the most memorable logos as being simple like the Nike and Coca-Cola stylized logos and the McDonald's arches and Apple symbol trademarks. As noted above, logos that are too simple risk being rejected for trademark registration because they are not considered to be distinctive. Logo designers seeking to design a simple logo need to make sure it is still visually distinctive.

Because logos are substantially verbal, they share many of the same legal issues as brand names. As noted above, purely descriptive or generic words may not be protected as word trademarks, but may still be narrowly protected as a logo (stylized drawing) trademarks. For example, a logo of the letters CVM was registered despite allegedly standing for "consumable vacuum melted" a descriptive method for making steel products. For that registration, trademark coverage for the letters themselves was disclaimed. However, for the standard character registration for the same three letters, which would have protected CVM in non-stylized formats, an appellate court held that evidence must be presented in the second proceeding to determine whether CVM is perceived as descriptive of the process (*United States Steel Corp. v. Vasco Metals Corp.* 1968).

A recent Supreme Court decision involved two marketers of tattoo ink. One had used "microcolors" to describe its products since 1991 and the other registered a logo mark of the words "micro colors" in 1992. The Supreme Court held that despite the possibility of confusion, the first firm was entitled to use "microcolors" as descriptive fair use of its product despite the second firm's logo mark (*KP Permanent Make-up, Inc. v. Lasting Impression I. Inc.* 2004). Thus while registering a logo of a descriptive term or letters prevents others from using a confusing similar trademark, it does not prevent others from using the terms or letters descriptively.

Logos have the advantage over brand names of being more protected against certain types of use by third parties. For example, an independent car repair shop that specializes in repairing Volkswagens may advertise that fact, but use of the "VW" logo is more likely to confuse consumers into thinking the shop is an official repair shop authorized by Volkswagen of America (*Volkswagen Aktiengesellschaft v. Church* 1969; *Volkswagen Aktiengesellschaft v. Uptown Motors* 1995).

Many logos incorporate company initials such as ABC and NBC (although the E.U. generally rejects applications for just two characters). The trademark question raised by such initials is whether they are confusingly similar because there is only one letter difference between the two. Having distinctive typefaces and graphic designs can diminish or even eliminate this issue (Hemnes 1985). For example, a recent European Court of First Instance Decision allowed registration for an "IDEA" logo for a furniture company, despite the aural and lettering similarities to the well-known IKEA community trademark for furniture.

Similarly, a recent U.S. court of appeals decision involved the following two marks (the left being black and dark red and the right colored blue):

The senior user Savin on the right had used its mark since 1959 in the sale of office equipment and it is quite well known. The junior user on the left is a civil engineering firm in New York who has been using its mark since 1987. It is the founder's nickname spelled backwards. Several hundred other businesses use the name Savin. The court affirmed dismissal of the infringement claim, finding no likelihood of confusion because of the distinctive logos and industries, despite the use of the identical name of SAVIN.

The court held that the dilution claim could go to trial to determine whether these logo marks should be considered identical in a dilution context. While the court suggested they may not be identical, it recognized that identicalness would create a presumption of actual dilution (*Savin Corp. v. Savin Group*, 2004). Similarly, the name CHARBUCKS was found not to be confusingly similar (nor dilutive) to STARBUCKS based on the distinctiveness of the logo and packaging. In contrast, a recent case in China found that the logo shown on the next page with a Chinese name that sounds similar to "STARBUCKS" was found likely to cause consumer confusion.

H. CONCLUSION

While the selection of a brand name and logo are important marketing decisions and should be made consistent with a larger brand identification strategy, sometimes a chosen verbal identifier may prove to be untenable under trademark law, typically for being too descriptive. As discussed in the previous chapter, rather than identify the source of the product, the proposed identifier merely describes the product or may describe all products in the category making it generic.

Brand managers who select and promote enforce-able identifiers are often thrilled when the brand name becomes a short hand term for the product itself, such as Coke, Xerox, Kleenex, Band Aid and Hoover in the United Kingdom. In fact Ries and Ries (2000, p. 41) declare this to be the ultimate sign of brand success. However, despite the marketing advantages of "owning the category," brands with this level of ubiquity run the risk of being declared generic even though when first used they were not generic. Thus, it is important for such ubiquitous trademarks to take action such as correcting the media and suing infringers to protect trademark status and minimize the risk of having the trademark declared generic.

CHAPTER 4

Sensory Brand Identifiers: Symbols, Characters, Product Design and Color, and Non-Visual Brand Identifiers

A. INTRODUCTION

Today, establishing an exclusive brand identity usually goes far beyond a name and logo. Marketers often seek to make an emotional connection to consumers through sensory brand elements. Marc Gobé (2001) argues that many non-verbal elements offer genuine marketing advantages. For example, research shows that sound, especially music, may add an emotional appeal to a brand. Similarly, colors may be used to communicate specific brand values such as green for the environment, white for purity, etc. Product scent may play a similar role with earthy scents or the smell of a new car. Lindstrom (2005, p. 3) warns: "In order to have a viable future, brands will have to incorporate a brand platform that fully integrates the five senses."

Sensory brand elements can communicate certain brand attributes. For example, Lageat et al. (2003, p. 104) found that two different sounds of the opening of cigarette lighters caused consumers to rate the lighter as luxurious. One sound was described as "matte, even and low in pitch" which the authors suggested was an unobtrusive sound of luxury. The other sound was a more conspicuous, "flashy perception of luxury" described as a clear resonant clicking sound. Thus with proper measurement of sound dimensions, a brand could develop a particular sound consistent with desired consumer perception of the brand and promote it as a brand identifier to obtain trademark protection. Of course during this process, there always is a risk that a rival will reverse engineer sound and imitate it on its brand, so that even though the sound communicates a particular value to some consumers, it never comes to identify a particular brand. A good example might be the sound of closing the door on luxury automobiles. The sound communicates high quality but few if any consumers could distinguish the sound of one luxury car door from another so the sound doesn't identify any particular brand.

Yet despite this interest, there has been little discussion in the marketing literature on how to protect sensory brand elements. Lindstrom (2005, p. 108) simply asserts that "[a]lmost every aspect of a brand's sensory appeal can be trademarked." It is true that trademarks have been broadly defined. As Chapter One explains, trademark law has expanded from protecting obscure marks and fanciful brand names to protecting a myriad of devices that identify the source of a product. A decade ago, the U.S. Supreme Court noted that the Lanham Act says that "trademarks 'includ[e] any word, name, symbol, or device, or any combination thereof.' . . . Since human beings might use as a "symbol" or "device" almost anything at all that is capable of carrying meaning, this language, read literally, is not restrictive" (*Qualitex Co. v. Jacobson Products Co., Inc.*, 1995, p. 162). Similarly in Europe, Article 4 of the Council Directive on the Community Trademark defines trademarks as "any sign capable of being represented graphically, particular words, including personal names, designs, letters, numerals, the shape of goods or their packaging, provided that such signs are capable of distinguishing the goods or services of one undertaking from those of other undertakings" (Council Regulation 40/94/EEC, 1994 O.J. (L11)). Thus both jurisdictions recognize non-verbal brand identifiers particularly those that are visual. Unfortunately, as this chapter demonstrates, trademark protection for other types of sensory brand elements is not as readily available as Lindstrom naively suggests.

One important limitation on all sensory brand elements is functionality. Just as verbal brand identifiers are not protected if they are purely descriptive or generic, sensory brand elements are not protected by trademark law if they occur naturally or are part of the product's function. The U.S. Supreme Court has defined functionality as "essential to the use or purpose of the device or when it affects the cost or quality of the device" (*Qualitex Co. v. Jacobson Products Co., Inc.*, 1995, p. 165; *TrafFix Devices, Inc. v. Marketing Displays, Inc.* 2001, p. 32). Lower court have examined whether competitors have available to them alternative functionally equivalent designs (*Morton-Norwich Prods.* 1982). An obvious example of sensory product functionality is the scent of a perfume. Even though many consumers can identify the brand of a perfume by its scent, the scent may not be trademarked because it is the function of the perfume.

In *TrafFix*, the Court held that product aspects protected by utility patents are strongly presumed to be functional and therefore unavailable for trademark or trade dress protection. The Court further noted that "[i]t is proper to inquire into a "significant non-reputation-related disadvantage" in cases of aesthetic functionality" (*TrafFix Devices, Inc. v. Marketing Displays, Inc.* 2001, p. 33). In other words, these two U.S. Supreme Court opinions suggest that sensory trademarks and trade dress may be functional in either a utilitarian way (e.g., the color of paint or scent of a perfume) or in a specific way that appeals to the senses—aesthetic functionality. For example, a court allowed the close imitation (rather than protection as a trademark) of baroque patterns in flatware because consumers bought that style of flatware because of its particular style of ornamentation. The ornamentation therefore was aesthetically functional (*Wallace International Silversmiths, Inc. v. Godinger Silver Art Co., Inc.* 1990).

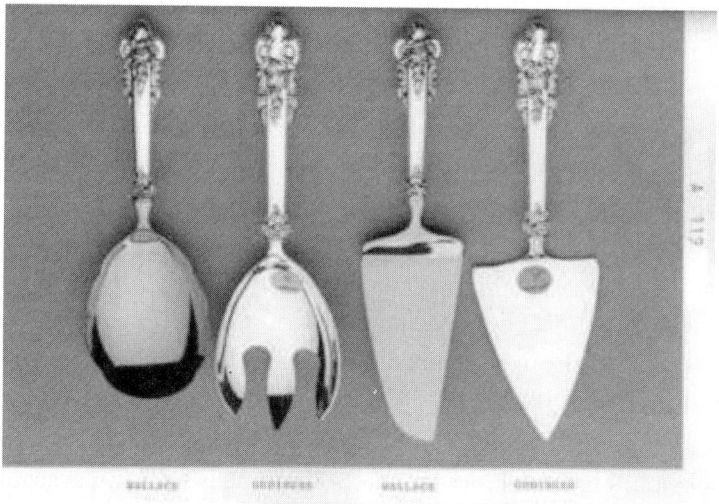

Similarly, people buy plastic planters that resembled Grecian stone urns because of their appearance so the product design itself is not protected as a trademark indicating origin with a specific company (*Duraco Products, Inc. v. Joy Plastic Enterprises, Ltd* 1994). In contrast, cracker marketers have a wide variety of colors and shapes from which to choose, so the appealing color and shape of Pepperidge Farm's goldfish snack crackers, which readily identifies the brand to consumers, is not available for imitation (*Nabisco, Inc. v. PF Brands, Inc.* 1999). A more questionable decision held that backgrounds of soft colors, calligraphy, florescent ink, high quality textured art paper and lengthy poetry were all trade dress for greeting cards rather than functional or ornamental elements that set a particular mood for the card message (*Hartford House, Ltd. v. Hallmark Cards, Inc.* 1988).

A second important limitation on protecting sensory brand elements under trademark law is the presumption that these elements are merely product attributes designed to increase the attractiveness of the product. The burden is on the brand owner to prove secondary meaning—that particular sensory elements actually identify the brand or source of the product to consumers. For example, athletic footwear is often decorated with attractive ornamental designs. Consumers might buy these shoes because they like the designs. However, that does not mean the design identifies a brand or product source with consumers (*Wal-Mart Stores, Inc. v. Samara Brothers, Inc.* 2000). In contrast, the Nike "swoosh" clearly does identify the brand and source of the product with consumers (*Nike Inc. v. "Just Did It" Enterprises* 1993). For this reason, trademark law prevents other brands of footwear or athletic clothing from using ornamental symbols that are confusingly similar to the Nike "swoosh."

The E.U. offers a third limitation on limiting trademark registration for sensory brand identifiers. Community trademarks must be capable of graphic representation (2008/95/EC). This requirement is not much of a limitation for visual marks but as explained below, it is problematic for other types of sensory marks under a recent European Court of Justice ruling (*Sieckmann v. Deutsches patent—und Markenamt* 2002).

Sensory brand identifiers can be divided into two categories. The first category is visual and is widely used. Visual trademarks may include color, two and three dimensional visual symbols, trade dress including packaging and non-functional product configuration and motion marks. The second category is other sensory marks including sounds, scents and possibly flavor and touch marks. These types of marks are not widely used, but Gobé (2003) and Lindstrom (2005) advocate and predict greater use in the future.

B. VISUAL MARKS

Visual marks are generally included in an area of trademark law known as trade dress. Trade dress refers to brand packaging and non-functional aspects of product design. One court of appeals defined trade dress as "encompass[ing] the design and appearance of the product together with all the elements making up the overall image that serves to identify the product presented to the customer" (*Fun-Damental Too Ltd. v. Gemmy Industries Corp.* 1996, p. 999). The Supreme

Court noted that trade dress "may include such features as size, shape, color, or color combinations, textures, graphics, or even particular sales techniques" (*Two Pesos, Inc. v. Taco Cabana, Inc.* 1992, p. 764). In 1992, the U.S. Supreme Court confirmed that trade dress could be inherently distinctive and therefore protected under trademark law without a showing of secondary meaning in the minds of consumers. The Court held the imitation of distinctive trade dress to be trademark infringement despite the non-confusing nature of the restaurant names (*Two Pesos, Inc. v. Taco Cabana, Inc.* 1992). It noted that the protections of the Lanham Act apply with equal force to trademark and trade dress infringement. Visual trademarks also include visual symbols (with no verbal content) such as the famous Nike swoosh and characters such as Kellogg's Tony the Tiger.

I. Trade Dress—Packaging vs. Product Configuration

Trade dress can often communicate some aspects of a brand to consumers. It can be innovative, bold, or artistic—thereby suggesting that the brand shares those attributes (Gobé 2003). Furthermore, packaging can help build brand identity both as a form of advertising, particularly at the point of purchase, and as part of brand use experience after purchase (Underwood 2003). For example, studies show that about 40% of all perfume purchases are based on the design of the bottle (Lindstrom 2005, p. 86).

Since the *Two Pesos* decision, the Court has clarified that product configuration trade dress, such as the product shape or color, may not be inherently distinctive under the law and must be proven to have secondary meaning in the minds of consumers. Only packaging may be inherently distinctive (*Wal-Mart Stores, Inc. v. Samara Brothers Inc.* 2000). Therefore, an important question for visual marks is whether they are part of product packaging and may be protected if inherently distinctive or whether they are part of product configuration and will only be protected if shown to identify the brand or source of the product in the minds of consumers.

A recent decision by the Federal Circuit Court of Appeals considered whether holes and flaps as part of the design of apparel such as pants and skirts could be inherently distinctive even though it was only part of the product design. The court said that product design did not need to "implicate the entire product." But consistent with the Supreme Court, it ultimately held that the hole and flap design was not inherently distinctive. The marketer must show that the hole and flap elements identified the brand source to consumers before trademark registration would be allowed (*In re Slokevage* 2006). In contrast, in an earlier case, the Trademark Trial and Appeal Board found that the shape of a container for bath products was not a mere refinement of a commonly used shape, but was in fact unusual for that particular type of product and therefore was inherently distinctive and did not require proof of secondary meaning in the minds of consumers (*Creative Beauty Innovations, Inc.* 2000).

For trade dress packaging that is not inherently distinctive and product design that can never be inherently distinctive, showing that trade dress identifies the product source rather than just serves as an attractive ornamentation can be done with a consumer survey. In addition, advertising that emphasizes the product's unique appearance and even emphasizes the appearance as a brand identifier (i.e., "look for . . . ") may help in this regard. Similarly, posting a trademark notice on the trade dress provides notice that the brand owner believes it is a source identifier (Hanson 1999).

Europe also recognizes that packaging might serve the function of a three dimensional trademark. Since consumers are used to seeing similar packaging on different brands of products, an applicant seeking to register packaging as a trademark must show the packaging has a distinctive character and significantly departs from other shapes used in the relevant market sector. Recently, the European Court of Justice affirmed the denial of trademark registration for a stand up pouches for fruit drinks and fruit juices. It held that the relevant sector was liquids for human consumption and that within that sector the pouches were not distinctive (*Deutsche SiSi-Werke GmbH & Co. Betriebs KG v. Office for Harmonization in the Internal Market* 2006). Previously, the ECJ had affirmed rejections of community trademarks for laundry tablets and a beer bottle with a slice of lime on its cap. The standard in Europe for such marks requires a significant departure from what is the norm in the respective section. This is an interesting contrast to word marks that must have a minimal degree of distinctiveness such as BABY-DRY discussed in Chapter Two (Klett and Lutz 2007).

Contrary to the U.S. Supreme Court's announcement that the Lanham Act applies with equal force to trademark and trade dress infringement (*Two Pesos, Inc. v. Taco Cabana, Inc.* 1992), most courts appear less willing to protect trade dress-packaging and non-functional product configurations than strong word marks. But a few lower courts have followed the Supreme Court and refused to allow trade dress imitation even with a distinctive name (*McNeil-PPC, Inc. v. Guardian Drug Co.*, 1997). However, if the name and packaging are similar, such as with Pecan Shortbread cookies imitating Pecan Sandies cookies, the courts more consistently enjoin the imitator for being confusingly similar (*Keebler Company v. Nabisco Brands, Inc.*, 1992).

Copying trade dress is allowed even when done intentionally (*Bristol-Myers Squibb Co. v. McNeil-P.P.C., Inc.* 1994) and is sometimes felt to be generic to the product. For example, a court refused to enjoin Mars' introduction of peanut butter M & Ms candies, even though it copied many aspects of the packaging of Reece's Pieces (*Hershey Foods Corporation v. Mars, Inc.*1998) finding that these aspects such as orange and brown colors were generically descriptive of peanut butter. Chapter Fifteen discusses trade dress imitation from the perspective of the imitating brand.

II. Color

While some colors such as brown and tan for peanut butter are considered generic or merely descriptive of the product, non-functional colors such as the green/gold color of an ironing board cover can act as trademarks if they identify a particular brand in the minds of consumers (*Qualitex Co. v. Jacobson Products Co., Inc.*, 1995).

Colors and product shape have been found functional (indicating dosage) for prescription drug pills (*Shire U.S. Inc. v. Barr Labs, Inc.* 2003) and color alone is functional for mouthwashes indicating flavor (*Warner Lambert Co. v. McCrory's Corp.* 1989). Colors are normally assumed to be ornamentation—attractive but with no secondary meaning to identify a particular source. In some cases, even when colors have secondary meaning, they will not be protected because they are aesthetically functional. The Eighth Circuit refused to protect "John Deere green" from imitation by tractor accessory marketers because consumers wanted to buy accessory equipment that matches their tractor (*Deere & Co. v. Farmhand, Inc.* 1983). Similarly, the Federal Circuit Court of Appeals affirmed refusal to register the color black for outboard boat motors because the color was functional in that it coordinated with many different boat colors (*Brunswick Corp. v. British Seagull Ltd.* 1994).

If secondary meaning is proven, both the U.S. and Europe will accept registrations for non-functional color trademarks. However, the E.U. accepts single color marks as a rare exception to its general rule that they are not distinctive (O'Reilly 2004). In the U.S., the drawings of the trademark must be in color and the color must be described in particular terms using generic language. In Europe, a sample of the color must be submitted and the color must be designated using an internationally recognized color code system such as the Pantone Color Code, RGB Color Code or RAL Color Code (Roth 1995). While the U.S. does not require the use of such a code system, the use of one is strongly recommended (Gilson and LaLonde 2005).

III. Symbols and Ornamental Designs

Overall trade dress can be viewed as a three dimensional symbol. Symbols, whether two or three dimensional, can be included upon product trade dress and as noted above are presumed to be ornamentation unless the user can show secondary meaning in the minds of consumers. For example, the sideways "V" figure used by Puma was held to be ornamentation rather than a trademark recognized by consumers (*Brooks Shoe Mfg. Co., Inc. v. Suave Shoe Corp.* 1983). Under some circumstances, such as Asics's stripe design first used for athletic shoes in 1966, a symbol may be deemed functional. In the case of the Asics design, the stripes were touted as reinforcement and support and the design was claimed as functional in two utility patents (*Asics Corp. v. Target Corp.* 2003). In contrast, Adidas zealously enforces its well-known three stripe trademark.

Some symbols such as the Nike "swoosh" and the McDonalds' golden arches are well known symbolic trademarks. When a computer company placed a single golden arch design on its product, it was found not to infringe upon McDonald's golden arches trademark, but did dilute it by blurring (*McDonald's Corp. v. Arche Technologies* 1990). Many estimate that most communication (perhaps 70–90%) is non-verbal (Aaker and Joachimsthaler 2000, p. 82). Use of a visual metaphor such as the Rock of Gibraltar for Prudential Insurance communicates strength, endurance and reliability more effectively than words.

It is the responsibility of the brand owner to prove that its symbol or shape has secondary meaning to identify the brand in the minds of consumers. In *Wal-Mart Stores, Inc. v. Samara Brothers, Inc.* (2000), the U.S. Supreme Court held that attractive pictures applied to children's clothing may not be deemed inherently distinctive and must be proven to identify the source of the product. It further noted that even unusual product shapes such as a cocktail shaker shaped like a penguin is presumed to be ornamental unless it is proven to identify a single brand in the minds of consumers.

IV. Character Marks

While abstract symbols can catch attention, characters also can serve that purpose while also adding a personality to the brand (Callcott and Phillips 1996). Research suggests that the use of likeable spokes-characters for a brand can enhance the favorability of brand attitudes (Garretson and Burton 2005), but it is not clear whether this leads to brand choice, at least for children (Neeley and Schumannn 2004).

Brand spokes-characters can be divided into four categories as illustrated by the table below:

Table One		
Brand Characters		
Brand Characters	**Inanimate**	**Live**
Created for the Brand	The Keebler Elves, Tony the Tiger, the Petco Sock Puppet	Mr. Whipple for Charmin, Uncle Ben for rice
Pre-Existing Characters	Snoopy, Superman	Captain Kangaroo for Schwinn bicycles; Celebrities—see Ch. 13

Characters vary in the degree to which they resemble living people. The Morton Salt Girl is a blue and white drawing that is limited to appearing on the package. Aunt Jemima and Betty Crocker are life-like drawings but still limited to appearing on the package. Uncle Ben is a photograph of an actual person, but he only appears on the package. In contrast, the Jolly Green Giant originally appeared on the package and only briefly in television advertising to laugh. The character Little Sprout was created to interact more fully with both the Giant and the TV audience. Tony the Tiger and the Trix rabbit are animated cartoon characters with well-developed personalities and distinctive voices and slogans that appear in television advertising as well as on packages. Bartel & Jaymes were two product spokespersons played by actors who did not appear on the package but did appear in television advertising and sometimes in point-of-purchase promotional materials. Wendy's character has appeared as the real daughter of company founder Dave, as a well-known picture of a young girl with red hair and freckles and as a young woman portrayed by an actor.

It is usually important for a brand to have exclusive rights to a promotional character. Buster Brown shoes learned this lesson the hard way when the brand adopted the comic strip character for its spokes-character in 1904. However, the character also began to be used by other products, including cigars and bourbon—far from ideal usages from the perspective of a children's shoe company (McCauley 1989).

The most direct way to insure exclusive rights to use a brand character is to create an inanimate character and register the drawing of the character as a trademark. As noted in Chapter Two, trademark rights accrue from use of the mark in commerce or its registration based on use or intent to use. When an artist initially draws, sculpts or otherwise creates an inanimate character, copyright law protects the work from imitation. If the artist is a full time employee of a company, then the copyright belongs to the company, but if the artist is an independent contractor then the company should only engage the artist in a written contract that expressly identifies the character as "work for hire" thereby assigning copyright protection to the employer (11 U.S.C. § 101). Similar copyright rules would apply to a commercial (storyboards or filmed) or package that is drawn or otherwise created by an artist. Copyright law also would apply to any two or three dimensional symbols that are separable from the product itself such as the McDonald's golden arches. Copyright law is discussed in more detail in the next chapter.

Some firms, such as Walt Disney Co., which now owns Marvel Entertainment, create characters that become brands in their own right. These companies may choose to license their character brands for advertising other brands such as Snoopy and other Peanuts characters which appear in advertising for Metropolitan Life. Such character brands also typically have active merchandise and multi-media licensing programs protected by both trademark and copyright law.

Character licensing does not always go smoothly. Since 1976, POPEYES brand fried chicken licensed both its name and the right to use the image of the cartoon character from the Hearst Corporation, paying over $1million annually in recent years. However, the restaurant discontinued using the cartoon character in 2012 and is seeking to let the licensing agreement expire but has filed a lawsuit seeking a declaratory judgment that it may continue to use the POPEYES name.

Actors who portray characters typically have no trademark or copyright rights to those characters. However, they might have some right against misappropriation or a right of publicity to the character. A 1928 court decision found that the commercial use in movies of the "Little Tramp" character by an actor known as Charles Aplin was misappropriation of the character created by and associated with Charlie Chaplin (*Chaplin v. Amador* 1928). Similarly, a Third Circuit opinion held that New Jersey right of publicity covered not only a celebrity's name but also the name of a character that was identified with that celebrity—in this case "Spanky" from the "Spanky and our Gang" series of movies (*McFarland v. Miller* 1994). Most recently, George Wendt and John Ratzenberger, the actors who played Norm and Cliff on the TV series, "Cheers" were able to successfully assert their right of publicity against a chain of "Cheers-like" bars that had copyright permission to build robots of Norm and Cliff to sit at the end of the bar (*Wendt v. Host Int'l, Inc.* 1999). The right of publicity is examined in more detail in Chapter Thirteen.

V. Motion Marks

One interesting aspect about character trademarks in particular is that they often move. If they move in the same way each time, these marks also qualify as motion marks. Such motion marks may be used in television or movie advertising as well as computer screens. Motion marks may include traditional word or logo marks along with a character mark that is animated to move. The motion adds visual interest as demonstrated by movie companies such as Columbia Pictures (U.S. Reg. No. 1,975,999) and 20th Century Fox (U.S. Reg. No. 1,928,424) that show their motion mark at the beginning of every movie. They also could include other sensory elements. The MGM lion not only moves its head, but roars creating both motion and sound trademarks (U.S. Reg. No. 1395550). Such motion marks may be registered by filing a description and perhaps a film strip or the digital equivalent of the mark in action.

Motion trademarks may be registered in both the U.S. and E.U. The U.S. accepted its first motion mark (a spinning coin) for registration in 1957. Both the U.S. and E.U. have registered car maker Lamborghini's trademark on the vertical movement of its car doors. (U.S. Reg. No. 2,793,439 and CTM 1400092).

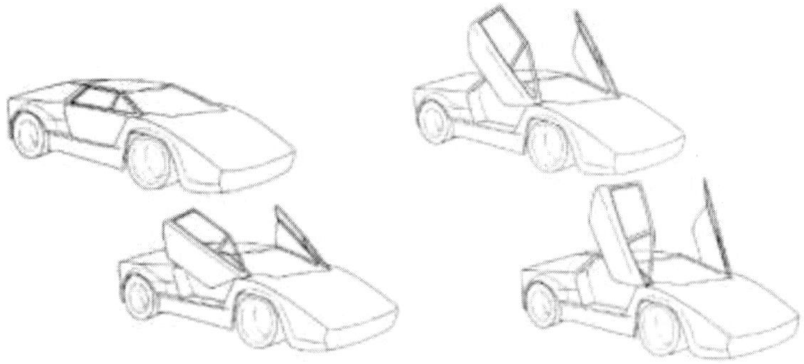

C. NON-VISUAL SENSORY MARKS

I. Sound Marks

Like non-verbal visual brand elements, sounds, scents, flavors and even tactile elements of a product or its packaging may be considered for trademark/trade dress protection if they are non-natural and non-functional and identify the product source or brand in the minds of consumers. The MGM lion and spinning coin trademarks both included sounds—the roar of the lion and sound of the coin spinning on a hard surface, respectively. The U.S. has allowed the registration of sounds marks since 1950 with the registration of the NBC three note chime mark. Less than 25 sound marks had been registered by 1990 (and one in Canada). Since then 254 sound applications have been filed in the U.S. resulting in 99 registered marks (McCormick 2006).

Such sounds must not be commonplace. The TTAB affirmed the denial of the sound of a ship's bell clock for radio broadcast services because it found the sound to be commonplace rather than inherently distinctive and there was no evidence of acquired distinctiveness (*In re General Electric Broadcasting* 1978). This reasoning was followed in a recent case involving duck calls as a possible trademark for duck boat city tours. The court held that duck calls were not inherently distinctive and lacked secondary meaning to identify any particular tour service (*Ride the Ducks. L.L.C. v. Duck Boat Tours, Inc.,* 2005). This suggests that more unusual sounds could be considered inherently distinctive and protected without proof of secondary meaning.

In 2004, the European Court of Justice confirmed that sound marks could be registered in Europe if they were distinctive and could be represented graphically. The court required detailed musical notation and rejected less detailed musical notation, word descriptions and onomatopoeia. These types of descriptions, along with a required sound recording, are all permitted in the U.S.—in fact a detailed written description accompanied the U.S. registration for the famous Tarzan yell in 1998. Europe also says it allows sonograms to be submitted for non-musical marks such as the roar of the MGM, but has not yet registered a sonogram supported mark. By the end of 2004, the European Community had registered forty-four sound marks (Roth 2005) of which 31 are still currently registered (McCormick 2006). Interest in sounds marks with Europe varies. The U.K. currently has a mere five registered sound marks, but Germany has about 166 such marks (McCormick 2006).

II. Scent Marks

Marketing literature suggests that product scent can be an important influence on product evaluation, particularly when the scent is deemed appropriate by consumers (Bone and Jantrania 1992). The U.S. also has allowed registration of scent marks for products that normally do not have a scent such as embroidery thread (*In re Clarke* 1990). Registration also has been allowed for scents that are arbitrary for a product class such as cherry, grape and strawberry scents for motor oils. The registrant must prove the scent functions as a mark rather than ornamentation and must provide a written description and sample of the scent (Gilson and LaLonde 2005). The embroidery thread registration was cancelled in 1997, leaving only 10 registered scent marks in the U.S., with another nine applications pending in early 2007. Verizon recently registered a trademark for its "flowery musk" scent used in marquee destination stores (Gershman 2015).

In theory scent registrations are allowed in Europe, but the graphic representation requirement appears to make such registrations difficult. In 1999, the Community Trade Mark Office Board of Appeal allowed registration for the smell of fresh cut grass as a scent trademark for tennis balls. The Board held that the scent was both well-known and distinctive and the word description qualified as sufficient graphical representation (Matheson 2003). To date however, this is the only registered olfactory community trademark and it has expired (Gershman 2015).

A 2002 decision by the European Court of Justice held that chemical formula, written description and sample of the scent all fail individually and collectively to satisfy the graphic representation requirement for a scent described as "balsamically fruity with a slight hint of cinnamon" (*Sieckmann v. Deutsches patent—und Markenamt* 2002). The court held that the graphical representation of a sensory trademark must be clear, precise, self-contained, easily accessible, intelligible, durable, unequivocal and objective. Shortly after this decision, the scent of raspberries for motor oil was recognized as a sufficient description for graphical representation, but rejected because it was not distinctive (*Myles Ltd.'s App.* 2003). In October 2005, the Court of First Instance rejected a mark for the scent of ripe strawberries because the description lacked precision given the number of varieties of strawberries (*Eden SARL v. Office for Harmonization in the Internal Market* 2005).

There is hope on the technology horizon. Computer generated scent stimulation technology is available to create consistent samples of scents. They would be represented graphically by gas chronomographs (Matheson 2003). Europe is currently considering removing its graphical representation requirement for community trademarks. However, the question of when a scent is functional requires further exploration and resolution. A fragrance would appear may be functional when it is a primary function of the product such as perfumes, air fresheners or cleaning products. Another likely functional purpose would be to mask other odors including an unpleasant odor of the product itself (e.g., some medicines). But questions remain. Since paper towels and toilet paper are used for cleaning, is a distinctive fragrance functional whereas a fragrance for napkins may be non-functional?

III. Flavor Marks?

Flavor trademarks are equally problematic in Europe because of the difficulty of representing such marks graphically with specificity. A 2004 decision denied trademark registration for a strawberry flavor for medicines because it lacked distinctiveness and could not be graphically represented as required by E.U. law (*Eli Lilly & Co's Community Trade Mark Application* 2004). In the U.S, there was a similar attempt to register an orange flavor created for a particular medicine as a trademark. The registration also was denied. The Trademark Trial and Appeal Board (TTAB) affirmed the trademark examiner's refusal of registration (*In re N.V. Organon*, 2006). It held that the flavor was functional in this case and there was no evidence that it served to identify the brand rather than being simply an attribute of the product. Careful analysis of this decision suggests that there is limited hope that a flavor might serve as a trademark in the U.S. under particular circumstances.

While the pharmaceutical company argued that flavor was non-functional because it did not impact the cost, quality, or therapeutic operation of the product, the TTAB took a broader view of functionality. Based on the applicant's own website, the TTAB held the flavor was functional because most doctors felt the pleasant taste was an advantage over conventional antidepressants. The taste made it more likely patients would continue to take the medicine and discontinuance is a substantial problem among depressed patients.

This broad view of functionality has been supported by past decisions, such as one that found the color black to be functional (matched a variety of boat colors) for outboard boat motors even though it had no effect on the operation of the motor (*Brunswick Corp. v. British Seagull Ltd.* 1994). The Board even cited an old 1924 Supreme Court decision that permitted competing liquid quinine manufacturers to both use chocolate because it functioned as a suspending medium for the medicine and masked the taste and therefore was not part of the trade dress that could be protected from passing off by a competitor (*William R. Warner & Co. v. Eli Lilly & Co.* 1924).

In addition, the TTAB found orange flavoring functional because there was some evidence it was more popular or better at masking the bitter flavor of most medicines and therefore was more effective than other flavors. To allow one company to have a monopoly for an indefinite period of time over orange flavor for antidepressants would be unfair because of the limitations of alternative flavors.

The Board also held that there was insufficient evidence that the orange flavor in this case functioned as a trademark to identify the source of the goods. It did note that the company advertised and promoted its unique orange flavor. However, the focus of such promotion was not on its distinctive flavor as identifying the brand, but rather on its functional benefits. It further found that many medicines employed an orange flavoring and there was no evidence consumers would perceive the flavor as a brand identifier rather than an attribute of the product. Because all pharmaceuticals, even pills, have some flavor, the TTAB held that flavors could never be considered inherently distinctive for this category of products. Therefore, the applicant had the burden of proving that its flavor had acquired distinctiveness so that consumers would identify the flavor with the brand.

Finally, the TTAB noted that while it recognized that colors and scents might under appropriate circumstances receive trademark protection, it had two reservations about flavor marks. First, flavor is complex and may be perceived subjectively very differently from person to person. Any flavor that is arguably a distinctive identifier according to the brand owner might be perceived by consumers as a flavor typical to the product category. Second, the Board noted that flavors are usually not accessible before product purchase and therefore may not function as a source identifier in the traditional sense.

Despite this denial of trademark registration for a medicinal flavor, there is limited hope for flavor trademarks for other types of products for several reasons. First, the Board admitted that any "device" might function as a trademark under appropriate circumstances. Second, in 1962, the trademark statute was amended to eliminate the requirement that brand confusion be proven among purchasers. Since then, a few courts have recognized post purchase confusion as trademark infringement which might help flavor trademarks that are only experienced after purchase. In addition, there is no reason why sampling programs for certain types of products could not be used to promote a distinct flavor to consumers. Various LISTERINE brand products have promoted their unique unpleasant taste that some rival advertising has called "medicine-y." Third, the lack of design alternatives argument was dismissed by the Supreme Court as it applied to colors (*Qualitex Co. v. Jacobson Products Co., Inc.*, 1995). The complexity of flavors noted by the Board suggests that an equally wide range of possible flavors with subtle differences are available.

Functionality appears to be the key sticking point for future "taste-marks" and would prevent food, candy, liquor and medicines from using a unique taste as a mark. However, flavor might still be available for other products, where taste is not a normal product function. For example, brands of sewing thread or skin lotion or even writing instruments might try to develop and promote a distinctive taste brand identifier that would be sensed during incidental contact. As noted above, the U.S. Patent and Trademark office did register the scent of Plumeria blossoms for embroidery thread (*In re Clarke* 1990).

Naturally occurring flavors also would not qualify for trademarks—e.g., if LISTERINE's "medicine" taste is simply the result of its ingredients. However, a distinctive added taste in a mouthwash or toothpaste could be promoted as a brand identifier. This is most likely to be successful if the taste is not perceived nor promoted as delicious (which would be ornamental or even functional). There is a judicial decision that supports the possibility of taste and flavor trademarks. In *Smith Kline & French Lab. v. Broder* (1959), a district court enjoined imitation of the cherry scent, flavor and color of liquid vitamins as unfair competition fearing that pharmacists would substitute the imitation product for the brand name product when dispensing liquid vitamins to consumers. While the court implicitly considered flavor and smell to be source identifiers for this brand of liquid vitamins, it did not explicitly consider whether taste and flavor were commonplace in this industry or whether they might be functional. It merely focused on the prevention of passing off a cheaper product to consumers.

IV. Tactile Trademarks

Currently, there is no separate category for tactile, texture or touch trademarks. However, some trademark registrations clearly describe tactile aspects of the mark. One of the earliest marks was applied for in 1996 to Louis Vuitton for its "distinctive man-made textured pattern utilized as a surface feature" for its luggage and leather products (U.S. Reg. No. 2,263,903). That same year, Dooney & Bourke sought to register features for its leather handbags including among other things their "pebble grained texture" (U.S. Reg. Nos. 2,252,278 and 2,252,280).

Other examples include marks consisting of raised Braille characters that have been registered to jewelry and clothing designers including blind entertainer Stevie Wonder who also markets a line of apparel. Alcoholic beverage marketers also have registered a few touch marks such as American Wholesale Wine & Spirits' trademark for its KHVANCHKARA brand of wine described as a "sensory, touch mark" consisting of "a velvet textured covering on the surface of a bottle of wine" (U.S. Reg. No. 3,155,702—cancelled May 2013), The David Group's similar mark with leather texture wrapping around the middle of a wine bottle (U.S. Reg. No. 3896100) and CROWN ROYAL'S purple and gold bag trademark (U.S. Reg. No. 3,137,914—the bag is described visually rather than by texture). Touchdown Marketing's registered a trademark for the "pebble-grain texture" and "soft-touch feel" of its basketball-shaped cologne dispenser (U.S. Reg. No. 3,348,363) and Fresh, Inc. registered a mark for the "cotton-textured paper" that wraps its soap products (U.S. Reg. No. 2,682,410).

Studies suggest that touch may increase a consumer's sense of ownership and willingness to pay. Scientists are developing the technology to artificially create a desired touch sensation on the surface of an object (Wassom 2014). However, like other sensory brand identifiers, the burden is on the applicant to show that a proposed trademark is not functional (e.g., makes the object easier to handle or pick up) nor mere surface ornamentation, but rather is distinctive from other similar products and used by consumers to identify the brand or source of the product.

D. CONCLUSION

Lindstrom (2005) argues that while vision usually is considered the most powerful of the five senses, its effectiveness as a branding tool for making an emotional connection to consumers is declining, perhaps because of overemphasis and marketing clutter. He suggests that brands may benefit from employing the other senses to make an emotional connection to consumers. While he may ultimately prove to be correct, it is clear that trademark law is based on history. Verbal trademark law is well developed historically and therefore reasonably predictable for brand managers. However, what used to be almost an exclusive focus on the verbal nature of marks is now being augmented by stronger consideration of non-verbal sensory elements, particularly non-verbal visual elements.

Not only is trademark less well developed for sensory brand elements compared to brand names and logos, but such elements are presumed to be ornamental rather than source identifying. Product color, shape, flavor, scent and touch also may be found functional for many products and therefore not entitled to trademark protection. For this reason, the brand manager seeking to register sensory marks bears the burden of proving that they are not descriptive, functional, or ornamental and do identify the brand as the source of the product. In Europe managers also face the challenge of developing a graphic depiction of sensory marks that will be sufficiently specific to be accepted for registration.

When selecting brand elements, managers should carefully consider the legal benefits of marks that are inherently distinctive. If a court finds a mark to be inherently distinctive, the owner does not have to prove that it has secondary meaning in the minds of consumers. The owner need only prove that its mark is infringed or diluted by a similar mark. Inherently distinctive marks include verbal marks that are suggestive, arbitrary or fanciful and unusually distinctive packaging elements, sounds and perhaps scents and flavors. Colors and product configurations in the U.S. may not be considered inherently distinctive and there is a strong argument that scents and/or flavors for products that normally have a scent or flavor would not be considered inherently distinctive unless particularly unusual.

Sensory branding may indeed be a growing phenomenon, but the law involving such the registration and protection from imitation of such brand identifiers is still uncertain and in its infancy. For example,

Gilson and LaLonde (2005) assert that at that time there were no U.S. trademark registrations or applications for tactile marks. As noted above, some marks that included descriptions texture were in fact registered in the 1990s. This uncertainty suggests that at least in the near future, an enforceable brand identification and differentiation strategy must still be based primarily on verbal and visual brand elements. Perhaps in time, the law of sensory trademark protection will develop to provide predictable protection for such brand elements. This is more likely if marketers make greater use of these elements despite the greater risk of lack of protection and therefore imitation by other marketers.

CHAPTER 5

Protecting Your Brand from Imitation—A Legal Portfolio Approach

A. INTRODUCTION

While trademark law, as discussed in the preceding chapters, is crucial to the protection of brand elements, particularly the brand name and logo, brand is only one aspect of a product's (or service's) unique Customer Value Proposition (CVP) (Reeves 1961). The product has functional, service, and aesthetic properties in addition to its brand identity. As Figure One on the next page illustrates, various laws may be used to protect some aspects of a product's CVP, but no single law or set of laws fully protects all aspects from imitation by competitors.

Figure One

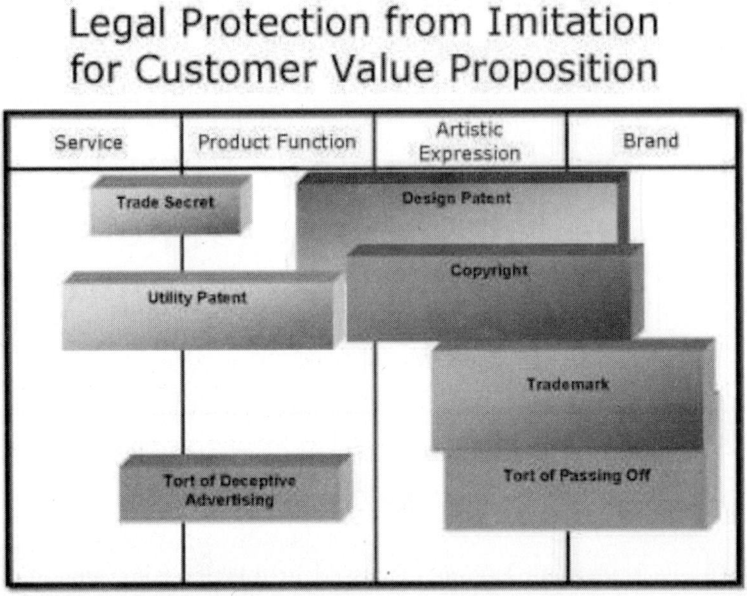

For example, trade secret law may be used to protect manufacturing and service processes as well as confidential encoded software code when these features add value because of their secrecy. The complaining party also must prove the trade secret was wrongfully taken. Processes as well as functional aspects of product designs may be protected by utility patents if they are new, useful and non-obvious. However, utility patents are expensive to obtain, expire after twenty years, and require disclosure of the invention so anyone skilled in the industry can make it after expiration. While trade secrets and patents can protect product and process functionality from imitation, brand managers are more concerned with the protection of brands and their promotion.

The figure above also illustrates that brand identity may be protected by trademark law and to some degree by other laws. The table on the opposite page summarizes non-brand name aspects of the brand that may be protected by trademark law as discussed in preceding chapters and Chapter Seven (slogans). In this chapter, we shall examine other ways to protect some of these aspects. For example, as explained below, symbols and ornamental designs associated with a brand may also be protected by copyrights and design patents under appropriate circumstances. In addition, copyright law protects the creative expression of brand advertising and promotional materials. Protecting brand identity and promotion should not be left solely to trademark law even if it usually does the heavy lifting.

Table One		
Trademark Eligible Brand Elements		
Type	**Marketing Variations**	**Legal Comments**
Logos	Many brand names are stylized, e.g., the Ford shield or Dell computer's name with the falling "E"	• Generally treated the same as word marks • Simple stylized components such as a square border or horizontal bands are weak and difficult to protect, but courts examine the entire combination of features
Symbols	• Pictures such as the girl with umbrella (Morton Salt) or abstract symbols like the CBS eye, Nike swoosh or Olympic rings • May be three dimensional (McDonald's golden arches) or animated • The NBC chimes may be considered a sound symbol	• Must be proven to have secondary meaning, rather than being merely ornamental—a pretty picture in advertising or on packaging • Simple figures are less protectable

Characters	Range from real people, e.g., Dave from Wendy's, to fictional characters such as Charmin's Mr. Whipple to animals like Budweiser's Spuds MacKenzie, to fictional animals like the Budweiser frogs or Pets.com's sock puppet to animated characters like Geico's Gecko and the Green Giant	• Must have permission to use name or likeness of living people • Many brands may use similar characters, e.g., Tony the Tiger and the cartoon Exxon Tiger, although when Exxon started selling food, Kellogg's objected to use of the Tiger
Slogans	May include brand name, "Bayer Works Wonders" or not, "Where's the Beef?"	• Presumed promotional rather than brand identifying • Simple descriptions or exultations ("The Player's Choice") are usually not protected (Byrt 2003) unless done distinctively such as McDonald's "TWO ALL BEEF PATTIES . . . "
Packaging	Includes label and container graphics and colors as well as unique package or container shapes, e.g., the Coca Cola bottle	• Only non-functional aspects of packaging may be protected under trademark law, but if sufficiently unusual, packaging may be deemed inherently distinctive
Product Design	Non-functional design characteristics of the product itself such as a particular scent of sewing thread (but not perfume) or the "tuned" sound of a motorcycle engine if consumers recognize it as identifying a particular brand	• Cannot be deemed inherently distinctive, secondary meaning must be proven • A single color such as pink for insulation may be trademarked if it is not the natural product color and not functional

It is important to note that protecting brand identity is not a one dimensional task. As noted in Chapter One, historically trademarks were just an indicator of product source like an artisan's name, initials or other mark. The mark itself often said nothing about the attributes of the product other than what was learned from product experience associated with the mark.

Today, however, brand elements, usually also communicate some aspects of brand positioning and values. For example, many brand names are no longer the name of the company or its owner, rather brand names often suggest some aspect of the product that is an important part of brand positioning (Keller et al 1998). Since brand elements not only identify but in many cases also communicate other information or values about the brand, it is even more important that brand managers pay attention to law beyond mere trademark law. A classic example of a brand element that usually communicates information about the brand is the slogan. Slogans are fully discussed in Chapter Seven, but will be included with other examples in this chapter as well.

The first section of this chapter examines the weaknesses of trademark protection for brand elements other than brand names. The next two sections suggest how trademark law may be supplemented by other laws in order to enhance the protection of non-name brand elements. Some of these supplemental brand protection laws, copyright and ornamental design patents involve registration of the brand elements. Other laws, passing off and deceptive advertising only provide protection through litigation after an offense has occurred. Conclusions are offered in the final section.

B. THE WEAKNESSES OF TRADEMARK LAW

As discussed in previous chapters, trademarks are defined broadly to cover signals or devices that identify product source (brand identity) in the mind of consumers. However, aside from names and obvious logos, most other possible brand identifiers (e.g., symbols, characters, packaging, sensory elements, and product design aspects) are presumed to be ornamental rather than source identifying. In addition, slogans, jingles and packaging are presumed to be promotional rather than source identifying. The burden is on the brand owner to prove that these elements do identify source in the minds of consumers and therefore are eligible for trademark protection. In cases such as logos, slogans and product packaging as well as sounds and scents, unusual elements for a product category may be deemed inherently distinctive and therefore presumed to identify the brand. Otherwise for brand elements that are not inherently distinctive, the brand owner also must prove that the element actually does identify a particular source of the product in the minds of consumers.

The weaknesses of trademark law in its ability to protect non-name brand elements from imitation by others may be summarized as follows:

- All brand elements must be shown to be inherently distinctive or proven to identify product source in the minds of consumers before they can be protected under trademark law.
- Aesthetic product or package designs are not necessarily trademarks; they are presumed to be ornamental and must be proven to identify the product source (brand) within the minds of consumers (*Qualitex Co. v. Jacobson Products Co., Inc.*, 1995).
- A distinctive brand name may dispel confusion over other trademarked brand elements, particularly product or package design (e.g., *Conopco, Inc. v. May Department Stores Co.* 1994; *McNeil Nutritionals, LLC v. Heartland Sweeteners LLC* 2007).
- Functional aspects of the product or package may not be trademarks (*TrafFix Devices, Inc. v. Marketing Displays, Inc.* 2001).
- For infringement, the trademark owner must prove likelihood of consumer confusion as to product source between the trademark and its imitator (15 U.S.C. § 1125(b)).

- When seeking protection from dilution, the mark must be proven to be famous (15 U.S.C. § 1125(c)).
- The typical remedy in trademark cases not involving intentional copying is an injunction rather than damages.

Three types of trademark fair use round out this list of trademark law weaknesses. First, fair use allows others to use descriptive words that may be part of a trademark such as playboy and fish fry. A toothpaste may claim to be "the dentists' choice" despite the trademark for Dentists' Choice toothbrushes (*Wonder Labs, Inc. v. Proctor & Gamble Co.* 1990).

Second, fair use allows nominal use where a trademark is used by another to identify a brand. Comparative advertising may claim one brand is better than a rival or merely comparable to a rival brand, typically with a lower price. In the U.S., a brand might also compare itself to a non-competing brand that is recognized as a market place standard such as a leather furniture company claiming "Only Revlon Has More Colors" (*Revlon Consumer Prods. v. Jennifer Leather Broadway Inc.* 1994).

Third, fair use allows for parody, particularly when offering social commentary upon a brand or its advertising (*L.L. Bean, Inc. v. Drake Publishers, Inc.*, 1987; *Girl Scouts of U.S.A. v. Bantam Doubleday Dell Publishing Group*, 1993). Shaughnessy (1986) suggests that parodies of the trademark owner using its own trademarks are more likely to be permitted as informational commentary than parodies that are merely play on words of the trademark itself. These types of fair use are examined further in Chapters Fifteen and Sixteen.

Lastly, brand marketers may consider jingles and distinctive advertising formats, such as the Energizer Bunny interrupting fake advertisements, as also being brand identifiers. However, trademark law traditionally has not protected longer jingles. Such protection may only come from copyright law. Similarly ideas, such as having the real advertisement interrupt a fake advertisement is not protected by copyright law which only protects the expression used to communicate the idea, not the idea itself.

C. SUPPLEMENTAL BRAND ELEMENT PROTECTION

The portfolio approach presented here suggests that brand marketers should design brand elements for maximum legal protection. While trademark law and trademark registration should be the first line of defense, these actions should not be the only line of defense. Two sets of laws can productively extent the protection of brand elements beyond that offered by trademark law alone. Copyright and design patent law protect creative expression in order to encourage artists and authors to pursue their crafts. Competitive torts or unfair competition protect rival business from unfair business practices. Each of these sets of laws is discussed in turn.

I. Protecting Expression—Copyrights and Design Patents

In order to make brand elements memorable, brand managers frequently seek to develop creative elements with some degree of originality and novelty. A classic example is advertising. Copyright law has protected original advertising expression from being copied for over 100 years (*Bleistein v. Donaldson Lithographing Co.* 1903). As noted previously, advertising jingles have traditionally been deemed too long to identify source in the minds of consumers and thus may only be protected under copyright law (e.g., *Dr. Pepper Co. v. Sambo's Restaurants, Inc.* 1981). However, a recent decision by the Second Circuit Court of Appeals conceded that musical compositions could function as a trademark for a brand, although not for the composition itself (*Oliveira a/k/a Gilberto v. Frito-Lay, Inc.* 2001). This would appear to open the door for trademark registration for jingles. In fact, as discussed further in Chapter Seven, the U.S. already has registered a number of trademarks based on the words of shorter jingles.

Advertising often includes background music to help consumers retain information or may feature music to add an emotional appeal to spur sales. Brands that align themselves with developing musicians appear to be cutting edge and may benefit in sales if the musician's popularity takes off. Of course the musician may benefit from the advertising exposure given to their music. In all of these cases, original music should be protected by copyright law and the advertiser will want to carefully craft a license to give it rights (probably exclusive) to use the music including melody and lyrics or a particular performance in advertising.

Copyright law also may be used to protect both expressive elements such as logos, label designs, jingles, and artwork of brand characters as well as artistic elements such as the product package and non-functional aspects of the product design that are separable from the functional aspects. A recent copyright case involving a camisole design found that embroidery on the edge of the garment was protected by copyright against close imitation and in fact was infringed by another camisole marketer (*Express LLC v. Fettish Group, Inc.* 2006). In contrast, copyright registrations for the SKYY vodka bottle and label and the Best Western logo pictured below were rejected because the name trademarks themselves may not be copyright protected and the remaining colors and graphics lacked minimal creativity.

When developing a unique product design or package, the brand marketer must be careful to distinguish functional aspects from aesthetic aspects. The former may be protected for 20 years (from the filing date) by a utility patent. The latter may be protected by a 15-year design patent in the U.S. For example, a design patent was issued for a hole and flap design on clothing such as pants and skirts (*In re Slokevage* 2006). Aesthetic aspects also may be protected by a copyright if the original and creative artistic expression of the product design or package may be separated from the functional aspects of the product such as a sculpture serving as the base of a lamp. Functional aspects may be advertised as such while aesthetic aspects should be advertised not only as attractive but also as brand identifiers ("look for . . . "). Once consumers come to associate particular non-functional aspects of a product design or package as identifying a particular brand, those aspects can also be protected under trademark law.

The famous building toy brick LEGO obtained utility patents on its brick design in the 1960s. These patents have long since expired, but have been successfully evoked in the U.S., Canada, Germany and the E.U. to deny trademark protection for the well-recognized appearance because the appearance of the brick is functional. Since then, LEGO has obtained utility patents on some brick improvements and is seeking to protect LEGO mini-figures with design patents and copyrights.

While some aesthetic aspects of product design or packaging may be protected by trademark law as well as both copyright and a design patent, aspects that do not yet identify the brand may only be protected by one of these latter laws. For example, the Coca-Cola bottle pictured on the opposite page was initially protected by a design patent, but then by copyright and in the 1960s, it was registered as a trademark. Other aspects of design or packaging may be functional and therefore ineligible for copyright protection (unless separable from functional aspects) or may not qualify as an article of manufacture and therefore be ineligible for design patent protection. Design patents can be somewhat functional but not predominantly functional.

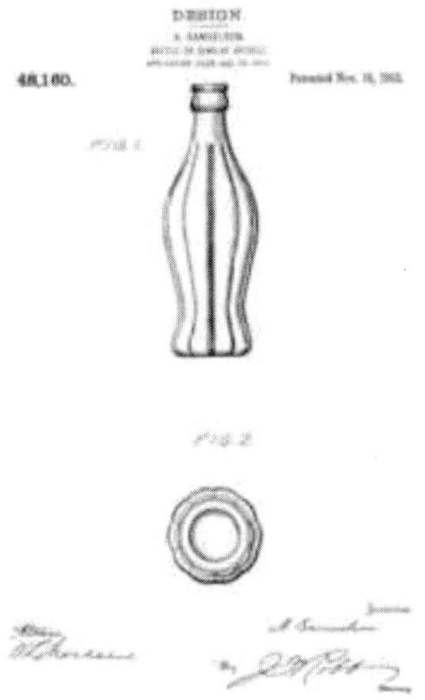

Although the international trend is to provide short term protection for unregistered designs (the E.U. provides three years—Alcock et al. 2003), the U.S. requires application to the Patent and Trademark Office in order to obtain a design patent. Thankfully, design patents are typically issued more quickly than regular patents, in 9–18 months and last for 15 years from date of issue (Moskin 2002). The applicant must show that compared with prior design art, the design that is subject of the patent application is both new and non-obvious to designers familiar with that particular field of design.

Unfortunately, older research suggests that while 60% of all design patent applications are granted, among those later challenged in court, nearly 80% were declared invalid, typically for being obvious compared with prior design art (Lindgren 1985). This result appears surprising since once the design patent is issued, it is then presumed to be valid and the challenger has the burden of proving invalidity (Moskin 2002). With the specialization of the Federal Circuit Court of Appeals to handle all patent appeals, the portion of utility patents that are declared invalid has been reduced. The same also may be true for design patents.

Protection of industrial designs in most other countries is more straightforward. For example, European Community Design protection begins the moment a new design becomes public. The prohibition against unlicensed copying lasts for three years unless within one year, the design is registered. Then it may last for up to five terms of five years each.

The design protection covers the appearance of a product and may include the lines, contours, colors, shape, texture and materials of the product or its ornamentation. It may also include logos, packaging, graphic symbols, typefaces and computer icons. Registration expands the scope of infringement to cover any close imitation whether intended or not. Infringement is judged from the overall impression of an informed user.

Like the U.S., the design cannot be dictated by function and it must be new. It must also have individual character. However, this novelty standard in Europe is much lower than in the U.S., only requiring that the new design not be practically identical with a prior design, differing in immaterial details (Aide 2003). In contrast, as noted above, U.S. design patents require a higher level of originality often described as a non-obvious improvement over existing design art as judged by someone familiar with the field. Finally, the U.S. just joined the Hague Agreement for the International Registration of Industrial Designs which allows filing in the U.S. and simultaneously in any of 63 other countries assuming the application satisfies any particular requirements of the other countries.

II. Advantages of Copyrights and Design Patents

Because copyrights and design patents require only original expression, not source identification (or fame for trademark dilution), they can be used in situations where a brand owner has difficulty proving that some brand elements actually identify the brand for consumers. This may be particularly useful for new brand elements that consumers do not yet associate with the brand or may never associate uniquely with one brand. For example, a logo that is a stylized letter or pair of letters may not be inherently distinctive as a trademark because the letters are just brand initials or may be a brand nickname. The European Union does not allow registration of single or double letter trademarks in most cases. However, a stylized version of these letters may still pass the minimal creativity and originality requirements to receive copyright protection.

Both trademark and copyright law allow for protection without registration. Copyright law protects original expression from the moment it is "fixed in a tangible medium" even without registration. However, in the U.S. copyright protected works do have to be registered before a federal copyright infringement lawsuit may be filed and registration before the infringement occurs also entitles the author/owner to statutory damages (without proof of actual damages) and attorneys' fees at the discretion of the court. Registration within five years of first publication creates a presumption of both validity and ownership. As with trademarks, items copyrighted after 1989 do not have to contain the copyright notice "© *author names, year of first publication*" but being copied despite such notice may be evidence of willful infringement leading to possible punitive damages.

Another advantage is that infringement of copyrights and design patents is judged by the hypothetical ordinary observer. The judge will hear argument and then exercise his or her own judgment. Copyright infringement is proven by showing access for copying (easily assumed in the case of advertising and labeling currently in use) or striking similarity at which point copyright is presumed such as a case where advertising or packaging is secretly being developed and not yet public. Trademarks typically require expensive consumer survey evidence to show likely consumer confusion and the validity of any such evidence is often rigorously (and expensively) contested during the course of litigation.

The final advantage of copyrights and design patents is the enhanced ability to get damages over trademark law. Lost sales are typically difficult to prove in trademark infringement or comparison advertising cases, so an injunction to stop the offending trademark use is the typical remedy in trademark cases. Occasionally the infringer's profits attributable to the infringement minus costs are awarded, but this amount also is not easily proven in most cases. Copyright law, assuming prior registration of the copyrighted material, allows for statutory damages of between $750 and $30,000 for infringement, plus an additional $150,000 if willfulness can be shown such as when the copyright notice was used on the product. Similarly, design patent infringement calls for a minimum award of a reasonable royalty or $250 statutory damages. Actual damages, if proven also may be awarded and any award may be trebled at the discretion of the judge. A reasonable royalty might exceed the infringer's profits, but, like trademark law, if the infringer's profits may be proven, they can be awarded as well.

III. Weaknesses of Copyrights and Design Patents

Descriptive trademarks such as the name of company founders lack any originality but are still protected once secondary meaning is shown. In contrast, copyrights and design patents only cover expression or art with some level of originality. Copyright law requires a minimum level of originality, something more original than arranging names in alphabetical order, to provide protection (*Feist Publications, Inc. v. Rural Telephone Service Co.* 1991). It typically won't cover (as too short) a brand name or slogans such as "The Most Personal Sort of Deodorant" (*Alberto-Culver Co. v. Andrea Dumon, Inc.* 1972).

For advertising, copyright law protects specific unique components such as photos and even a creative arrangement of photos or scenes, but copyright law does not protect expression of product facts and the use of common scenes in advertising (such as showing a product in typical use), called scenes a faire (*American Direct Marketing, Inc. v. Azad Int'l, Inc.* 1992). These are considered ideas rather than expression. A 30 second TV ad is far less likely to infringe another by the mere arrangement of common scenes than a 90 minute movie that may prove infringement by a second movie with a myriad of parallel incidents and scenes (*Miller Brewing Co. v. Carling O'Keefe Breweries Ltd.* 1978).

Copyright law, like trademark law, does allow fair use. However, copyright fair use analysis focuses on four factors: purpose and character of the second use, the nature of the copyrighted work, the amount and substantiality of the work that was copied and the effect on the value of the copyrighted work (17 U.S.C. § 107). In the comparative advertising context, which is of particular concern to the brand owner (Grewal et al. 1997), copyright and trademark law both often allows fair use. For example, when a newspaper compared its weekly TV section with TV Guide, it showed side-by-side pictures of the two. Even though the advertisement showed the entire copyrighted cover of TV Guide, the court found fair use because none of the inside of TV Guide was shown and there was no detriment to the market for TV Guide covers (*Triangle Publications Inc. v. Knight-Ridder Newspapers, Inc.* 1980). More recently, the Ninth Circuit also found fair use of "screen shots" of a copyrighted video game in comparative advertising (*Sony Computer Entertainment America, Inc. v. Bleem, LLC* 2000).

However, copyright fair use in comparative advertising is not absolute. In *Southco, Inc. v. Kanebridge Corp.* (2000), the court issued a preliminary injunction against the use in comparative advertising of a copyrighted parts numbering system for industrial fasteners. The court held that the system was sufficiently creative for protection and the four copyright fair use factors all favored or were neutral toward disallowing the comparative advertising use. Similarly, although not comparative advertising, the Second Circuit has held that copyright law may prevent the prominent depiction of a copyrighted item, i.e., sunglasses, in a clothing advertisement (*Davis v. The Gap, Inc.* 2001). These two decisions suggest that fair use for commercial purposes is not highly valued and that using the entirety of a creative copyright work also is not appreciated. However, these cases also generally recognize under the fourth factor of effective on the market for the original work that increased competition because of comparative advertising, even if it diminishes the value of the original work is at least neutral if not positive in favor of fair use.

Trademark and copyright fair use also often allow for parodies. The movie "Naked Gun 33 1/3" developed an advertising poster that parodied a famous Vanity Fair magazine cover that was a photograph of the actress Demi Moore, naked and pregnant. The poster was a very similar picture of the actor Leslie Nielsen, star of the movie, also naked and apparently pregnant. The court held this was parody and fair use (*Leibovitz v. Paramount Pictures Corp.*, 1998).

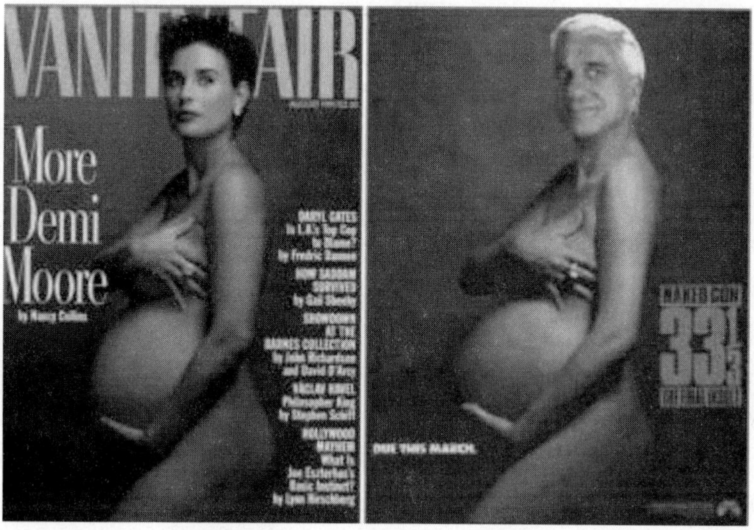

Leslie Nielson also appeared in a Coors beer advertising parody of the Energizer Bunny and the related slogan that it "keeps on going and going." Mr. Nielson appeared in a business suit with bunny ears and feet and the tagline that Coors beer "keeps on growing and growing." The court found fair use under both trademark and copyright law since only enough bunny elements were copied so that consumers would understand the parody (*Eveready Battery Co. v. Adolph Coors Co.* 1991).

Original Energizer Battery commercial   Coors Light parody commercial

Thus, both trademark and copyright law allow advertising parodies but trademark law may be a bit stronger in protecting a brand owner from an advertising parody that tarnishes the brand as illustrated by the preliminary injunction issued against an American Express condom that also used the slogan "Don't Leave Home Without It" (*American Express Co. v. Vibra Approved Laboratories Corp.* 1989). In contrast, copyright law emphasizes the amount of the copyrighted material used by the other party. If the brand owner can argue that the imitation borrowed so much of the original that the likely effect on the market is to eliminate the original advertisement, then copyright law could conclude that this is not fair use and disallow the imitation even when trademark law finds descriptive fair use. Unfortunately, there have been no legal decisions to date involving this specific set of set of facts.

Both trademark and copyright law will not protect functional product design or features of the product or its packaging. Copyright law specifically requires that any protected artistic expression in the product design must be separable from any functional aspects. Design patents offer a significant advantage here because they can be partially functional, just not primarily functional. For example, perforations on the body of an athletic shoe and various elements on the sole do serve a function on the shoe (ventilation and support), but the design patent was held to be valid because they were primarily ornamental. There were many alternative arrangements and methods for achieving the same functionality (*Avia Group Int'l. v. L.A. Gear* 1988).

A significant disadvantage of design patents is the requirement that all the features claimed in the patent be infringed. If the imitator decides to only infringe some of the claimed features, courts will typically hold the design patent was not infringed. This problem can be addressed by filing multiple patents, one to cover each unique ornamental feature of a product. In such a case, when an imitator only copies selected features, those features should be the subject of their own design patent (Hanson 1999).

Table Two summarizes the requirements for trademark protection and compares them to those of copyrights and design patents.

Table Two			
U.S. Registration-Based Protection for Brand Identifiers			
Requirements	**Trademarks**	**Copyrights**	**Design Patents**
Coverage	Distinctive words, pictures, logos, symbols, sounds, colors	Original expression including, writings, music, advertising and artwork	New ornamental product shapes and packaging
Limitations	• Must identify product source in the minds of consumers • Can't be part of product function • Can't be generic	• Does not protect ideas or facts • Does not protect functional aspects of product	• Must be primarily ornamental rather than functional • Must not be obvious to ordinary designer
Registration	Recommended	Recommended	Required
Duration	As long as used in commerce	• Life of author plus 70 years • Work for hire—the shorter of 120 years from creation or 95 years from first publication	15 years from issuance

Infringement	Confusingly similar to consumers	Substantially similar to ordinary person	Substantially similar to an ordinary person
Fair Use	Yes, for descriptive, nominal, and parody use	Yes, depending on purpose and character of the second use, the nature of the original work, the amount and substance taken and the effect on the potential market for the copyrighted work	Only upon expiration

D. PROTECTION FROM UNFAIR COMPETITION

Torts of unfair competition have evolved to protect one business from having its business unfairly diverted by another. As noted in Chapter One, the tort of passing off one's products as being those of another served as the basis for modern trademark law. Similarly, the torts of commercial disparagement and trade defamation also have evolved into modern actions against deceptive advertising. None of these torts require or even provide for registration before bringing the lawsuit. However, brand owners must prove each element of the tort in order to obtain a legal remedy. While an injunction may be obtained upon proof that consumers are likely misled, additional remedies may be difficult to obtain. Proof of actual lost sales or a quantifiable devaluation of a brand owner's reputation typically is required for damages and proof of both the deliberate nature of the conduct and the amount of money earned by the conduct is needed to award the wrong-doer's profits. Deceptive advertising is the subject of Chapter Eight.

I. Passing Off

The tort of passing off requires that the plaintiff prove that the accused party made some sort of representation that was likely to mislead consumers into the mistaken belief that the actor's products were those of the plaintiff or sponsored by or affiliated with the plaintiff (American Law Institute 1995). A typical case involves trade dress imitation where the imitator's product looks deceptively similar to that of the brand owner. Obviously, this may entail the use of a confusingly similar trade name or other trademarked brand elements.

However, the tort of passing off is broader than trademark infringement or dilution for two reasons. First, it encompasses misrepresentations beyond the imitation of someone else's distinctive trademarks. For example, a firm that misrepresents that its goods are used by a celebrity is passing itself off as the firm whose goods are actually used by the celebrity. Similarly, if a customer requests a Coke in a restaurant but is served a Pepsi in an ordinary glass, passing off has occurred without imitation of any of Coke's trademarks by the seller. Lastly, if a firm uses a picture or actual sample of someone else's product, it is passing itself off as the source of those products even if no brand elements are contained on the product or shown in the picture.

The second reason why passing off is broader than trademark infringement is that the latter only asks if consumers are likely to be confused after the trademark in question has been proven distinctive. If the trademark is not distinctive, the brand owner loses. In contrast, passing off focuses on whether a significant proportion of potential consumers are likely to believe that the passed off product actually came from the well-known brand source. Passing off does not necessarily ask whether a name or trade dress is distinctive, although evidence of distinctiveness would suggest likely consumer confusion.

This raises the question of whether generic trade names, trade dress or domain addresses can be protected from imitative use under unfair competition law, despite their generic nature. Nguyen (2001, pp. 972–978) suggests that the Second Circuit, as well as New York state law, protects generic brand elements from unfair competition even though they are not protected under trademark law. Furthermore, the Fourth Circuit recently held that a firm with a registered Mexican trademark for FLANAX could sue for unfair competition in the U.S. against a firm that claimed its Flanax™ was from the same producer as the Mexican brand.

The focus of passing off on confusion about source or sponsorship also allows passing off to be used to challenge some fair use situations such as nominal fair use where consumers might be confused about sponsorship. Similarly, when a trademark is used to trigger advertising through a search engine search or spyware, consumers might believe the pop up advertising is being sponsored by the brand even if the ad does not explicitly contain the trademark in question.

II. Disparagement

The earliest false advertising torts of commercial disparagement of someone's products and commercial defamation of someone's business reputation both required proof that the statements were false and made either deliberately or carelessly. In addition, actual damages from lost sales must be proven in order to recover damages (although defamation might allow nominal damages). While these torts could still be applied to advertising today, the modern laws against deceptive advertising (discussed in Chapter Eight) do not require proof of intent and often substitute lack of reasonable substantiation by the advertiser for proof by the challenger that a particular factual statement is false.

However, these old torts may still be useful to modern brand managers for dealing with statements arguably made outside the advertising context such as on websites or blog pages. Sometimes competitors disguise their true identities to appear as disinterested consumers who negatively examine a particular brand's products. If this can't be proven as advertising, it may still qualify as disparagement or defamation.

III. Brand Criticism

Even extremely popular and successful brands face criticism, sometimes simply because they are popular and successful. The low cost and proliferation of internet use allows the message of complaining parties to easily reach thousands of people making brand criticism a more significant issue than in the past. It is relatively easy for critics to set up their own website or blog, post negative messages on bulletin boards or even start a chain e-mail. Unwanted criticism may come from review websites, normally considered neutral, or even fan sites where brand fans sometimes offer criticism. Serious critics may file a lawsuit and seek publicity about the wrongs alleged in the lawsuit. Brand criticism may come from a number of sources: competitors (often without disclosing this fact), disgruntled former employees, or consumers or political groups who oppose consumption generally or particular aspects of a brand such as an alleged exploitation of the environment or third world labor.

It should be noted at the onset that in the U.S., the First Amendment generally favors allowing brand criticism. This is particularly true if the criticism is a complaint to a government agency. For this reason, the best response may be addressing the criticism. It may mean improving the product or its method of production or simply attempting to placate disgruntled commenters.

Should the brand marketer choose to respond with a lawsuit, approximately half the states have anti-SLAPP (Strategic Laws Against Public Protest) laws that provide additional protection for critics beyond the high burden of proof for libel and disparagement. While some of these statutes are relatively narrow, applying to specific situations such as criticism made before a governmental agency, others are broad, applying to speech about an issue in the public interest. Such statutes typically call for early procedural review, possible injunction of the SLAPP lawsuit, and attorneys' fees paid for the victims of SLAPP lawsuits who avail themselves of anti-SLAPP protection (Hartzler 2007).

There are essentially two modes of response to brand criticism: challenge the message and/or challenge the use of the target brand's trademarks. Messages may be challenged as libelous or disparaging, both of which are difficult to prove. The complaining party must first prove that the critic made a false statement of fact (as opposed to opinion) that defamed a person or her commercial activities or products. Printed false statements about a particular person are usually referred to as libel.

Next, the statements must be proven to be defamatory—they may be reasonably understood as casting dispersions about the person's character or the quality of the goods and services being criticized. Puffing or general sales talk that one product is "best" or another is "not very good" are not considered statements of fact, but merely statements of opinion that are common in the marketplace (*Groden v. Random House* 1995).

People who are criticized because of their association with particular brands, such as Bill Gates and MICROSOFT, will usually be considered public figures because they invited public exposure and scrutiny. For such people to win a libel lawsuit, they also must prove that the defamatory statement was made with malice, meaning the critic knew the statement was false or made the statement in reckless disregard of whether it was true or false. The burden of proving falsity is placed upon the complaining party, but the critic often relishes the opportunity to prove the statement is true. The Supreme Court has held that proving the statement is substantially true is sufficient even if some details are incorrect (*Masson v. New Yorker Magazine, Inc.* 1991).

If the statement is about a product or commercial activities, it is typically referred to as disparagement or trade libel. Not only must the brand owner prove the statement was false, defamatory, and made with malice, the brand owner also must prove special damages. Special damages are actual and specific economic harm caused by the statement, such as customers who didn't purchase the product because of the statement (*Bose Corp. v. Consumers Union* 1982). Brand owners may be entitled to nominal damages if the statements are deemed defamatory on their face. For example, this standard was reached when a customer set up a website about a builder and made false statements about building code violations and poor workmanship (*Taylor Building Corp. v. Benfield* 2007).

The other legal strategy against brand criticism is to challenge the use of brand trademarks in the criticism. However brand marketers must be prepared for a fair use defense as discussed in Chapters Fifteen and Sixteen. Just as comparative advertising can name rival brands, so can critics. Trademark use by critics typically involves using a targeted brand's trademark in a domain name for a protest website or in some form of parody, e.g., "brandsucks.com." The brand owner can challenge these uses as diluting or infringing its trademarks, but confusion seems unlikely in most cases and the federal dilution statute specifically exempts criticism.

Brand marketers can also challenge the media that publishes the statement, but generally speaking, a third-party publisher that lacks knowledge of falsity is not responsible for publishing a defamatory statement, such as a newspaper that publishes a letter to the editor. A 1996 statute explicitly applies this defense to internet service providers. So when an anonymous subscriber repeatedly posted allegedly defamatory statements about Zeran on an AOL bulletin board, a court refused to hold AOL liable even though Zeran had informed the service after the first posting that it was defamatory (*Zeran v. America Online* 1997).

Courts have recently held in the context of copyright law that internet search providers can't simply remove postings because of a request, but rather they must consider fair use arguments. Most ISPs prohibit the posting of defamatory statements in their terms of service and, when pressured, may reveal the identities of posters of such statements, despite privacy policies that promise anonymity. This allows a brand owner to threaten to sue the person making the statement.

E. CONCLUSION

As the late Professor Cohen (1986) observed, trademark law is a powerful method for protecting trade names and other brand identifying elements. However, since brand elements typically contribute to brand positioning and communicating brand values in addition to identifying product source, brand managers today should be familiar with an entire legal portfolio of laws that can be used to protect brand identifying elements. Some laws, like trademark law, require or encourage registration of brand elements as they are adopted. Brand managers should carefully design such elements to both meet legal requirements and to maximize overall protection.

Of course, brand managers also must watch rival products to make sure they don't violate the legal protections granted to registered elements. Brand managers also must be vigilant that rivals are not taking other actions that may injure brand value that can be challenged under unfair competition law. The advantages of this legal portfolio approach over trademark law alone are summarized in Table Three on the next page.

Table Three	
Trademark Law Augmentation	
Trademark Law Weaknesses	**Supplemental Protection**
Trademark must be distinctive and identify the product source.	Copyright requires only originality; design patents must be novel in a non-obvious way; passing off requires likely consumer confusion of product source. None of these explicitly requires distinctiveness or source identification.
Trademarks may not be functional.	Design patents must be primarily ornamental but may have some functionality; passing off examines likely consumer confusion rather than functionality, but protecting entirely functional elements under passing off would be pre-empted by federal patent law.
Infringement is proven by likely consumer confusion concerning the imitation and the trademark, but a distinctive name or disclaimer may dispel confusion.	Use of ornamental elements covered by copyrights or design patents could be infringed regardless of consumer confusion about product source. Passing off examines the overall likelihood of confusion between products without special significance to the name.
Dilution under federal law requires proof that the mark is famous.	Neither fame nor dilution must be proven under other laws.
The typical trademark remedy is an injunction rather than damages unless the copying is intentional.	Copyright and design patent registration provide for minimum statutory damages.
Trademark law permits nominal fair use.	Design patents require permission for non-owner use. Nominal use may result in confusion of sponsorship under passing off. Nominal use in comparative advertising may result in liability for deceptive advertising.
Trademark law permits descriptive fair use of words that are part of a descriptive trademark.	Descriptive use may result in confusion of sponsorship under passing off or may be challenged as deceptive advertising.
Trademark use permits some parodies.	Copyright law may condemn advertising parodies that use more of the copyright protected feature than needed to identify the target brand to consumers.

CHAPTER 6

Domain Names and Product Category Names

A. INTRODUCTION

As preceding chapters have demonstrated, various brand elements may be protected by trademark law and other forms of legal protection. This chapter first examines how domain name registration regulated by the Internet Corporation for Assigned Names and Numbers (ICANN) may control online use of website addresses containing brand or product category names. It then examines other methods of exercising a limited amount of control over the use of product category labels.

Suarez and Grodal (2015) suggest that by monitoring the use of proposed category labels for new products, a firm can increase the probability of it adopting what ultimately becomes the dominant category label. This may enhance commercial success as consumers associate the firm's product design with the dominant category label. (Petty 2015b) argues there are at least four methods for a marketer to exercise some control over which other firms (and which product designs) can and cannot use a particular product category label. Each of these will be discussed in turn after examining domain names.

B. DOMAIN NAMES

Given the ubiquity of the World Wide Web, most businesses of significant size use at least one domain name address to establish a web presence. Firms might connect a variety of domain addresses to one primary website or they may design a variety of websites to appeal to different market segments. If a firm develops a new product, it may well wish to create a website and unique domain name address for that product (probably with links to its other webpages). The traditional approach has been to match a second level name with a top level domain name in the form brandname.com or trademark.com. Until recently, top level domain names have been limited to twenty-two specific words such as "-.net," "-.biz" and "-.com," with the latter being far and away the most popular choice. The popularity of dotcom addresses has led to "insure.com" selling for $16 million and "hotels.com" selling for $11 million.

Because of a perceived shortage of "-.com" addresses, ICANN recently decided to expand the number of available domain names through its new generic top-level domain name (gTLD) program. Under this new program, applicants may seek to operate a domain name registry for an address ending in virtually any word or set of letters including brand names like "-.ford" or generic/descriptive words such as "-.car." These new options may be particularly attractive to firms that do not currently control their "brand.com" or "categorylabel.com" domain name (Petty 2015b). Initial fees for operating a new gTLD registry are expected to be $185,000 with continuing annual fees of at least $25,000. It remains to be seen, what registrars will charge for new gTLD domain names, but recently the registrar of "-.car," "-.cars," and "-.auto" announced annual fees will start at $3000, significantly higher than most other annual registration fees. Preliminary studies suggest that internet users find these new domain name forms are more noticeable in ads, more memorable and more convenient (Birkner 2012). Whether this will be true in practice after the novelty wears off remains to be seen.

There was some resistance to and criticism of the proposal from brand marketers based in the U.S. These marketers feared they may be forced to set up one or more new and expensive registries or register various domain names with various new registries to preempt cybersquatting. For example, the domain name "-.xxx" was added in 2004 and as of 2012, it had 215,835 domains, the majority (132,859) of which are adult websites, but a sizeable minority (82,976) are defensive registrations to prevent cybersquatting adult websites. These defensive registered sites typically redirect visitors to a non-adult website (Matyszczyk 2012).

Despite or perhaps because of these concerns, ICANN's received 1930 applications for this new program—almost twice what experts predicted. These applications covered just over 1400 proposed gTLDs because 230 of the proposed gTLDs had multiple applicants (Birkner 2012). As of March 2015, over 500 strings have been assigned to registries (http://newgtlds.icann.org/en). Some estimate that only about 600 of the original applications were for trademarked brand names and nearly 1300 for generic categories such as "-.book," "-.store" and "-.app" (Calvaruso et al. 2012). The latter was the most contested name with thirteen applicants.

I. Selecting a Domain Name

As noted in Chapter Three, several factors should be considered when selecting a brand name and the same factors normally would apply to domain name selection as well. One additional factor of increasing important is e-commerce compatibility. Choosing a multiple word domain name such as AMERICAN AIRLINES may require consumers to type both words correctly (and figure out if there is any punctuation between them) to find the desired site. Mis-typings may lead to the wrong site or a site disguised to look like the desired site ("typosquatting"). Common typographical mistakes include hitting a key next to the intended key and switching two adjacent letters in simple words that most people type rapidly such as "hte" instead of "the." Even prior to e-commerce many companies shortened the company (and brand) name to just initials both for greater simplicity and "memorability" as well as more flexibility to expand into new business areas. CBS, IBM, AT & T and NCR are just a few examples. Brand owners should also consider fanciful names such as KODAK or XEROX or a misspelled word such as COMPAQ or NUMB3RS. These often are more memorable than ordinary words and can be more easily and accurately found using an internet search engine. Of course if such words are not common on the web, the searcher may receive a search engine query asking whether the spelling was really intended. Another partial solution is to adopt, trademark and publicize a shortened website name such as AA.COM for American Airlines or BN.COM for Barnes and Noble Booksellers. With the rise of e-commerce on mobile devices, marketers should also consider how well their name or logo will present on a small cellphone display screen. Google just changed the typeface of its logo and name to be more visible on a small screen.

It should be emphasized that court decisions have consistently held that the mere registration of a trademarked word or phrase as a domain name does not constitute use of the mark in commerce that is required for trademark protection (*Academy of Motion Picture Arts & Sciences v. Network Solutions, Inc.* 1997). Marketers must present evidence that the domain name is actually used by consumers as a source identifier and therefore merits protection as a trademark (*In re Eilberg* 1998). Consistent with these holdings, a recent Federal Circuit opinion confirmed that use of a proposed trademark on a website "in progress" is not sufficient for trademark use. Rather the mark must be used on or associated with goods and services being offered in commerce (*Couture v. Playdom, Inc.* 2015).

Clearly it makes sense to coordinate trademarks, domain names and even company names into a comprehensive naming strategy. Therefore brand marketers typically check the availability of both trademark and domain name registration when considering a new brand name. Both can be searched through various databases and often a simple web search will reveal prior registration and use. Sometimes a web search reveals a domain name that is reserved but not in use. The party currently holding rights to the domain name may be willing to license it. If the desired domain name is a registered trademark or a close variation thereof, the trademark owner may be able to obtain domain name rights through the domain name dispute resolution system or by suing the registrant for cybersquatting as discussed in the next section.

It is important to remember that the international system for registering domain names is distinct from various national (and the European Community) systems for registering trademarks. Domain name registrars do not conduct trademark searches before assigning a requested domain name. The differences in these two systems are summarized in Table One on the following page.

While all word trademarks may potentially be registered as domain names with the addition of a top level suffix such as "-.com," not all domain names may be eligible for trademark protection. As discussed in the table above, generic or purely descriptive domain names such as "patents.com" will not also be protected as trademarks (*In re Oppedahl & Larson LLP* 2004). The addition of a top level domain name such as "-.com" does not affect trademark analysis in determining whether a word is generic or pure descriptive. The fact that generic category labels can be assigned as domain names has meant that one party would control a specific website like bookstore.com. Courts even have protected generic domain names from misappropriation by another party (*Kremen v. Cohen* 2003).

Non-generic domain names may receive trademark protection if they are distinctive and function to identify the source of products (brand) for consumers. This issue was resolved even before domain names came into use by courts and the trademark office considering an earlier technique for simplifying commerce—the use of vanity or mnemonic telephone numbers, e.g., "1-800-SLEEPY'S" which was registered as a trademark (U.S. Reg. No. 1,946,855). Like domain names, vanity phone numbers are registered/issued by companies that

Table One		
Domain Names Compared to Trademarks		
Issue	**Domain Names (DNs)**	**Trademarks (TMs)**
Similarity	DNs do not conflict as long as they are not identical. However cybersquatting covers DNs that are either identical or similar to TMs.	TMs conflict if they are confusingly similar to each other in meaning, sound or appearance (including typeface, color, logo design, etc.).
Descriptiveness	DNs may be generically descriptive such as drugstore.com	TMs may not be generic and may only be descriptive if secondary meaning is shown. However, a generic term may be used as an arbitrary mark for an unrelated product category such as APPLE computers and APPLE records.
Classes of Goods and Services	DNs may only be assigned to one user and therefore cover all goods and services.	TMs are registered for specified classes of goods and services, so that the same mark may be registered by different parties in different classes of goods and services. There may still be an issue of infringement if the classes are sufficiently close to confuse consumers or issues of dilution.
Geographic Scope	DNs are registered once for a period of time, may be renewed and are good throughout the world.	TMs must be protected on a country by country basis. The TRIPS agreement requires protection of famous, but unregistered marks and the Madrid Protocol allows for a single application to be used for multiple countries.

are completely independent of entities that register trademarks. Vanity phone numbers found to be generic have not been protected against spelling variations by competitors (*Holiday Inns, Inc. v. 800 Reservation, Inc.* 1996; *Dranoff-Perlstein Assoc. v. Sklar* 1992). In contrast, 1-888-M-A-T-R-E-S-S was held to be register-able because it was not generic, but rather descriptive with acquired secondary meaning (*In re Dial-A-Mattress Operating Corp.* 2001). Vanity numbers with acquired secondary meaning have been protected against the use of slightly misspelled vanity phone numbers (*Dial-A-Mattress Franchise Corporation v. Page* 1989; *American Airlines, Inc. v. A-1-800-A-M-E-R-I-C-A-N Corp.* 1985).

II. Cybersquatting

A specific U.S. statute condemns cybersquatting, the bad faith registration or selling of a domain name that is identical or confusingly similar to a registered trademark or dilutive of a famous trademark (15 U.S.C. §§ 1125(d) and 1129). Even before this statute was enacted, courts condemned domain names that infringed or diluted trademarks. The statute specifically includes typosquatting—the intentional misspelling of a trademarked in a domain name mentioned above. The misspelled word is almost always confusingly similar to the trademark. The statute lists nine non-exclusive factors that courts may consider when determining whether there is "bad faith intent to profit." Essentially the factors boil down to whether the registrant has a legitimate interest in the domain named as evidenced by prior use or perhaps non-commercial use versus evidence of bad faith such as false contact information, offer to transfer the domain name to the owner of a closely similar or identical trademark, intent to divert customers from the trademark owner's website, or the registration of multiple similar names.

Originally these practices involved the registration of domain names, but little use of the web addresses beyond trying to sell them to brand owners. ICANN developed uniform dispute resolution procedure to consider disputes between domain name registrants and trademark registrants (http://www.icann.org/udrp/udrp.htm). It licenses organizations such as the World Intellectual Property Organization Arbitration and Mediation Center to perform this service and results may be achieved in as quickly as one month. This system has awarded trademarked (or closely similar) domain names to the trademark owners about 80% of the time. In situations where several trademark owners may have interests in a domain name, the domain name will generally stay with the first to seek registration for it.

Since cybersquatting generally was not successful, domain address entrepreneurs turned to typosquatting where they could try to argue the (minor) difference in spelling caused consumers not to be confused between the domain name and trademarks. Experts suggest that as high as 20% of all hand typed URLs are misspelled with the most common misspelling being an extra letter, an incorrect letter and omission of a letter (FairWinds Partners 2008b). However, different domain names will likely have different most common spelling errors, e.g., youtub.com for youtube.com and mysapce.com for myspace.com, so brand owners should conduct tests to determine the most likely misspellings and consider registering those domain names in order to direct people from those URLs to the brand webpage without paying third parties.

Initially typosquatters, like their predecessor cybersquatters, also sought only to sell back the domain name to the trademark owner. Today, the more common model is to set up the domain site with advertising where the advertisers pay for each click through they receive. Most people will click on at least one link when they get to such sites.

Most recently, some firms have been registering domain names that contain a well-known trademark plus a generic keyword—a practice called "combosquatting" (FairWinds Partners 2008a). For example, Verizon recently obtained a default judgment awarding $31.5 million against internet registrar and typosquatter OnlineNIC. According to Verizon, OnlineNIC had registered more than 900,000 domain names that were similar to large companies including 663 Verizon-related names such as buyverizon.net (Masters 2008). While most squatters set up pay per click advertising websites, some set up pornographic sites or "phishing" sites that look like a genuine site but seek to collect name and password information for identity theft.

III. Brand Marketer Protection for the Generic gTLD Program

ICANN appears to be sensitive to brand marketer concerns with trademark protection and has established a multi-level system to protect trademark rights. The first concern it addressed was the possibility of "squatters" attempting to establish a registry for someone else's brand after the dot such as "-.coke." Given, the expense of setting up the registry, this seems unlikely and there is little evidence of firms actually attempting this. Nevertheless, to address this possible issue, ICANN provided for a Legal Right Objection that could be filed for fees ranging from $10,000 to $23,000. The objector would have to prove that a proposed gTLD registry (1) took unfair advantage of, (2) unfairly impaired the value of, or (3) created a likelihood of confusion with their trademark, e.g., "-.trademark." The filing date for these objections for this first batch of proposed gTLDs lapsed in March 2013. The majority of objections involved descriptive terms that were not entitled to trademark protection and only four objections were upheld (WIPO Arbitration and Mediation Center 2013).

The next concern ICANN addressed was the possibility that a trademark name could be registered before the dot within one of more new registries such as "coke.beverage." As the time for Legal Rights Objections for this round of applications lapsed, ICANN launched its Trademark Clearinghouse. Brand marketers can register their established trademarks with the Clearinghouse for about $150 per year per mark. Trademark Clearinghouse registrants are provided with Sunrise Service for at least 30 days before any new gTLD registrar is open to the public in order to receive notice of the new registry and apply to register their trademark with that new registry (assuming the registrar takes applications from the public). In addition, Clearinghouse registrants will receive notice during the first sixty days that a new gTLD register is open if anyone tries to register the Clearinghouse-registered trademark (e.g., "burberry.clothing"). Early reports suggest that if a proposed domain name conflicted with a Clearinghouse-listed trademark, 90% of the time, the domain application was withdrawn.

In the first year of the Clearinghouse over 28,000 trademarks were registered for over 10,000 brands and more than 500,000 notices were sent to Clearinghouse registrants (Trademark Clearinghouse 2014). It is important to note that these courtesies only applied to applications for the exact trademarked word in a domain name. One letter misspellings and even plurals received no benefit under this program unless they were also registered trademarks. However, new registries must provide a Trademark Claims Service for at least 90 days after the end of the Sunrise period whereby they identify registrants in the Trademark Clearinghouse of near identical registrations for no additional cost. Some registries are going beyond ICANN requirements by offering fee-based blocking services for domain names containing Clearinghouse registered trademarks. For example, the registry Donuts charges about $3 per year for a five year block on any domain name containing a trademark or a variation on the trademark that contains the trademark, e.g., "buyford." Blocking is significantly less expensive then registering the same combination and having it link to a brand's main website.

A third stage of protection for brand marketers occurs after a registry has registered a domain name. The Uniform Rapid Suspension System is relatively fast and inexpensive ($300–$500) and will "lock" a challenged domain name within 24 hours of complaint, while the complaint is being considered. After six months of operation, the URS system has decided 80 cases issuing suspensions in 72 of them, sometimes as quickly as seven days after the initial filing. Registration suspension makes the challenged domain name re-available for registration by the complainant or anyone else (INTA Internet Committee—Domain Disputes Subcommittee 2014).

A second post registration option involves paying higher fees ($1500–$2000), and using ICANN's current Uniform Domain Name

Dispute Resolution Policy (UDRP) to challenge a domain name registration. Historically challenges have been successful about 80% of the time and the remedy is the award of registration rights to the challenger rather than mere suspension. In 2015 just over ten percent of all UDRP disputes filed with the World Intellectual Property Organization (WIPO) involved new gTLDs with .XYZ, .CLUB and .EMAIL with the most disputed names. So cybersquatters are not becoming gTLD registrars (which would cost $285k), but are using newly created gTLD registrars to obtain domain names related to trademarks of other parties.

C. PRODUCT CATEGORY LABEL SELECTION AND POSSIBLE PROTECTION

In contrast to trademarks and domain names that are assigned to particular users and protected from unauthorized use by others, product category labels are thought to be generally available for all to use. Indeed, as noted in Chapter One, court cases involving the name of products whose patents had expired consistently held that others could use the product name (e.g., shredded wheat and cellophane) when the marketer had not created a category label for the product. The name had become the generic category label (*Kellogg Co. v. National Biscuit Co.* 1938; *Dupont Cellophane Co. v. Waxed Products Co.* 1936).

Suarez and Grodal (2015, pp. 27–29) offer two sets of suggestions for developing a dominant product category label. First they suggest that a successful label balances the familiar and the novel. The label "snowboard" does that while directly communicating what the product is and what it is used for. The earlier proposed label of "snurfing" combined snow and surfing but consumers did not directly understand the reference to snow. So "snurfing" was novel but not sufficiently familiar. Both "snowboard" and "snurfing" illustrate one technique for label creation—compounding two separate words into a single new word. Other examples include "laptop," "voicemail," and even the old "typewriter."

A second technique they call deriving a new word such as transforming the verb browse into a category label noun "browser" (Suarez and Grodal 2015, p. 29). These techniques are similar ones discussed in Chapter Three for use in developing brand names. Marketing concepts for brand name selection can be adopted for category labels provided that the difference between the two is kept in mind. The product category label should be descriptive but also should be attractive (interesting) and memorable to consumers. Most product category labels are descriptive and boring, but competition among possible labels can lead to a label that consumers find meaningful and memorable.

Once a product category label becomes generally adopted, it generally becomes available for all to use. However, there are four strategies that may be used by brand marketers under some circumstances to control the use of a category label by other firms (Petty 2015b). Each of these strategies is discussed below.

I. Top Level Domain Names

Depending on how it finally develops, the nascent generic top level domain program may prove to be the most significant strategy for controlling competitor use of a category label. Analysts did not foresee the popularity of generic product labels that resulted in about 1300 applications in the first round of this new program.

Once a firm registers a particular category label as a top level domain name, it will only face competition from somewhat substitutable terms unless those alternatives also are controlled by on firm. For example, Fidelity is seeking registries for "-.ira," "-.retirement," and "-.mutualfunds." If granted to Fidelity, Fidelity will determine the price and availability for competitors to obtain a name from its registry such as Vanguard.ira, Vanguard.mutualfunds, etc. It is not clear whether ICAAN rules that require registries to grant applications on a non-discriminatory basis will be effective or whether some applications can be arbitrarily rejected (Petty 2015b). Novelist and lawyer Scott Turow, president of the Authors Guild, wrote a letter to ICANN noting that he felt troubled that he might have to pay Amazon a fee to set up www.scotturow.author (Longstreth 2013). Amazon might condition granting "-.author" or "-.publisher" domain name addresses by requiring links to its website and banning links to websites for other online booksellers. Similarly, the firm operating a registry might "cherry-pick" the best domain names for itself, e.g., "life.insurance," "health.insurance," etc. Competitors may still be able to obtain their "brand.insurance" but still face a competitive disadvantage if descriptive names are controlled by a rival (Berkens 2013).

These examples all involve established category labels, but a firm in a developing industry faces similar options. If it is willing to spend the money (at least $185,000) to become a registrar, a firm could gamble on one (or more) developing category names. It seems likely that establishing a "-.newproduct" registry would contribute toward establishing that category label as the dominant label. Firms less willing to gamble can wait until they feel the category label has become clear and then try to register that label as a top level domain name. ICANN has a system for deciding who is chosen from multiple applicants for the same term (Petty 2015b).

By awarding such generic registries to marketers of the product, ICANN may be doing what trademark law has attempted to prevent for over a century—deny exclusive rights to a generic product category to a single firm in that category for fear that such a "trademark monopoly" would make it more difficult for competitors to promote their products to consumers (Folsom & Teply 1980). Trademark law does allow generic terms to be used in collective and certification trademarks, as discussed below, but such marks must be available to qualified organization members or firms rather than arbitrarily allocated to some but not others. It remains to be seen whether ICAAN will impose similar open availability requirements.

II. Collective and Certification Trademarks

Marketers may also adopt collective or certification trademarks of product category labels in order to control who may use them. For example, Darjeeling is an area located in West Bengal, India and is famous for producing a distinctive tea that is known and sold throughout the world. The Tea Board of India has registered the name Darjeeling as either a collective mark (continental Europe) or certification mark (most common law countries including India and the U.S.) to prevent unqualified tea firms from using that term as a specific category label (*Tea Board of India v. The Republic of Tea, Inc.* 2006).

Collective trademarks are owned by membership organizations and are used by the organization or its members to promote goods or services provided by the members. The membership organization must exercise control to insure its members properly use the mark (15 U.S.C. § 1127). Certification marks are similar except they may not be used by the certifying organization on any goods that it might sell and must be licensed for use to all qualified third parties not just organizational members. If a certifying organization is not able to legitimately exercise control over a descriptive mark or discriminately refuses to certify goods or services that satisfy the certification standard, the mark may be cancelled (15 U.S.C. § 1064(5)). Certification marks also may certify material content or mode of manufacture as well as quality, accuracy or other characteristics (15 U.S.C. § 1127).

Technology standards such as DOLBY and JAVA are often protected by a trademark or certification mark. When Fuji Film developed its DPOF (Digital Print Order Format) for digital cameras and printers, it sought trademark protection. However, the trademark examiner argued the mark was merely descriptive of the standard not identifying the source of the standard—Fuji Films. The TTAB overturned the examiner and held that trademark protection was appropriate because DPOF could distinguish goods using the format from those that did not and that such goods were from Fuji or licensed by it to use the mark (*In re Fuji Photo Film Co.* 2006).

III. Deception and Identity Standards

In the food and drug industries in particular and to a lesser degree in some other industries such as automobiles, the product category label may only be used by products that satisfy specific government standards. From 1938 through the early 1960s, the FDA promulgated "recipe" standards of identities for over one hundred canned and packaged foods. These standards specified exact recipes for products, such as requiring peanut butter to contain 90% peanuts. Any product with more or less peanuts could not identify itself as peanut butter and gain the favorable association that many consumers have with that type of product. In more recent years, the FDA has created more flexible standards and allowed some products to be labeled imitation under specific conditions so that standards of identity could be used by a broader variety of products (Chen 1992). As Europe moves toward a single market, it faces similar issues with incompatible food identity standards enacted by various member states that specify with precision appropriate types and levels of ingredients in such popular commodities as beer and chocolate.

One example of the importance of controlling the product category label is the National Milk Producers Federation that worked closely with the FDA to ensure that government identity standards for dairy and milk products must include cow's milk rather than milk from coconuts or other mammals. Milk, cheese, yogurt, ice cream and similar products that are not based on cow's milk must clearly indicate they are imitation or non-diary and also indicate what ingredient substitutes for cow's milk such as soy.

Outside of the food area, many products are subject to government or industry safety standards. If a new product fit into a broad product category label but did not satisfy the safety standards, a more specific category label would have to be careful not to suggest safety standard compliance. Fortunately, from the perspective of nascent products, it takes time to develop and adopt identity or safety standards. Whether the SEGWAY brand human transporter can be operated on roads or sidewalks is currently subject to regulation in some localities. The proposed category label of human transporter does not suggest where it might (or might not) be used.

Brand owners are well aware that they must create a brand name that is easily distinguishable as a source identifier rather than the name of the product category. Yet occasionally private parties sue brand marketers for alleged inappropriate and deceptive product identification. For example, the Potato Chip Institute sued General Mills for marketing its CHIPOS brand product, similar to PRINGLES, as potato chips when in fact the product was made from dehydrated potato granules rather than slices of raw potato. The Eighth Circuit upheld a trial court decision that allowed use of the term potato chip as long as there was a prominent disclosure that CHIPOS were made from dried or dehydrated potatoes. This was consistent with FDA guidelines that had been issued after a survey showed that 98% of all consumers were not deceived by PRINGLES brand potato chips into thinking they were made from slices of raw potato (*Potato Chip Institute v. General Mills, Inc.* 1972).

Similarly, Hampton Creek Foods is currently selling a product called JUST MAYO (pictured opposite). The product label prominently features an egg, yet this product is egg-free. Hampton Creek was briefly sued by Unilever, the marketer of HELLMAN'S and BEST FOODS mayonnaise. Unilever withdrew its complaint after criticism for attacking a small start-up. Hampton Creek still faces consumer class action lawsuits and had received a warning letter from and then negotiated label changes with the FDA to avoid consumers being falsely misled into thinking the product contains eggs. Mayonnaise must contain eggs under FDA regulations (21 C.F.R. 169.140(c)) (Entis 2015). In both of these examples, marketers of traditional products attempted to block a new product from using a traditional category label and force them to use a less familiar description of the new product.

IV. Geographical Indications

As the Darjeeling tea example illustrates, in the U.S. certification marks may be used to protect geographic names (Shalevich 2008). However, even without a conflicting registered certification or collective trademark, U.S. deceptive advertising law (Chapter Eight) can condemn misleading geographic representations. In 2015, the National Advertising Division recommended the company importing DANISA brand butter cookies (pictured on the previous page) from Indonesia stop using indicia of Danish origins. It also questioned whether the product complied with an FDA standard for use of the word "butter" in a product name. Similarly way back in 1942, a group of furniture producers from Grand Rapids, Michigan joined together to sue several Chicago-based companies and individuals for using "Grand Rapids" in their store names falsely representing they sold furniture produced in Grand Rapids (*Grand Rapids Furniture Co. v. Grand Rapids Furniture Co.* 1942).

However, U.S. law considers some names that sound geographically descriptive to be generic—describing a category of goods rather than goods from a specific source. Examples include French fries, Danish pastry and Bermuda shorts. Few, if any consumers believe these items necessarily come from the geographic area suggested by the name so that these terms are not considered misleading as to geographic origin under U.S. law. U.S. courts also have declared Swiss cheese and Worcestershire sauce to be generic. Food and Drug Administration regulations allow advertisers to use terms that arguably have geographic significance to describe products that are made in a specified manner. These include the following cheeses: Edam, Gorgonzola, Gouda, Gruyere, Limburger, Mozzarella, Muenster, Neufchatel and Roquefort. Similarly, the Bureau of Alcohol, Firearms and Tobacco considers vermouth and sake to be generic beverages and considers Burgundy, Chablis, Champagne and other names to be "semi-generic." The latter names may be used only in direct conjunction with an appropriate indication of geographic origin such as California Champagne (Bendekgey and Mead 1992).

Since many of these descriptive terms suggest European origin, it is not surprising that Europe is more protective of what it calls geographical indications (GIs). In fact Europe allows registration of

GIs for wine and spirits as well as agricultural products and foodstuffs and, in cases of conflicts with trademarks, Europe generally considers rights in GIs to be superior (Goebel 2003). The E.U. allows terms to be registered as one of two forms of GIs. First is protected geographic indication of a food that must have been produced, or processed or prepared within a defined geographic area. The second more restrictive category is the protected designation of origin where production, processing and preparation of the product all must take place within the defined geographic area (Byrne 2006). Europe is negotiating to have the U.S. recognize nearly 3000 GI registrations that it has for agricultural products, wines and spirits.

Thus, Europe would restrict the use of "Champagne" among wines to only those sparkling wines produced in that region of France, while the U.S. allows terms like "California Champagne" believing that few consumers would think the product came from France rather than California. However, even Europe does not totally restrict GIs, The European Court of Justice decided that under the Comparative Advertising Directive, it would allow a Belgian beer to advertise itself as "Champagne beer" (*De Landtsheer Emmanuel SA v. Comité Interprofessionel du Vin de Champagne* 2007).

The European system has been criticized for discriminating against foreign firms and products by making European GI available only to firms whose home country offers reciprocal GI protection and by allowing only foreign governments not firms to register and oppose GIs in contrast to European firms that can participate directly in the GI system. In contrast, the U.S. claims it is fully addressing GIs under its system of trademark registration fully satisfying its obligations under the 1995 Agreement on Trade Related Aspects of Intellectual Property Rights (United States Patent and Trademark Office, n.d.)

The E.U. is now considering whether to extend GI protection to some 800 non-food products such as Donegal tweed, Scottish tartans and Newbridge silverware. While GI protection has been used to protect historical product geographic labels, once a system is in place, they might be used for newly developed category labels as well. Still they are limited to locational labels rather than product category labels and presumably would be of more limited use than the other alternatives for exercising some control over who can use a category label.

D. HASHTAGS

Hashtags "#" are used in social media to link postings of related content together. Traditionally they may be used by anyone who wishes to post something related to a particular hashtag. However more and more brand marketers are seeking trademark protection for particular hashtags involving their brands. In 2010, four years after the launch of Twitter, only seven companies had submitted trademark applications for hashtags. Five years later in 2015, there were 1400 global trademark applications for hashtag trademarks (Brooke 2016).

The USPTO first recognized the possibility of hashtag trademarks in 2013. Like company designations, the addition of a hashtag does not change the trademark potential of the accompanying word. A generic or purely descriptive term with the addition of a hashtag is still generic or purely descriptive and not eligible for trademark protection (Brooke 2016). Indeed, it seems likely that most consumers perceive most hashtags as social media organizers rather than as brand identifiers. However, hashtags with well-known brand identifiers such as #ILikeCoke may be perceived by consumers as trademarks because of the prominence of COKE. Although hashtag trademark law is just beginning to evolve, it seems likely that the normal presumption will be that hashtags are not trademarks and the trademark applicant must bear the burden of proving that the social media use of a particular hashtag is brand identifying.

E. CONCLUSION

While trademarks should be the first tactic considered for protecting brand identity from unauthorized imitation, this chapter and the preceding one suggest that brand marketers may benefit from additional protections. Today e-commerce mandates website usage for most marketers so that domain name protection is a crucial consideration. It is important to remember that obtaining a domain name does not establish any trademark rights. Those are determined by each country's trademark laws. It remains to be seen what impact the new gTLD program will have on brand marketing. A number of well-known brands are adopting "-.brandname" or "-.productname" web addresses, but many others are adopting a wait and see strategy.

In addition, brand marketers used to be only minimally concerned with product category labels. The primary concern was distinguishing their brand name from the generic category label. However, today experts suggest that marketers become involved in the development of category labels for new products which leads to the question of whether some marketers and their products can be excluded from using particular labels. In the U.S., product identity standards and geographic indications of origins are no longer as strongly protected as they used to be, but Europe still believes that such regulations are important. How these issues will develop on the world stage, like the use of the new gTLDs, remains to be seen.

CHAPTER 7

Slogans—Brand Promotors and Possible Brand Identifiers

A. INTRODUCTION

Brand managers as well as attorneys tend to distinguish tactics such as brand names that identify the brand from those that promote the brand and its attributes. Yet often there is overlap between these two categories. Many brand names are descriptive or suggestive of brand attributes and therefore promote those attributes. Similarly, some forms of brand promotion may come to identify the brand in the minds of consumers. Slogans are the epitome of a tactic that may perform both tasks (Petty, Leong and Lwin 2010). Just as Warner-Lambert advertised its CERTS brand mint in the U.S. in the 1990s as being "two mints in one" (both a breath mint and candy mint—U.S. Reg. No. 1676941, cancelled Sept. 1998), a slogan may perform two functions as both a brand promoter and brand identifier.

For a slogan to be protected from imitation by a competitor, it must be sufficiently complex to qualify for copyright protection or it must identify the source of a product (the brand) to qualify for trademark protection. As noted in Chapter Five, short phrases such as slogans are generally thought to be too short and uncreative for copyright protection (*Kitchens of Sara Lee, Inc. v. Nifty Foods*, 1959; see also 37 C.F.R. § 202.1). Similarly, slogans are presumed to be promotional but not brand identifying. However, this presumption may be rebutted by proving that a particular slogan does identify the brand in the minds of consumers. Any such slogan also must satisfy other requirements for trademark protection such as not being merely descriptive, scandalous or misdescriptive. Slogans that do not satisfy this standard for trademark protection may still be used for brand promotion, but like other forms of brand promotion such as advertising, they must not be deceptive. Deceptive advertising is discussed in Chapter Eight.

B. BACKGROUND ON SLOGANS

While slogans can be used for many marketing purposes such as a humorous slogan that grabs attention or is memorable, it would appear that many marketers overlook the value of using slogans to promote a brand's unique selling proposition (Reeves 1961). Brand names might suggest the USP, but slogans can present the brand's USP more fully. David Aaker (1996, p. 58) implicitly suggests that slogans may embody a brand's USP: "A slogan can capture the essence of a brand and become an important part of the brand equity. If a brand is 'packaged meaning', a slogan can be the ribbon that ties the package together and provides an extra touch." Many advertisers believe that slogans work best when they reflect both the soul of the brand and the company's reason for being in business (Kiley 2004). Therefore most brands try to associate itself with a specific benefit, which over time acts like a stake in the ground, claiming territorial rights over its value proposition (Dawar 2004).

Alreck and Settle (1999) note that slogans can communicate not just a factual product benefit but also an emotional benefit e.g., "The night is made for Michelob" or THE GREATEST SHOW ON EARTH. A brand's USP may well have an emotional component. For example, Allstate Insurance's famous slogan: YOU'RE IN GOOD HANDS WITH ALLSTATE communicates a USP of reliable insurance protection, but with a strong emotional tone of re-assurance. Of the various components which make up marketing communications, slogans appear to play a crucial role in contributing to brand building and are important in generating and sustaining the financial performance of a brand (Haigh and Knowles 2004).

Researchers have found that brand recognition of slogans can vary widely. For example, a survey found that Wendy's newly coined "It's Better Here" had zero recognition, while Allstate's "You're in Good Hands" enjoyed a high level of recognition of 87% (Kiley 2004). This means that Wendy's should have a difficult time obtaining trademark protection for this slogan. However, it was successfully registered based on its use in commerce from June 2003 through January 2011 when it was cancelled (U.S. Reg. No. 2847387). Apparently no one questioned whether consumers identified the slogan with the WENDY'S brand. In contrast, Allstate registered its YOU'RE IN GOOD HANDS trademark in 1979 (U.S. Reg. No. 11222022) which was highly recognized as a brand identifier in a study over twenty years later. Whether a slogan is well recognized depends greatly on a host of variables such as distinctiveness and memorability as well as how long and often it has been used to market the brand. When slogans are effectively utilized, they add greatly to the market values of firms (Mathur and Mathur 1995).

C. TRADEMARK PROTECTION OF SLOGANS

As noted above, trademark law presumes that slogans are promotional rather than brand identifying. For example, Volvo's slogan of "Drive Safely" was refused registration in the U.S. for being informational but not distinctive. Similarly, in Europe the slogan "Safety 1st" also was denied trademark registration. When Oldsmobile adopted the slogan "Escape from the Ordinary," a court denied trademark protection for a clothing outfitter that claimed prior trademark rights in the same slogan. The court held that there was insufficient evidence that it had secondary meaning for the outfitter in the minds of the public or that the public would likely be confused about source or sponsorship from these two uses. The court also found the slogan was descriptive for the clothing outfitter because it carried outdoor clothing (*Norm Thompson Outfitters, Inc. v. General Motors, Corp.* 1971). The burden of proving a slogan functions as a trademark is on the slogan user (*Microstrategy Inc. v. Motorola, Inc.* 2001).

Slogans are often used in conjunction with brand names such as "British Airways: The World's Favorite Airline." However, such a slogan may not be protected from imitation by other airlines also claiming to be "The World's Favorite." If British Airways wants to protect this three word phrase as its trademark, it must prove that the phrase without the company name identifies the brand by itself.

In the E.U. case of *Nestle SA's Trade Mark Application (Have a Break)* (2003), one of the questions that the courts had to consider was—is the mark HAVE A BREAK which is a portion of the well-known slogan HAVE A BREAK . . . HAVE A KIT KAT sufficiently distinctive to identify the brand on its own? Although lower decision makers denied registration, claiming the phrase was devoid of any distinctive character, the European Court of Justice disagreed concluding that even though the slogan had not been used without the brand name, the slogan by itself still functioned as a trademark. The court found that due to repeated exposure to the slogan, consumers actually perceived the slogan as identifying the Kit Kat brand (*Nestle SA's Trade Mark Application (Have a Break)* 2005). In the U.S., Hershey was able to register part of its jingle GIMME A BREAK as a trademark slogan for Kit Kat bars without opposition (Reg. No. 2175506).

I. The Source Identification Function

In order for a slogan to function as a trademark it must stand out from advertising copy and must identify the product source rather than merely describe its properties. Longer phrases are less likely to perform this function (and more likely to be promotional) than shorter phrases (*Smith v. M & B Sales and Manufacturing* 1990). Comedian Jeff Foxworthy successfully sued a t-shirt company for copying his "redneck" jokes. The court held that the phrase at the beginning of all of his jokes, "you might be a redneck" acted as a trademark and was well recognized by the public as identifying Mr. Foxworthy. The rest of the numerous jokes (e.g., "if your two year old has more teeth than you do") were held to be protected under copyright law (*Foxworthy v. Custom Tees, Inc.* 1995).

As noted in Chapter One, for a long time the USPTO refused to register slogans as trademarks, considering slogans to be mere promotion rather than source identifiers. This changed in 1952 when a court granted trademark registration for the slogan "The Fate of a Fabric Hangs by a Thread" for rayon yarn. Because this slogan did not describe the product or its function in any way, the court held the mark was arbitrary and therefore inherently distinctive. Given that slogans communicate a brief message this is probably the highest category of distinctiveness available for slogans.

After the 1952 decision, the U.S. Patent and Trademark Office (USPTO) began to register clever marks with double meanings such as "Tops for Good Drinks" by a bottle cap company and "No Bones about It" for a boneless ham. These marks would qualify as suggestive rather than merely descriptive. In 1954, it also registered Ivory Soap's descriptive slogan: 99 44/100% PURE. In 1970, a court upheld the registration of Clairol's famous slogan: "Hair Color So Natural Only Her Hairdresser Knows for Sure." While the court agreed with the USPTO that the slogan was descriptive, it was persuaded by evidence that consumers identified the mark with the Clairol brand—which is secondary meaning in trademark law parlance (Grover 1991). Thus in the U.S., slogans now are treated like other trademarks. They may be registered and protected if they are deemed distinctive and brand identifying by the USPTO or the courts.

The same is true for slogans in the E.U.—they must be capable of performing the essential function of a trademark—to identify the goods or services of a particular firm or brand and enable consumers to distinguish the firm's goods or services from those of its competitors. Besides seeking individual national registrations within the E.U., marketers may also apply for a community Trade Mark with the Office of Harmonization in the Internal Market (OHIM). The community trade mark is a single trademark which operates for the whole of the European Community and the laws governing community trade marks are found in the Council Regulation (EC) No. 207/2009.

II. Slogans Must Be Distinctive for Trademark Protection

Both the U.S. and E.U. allow registration and trademark protection for descriptive slogans that have proven secondary meaning, but not for common commercial phrases such as "Why Pay More?" (*In re Wakefern Food Corp.* 1984). Similarly, SAY IT WITH CHOCOLATE was registered in the U.S. (U.S. Reg. No. 1969797) but registration was disallowed in the United Kingdom for being a mere promotional phrase. The E.U. registers slogans only if they possess the inherent property of distinguishing goods by their source. For example, in the case of *Masterfoods Ltd v. Controller of Patents, Designs and Trade Marks* 2003, the slogans in question were TOP BREEDERS RECOMMEND IT and DEVELOPED BY VETS, TOP BREEDERS RECOMMEND IT for animal foods. The Controller of Patents, Designs and Trade Marks refused the applications of both slogans on the ground that they were devoid of any distinctive character. The objections raised by the Controller for both slogans are similar, namely that they are composed of ordinary English words and were statements of fact that could be validly made by any other producers of dog food who wish to attract customers by claiming their product to be recommended by top breeders.

On appeal, the High Court of Ireland found the slogans to be inherently distinctive because the slogans were not a normal way of referring to pet food. The court also found that the slogans did not represent the essential characteristics of pet food as a matter of every day common speech. Furthermore, no other manufacturer of pet food used these phrases. In the U.S., Kal Kan registered the similar slogans RECOMMENDED BY TOP BREEDERS and DEVELOPED WITH VETS, RECOMMENDED BY TOP BREEDERS without opposition (Reg. Nos. 1557104 and 2073460, respectively). In contrast, the E.U. denied a telemarketing service firm's attempt to register its slogan "Real People, Real Solutions" as being non-distinctive of a particular brand (*Sykes Enterprises, Inc.* v. *Office of Harmonization in the Internal Market* 2003). More recently, European courts have affirmed findings that proposed trademarks "Investing for a New World" and "Equipment for Life" were devoid of distinctive character.

III. Merely Descriptive Slogans Are Not Protected as Trademarks

In general, proposed marks that are only descriptive in nature may not be registered nor protected as trademarks because public policy considerations dictate the need of preserving a public commons for words free for all to use. The European Court of Justice set a low threshold for registration of such descriptive slogans in the recent case of *Procter & Gamble Company v OHIM (BABY-DRY)* (2002). As described in Chapter Three, the proposed trademark at issue, BABY-DRY for diapers, is probably best considered a brand name mark, but the decision has relevance for descriptive slogans as well.

The ECJ found that even though individually the words 'baby' and 'dry' could be used to describe diapers, once they are placed together in the order and form of BABY-DRY, they ceased to be descriptive. The reason was that it was unlikely that other brands would use this combination of words to describe diapers. The court noted that "any *perceptible difference* between the combination of words submitted for registration and the terms used in the common parlance of the relevant class of customers to designate the goods or services or their essential characteristics is apt to confer distinctive character on the word combination enabling it to be registered as a trade mark."(Emphasis added) (*Procter & Gamble Company v OHIM (BABY-DRY)* 2002, Para 40).

The unusual juxtaposition was an unfamiliar expression in the English language and was not therefore exclusively descriptive. Instead, the court found that the combination should be regarded as a 'lexical invention bestowing distinctive power' (*Procter & Gamble Company v OHIM (BABY-DRY)* 2002, Para. 44) on the trademark. Although it remains to be seen what exactly the terms 'syntactically unusual juxtaposition' and 'lexical invention bestowing distinctive power' really mean, they have been relied upon in subsequent cases seeking registration of slogans.

In contrast, one year later, the ECJ found the trade name "Doublemint," registered in the U.S. since 1915 (U.S. Reg. No. 0102001) and many European countries, to be merely descriptive in *OHIM* v *Wm. Wrigley Jr. Company* (2003). The Advocate General argued that 'Doublemint' was not a 'lexical invention' like BABY-DRY which he thought was rightly held to be registered. Wrigley argued that "Doublemint" was similarly unusual compared with more typical descriptive phrases such as "double the mint" or "twice the mint" but the two words double and mint are rather common. The ECJ, following the Advocate General and the First Board of Appeal at OHIM holding that the term 'Doublemint' should not be registered for being descriptive. It found the proposed mark consisted "exclusively of descriptive" words. However, other OHIM appeals boards have allowed registration of other seemingly descriptive combinations of two words such as ALLTRAVEL and NETMEETING (Ryan 2004). This suggests that a little bit of lexical invention or syntactically unusual juxtaposition can go along way for slogan trademarks as well as name trademarks.

IV. Use of Descriptive or Common Words

Slogans are often made up of descriptive or common words suggesting that the slogan is not distinctive. However, unusual phrasing may be sufficient for trademark protection as illustrated by the examples BABY-DRY and TOP BREEDERS RECOMMEND IT. Although the U.S. has registered DOUBLEMINT, it still has limits on descriptive slogans. For example it denied registration for the slogan: "The Baby Bootie Sock that Will Not Kick Off" (*In re Sandra Hosiery Mills* 1967).

Common descriptive words are more likely to be acceptable if they are used in an unusual context for the goods or services in question. For example, the USPTO has registered WE SMILE MORE for the Marriott Corporation demonstrating its acceptance of "ordinary word" slogans. The PTO found the slogan was suggestive of the facial expression of the service providers rather than merely descriptive of the services being provided (Grover 1991).

The U.S. and E.U. have registered phrases consisting of common words such as: TAKE IT AS IT IS, TAKE IT EASY, and WE'LL TAKE IT FROM HERE presumably because they are vague and suggestive rather than descriptive. Similarly, in the E.U., the slogan BEAUTY ISN'T ABOUT LOOKING YOUNG BUT LOOKING GOOD was allowed to be registered as a trademark because it did not describe the cosmetics being sold, but was rather a statement of the brand's philosophy (*Clinique Laboratories, Inc.'s Application* 1999). Similarly, the slogan DAS PRINZIP DER BEQUEMLICHKEIT (THE PRINCIPLE OF COMFORT) was eventually allowed to be registered. Although it was composed of common words, the ECJ felt that it did identify a particular source of product in the minds of consumers (*OHIM* v. *Erpo Mobelwerk GmbH* 2004). Typically when common words are used in a slogan, the trademark application must disclaim protection for each of the words individually.

V. Purely Laudatory Phrases Are Disfavored

Trademark law also does not protect general laudatory slogans such as "America's Freshest Ice Cream" (Grover 1991), "the player's choice" for musical instrument strings in Europe (Byrt 2003), or "Number One in Floor Care" (*Hoover Co. v. Royal Appliance Mfg. Co.* 2001). The phrase "The Best Beer in America" was incapable of being registered as a trademark because it was laudatory and descriptive (*In re Boston Beer Co.* 1999). However Anheuser-Busch was allowed to register its slogan KING OF BEERS as a trademark (U.S. Reg. No. 0847980) and is currently opposing trademark registration of "Queen of Beers" by another firm. Similar slight changes are sufficient for registration in some cases such as THE FIRST NAME IN FLOORCARE (*Hoover Co. v. Royal Appliance Mfg. Co.* 2001) or AMERICA'S BEST CHEW. Using "chew" for chewing tobacco was found to advance the slogan beyond merely descriptive (Grover 1991).

Hammond and Schmitz (2003), note that the E.U. may be tougher than the U.S. in this regard. They cite the difficulty PT Barnum also had difficulty registering its slogan "The Greatest Show on Earth" as a European Community Trademark, although the Board of Appeal ultimately allowed registration because the slogan was distinctive in the minds of consumers identifying the circus (Bryt 2003). The E.U. also refused to register Visa's proposed slogan: "The World's Best Way to Pay and Be Paid" as a trademark for being purely laudatory. The Appeal Board was not impressed by the rhyme between "way," and "pay" and near rhyme with "paid" (*Visa International Service Association's Application* 1999).

Table One	
Slogans Afforded or Denied Trademark Status	
Afforded Trademark Protection	**Denied Trademark Protection**
America's best chew	America's freshest ice cream
America's favorite way to fly	The players' choice*
The first name in floorcare	Number one in floor care
The Greatest Show on Earth	The world's best way to pay and be paid
The toughest glue on the planet earth	The most personal sort of deodorant; Substance for success*
Top Breeders Recommend It	Why pay more?
Always low prices	Brand names for less
Better ingredients. Better pizza	Real people, real solutions*
Hair Color So Natural Only Her Hairdresser Knows for Sure	The baby bootie sock that will not kick off.
No bones about it (ham)	Never clean your shower again*
We smile more	We make it, you bake it.
Just do it; Take it easy	Live richly*
Take it easy	Drive Safely; Safety First*
* Trademark status denied in Europe, but registration allowed in the U.S.	

VI. Slogans vs. Jingles

Advertising songs, known as jingles, also may become well known to consumers and identify a particular brand. As noted in the previous chapter, they are typically considered too long to be protected under trademark law. Rather, like advertising, they are protected from imitation by copyright law. In contrast, it should be noted that slogans are generally considered too short to be protected under copyright law. They are therefore only protected against imitation by trademark law. However, a recent decision by the Second Circuit Court of Appeals conceded that musical compositions could function as a trademark for a brand, although not for the composition itself (*Oliveira a/k/a Gilberto v. Frito-Lay, Inc.* 2001). Furthermore, Mattress Discounters registered both its word slogan and the musical sound recording version of the most notable line of its jingle HAVE A GOOD NIGHT'S SLEEP ON US, MATTRESS DISCOUNTERS (U.S. Reg. No. 1754344).

The U.S. has registered a number of slogan trademarks based on the words of shorter jingles as illustrated in the table below. For example, although the Dr. Pepper jingle was denied trademark protection, the company did register the slogan BE A PEPPER taken from the jingle (U.S. Reg. No. 113673). These registrations appear not to include the music so technically they are slogan trademarks rather than jingle trademarks. However, it seems likely that these trademarks could protect against confusingly similar words or words of jingles, even if they don't protect against the use of a similar melody with distinctive words.

Table Two			
U.S. Slogan Trademarks Derived from Jingles			
Word Mark	**Owner**	**Year**	**Reg. #**
Have it Your Way	Burger King	1973	0961016
Plop, plop, fizz, fizz, oh what a relief it is	Alka-Seltzer	1977	1079406
Be a pepper	Dr. Pepper	1980	1136373
Have a good night's sleep on us	Mattress Discounters	1989	1676268
Like a good neighbor, State Farm is there	State Farm	1991	1668793
The best part of waking up is Folger's in your cup	Folger's Coffee	1992	1567395

D. TRADEMARK ENFORCEMENT

Once a slogan comes to identify a product source in the minds of consumers, it may be registered as a trademark and may be protected as such. As noted in Chapter Two, often trademark infringement is found based on similar wording. For example, the slogan GATORADE IS THIRST AID was found to infringe the trademark brand name THIRSTAID, because the slogan was found to function as a trademark (*Sands, Taylor & Wood Co. v. The Quaker Oats Co.* 1992). Trademarks also may be considered confusingly similar to each other if they sound similar when spoken out loud such as WHERE THERE'S BUD, THERE'S LIFE and WHERE THERE'S BUGS, THERE'S LIFE (*Chemical Corp of America v. Anheuser-Busch, Inc.* 1962). They may be confusing similar if the words look similar such as KING OF BEERS and BEER OF BEERS (*Anheuser-Busch, Inc. v. Customer Co., Inc.* 1996). Finally, marks may be similar if they are conceptually similar, even if otherwise dissimilar such as I GIVE MY MAN ENGLISH LEATHER EVERY CHANCE I GET and YARDLEY LEATHER: GIVE IT TO YOUR MAN TONIGHT (*Mem Co. v. Yardley of London, Inc.* 1981).

Although trademark law provides greater protection from imitation than copyright law, it is important to note that trademark law does not provide complete protection. The slogan YOU GOTTA EAT was found not to infringe on the website name YouGottaEat because the latter was descriptive and had not come to identify a particular brand in the minds of consumers (*YouGottaEat, Inc. v. Checkers Drive-In Restaurants, Inc.* 2003).

Similarly, the company name "Just Did It" was found not to infringe Nike's slogan, JUST DO IT, because the company name functioned as the mail order source of the product rather than as a brand identifier (*Nike, Inc. v. Just Did It Enterprises* 1993). Nike did not object to registration of DO IT JUST by a hospitality consulting group, but is contesting the proposed trademark "Just Do IT" by an IT consulting firm. A trademark examiner found "Just Doo It" to likely infringe so a company making a dog pack that could hold dog droppings abandoned that application.

Recently, the Federal Circuit vacated the denial of trademark registration for Juice Generation's slogan: "Peace, Love and Juice." The TTAB found this slogan would likely cause consumer confusion with previously registered PEACE AND LOVE registered trademarks (both standard character and color/design marks) in the same industry. However, the appellate court held that the TTAB did not properly consider the differences between the two marks as a whole (i.e., two words vs. three words) and evidence that many similar slogans were used in the food industry such as "Peace, Love and Popcorn" and "Peace, Love and Pizza." Furthermore, PEACE AND LOVE was suggestive or descriptive and therefore entitled to narrow protection (*Juice Generation, Inc. v. GS Enterprises, LLC* 2015).

Finally as suggested by the preceding case, trademarks may be the subject of a descriptive fair use defense. For example, a court refused to find either infringement or dilution of Carnival's FUN SHIP trademark from SeaEscape Casino Cruise's use of the slogan SEAESCAPE TO A SHIP FULL OF FUN. The court based its conclusion in part on the common use of the word "fun" in the travel and entertainment industries rather than a formal fair use analysis (*Carnival Corp. v. SeaEscape Casino Cruises, Inc.* 1999). Similarly, a court allowed CREST brand toothpaste to use the slogan that it was "The Dentist's Choice for Fighting Cavities," despite protests from DENTIST'S CHOICE brand toothbrushes (*Wonderlabs, Inc. vs. P & G Co.* 1990).

U.S. courts also allow some leeway to parody famous slogans such as when the slogan THE JOY OF SIX was used in a newspaper article and related sports memorabilia to celebrate the six championship victories of the Chicago Bulls basketball team (*Diana Packman v. Chicago*

Tribune Co. 2001). Similarly, a florist association was allowed to advertise "This Bud's for you and 11 More Rosebuds" (*Anheuser-Busch, Inc. v. Florists Association of Greater Cleveland, Inc.*, 1984) and a marketer of t-shirts could advertise Myrtle Beach using the slogan "This beach is for you" (*Anheuser-Busch, Inc. v. L & L Wings, Inc.*, 1992). Lastly, a printing company producing pocket calendars and address books was allowed to use the descriptive slogan "Don't Leave Home without Me Pocket Address Book" despite the similarity to American Express' well known slogan (*American Express Co v. CFK, Inc.* 1996). However, other countries are less permissive with parodies of trademarked slogans. France did not allow Air France's slogan MAKING THE SKY THE BEST PLACE ON EARTH to be parodied by discount carrier Ryan Air's "Making the Sky the Cheapest Place on Earth." Parodies are discussed in more detail in Chapter Sixteen.

Ringling Brother's Circus also has struggled in trying to prevent imitation/parody of its famous slogan. In 1988, it won a dilution by blurring case against a firm proclaiming "The Greatest Used Car Show on Earth" (*Ringling Bros.-Barnum & Bailey Combined Shows, Inc. v. Celozzi-Ettleson Chevrolet, Inc.* 1988). However, it has lost later cases because the slogan is laudatory and courts are reluctant to restrict the use of the phrase "The Greatest _______ on Earth." U.S. courts allowed the use of slogans "The Greatest Bar on Earth," "The Greatest Snow on Earth," and "The Great Show on Earth Isn't" (*Ringling Bros.-Barnum & Bailey Combined Shows, Inc. v. B.E. Windows Corp.* 1996; *Ringling Bros.-Barnum & Bailey Combined Shows, Inc. v. Utah Div. of Travel Dev.* 1999; *Ringling Bros.-Barnum & Bailey Combined Shows, Inc. v. Chandris American Lines, Inc.* 1971).

Imitative slogans that contain a negative connotation may be more readily condemned under trademark law. Even before the federal prohibition of dilution by tarnishment, courts are were more protective of slogan imitations that may harm the value of the original slogan such as "Where there is life, there's bugs" instead of "where there is life, there's Bud" and a condom maker's slogan "Never Leave Home

Without It" imitating American Express' slogan (*American Express Co. v. Vibra Approved Laboratories Corp.* 1989). However, this protection was not absolute. A court allowed a parody poster of the Girl Scouts' motto "Be Prepared" showing a pregnant girl in a uniform similar to a Girl Scout uniform. The court held that consumers were not likely to be confused into thinking the source of the poster was the Girl Scouts (*Girl Scouts v. Personality Posters Manufacturing* 1969).

E. SLOGANS MUST NOT BE DECEPTIVE

As with brand names, both the U.S. and E.U. prohibit the registration of misdescriptive (the term used in the U.S. statute) or deceptive slogans as trademarks. However, given that many slogans are not registered as trademarks, registration challenges of slogans for being misdescriptive are rare. One exception was Hoover's challenge to competitor Royal's attempt to register the slogan "First Name in Floorcare." The Federal Circuit upheld the TTAB's affirmation of dismissal of the opposition holding the proposed mark was not misdescriptive. Hoover contented it rather than Royal was the number one brand in floorcare, but failed to prove that was the likely meaning of Royal's slogan. "First name" might also connote general familiarity such as being on a first name with someone. Such general familiarity does not misdescribe "the character, quality, function, composition or use of the goods" (as specified by the U.S. statute). Even if it did, Hoover would have to prove that the prospective purchasers would believe the misdescription actually described the goods and that the misdescription would likely affect the decision to purchase (*Hoover Co. v. Royal Appliance Mfg.* 2001).

Because slogans are a form of advertising, challenges for deceptiveness are more commonly made under advertising law (discussed in more detail in the next chapter). For example, the United States Federal Trade Commission (FTC) condemned advertising for Aspercreme that proclaimed Aspercreme concentrates "All the strong relief of aspirin directly at the point of pain." The FTC found the message was false because the product did not contain aspirin and misleading because the advertiser had no clinical studies to support its claim that the product provided relief (*Thompson Medical Co., Inc. v. FTC* 1986).

Advertising self-regulation also challenges misleading slogans. The National Advertising Division of the Council of Better Business Bureaus (NAD) supported Wal-Mart's argument that its slogan "Always The Low Price. Always" was understood by consumers to mean it had a general policy of offering low prices, but did not mean it would always have the lowest prices on all items. The National Advertising Review Board, on appeal however, felt it might be misleading so Wal-Mart agreed to change its slogan to "Always Low Prices" (*Wal-Mart Stores, Inc.* 1994). In contrast, Winn-Dixie's slogan of "Everyday Lower Prices" in conjunction with specific price comparisons to Wal-Mart prices was thought to deceptively communicate that its prices generally were lower than those of Wal-Mart (*Winn-Dixie Stores, Inc.* 1996).

Although slogans may be challenged as false advertising, because they are short and typically not very specific, they may be permitted as mere puffing—seller's talk too vague to be relied upon as a factual statement by consumers. Puffing generally is defined as a vague opinion of quality (e.g., "Deluxe" or "Best Quality") as opposed to a statement of fact. As discussed above, slogans that were purely puffing would probably be considered self-laudatory and might be denied trademark protection on that basis unless they had at least slightly unusual wording.

Yet even claims that might be puffing must be interpreted within the context of the entire advertisement. Although "best quality" is often considered puffing, the FTC found that the advertising claim "world's best" safety helmet was a factual statement about the level of protection provided by the helmet rather than puffing (*Payless Drug Store Co.* 1972). The FTC also found a claim that a brand of yogurt was "nature's perfect food that science made better" was a statement of fact rather than puffing (*Dannon Milk Products, Inc.* 1962).

In contrast, an FTC administrative law judge dismissed a complaint that the statement "Everybody Needs Milk" was deceptive because some people are allergic to milk (*California Milk Producers Advisory Bd.* 1979). Essentially it treated the slogan as puffing. Similarly, a court found that Papa John's slogan "Better Ingredients. Better Pizza" was puffing, if used by itself. However, the court noted that the slogan could contribute to a false or misleading message if used in advertising that factually discussed particular ingredients but communicated a false or misleading message about them (*Pizza Hut, Inc. v. Papa John's Int'l Inc.* 2000).

The NAD referred a complaint to the government when an advertiser refused to cooperate after claiming to offer "America's Best Online Banking" and claiming to be "American's Leading online banking service." The NAD apparently supported the challenger who argued such slogans should be supported by current industry ratings (*Commerce Bank* 2004). The NAD also felt claims to be the "No. 1 seller" should be substantiated by evidence (*General Steel Corp.* 2003). In a case involving the slogan "America's Favorite Way to Fly," the NAD asserted the slogan by itself could be merely a statement of corporate pride, but in the context of other statements that more passengers flew this airline than any other airline, it was a statement of fact (*Eastern Airlines, Inc.* 1982). This slogan was registered as a trademark in 1983 (Reg. No. 1227143), but cancelled in 1989. Similarly, the NAD held that the slogan THE TOUGHEST GLUE ON PLANET EARTH (Reg. No. 0868481) was an unsubstantiated and therefore deceptive superiority claim rather than puffing as argued by the brand owner (*Gorilla Glue Co.* 2006).

Taste claims also are difficult to analyze. The NAD found the statement "America's best loved coffee" to be puffing (*Kraft Foods, Inc.* 1995). A recent Lanham Act decision agreed finding the phrase

"America's Favorite Pasta" to be mere puffing, particularly in the context of the advertisement which emphasized taste rather than sales data (*American Italian Pasta Co. v. New World Pasta Co.* 2004). However, in an earlier case, the NAD treated statements: "Taste it yourself and you'll agree Jolly Time is the world's favorite popcorn. The Taste is why" as a factual claim about taste that required substantiation (*American Pop Corn Co.* 1979).

Finally, a series of three U.S. court cases in the 1970–80s analyzed slogans for copycat perfumes that took the form of "If you like [famous brand name product], you'll love [our copycat product]". Two cases allowed the use of such slogans, particularly when the maker of the copycat product is clearly disclosed and obviously different from the maker of the famous brand product. However, one court of appeals affirmed a trial court finding that use of such a slogan that included both company names and a disclaimer that the famous brand company was not related in any way to the copycat company was confusing to consumers (Reed 1989).

F. CONCLUSION

There is no doubt that that from a business viewpoint, slogans serve to promote brands and can add greatly to the market values of firms (Mathur and Mathur 1995). The brand promotion message is regulated under both trademark prohibitions against misleading marks and general advertising law discussed in the next chapter. However, the promotional aspect of slogans can interfere with their ability to distinguish one brand form others. For this reason brand managers must be cautioned to avoid clichés, pure laudation and purely factual statements. A modicum of creativity and distinctiveness in slogan phrasing should be sufficient for trademark protection, particularly in the U.S.

PART 2

Promoting the Brand

Once a brand's identity is protected from unauthorized imitation, the brand marketer is free to promote the brand to consumers to induce them to first try and later re-purchase the product, hopefully becoming brand loyal customers. Media advertising, the subject of the first chapter in this part, arguably is the most ubiquitous form of brand promotion, but there are several other important forms of brand promotion. In order to develop a categorization scheme useful to marketing managers and reflective of legal issues, Joan Lindsey-Mullikin and I developed the 3 Cs matrix of non-advertising brand promotion that illustrates how these topics are treated in Chapters Nine through Thirteen (Petty and Lindsey-Mullikin, 2006):

Table One		
The 3 Cs of Attracting Brand Interest		
Cajolery (Chapter 9)	**Compensation (Chapter 10)**	**Connection (Chapter 11)**
Personal Selling	Price Promotions	Personalized Recommendations
Pressure to Buy	Samples, Bundles, Premiums	Masked Marketing
Targeting	Sweepstakes/Prize Promotions	Secondary Brand Associations (Chapter 12)
Repeat Solicitations	Loyalty Programs	Celebrities (Chapter 13)

Nearly all brands engage in some form of media advertising. One way to think about brand promotion is called the FCB grid as illustrated below. This grid was developed by the advertising agency—Foote, Cone and Belding—as an advertising planning tool. It is a simple matrix in which advertisers can categorize products and services along two dimensions: thinking-feeling across the top and high-low involvement down the side (Ratchford 1987).

Table Two

FCB Grid

	Thinking	**Feeling**
High Involvement	INFORMATIVE (THINKER) Examples: car, house, consumer electronics Copy: specific information	AFFECTIVE (FEELER) Examples: jewelry, fashion, cosmetics Copy: executional impact
Low Involvement	HABIT FORMATION (DOER) Examples: food, household items Copy: reminder	SELF-SATISFACTION (REACTOR) Examples: cigarettes, candy, liquor Copy: attention

This grid suggests that promotional approaches for a brand may vary depending on whether consumers are likely to be highly involved when purchasing the product type and whether they are likely to try to make a well-reasoned decision about purchase or simply select a brand for which they have positive feelings. The left hand column focuses on informational advertising that is the focus of Chapter Eight and probably over 90% of all advertising lawsuits and challenges brought in the United States. Occasional challenges are brought against advertising covered by the right hand column. These situations are addressed as cajolery in Chapter Nine.

It should be noted that the current popularity of the "Native Advertising" concept where commercial messages are formatted to blend into the background media of a website or magazine for example, has also led to greater scrutiny of deception in format rather than deception in facts being claimed in an easily-recognizable advertisement. The policy concern is with format deception is that consumers may not realize that a particular message is an advertisement and therefore won't engage their normal skepticism defenses against the message (Petty and Andrews 2008). Petty (2013) suggests that some messages are fully masked as non-commercial information from objective third parties and some messages are partially masked such as an obvious advertisement that purports to contain objective third party endorsements but the endorsements are either fictional or from non-objective parties. This issue of masked marketing is examined in Chapter Eleven.

CHAPTER 8

Avoiding Deceptive Advertising When Promoting Brand Attributes and Performance

A. INTRODUCTION

Challenges to factually deceptive advertising can be examined in five stages: (1) how advertising challenges are brought—Initiation, (2) what message is conveyed to consumers—Interpretation, (3) what is the likelihood the message will mislead consumers—Deception, (4) the accuracy of the advertising claims—Verification, and (5) what remedy, if any, is appropriate—Remediation (cf. Petty & Kopp 1995; Petty 1997).

B. INITIATION—CHALLENGING DECEPTIVE ADVERTISING

Advertising is policed for deception through industry self-regulation, government regulation, or private lawsuits (most commonly by competitors, but sometimes by consumers or consumer organizations). In the U.S., advertising legal challenges arise from all three sources. Given, this level of scrutiny, advertisers often conduct their own internal review of advertising before it is released to the public (Zanot 1985).

Media also can play an important role through self-regulation—screening out ads that might mislead consumers. Twenty years ago the major U.S. television networks reviewed about 50,000 advertisements and received challenges to less than 100 of those advertisements. More recent figures are not available, but in the late 1980s networks cut the number of people employed to scrutinize ads for problems (Gordon 1988). Some individual television stations (Rotfeld, Abernathy and Parsons 1990) and magazines also review advertising before accepting it (Rotfeld and Parsons 1989).

The primary mechanism for industry *self*-regulation in the U.S. is the National Advertising Division (NAD) of the Council of Better Business Bureaus (CBBB). It receives about 200 advertising complaints each year and opens about half that number into formal cases (Villafranco and Riley 2013; Boddewyn 1988). About 60% of NAD challenges are initiated by competitors and the rest from routine monitoring (usually about one complaint a year from consumers groups) (Villafranco and Riley 2013).

These cases target around 60 days to produce a recommendation that can be appealed to the National Advertising Review Board, although this rarely happens. Rarer still, if the advertiser does not comply with its recommendation or participate at all in the process, the NAD can refer the case to the appropriate government authority. This happened for the first time in 1992 (*Sunshine Makers, Inc.* 1992) and typically amounts to 1–2 cases per year. This may also happen informally as when the FTC settled with Airborne for $30 million in 2008 after it failed to comply with a 2002 NAD recommendation that all future advertising be substantiated (Villafranco and Riley 2013).

The Federal Trade Commission is the main source of formal U.S. *legal* regulation of advertising. It opens about 50 advertising investigations and issues 10–15 orders annually. It can try advertising cases administratively before its own Administrative Law Judges, or it can seek injunction in federal district court (Petty 1992). The FTC seldom loses advertising challenges but it may take a couple of years to obtain a consent agreement, while other U.S. forums may resolve issues in a couple of months. Competitors sue one another for misleading advertising under section 43(a) of the Lanham Act at least as frequently as the FTC brings cases (Petty 1992, pp. 58, 98–99). Specialized agencies address advertising issues for particular products (Food and Drug Administration, Bureau of Alcohol, Tobacco and Firearms) or media (Postal Service).

In recent years, both state attorneys general and consumer class action attorneys have become active pursuers of deceptive advertising. The state AGs became more active in pursuing national advertising during the 1980s when it was widely perceived that the FTC became less active. They typically settle for advertising changes and the costs of their investigation and litigation (Beales 1991; McKinney and Dewey 1990).

Class action lawsuits for false advertising are even more recent, growing in popularity in the past few years, particularly for "natural" and other claims about food (Petty 2015a). Although there have been a handful of settlements, most of the litigation has involved questions of whether class action certification is appropriate—can you define a class of misled purchasers and were they all misled in the same way to cause them the same amount of damages. Some other countries allow consumer groups to bring and litigate advertising complaints (Petty 2014).

Outside the United States, the E.U. has adopted its Misleading and Comparative Advertising Directive (2006/114/EC) instructing member states to adopt comparable country laws. It requires laws to challenge misleading advertising before either a court or an administrative authority by "persons or organizations regarded under national law as having a legitimate interest in" prohibiting misleading advertising. The United Kingdom insisted that the directive also recognize the validity of self-regulation. The U.K.'s Advertising

Standards Authority (ASA) is the largest, most active, and best financed self-regulatory system in the world, and is supported by the government. Its authority is derived from the British Code of Advertising Practices (Boddewyn 1988, pp. 267–94). Consistent with the directive, ASA decisions can be appealed to a court for review (Newell 1989). Legal actions in Great Britain generally follow only after self-regulatory solutions are sought.

A similar process is followed in Ireland (Boddewyn 1988). Italy, Belgium and Switzerland likewise have active industry self-regulation (Maxeiner and Schothofer 1992). Italian law allows competitors (not consumers) to sue privately, but courts seldom find advertising to be misleading. So self-regulation handles about 80% of all advertising disputes (Schricker 1990, pp. 631–636). In the Netherlands both private lawsuits and industry self-regulation are active arbiters of advertising challenges. But like the U.K., the Dutch self-regulatory body can be overruled by the courts (Dommering 1992, p. 269). Scandinavian countries actually have displaced industry self-regulation with a consumer ombudsman who functions much like the U.S. FTC by receiving advertising complaints, attempting to resolve them, and litigating if necessary. Many of its guidelines were based on prior industry self-regulation, so industry supports and cooperates with the ombudsman (Boddewyn 1985).

In contrast, Germany, Austria, and Spain base ad regulation on private lawsuits by competitors and consumer organizations. Indeed, advertising litigation is more prevalent in Germany than in any other country, but roughly 90% of these disputes end in a settlement between the parties (Maxeiner and Shotthofer 1992, p. 170). The German Weberat is the primary self-regulatory body, and it complements the legal system by focusing on questions of taste and opinion, rather than deceptiveness (Horn, Kotz, Leser 1982, pp. 284–287).

France, Luxembourg, and Belgium also allow recognized consumer organizations to bring lawsuits challenging advertising.

These three countries and the rest of Western Europe generally fall somewhere in between the two extremes of Italy (predominantly industry self-regulation) and Germany (private lawsuits) with more balance of private lawsuits, self-regulation, and government regulation (Petty 1997).

In all countries, the advertiser can be held liable for its advertising. In the U.S., the FTC also pursues advertising agencies that were active participants in creating the ads and knew or should have known of the legal problems. Similarly, under the U.S. Lanham Act, advertising agencies may be sued, although this is rare. In Europe, ad agencies may be sued in Belgium (in lieu of an advertiser located in another country), Denmark, Ireland, Italy, France (if negligent), Germany, Austria, Portugal, Switzerland, and the U.K. In Germany, Ireland, Italy, Switzerland, and the U.K., the magazine, TV station, etc., also may be held liable (Maxeiner and Schotthofer 1992). In the U.S., agencies can be held liable but media generally are not, although the FTC has started encouraging media to take more responsibility for the ads they publish (Galloway et al. 2005).

C. INTERPRETATION—MESSAGE CONVEYED TO CONSUMERS

To find an advertisement misleading, it must first be "interpreted" to determine what message(s) is communicated to consumers. For explicit claims, the regulator need only look at the advertisement itself to determine the literal messages. However, such literal interpretation may miss messages that are implied. (Preston & Richards 1986). For example, when newspaper ads proclaimed "Hertz has more new cars than Avis has cars," the trial court interpreted the ads literally and counted the cars owned by each company. It found the ad to be literally false and ordered a permanent injunction and required Hertz place corrective notices in the same newspapers where the ad ran. In contrast, the court of appeals found that the message conveyed to consumers was that Hertz had more cars available for rent than Avis.

This interpretation was found true since Avis was in the process of selling a large number of cars that it still owned but were not available for rent. The appellate court dismissed the complaint (*Avis Rent-a-Car System, Inc. v. Hertz Corp.* 1986). One ad, but two diametrically opposed interpretations!

Most cases involving implied claims involve the opposite situation—the advertising is literally true, but the implied claim is false. For example, an ad proclaiming: "Robot-Coupe 21, Cuisinart 0. When all 21 of the three-star restaurants in France's Michelin Guide chose the same professional model food processor, . . . —shouldn't you?" was found to be literally accurate because no three-star restaurant had chosen a Cuisinart food processor. However, the undisclosed reason for that result was that Cuisinart did not make a professional model food processor. The court held that the advertisement was false by necessary implication because the ad must be interpreted to imply Cuisinart made a professional grade food processor when it did not (*Cuisinarts, Inc. v. Robot-Coupe Int'l Corp.*, 1982).

If an ad is ambiguous and subject to several possible consumer interpretations, courts have long recognized that the FTC may use its own expertise rather than marketing studies to determine the meaning of an advertisement. In the 1980s, the FTC exercised this prerogative in about 80% of the advertising cases it litigated. However, the FTC always considers marketing studies when introduced by the advertiser and, in cases disputing implied claims, often conducts its own studies. Unlike the FTC, Lanham Act judges are reluctant to interpret the meaning of advertisements, except in cases where the meaning is obvious. As the Southern District of New York noted: "The court's reaction [to the advertising] is at best not determinative and at worst irrelevant" (*American Brands, Inc. v. R.J. Reynolds Tobacco Co.*, 1976, p. 1357). Following this reasoning, courts considering implied claims under the Lanham Act usually require the competitor-plaintiff to introduce evidence, typically marketing studies, concerning how consumers interpret the challenged advertising.

The 2006 EC Directive is silent on interpretation and the regulation of implied claims (2006/114/EC). Not surprisingly most European countries also do not explicitly address these issues. Most simply have the judge or other authority examine the advertisement and apply their personal judgment to interpret it. However, the 2006 Directive:

> 'misleading advertising' means any advertising which in any way, including its presentation, deceives or is likely to deceive the persons to whom it is addressed or whom it reaches and which, by reason of its deceptive nature, is likely to affect their economic behaviour or which, for those reasons, injures or is likely to injure a competitor (2006/114/EC).

That language closely mirrors the policy followed by the U.S. FTC that it is the meaning of ads to consumers and their likely impact on consumer behavior that is important. At present, Germany and the U.S. are the only countries that routinely use consumer research to help determine the meaning of advertising (Petty 2014).

I. Types of Implied Claims

Communications scholar Ivan Preston has identified fifteen ways by which advertising makes implied claims (Preston 1990). Because of similarities between many of his classifications, they can be synthesized into four reasonably distinct, fundamental categories of implied claims (Hastak and Mazis 2011; Petty and Kopp 1995).

a. Exaggerated Significance

In this type of advertising claim, the literal claim is often true but implies a broader false claim to consumers. This may occur because promotion emphasizing a particular attribute may falsely suggest to consumers that only the advertised product has that attribute. Alternatively, consumers may have previously formed false beliefs that associate particular attributes with other attributes. For example, foods advertising they are low fat may cause consumers to believe they are also low in cholesterol and perhaps low in calories as well (Hastak and Mazis 2011, pp. 162–163). Advertisers also occasionally make "straw man" comparisons such as the FTC case challenging the claim that Carnation Instant Breakfast has as much mineral nourishment as two strips of bacon. This ad suggests Carnation Instant Breakfast is high in mineral content when in fact, like bacon, it is a poor source of minerals (*Carnation Co.* 1970).

Lastly, sometimes promotion of a particular attribute suggests to consumers that overall performance will be superior. For example, when Wilkinson advertised that the lubricating strip on its razors was six times more slippery than that of rival Gillette, it was suggesting to consumers that they would get a noticeably smoother shave (*Gillette Company v. Wilkinson Sword, Inc.*, 1989). While the ad only discusses the lubricating strip as being smooth, it subtly presents the implied message of a smooth shave by showing a man rubbing his face in apparent appreciation of the smoothness of his shave. Wilkinson had no support for a claim of a smoother shave than rival razors (*Gillette Company v. Wilkinson Sword, Inc.*, 1992).

b. Confusing Presentation

Some advertising contains confusing language and/or pictures that mislead consumers who often impose an expected practical implication from confusing language or pictures they perceive (Hastak and Mazis 2011, p. 160). The Carnation Instant Breakfast example of exaggerated significance could also fit in this category because it falsely suggests that bacon is a good source of minerals. The FTC more recently found that Stouffer's claim that its Lean Cuisine prepared meals contained less than one gram of sodium, confusingly implying they were low in sodium when they were not (*Stouffer's Food Corp.* 1994). Other advertisements use confusing language or pictures alone to imply claims. For example, Elliot Knitwear sold a sweater made of "Cashmora." Despite a fine print disclaimer, 22% of consumers surveyed thought it contained cashmere, so the FTC held the company liable for misleading advertising (*Elliot Knitwear, Inc.,* 1961).

Sometime advertising language is confusing to challengers as well as consumers. Fruit of the Loom unsuccessfully challenged advertising by rival Hanes that Hanes T-shirts shrank 38% less than those of Fruit of the Loom. Fruit of the Loom argued that consumers understood these ads as saying that Fruit of the Loom shirts shrank 38%. Because the advertising clearly indicated 38% *less* shrinkage, the judge discounted the validity and significance of the plaintiff's survey which showed that 18% of consumers agreed with its interpretation of 38% shrinkage.

Fruit of the Loom's challenge might have been more successful if it had simply challenged the exaggerated significance of the "38% less shrinkage" claim which falsely suggests shrinkage consumers would notice. The court was troubled by the insignificant difference in shrinkage: i.e., Fruit of the Loom T-shirts started out one inch longer than Hanes and, after five washings, shrank to be 7/8 of an inch shorter (*Fruit of the Loom, Inc. v. Sara Lee Corp.*, 1986).

A common example of confusing language is implied superiority claims such as "No product is better than _______." When read literally, such claims are only claiming product parity, not superiority. For example, a Sunoco claim, that its gasoline had "the world's highest octane," was successfully challenged for implying higher octane than competitors by FTC based on the Commission's finding that competitors' fuels possessed equal octane ratings (*Sun Oil Co.* 1974). Recent research has shown that advertising messages which are literally parity claims, but which employ comparative language such as "no product is better," may mislead as many as 55% of consumers tested into believing they are actually superiority claims (Wyckham 1987; Buchanan and Smithies 1989).

Other examples of confusing presentation include the Milk Duds advertisement where a famous baseball player is asked: "Milk Duds with energy for speed; is that where you get your speed, Lou?" The athlete responds "Well, I sure do like them." He does not affirm that Milk Duds are the source of his athletic ability but does not deny it either. The FTC ruled that the ad suggests this product benefit merely by asking the question (*Beatrice Foods*, 1972). Similarly, a common technique of misdirection in food advertising is to compare or picture a natural, or well accepted, food with the advertised food to wrongly imply they are nutritional equivalents (Preston 1990, p. 1299). The FTC recently challenged a fortified (high alcohol) wine cooler for presenting itself as a regular wine cooler (*Canandaigua Wine Company*, 1991).

One final example of confusing language is the advertisement for Kraft Singles Cheese shown in print format on the next page. The ad truthfully explains that imitation cheese slices are made with hardly any milk, but that Kraft uses five ounces of milk in every slice. It continues that the child can then get calcium for bone growth. This confusing language falsely implies that imitation slices contain virtually no calcium since they contain little milk. However, imitation slices are required by the Food and Drug Administration to be fortified with calcium to the same extent as natural cheese. This implication is visually reinforced by the pictures of a glass with little milk (imitation slices) and a glass nearly full with milk (Kraft). This ad also falsely suggests that each slice of Kraft Singles has the same amount of calcium as five ounces of milk. In fact, about thirty percent of the calcium is lost in processing (*Kraft, Inc. v. FTC* 1992).

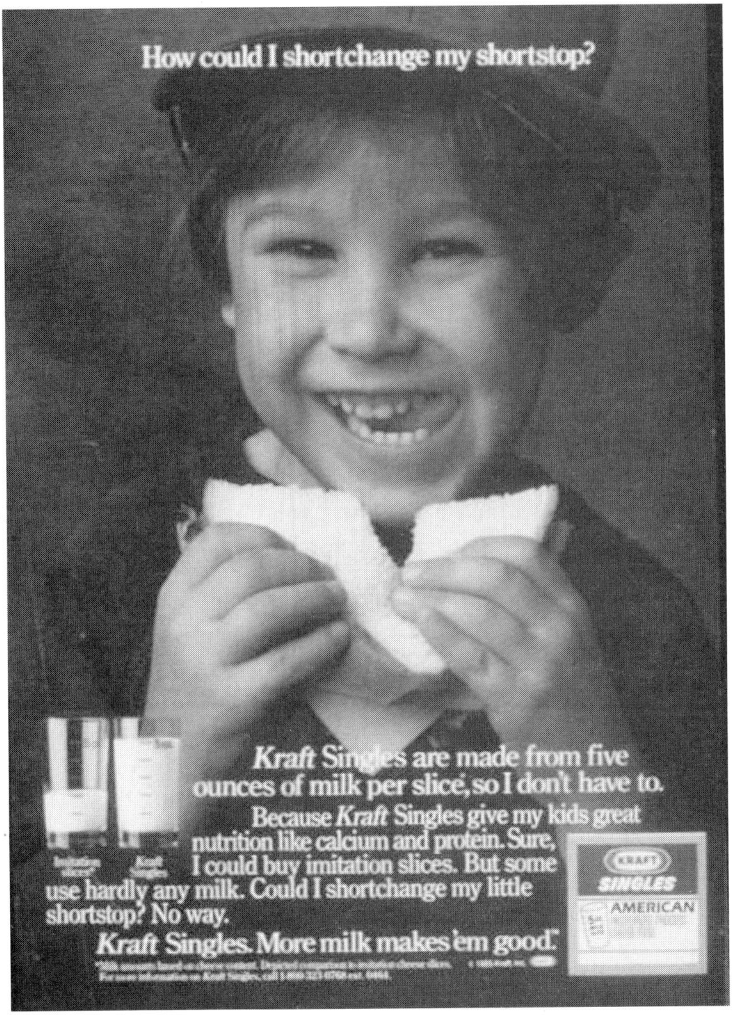

The FTC has numerous guides (which it changes occasionally) and some rules to inform marketers how to avoid deception by confusing language in particular industries. These guides often explain what terminology may be misleading in such varied industries as nursery (plants), hosiery, jewelry, luggage, automobile tires, adhesives, pet food, wall paneling and textiles. Some guides and rules attempt to set standards for advertising size such as sleeping bags, television screens and extension ladders in order to facilitate comparisons and avoid consumer confusion.

c. *Promises of Proof*

Some advertisements imply that a product performance claim has been substantiated when in fact the advertiser has no such proof. For example, the two glasses of milk filled to different levels in the Kraft ad above suggest that a careful measure of milk content was made. When Firestone advertised that its tires stop 25% quicker, the use of a precise percentage falsely implied to consumers that the number was based on scientific tests (*Firestone Tire & Rubber Co. v. FTC*, 1973). Similarly, when Body on Tap shampoo stated that 900 women had tried the shampoo and found it superior to Vidal Sassoon and other shampoos in several categories of conditioning and cleaning hair, the court held this advertising implied that pairwise comparison testing was done. In fact, the 900 women were divided into groups that only tried and rated one brand of shampoo (*Vidal Sassoon, Inc. v. Bristol-Myers Co.* 1981).

One final example is an Aspercreme advertising campaign. By announcing a "remarkable breakthrough" for arthritis pain, the ad is promising scientific proof that the product works. Moreover in television advertising, the ads showed tablets of aspirin dissolving through the skin to bring relief to arthritic joints while stating: "Aspercreme concentrates all the strong relief of aspirin directly at the point of pain." This suggests scientific tests determined how Aspercreme works. Note this tagline also is a prime example of carefully selected confusing language falsely implying, as the name Aspercreme itself does, that the product contains aspirin. The FTC found that the advertiser had no substantiation that the product worked better than simply rubbing arthritic joints or that it worked as a topical pain reliever (*Thompson Medical Co. v. FTC* 1986).

d. *Ineffective or Nonexistent Qualification*

This fourth category of implied claims is related to the first four. Any of these examples could have been cured by a "clear and conspicuous" disclosure that qualified or limited the challenged claim. The FTC examines the 4 Ps to see if a disclosure is clear and conspicuous: Prominence, Presentation (easy to understand), Placement (noticeable), and Proximity (the disclosure should be close to the claim it is qualifying). If the disclaimer about "Cashmora" containing no cashmere was conspicuous enough, few consumers would have been misled. Similarly, the Aspercreme print ad disclosed in small print that it contained an "aspirin-like" analgesic, which the FTC proved did not overcome the aspirin ingredient claim of the name. Later television ads ran a less ambiguous disclaimer that the product did not contain aspirin as required by the FTC order.

Both the NAD and the FTC can pursue omissions of material information which is necessary to prevent consumer deception regardless of what claims are made in advertising. An omission of information may be misleading because consumers have a baseline product understanding but the advertised product is materially different and does not disclose the difference or because consumers assume advertisers that provide information will provide all the information needed to draw accurate inferences about the product (Hastak and Mazis 2011, pp. 158–159). The Lanham Act does not condemn omissions of material information unless claims in the advertising are deemed misleading without disclosure of additional, omitted information.

A classic example of an omission of material information is a Canadian case condemning a truthful claim that houses were being offered for sale for $24,900. The claim was literally true but failed to note that these houses had already been built on particular tracts of land and the purchaser also had to purchase the land the house was located upon for a substantial amount more (Black 1988, p. 534).

Additionally, the FTC challenged advertising of Campbell Soup for proclaiming that certain of its soups were low in fat and cholesterol which may reduce the risk of certain forms of heart disease. While the statement was true, the FTC alleged it was deceptive not to disclose that these same soups were also high in sodium which may increase the risk of other types of heart disease in some people (*Campbell Soup Co.* 1991). Although this may be characterized as exaggerated significance, it is deceptive not only because of the implication that the soups were good for all heart disease, but also because of the failure to disclose the heart disease risk from the high levels of sodium.

A second example in this category is advertising for Tropicana orange juice showing an orange being squeezed so that its juice pours into a Tropicana container while Olympic decathlete Bruce Jenner says; "Its pure, pasteurized juice as it comes from the orange." Pasteurization contradicts both the rest of the sentence and the visual image. This could be an example of confusing language, but it is confusing because of the attempt to use the word "pasteurized" to qualify the claim that the court held was ineffective and did not prevent deception (*Coca-Cola Co. v. Tropicana Prods. Inc.*, 1982). Similarly, the FTC's challenge against Stouffer might have been avoided if the fine print explanation that sodium content is usually measured in milligrams had been conspicuous and provided sufficient clarification to prevent consumers from being misled.

II. Visual Claims

Advertising regulators traditionally have struggled with visual messages. But visual content certainly can deceive, so it is regulated in some cases (Richards and Zakia 1981). For example, the FTC and the Texas State Attorney General both challenged Volvo advertisements as deceptive for showing a "monster" truck rolling over a line of cars, all of which were crushed except the surreptitiously re-enforced Volvo. For over fifty years, advertising regulators have required television demonstrations to be bona-fide or disclose they are dramatizations of a genuine demonstration or test (Petty 1997). More recently, Clorox, maker of Glad storage bags, ran an advertisement with two fish in water, one in a glad bag and one in a Slide-Loc bag, made by S.C. Johnson & Son, showing "a substantial and rapid decline" in the water level in the rival bag. This ad was enjoined for being literally false because tests showed that most leaks are small and occur at a very slow rate (*S.C. Johnson & Son, Inc. v. Clorox Co.* 2001).

However, not all demonstrations are deemed false. For example, the FTC refused to pursue animated visual claims by Perrier that arguably falsely told consumers Perrier water was unprocessed, by showing historical figures such as Napoleon dipping a cup into an unrefined natural spring and drinking the Perrier water. Similarly, in a case brought by the maker of Lysol Deodorizing Cleaner against the maker of Spic and Span products, advertising showed two people cleaning a bathroom surface, one using the Lysol product and the other using a Spic and Span product. Then two new people wipe the just-cleaned surfaces with clean cloths and the Lysol cloth appears dirty while the Spic and Span cloth appears clean. Lysol argued that the addition of carbon black to bathroom soap scum was misleading, but the court held it was permissible to allow viewers to see the residue that remained. The court further held that Lysol failed to prove the ad implied to consumers that Lysol merely appeared to clean (but did not), and that Spic and Span cleaned better (*L & F Products v. Proctor & Gamble Co.*1995).

Other countries such as Germany and France occasionally condemn visually misleading advertising (Petty 2014). For example, French authorities challenged the advertising of TANG drink mix that showed an empty orange peel, a glass of TANG surrounded by green leaves, and the slogan: "the taste of fresh squeezed oranges." This advertising was found to falsely claim TANG contained orange juice, despite a fine print listing of TANG's artificial ingredients (Baudot 1989, pp. 136–37). French courts also condemned an ad for a legal advisor shown wearing a robe, creating the false impression the advisor was an attorney (Maxeiner and Schotthofer 1992, p. 125).

D. DECEPTION—LIKELIHOOD OF MISLEADING CONSUMERS

Once the claims in challenged advertising have been proven false or unsubstantiated, it is almost certain that *deception* will be found and a remedy will be imposed (Richards and Preston 1992). Technically, a false message would not constitute deception if it were not material to the purchase decision or were not believed. Despite these technicalities, the NAD appears to assume deception once it finds claims to be false or unsubstantiated. It does not inquire whether consumers were actually misled. Under both the Lanham and FTC Acts, deception is similarly presumed from false or substantiated claims in advertising in most cases. In fact, the Supreme Court has held that the FTC has the expertise to determine whether an advertising claim is material without evidence.

Occasionally, however, defendants have formally contested the deception stage of an advertising challenge. For example when the FTC challenged Kraft for making false claims about the relative calcium content of its product (as discussed above), Kraft argued that the exact amount of calcium was an immaterial or unimportant product attribute to consumers. The FTC found that the attribute was material to reasonable consumers and that consumers would likely believe Kraft's advertising so that they were "likely to be misled" (*Kraft Inc. v. FTC* 1992). Similarly, Doan's Pills unsuccessfully argued the claim of superior back pain relief was immaterial to consumers given the truthfulness that the product was an effective pain reliever (*Novartis Corp. v. FTC* 2000). One (perhaps the only) example where an arguably false claim would not mislead consumers was an FTC Administrative Law Judge's dismissal of a challenge to advertising that claimed milk was good for everyone. The ALJ found that the small minority of people who are allergic to milk would know from experience not to believe the claim (*California Milk Producers*, 1979).

Because of its focus on competitor injury, the Lanham Act has particular requirements for the deception stage of an advertising challenge. Challengers must show that they were injured by consumers being deceived and diverting their purchases away from the challenger toward its rival. Injury is *presumed* in injunction cases where the plaintiff's brand is explicitly compared to the defendant's brand (*McNeilab, Inc., v. Am. Home Prods. Corp.*, 1988). Injury can otherwise be proven in such cases by establishing direct competition between plaintiff's products and defendant's advertised product (*Vidal Sassoon, Inc. v. Bristol-Myers Co.*1981).

For example, when Nair depilatory falsely claimed that baby oil within the product had a moisturizing effect, the court found Johnson & Johnson had shown injury with evidence that consumers otherwise would use J & J's Baby Oil as an aftershave moisturizer (*Johnson & Johnson v. Carter Wallace, Inc.* 1980). In damage cases, the courts under the Lanham Act require proof of lost sales caused by defendant's advertising. Proving a precise amount of lost sales is difficult because many market factors other than competitor advertising can affect sales (*Coca-Cola Co. v. Tropicana Prods. Inc.* 1982).

While Lanham Act cases have found deception when as little as fifteen percent of consumers perceive a particular implied claim in an advertisement, typically courts prefer to see at least 20–25% of consumers identifying a deceptive implied interpretation. Based on their finding that message miscomprehension typically occurs among 15–23% consumers for television advertising and 12% for print, Jacoby and Hoyer (1990) have urged the courts to exercise some caution in this area.

As noted above, the 2006 Directive also adopts a likely to deceive rather than actual deception standard. It defines misleading advertising as that which deceives or is likely to deceive persons to whom it is addressed or whom it reaches and which by reason of its deceptive nature, is likely to affect their economic behaviour or which, for those reasons, injures or is likely to injure a competitor (2006/114/EC).

The U.S., Belgium, France, Greece, Ireland, Italy all recognize the defense of "puffing"—claims of quality too vague to be relied upon by consumers (Petty, 2014, pp. 399–400). Puffing occurs when advertisers obviously exaggerate, state opinions, or make vague quality claims such as that a product is "best" (Richards 1990). France explicitly requires that superlatives be verified.

One example of visual puffing occurred in France when a competitor challenged Samsonite luggage advertising that showed a pair of bulldozers "playing" with a suitcase that was shown undamaged. The lower court found the commercial misleading because many suitcases had been used and damaged during the filming of the commercial. The court of appeals held that the average consumer would recognize this as exaggeration, and not take it as literal truth (Rijkens and Miracle 1986, p. 150). A claim not believed by consumers is unlikely to play a material role in their purchase behavior. Denmark, Portugal, and Germany do not recognize this defense (Maxeiner and Schotthofer 1992).

E. VERIFICATION—ACCURACY OF THE ADVERTISING CLAIMS

Once the conveyed meaning of an ad is determined (and presumed material to consumers, it is compared to the reality of the product (or service) attribute or characteristic. Historically, challengers had the burden of proving falsity rather than advertisers needing to prove the truth of their claims. This rule is still applies in the U.S. for Lanham Act cases—the plaintiff must conduct its own tests or use those of the defendant to disprove the challenged advertising.

The Fourth Circuit Court of Appeals recently announced an "all reasonable experts" standard. To prove falsity, the Lanham Act plaintiff must prove that all reasonable experts believe the advertising claim is false. If there are some that believe the claim is true, then the claim is not proven false and may continue to be made. Of course, a Lanham Act challenger may allege advertising claims are true but misleading to avoid this requirement of reasonable expert consensus (*GNC Corp.: Triflex Prods. Mktg & Sales Practices Litigation* 2015). However, as discussed under interpretation, the challenger then must present evidence and prove consumers do receive the allegedly misleading message from the advertising and then the challenge must prove that the implied message is false.

Beginning in the 1970s for the FTC, state attorneys general, and NAD, as well as in Europe under the 1984 Directive, the burden of proof has shifted so that advertisers must now have a reasonable basis for their advertising claims before they actually make the claims. The 2006 Directive (2006/450/EEC) authorizes member states to require advertisers to provide evidence of the truthfulness of advertising claims in appropriate circumstances, but various countries both in Europe and beyond vary in whether this is always required or just under particular circumstances such as comparative advertising (Petty, 2014, pp. 404–405).

The FTC wrote a policy statement to clarify its policies regarding advertising substantiation (Federal Trade Commission 1983). It states that if the advertiser led consumers to believe a claim is based on a specific type of evidence (e.g., "According to tests by an independent laboratory. . . ."), the advertiser must have that exact evidence. In all other situations the advertiser must have *at least* a "reasonable basis" for believing the claim to be true. In deciding what is reasonable, the FTC will look at six factors to make this determination: (1) the type of claim, (2) the type of product, (3) the consequences of a false claim, (4) the benefits of a truthful claim, (5) the cost of developing substantiation, and (6) the amount and type of substantiation that experts feel is reasonable. Despite paying lip service to all six factors, the Commission appears to focus on the last two as well as on possible health risks from false claims.

The requirement to have a reasonable basis in support of advertising claims also can apply to survey claims. For example, in 2015, the U.S. NAD requested that advertising for SleepRight dental guards discontinue the claim that it was the #1 brand prescribed by dental professionals. The claim was based on an in-house survey of 1000 dental professionals in which 111 individuals responded but were not asked to verify they were dental professionals. Of the 111 respondents most said they did not prescribe dental guards and only 14 said they prescribed SleepRight (Advertising Self-Regulatory Council 2015).

F. REMEDIATION

This final phase of advertising challenges determines what remedy is appropriate if the challenger has been successful in the prior stages. In some cases, an appropriate remedy can be readily determined. In a case under the New Jersey Fraud Act, the court ordered a company that had advertised a "going out of business sale" to actually cease doing business at that location (*Giant Carpet Stores of American Inc. v. Retail Kane Carpet, Inc.*, 1991). However, other than cases involving advertising of warranty or credit terms, it is typically difficult to make the advertised product or service conform to its advertising boasts.

NAD finds about 40% of the advertisements it reviews to be acceptable; the remaining 60% are withdrawn or voluntarily modified. As noted above, if an advertiser refuses to cooperate, the NAD may refer the case to an appropriate government agency. Lanham Act plaintiffs are successful in two thirds of cases that are litigated. While the FTC closes most of its advertising investigations without taking action, when it opens a case, it nearly always obtains an order against the advertiser.

I. Injunctive Relief

An order (or request in the case of the NAD) to stop disseminating the misleading claims is the most common remedy imposed in advertising challenges. To obtain an injunction, the FTC has an easier burden than a Lanham Act plaintiff. For an administrative proceeding, the FTC need only prove deception, i.e., that reasonable consumers are likely to be misled in a way that is material to the purchase decision, in order to be entitled to a remedy. Similarly, to obtain a preliminary injunction in federal court, the FTC need only prove a likelihood of ultimate success in the underlying case to obtain this relief (*FTC v. Pharmtech Research, Inc.,* 1983).

In order to obtain a preliminary injunction, the Lanham Act plaintiff must prove that:

(1) the plaintiff will likely win the lawsuit because the advertising is false,

(2) the defendant's advertising is likely to cause or have caused injury to the plaintiff, and

(3) the plaintiff's injury without the injunction is likely to be higher than the advertiser's injury from the advertisement being enjoined, i.e., "balancing of the hardships" (*Coca-Cola Co. v. Tropicana Prods. Inc.*, 1982).

As noted under deception, proving likelihood of injury caused by the challenged advertising can be relatively straightforward in injunction cases. Even though the injunction is only preliminary, lasting until the full trial of the challenge is concluded, this remedy frequently ends a Lanham Act challenge. Advertisers often prefer to develop new or modified advertising rather than have no advertising during the trial. The advertiser simply agrees to abide by the injunction permanently to settle the case.

Relief for FTC administrative proceedings and injunction proceedings under both the FTC and Lanham Acts typically is an order stopping the advertising from being further disseminated. The FTC administrative "cease and desist" order typically prohibits claims that have been proven false or misleading and also prohibits other claims without a reasonable basis. Often the type of reasonable basis is specified, i.e., drug efficacy claims must be substantiated by well-controlled, double-blind clinical tests. Should the company violate either a cease and desist order or an FTC injunction, it would be subject to civil penalties of up to $10,000 per day, per violation.

Another difference between FTC and Lanham court orders is that the FTC order is typically broader to "fence in" the advertiser to prevent it from making similar deceptive claims for related, albeit currently unchallenged, product lines. The advertiser with a broad product line faces the risk for civil penalties for products other than the one falsely advertised. For example, Sears unsuccessfully appealed the scope of an FTC order covering all Sears "major appliances" even though its liability for falsely advertising dishwashers was clear. Sears had advertised that dishes placed in its Lady Kenmore dishwasher did not have to be scraped while the owner's manual clearly advised to the contrary (*Sears, Roebuck & Co. v. FTC* 1982).

II. Other Remedies

Relief beyond the usual injunctive order is more common in FTC than Lanham Act cases. Such relief may include monetary penalties such as the payment of restitution to injured consumers (FTC Act) or damages to competitors (Lanham Act); the disclosure of information to prevent deception from future advertising; or even corrective advertising to correct continuing deception caused by the prior false product claims.

In about one third of FTC cases, the FTC will order affirmative disclosures of information necessary to prevent future deception. Such disclosures may be ordered for all advertising, often for a limited period of time, or whenever a specified claim is made. Courts under the

Lanham Act seldom order such relief. One explanation for this difference is the FTC's greater ability to challenge omissions of information. Omissions are typically corrected by ordering a disclosure.

Corrective advertising is a special type of affirmative disclosure that is intended to remedy "lingering false beliefs" created by past advertising rather than ongoing deception from continuing advertising. For example, Listerine was ordered to correct its past advertising by disclosing that "Listerine will not help prevent colds or sore throats or lessen their severity" (*Warner-Lambert Co. v. FTC*, 1977).

The FTC has rarely ordered corrective advertising since this case but ordered it again after stopping an eight-year campaign by Doan's Pills that claimed the pills were more effective than other pain relievers for back pain. The Commission majority disagreed with the Administrative law judge's characterization of corrective advertising as a drastic remedy. Rather, it described corrective advertising as an appropriate method of restoring the *status quo ante* in cases where the advertisements substantially created or reinforced the misbelief and the misbelief was likely to linger into the future if not corrected. The Commission ordered a corrective message to appear in advertising and packaging for one year and until $8 million of advertising had occurred, the average amount of annual advertising spending during the 8 year campaign (*Novartis Corp. v. FTC* 2000).

Occasional Lanham Act cases (including some for trademark infringement) have awarded corrective advertising damages in cases where actual consumer deception is proven. To determine how much to award for corrective advertising, some courts have followed the FTC's *Warner Lambert* "rule" to award 25% of the amount expended in the deceptive advertising campaign. Another approach is to award compensation for corrective advertising expenditures made at the time to rebut or correct the deceptive advertising. For example, in the case of *Pizza Hut Inc. v. Papa John's International, Inc.* (2000), the federal district court of Northern Texas ordered Papa John's to pay nearly one half million dollars to compensate Pizza Hut for running "corrective advertising" that Pizza Hut would not have run if not for misleading claims concerning better ingredients being made in Papa John's advertising. However the ruling on liability was overturned by a Court of Appeals. Because of their focus on competitor injury, Lanham Act cases do not require lingering consumer beliefs.

The FTC also more commonly obtains monetary relief than do Lanham Act plaintiffs. Since 1983, the FTC has used its authority to seek court injunctions and asset freezes and obtain consumer refunds using those frozen assets ("disgorgement of illgotten gains"). By the 1990s, consumer redress cases accounted for about twenty percent of advertising cases. Since 2011, the FTC also has sought consumer refunds in advertising substantiation cases (Beales and Muris 2015). The state attorneys general typically ask for costs in the tens of thousands of dollars for matters in which they have invested significant time and resources before settlement (McKinney and Caton 1990–91).

Proving injury in Lanham Act cases where damages are being sought is very difficult and often precludes this remedy altogether. Presenting such proof may expose the complainant to broad discovery, by its rival, of its own sales figures and planning documents. For these reasons, relatively few Lanham Act cases have sought much less awarded damages.

Perhaps because the amount of the challenger's loss is difficult to prove, an alternative remedy, i.e., awarding the challenger the amount of the defendant's profits, is emerging in Lanham Act cases. For example, when Jartran deceptively compared its rental trucks with those of U-Haul, it was ordered to pay U-Haul $40 million based on both damages and wrongfully gained profits theory (*U-Haul Int'l Inc. v. Jartran, Inc.* 1986).

Outside the U.S., the 2006 Directive on Misleading Advertising similarly calls for injunctions both potentially before an ad runs and certainly to stop it from continuing to run. It permits interim injunctions while the case outcome is pending and if needed, the Directive authorizes authorities to require publication of a corrective statement. Injunctions are the primary formal remedy in most European countries for misleading advertising. When self-regulation is ignored in the U.K., its Director of Fair Trading is authorized to seek an injunction. In Germany, approximately 80% of misleading advertising cases include an injunction during the trial, which often becomes permanent (Schricker 1990, p. 630).

Most European countries also have a provision allowing the advertiser to simply publish a retraction (called rectification in the Netherlands) but this remedy is rarely used. Plaintiffs also may request that a court's decision be published at the advertiser's expense. This is essentially a form of corrective advertising. Most European countries allow for the awarding of money damages if they can be proven, but such awards also are rare in advertising cases (Maxeiner and Shotthofer 1992).

Finally, a few countries invoke *criminal* penalties at least on occasion. In Great Britain, fines are typically ordered (and possible jail time) for explicitly false advertising claims. Similarly, France and Greece can impose jail time or criminal penalties (Maxeiner and Shotthofer 1992). In the U.S. the FTC Act does not permit criminal penalties (except for violating a prior order), though there are occasions where criminal penalties may arise under a separate set of laws concerning mail fraud. A number of U.S. states do have old criminal laws on the books but today, these are rarely the basis for a prosecution.

CHAPTER 9

Cajolery—The First of the 3 Cs of Attracting Brand Interest

This chapter starts our examination of what I call the 3 Cs of attracting brand interest: Cajolery, Compensation, and Connection. Cajolery covers higher levels of persuasion (sales pressure) than mere occasional exposure to advertising to include personal selling (whether in person or through electronic media) and repeated solicitations and targeting vulnerable consumers. Compensation involves some additional reward (immediate or promised in the future) for purchase. Connection tactics try to make a personal appeal for purchase to circumvent consumer skepticism of marketing appeals generally. Forms of each of these practices may be used in the short term to stimulate trial of the brand or over the longer term to develop brand involvement and hopefully create brand loyalty.

The 3 Cs are summarized again in the following table:

Table One		
The 3 Cs of Attracting Brand Interest		
Cajolery (Chapter 9)	**Compensation (Chapter 10)**	**Connection (Chapter 11)**
Personal Selling	Price Promotions	Personalized Recommendations
Pressure to Buy	Samples, Bundles, Premiums	Masked Marketing
Targeting	Sweepstakes/Prize Promotions	Secondary Brand Associations (Chapter 12)
Repeat Solicitations	Loyalty Programs	Celebrities (Chapter 13)

Brand marketing is not solely about rational appeals to position a brand based on its performance and attributes. Brands are well recognized as platforms for building customer relationships (Dawar 2004). Strong brands have been shown to attract consumer attention, lead to favorable consumer evaluations, and engender consumer loyalty (Hoeffler and Keller 2003). Connection tactics seek to initiate and develop this consumer-brand relationship.

A. INTRODUCTION

The term "cajolery" may be defined in various ways to include flattery, wheedling, coaxing, and pleading in an effort to persuade someone to take a particular action. As applied to consumer protection situations, none of these terms are recognized as illegal. The beauty of the term cajolery here is that its vagueness illustrates the difficulty of determining when a practice crosses the line between typical "hard sell" marketing practices that consumers are expected to be able to resist and practices that actually reduce consumers' freedom of choice and should be legally condemned.

For example, the tactic of "selling up" involves showing consumers the deficiencies of a low priced model (typically emphasized in price advertising) and how higher priced models offer more features or better performance. "Selling up" is a legitimate personal selling technique when the consumer is free to choose among the alternatives. But "selling up" crosses the line to become illegal "bait and switch" when the seller essentially refuses to sell the advertised low price model and insists that the customer may purchase only a higher-priced alternative. For this reason, it is common for price advertisements to indicate that "supplies are limited" or only one or two models are available at the low advertised price. Price promotion is discussed in detail in the next chapter.

Both the FTC (16 C.F.R. § 238) and Council of Better Business Bureau (BBB) (Better Business Bureau 2005) Guidelines condemn bait and switch practices and provide numerous examples of practices to help managers distinguish legal from illegal. While Hess and Gerstner (1998) have argued that under limited circumstances, bait and switch might benefit consumers, it is generally agreed that if consumers lack choice, then they are misled about purchase options and the practice should be condemned (Wilke, Mela, Gundlach 1998). In most cases, bait and switch may lead to the short term purchase of the "switched" brand, but for many the shopping experience is negative. Only a very positive usage experience with the purchased brand might overcome the negative shopping experience making a repeat purchase likely. For this reason, bait and switch is more commonly observed for consumer durable products rather than convenience products that are less expensive and purchased regularly.

Cajolery tactics are used to overcome consumer disinterest in and resistance to more traditional forms of brand promotion. Personal selling is difficult to ignore and is just one method to apply pressure to buy upon consumers. Repeat solicitations may be used to try to catch consumers at a time when they are interested in the solicitation such as when they run out of a convenience product and need to purchase more. Finally, consumers may be explicitly targeted by preying upon their weaknesses as consumers to sell a particular brand. Each of these techniques is discussed in turn below.

This topic includes techniques involving explicit customer coercion, although they may be challenged as assault and battery in some cases. The classic bait and switch scenario, discussed above, is one example that borders on coercion if the customer is pressured until they buy. Another is a couple of cases condemned by the FTC in the 1950s where furnace repair companies would offer free furnace inspections but then refuse to reassemble the furnace until a service contract was purchased (e.g., *Davis Furnace Co.* 1961, *Holland Furnace Co.* 1958). More recently, the FTC has pursued internet cases that at least approach a similar level of coercion. In one case internet surfers have been "mouse-napped" to webpages, bombarded with ads, and not allowed to escape (*DSquared Solutions, LLC* 2004). In an earlier case consumers who downloaded a free image viewer were secretly reconnected to the internet through expensive international phone routes (*Beylen Telecom Ltd.* 1997). Ad-ware issues beyond such coercion are discussed at the end of this chapter.

B. PERSONAL SELLING

Today personal selling to consumers does not occur very often with traditional door-to-door peddlers, but may occur through telemarketing and various forms of "Buzz Marketing," discussed in Chapter Eleven, where potential buyers interact either in person or electronically with marketing agents. This issue of disguising marketing agents in some other form is not new. Early cases prohibited "misleading door openers" when sales agents would misrepresent their status as being something other than a sales agent (such as conducting a survey) and required immediate disclosure of their true sales purpose (*Encyclopedia Britannica, Inc. v. FTC* 1979).

Personal selling is included here as a cajoling technique because a salesperson can interact with potential purchasers adapting their sales pitch to each potential purchaser. Of course, the salesperson also can attempt to establish a personal connection with each prospective purchaser and might offer purported special compensation for completing the purchase so that the other two Cs may also apply.

Sales people who mislead consumers are subject to the same laws as misleading advertising discussed in Chapter Eight. However, it may be more difficult to prove what a salesperson actually said if the exchange was oral. In such cases, evidence of training materials and testimony of former sales people along with consumer testimony may carry the burden of proof. In the U.S., marketers are allowed to disclaim responsibility for representations made by sales agents as long as they do so clearly and conspicuously within a written contract. In contrast, under European law marketers are responsible for statements made by sales agents when selling consumer goods (Petty and Hamilton 2004).

Traditionally there also have been concerns that all provisions of the sales contract are clearly disclosed and that the quality of the delivered product is the same as promised to the consumer. Such concerns are addressed toward "fly-by-night" marketers primarily interested in the quick sale rather than long term brand loyalty. The European Union takes the most comprehensive approach to this did consumers "get-what-they paid-for" question by simply requiring that member states enact laws establishing a 14 day (formerly 7 days) refund period for nearly all "distance" sales. In this way, the Consumer Rights Directive (2011/83/E.U.), allows consumers to examine the product and carefully review the sales contract and then decide to keep the product or not. The FTC Door to Door Sales Cooling Off Rule (16 C.F.R.§ 429) provides a three day cooling off period for sales made outside the ordinary place of business, but unlike the E.U., the FTC has not extended cooling off protection to sales made by mail, telephone, or internet.

C. PRESSURE TO BUY

The other concern with personal selling is that the live salesperson will pressure consumers to buy something that upon reflection they did not want to buy. The European Unfair Commercial Practices Directive (2005/29/EC) condemns misleading and aggressive practices that are contrary to professional diligence and likely to change transactional decisions such as harassing, threatening, or coercive behavior. It further condemns harassing or coercing consumers into purchase, making an inaccurate claim about risks to the consumer's personal security, or threatening that the salesperson will lose his job if the consumer does not buy.

Because the Directive establishes a minimum level of European-wide protection, other countries are free to continue their more specific prohibitions. Several European countries also ban solicitations that are considered too aggressive or surprising or invasive of consumers' privacy. Austria, Germany, the Netherlands, and Greece also prohibit using psychological pressure to buy, such as using gratitude for a free gift or the exploitation of emotions like compassion, fear, or superstition (Maxeiner and Schotthofer 1992). U.S. law also prohibits sending unordered merchandise through the mail and then requesting payment. Recipients may keep such merchandise considering it a gift (39 U.S.C. § 3009).

Two European court decisions illustrate these concepts. The European Court of Justice affirmed a ban on door-to-door sales of English language courses to unemployed French citizens despite their right to cancel the transaction because they were particularly vulnerable to this appeal. Similarly, a Belgium court condemned the advertising of prizes by a mail company that made the prizes appear meaningful when in fact most were of low value. It found that some consumers were sufficiently naïve to be vulnerable to this practice and that this group merited protection (Micklitz, Stuyck and Terryn 2010, pp. 43–47).

At one time, the FTC also was concerned with high pressure interactive sales tactics. This was one justification for enacting the 3 day cooling off in Door to Door Sales Rule (16 C.F.R. § 429). No matter how insistent, persuasive, or simply effective a sales person was the consumer has the right to cancel the order within three days after the salesperson has departed and the consumer has "cooled off."

In the early 1970s, The FTC did pursue a few cases where the exploitation of emotional desires and weaknesses were alleged to be unfair practices. Its greatest success among these cases was in *Arthur Murray Studio of Washington* (1971) where dance salespeople pressured elderly widows to purchase exorbitant amounts of lessons through flattery, playing on their loneliness, and coercion. The Fifth Circuit Court of Appeals affirmed the FTC's decision. Similarly, in *J.B. Williams Co.* (1972), the Commission accepted a consent agreement that prohibited the marketer of Vivarin, an over the counter stimulant, from advertising that use of any such product would solve any individual's marital, sexual or personality problems or improve their personality, physical appearance, marriage, or sex life. A more recent state law case did condemn the use of scare tactics to sell a termite protection plan (*Bandura v. Orkin Exterminating Co.* 1987), but such cases are rare in the U.S

The FTC interest in such cases has never been strong. While the Commission initially approved issuance of the complaint, it ultimately dismissed allegations that advertising for Wonder Bread exploited parental vulnerability regarding the healthy growth of their children and advertising for Hostess Snack Cakes exploited mothers' feelings of guilt for providing snack foods. Over the dissent of Chairman Engman, the Commission also dismissed allegations that rapid growth portrayal sequences in the television advertising were unfairly appealing to small children who have strong desires to grow and may not understand how long growth takes (*ITT Continental Baking Co.* 1973).

Television home shopping shows have similarly been accused of preying on the vulnerability of elderly shut-ins by providing both excitement and television-based "friendship." They often cajole viewers into purchase by emphasizing the number of items or minutes left for the current offering. Yet when the FTC recently investigated a shopping network, it obtained a consent order that only addressed advertising substantiation concerns (*Home Shopping Network, Inc.* 1996). Similarly, a recent consent agreement with the marketer of Wonder Bread challenged advertising allegations that as a good source of calcium, Wonder Bread helped children's minds work better or improved memory, but did not allege an unfair emotional appeal had been made to either parents or children (*Interstate Bakeries Corp.* 2002). Thus it would appear that the FTC has little current interest in trying to curtail emotional appeals.

D. TARGETING TO EXPLOIT VULNERABILITIES

Pressure to buy can be more effective if targeted toward a specific group. Many of the examples in the preceding section included allegations not only of pressure to buy but also unfair targeting of vulnerable audiences. Some forms of targeting such as direct mail and e-mail can appear to include a personalized message in which the prospective customer is identified by name. These Connection techniques are discussed in Chapters Eleven through Thirteen. The main issue is whether such techniques are used deceptively.

There is concern over the targeting of vulnerable audiences e.g., alcoholics with liquor advertising, gambling addicts with state lottery ads, etc. For example, as noted above under pressure to buy, some older FTC cases involved preying on emotional weaknesses of adults. Similarly, the FTC Funeral Rule (16 C.F.R. § 453) seeks to protect the recently bereaved who are purchasing funeral services by requiring itemized prices and the availability of price lists and price information over the telephone. Furthermore, the Supreme Court has recognized that under the First Amendment, state bar associations may regulate in person attorney solicitation for personal injury cases. Unlike informational advertising for the same services, in person solicitation seeks to pressure consumers to agree and therefor has the potential for abuse (*Ohralick v. Ohio State Bar Ass'n* 1978, p. 457). Occasionally such stories of targeting make the news such as the elderly man who used his meager savings to fly to Florida because he incorrectly thought he had won the grand prize once he received a misleading solicitation to enter the contest (Cyr 1999).

Nearly all of the actual legal challenges involve the alleged targeting of children with advertisements for adult products, most often cigarettes. For example, a California court in *Mangini v. R.J. Reynolds Tobacco Co.* (1993), found that the targeting of minors with cigarette advertising would be unfair. The court relied on an old FTC case, *FTC v. Keppel & Bro.* (1934). This case concerned the use of a lottery to market candy to children. The Supreme Court affirmed the Commission's holding that this practice encouraged gambling among children which induced children to buy a lower quality product. It held that such a practice violated established public policy against gambling, was unethical, and therefore was unfair under the FTC Act.

The California court also relied on the three part test for unfairness under the FTC Act adopted by the U.S. Supreme Court in *FTC v. Sperry & Hutchinson Co.* (1972). The California court held that targeting minors with cigarette advertisements: (1) offends public policy; (2) is immoral, unethical, oppressive or unscrupulous; and (3) causes substantial consumer injury. This case later was settled with an injunction, attorneys' fees of $1 million and $9 million for education and enforcement programs in California *Mangini v. R.J. Reynolds Tobacco Co.* (1997).

A similar FTC complaint was ultimately dismissed (Petty 1993). The multi-state tobacco settlement also prohibits the targeting of children, but failed to define targeting (Petty 1999). Since that time, tobacco companies have agreed to avoid or been held liable for advertising in magazines with more than 15% of their readership below the age of 18 (California Attorney General 2002).

The guidelines of the Children's Advertising Review Unit of the National Advertising Division of the Council of Better Business

Bureaus (2009) also recommend against certain unfair practices when targeting children. For example section 2(b)2 of the guides state that advertising should not mislead children about the benefits from using a product, particularly benefits such as the acquisition of strength, status, popularity, growth, proficiency and intelligence. The guides also prohibit use of programming personalities, alive or animated, to sell products adjacent to TV programming directed to children under 12 years of age. Similarly, the multi-state tobacco settlement prohibits the use of cartoon characters in tobacco advertising and several companies are voluntarily restricting the licensing of characters for using in advertising or packaging of unhealthy foods.

The FTC also has taken action against the unfair targeting of children. For example, the FTC obtained a consent agreement with *Hudson Pharmaceutical Corp* (1977) for using the Spiderman comic book character to sell vitamins. The complaint first alleged that children were not capable of deciding whether they should use a vitamin supplement, so that targeting of children in advertising for such a product was challenged as an unfair practice.

The complaint also alleged that the use of the cartoon hero would be particularly appealing to children and might cause them to believe the product had attributes it did not have (e.g., the ability to grant super-powers) and it might cause children to take excessive amounts of the vitamin thereby injuring their health. However, Flintstone vitamins went unchallenged apparently limiting this consent to the targeting of advertising at children rather than the use of character shapes attractive to children. Furthermore in 2010, the FTC obtained a consent agreement calling for consumer refunds with a marketer of children's character vitamins, including Spiderman, for making exaggerated claims about the benefits of vitamins. This consent agreement did not mention the use of characters to market vitamins to children (Federal Trade Commission 2010). The Council of Better Business Bureaus has established the Children's Food and Beverage Advertising Initiative to champion industry self-regulatory efforts to avoid targeting children with advertising for less healthy foods and beverages.

The European Union also is interested in protecting children from being targeted with inappropriate ads. Article 16 of the European Television Directive addresses fairness concerns with television advertising directed towards children. It requires that such advertising not cause moral or physical detriment to minors. Specifically, it states that television advertising not:

(a) directly exhort minors to buy a product or a service by exploiting their inexperience or credulity;

(b) directly encourage minors to persuade their parents or others to purchase the goods or services being advertised;

(c) exploit the special trust minors place in parents, teachers or other persons;

(d) unreasonably show minors in dangerous situations

Hungary expands on the ban of showing kids in dangerous situations to include anything that might harm their physical, emotional or moral development including dangerous, violent or sexual situations. Portugal prohibits physical or moral harm and the U.K. disallows physical or mental harm. Italy also precludes inducing antisocial behavior (Henning-Bodewig 2006).

China, Hong Kong and Taiwan also seek to protect children physically, mentally and morally. Advertising directed at children must not depict dangerous or unhealthy behaviors. It must not exploit their credulity or loyalty to teachers or favorite celebrities. Lastly, to protect children morally, advertising must not depict children with bad manners, interfere with parental upbringing or instill bad values such as feeling superior because of ownership of a particular product (Gao 2005).

Canada also prohibits taking advantage of the credulity of children, direct appeals to purchase or emotional appeals based on popularity or ridicule, and the use of TV personalities or characters from children's programs in children's advertising. Norway also prohibits endorsement by TV personalities in children's advertising and with Denmark bans the use of children in children's advertising unless they are naturally part of the environment of the ad (a playground or school). Finland doesn't allow the use of teachers or parents. Some jurisdictions go even further and prohibit at least some forms of children's advertising. Quebec and Sweden prohibit TV ads directed at children, Italy bans children's advertising during cartoons and Sweden prohibits direct advertising to children under the age of 16 (Henning-Bodewig 2006, Maxeiner & Schotthofer 1999). Greece prohibits advertising toys to children between 7 a.m. and 10 p.m. (Campbell & Yaqub 1999, p. 31).

All of these actions suggest that targeting minors with inappropriate advertising is likely result in legal challenge. For example alcoholic beverage websites often contain content such as games that would appeal to minors. Drinking games may encourage excessive drinking and appeal to minors (Pridgen 1997).

It has proven difficult to distinguish between messages and promotions that appeal to adults but have an acceptable level of spillover to minors from appeals which unacceptably target minors. Currently two different tests have been suggested. The first approach simply examines the audience of the media in which advertising is placed. In adopting the 900 Number Industry Rule, the FTC prohibits advertising in a vehicle where half of the audience or more is under the age of twelve (16 C.F.R. § 308). The FTC followed its fifty percent test in *Global World Media Corp.* (1997).

In contrast, the FDA's cigarette proposal, which was overturned by the Supreme Court, banned event sponsorship promotional items such as clothing in cigarette brand names/logos. It also limits advertisements to text-only, black and white format, if in a publication where more than 15% or 2 million of the readers are below the age of 18. Perhaps the more stringent 15% test for cigarettes is justified by the health consequences of smoking. Advertising has been found deceptive when as little as 15% of the audience perceives a misleading message when the message involves health or safety (*Firestone Tire & Rubber Co v. FTC* 1973, p. 249).

The second test is a typical Commission-expertise test. To determine if advertising targets children the Commission will examine a variety of factors such as the placement of the ad., subject matter, visual content, language, the age of any models and any characters used in the ad.

E. REPEAT SOLICITATIONS (WITHOUT PERMISSION)

Brand interest programs may include periodic catalogs, newsletters or special offers that are communicated to past customers by mail, e-mail or telephone. In general such programs are allowed, particularly if the consumer has consented to receive future brand solicitations. Even repeated solicitations to potential new customers, while often disliked by consumers, may not result in much reduction of goodwill toward any particular brand because consumers have difficulty keeping track of particular solicitations since they receive so many.

An exception occurs with unsolicited e-mail where a marketer may receive few orders, but lots of negative reply e-mail (Headden 1997, p. 48). In the extreme case, such as "spam king" Sanford Wallace, return e-mail was so overwhelming that after a while he could no longer find a company willing to connect him to the internet for fear of the return bombardment (Weber 1999).

Repeated exposures to advertising have been proven to be effective. In one study, as advertising exposure increased from one to four times, recall, attitudes toward the product, and purchase intentions all increased. Swinyard (1979) roughly equated four exposures to advertising as equal to one personal sales call. Similarly, a study of brand extensions showed that repeat exposure to advertising improved the perceived fit and use intentions for potential buyers of incongruent brand extensions (Lane 2000). To the extent that these solicitations engage the consumer to evaluate the brand in isolation, a recent study suggests that such an evaluation may be more positive than when the brand is considered as one of several rival products (Posavac et al. 2004).

However, the sheer volume of repeated solicitations may cause each solicitation to be less effective. In 1998, the credit card industry sent 3.4 billion solicitations by mail, nearly four times as many as it sent in 1992. However, the response rate slipped from 2.8% down to 1.2% (Sanders, 1999). In 2005, the acceptance rate dropped to 0.3%. Yet direct mail is still the most effective method of selling new cards generating more than 60% of new applications (Enrich 2006).

As this example of credit card mail solicitations illustrates, direct mail is the traditional vehicle for repeat solicitations. According to the Direct Marketing Association (2005), the marketers spent $48.6 billion for direct mail in 2003 in order to make over $689 billion in sales. In 1992, the 62 billion pieces of third class mail accounted for nearly 40 percent of postal volume (Jacobson & Mazur 1995, p. 123). Some estimate that 4.5 million tons of such mail is sent annually with nearly half going straight to the trash (Headden 1997). With growing restrictions on solicitation by telephone and e-mail, direct mail in 2004 was on the rise, totaling 96 billion pieces. However, according to the FTC in 2015 only about 4% of consumer fraud complaints used mail as the method of initial contact. Furthermore, as discussed in Chapter Eleven, there also appears to be an increasing tendency to disguise mail solicitations to look like an official notice or personal mail such as a greeting card complete with what appears to be a handwritten address and a postage stamp rather than postal meter cancellation (Abelson 2005).

Direct mail solicitation of consumers is almost completely unrestricted. The only exception occurs if customers refuse delivery of materials they declare to be obscene and require such mailers to stop mailing materials to them (39 U.S.C. §§ 3008–12). As noted above, it also is illegal to send unsolicited merchandise through the mails and then request payment. The law allows consumers to treat such merchandise as a gift.

The latest effort to repeatedly solicit sales is through e-mail and the internet. One study estimates that senders of direct mail bear 88% of the total costs of direct mail, but senders of unsolicited commercial e-mail (UCE) bear only 0.1% of the total costs of dealing with UCE (Lieb 2002). The Federal Trade Commission monitors UCE and receives between 3,000 and 4,000 messages forwarded from consumers each day (Federal Trade Commission 1998). However, FTC consumer fraud complaints have fallen from 32% by e-mail in 2013 to 8% by e-mail in 2015.

As noted above, the FTC has pursued cases where internet surfers have been "mouse-napped" to webpages, bombarded consumers with ads, and not allowed them to escape these webpages. In addition, the FTC challenged a company that used Windows Messenger Service to repeatedly send ads (as often as every 10 minutes) for software that would stop "pop up spam" at a cost of $35 to $30, which also caused computers to crash in some cases (*DSquared Solutions, LLC* 2004).

In April 2004, 83% of all e-mail in the U.S. was unsolicited commercial e-mail commonly known as spam according to MessageLabs (TechWeb News 2004). In 2015, spam finally fell below 50% of all e-mails received according to monitoring services. A list of one million e-mail addresses costs only about $7, making this medium very attractive to marketers (Leibowitz 1999). With such low acquisition and use costs, a small response rate may still make UCE profitable for marketers.

However, UCE is controversial because of high costs for recipients who buy their computer and internet connection and increasingly pay for some sort of UCE filter (Petty 2000). They therefore feel they have some right not to receive unsolicited messages. According to polls, 70% of all e-mail users say spam makes using the internet annoying and 25% of users say they have reduced their usage of e-mail because of spam. Many consumers pay for spam filtering, but the technology of filtering is unable to catch all spam and can filter out legitimate e-mail as well. (Spring 2004; MacMillan 2004). A University of Maryland study estimated that the average U.S. employee receives 18.5 spam messages each day and spends on average 2.8 minutes deleting them. This amounts to $21.6 billion annually in lost productivity (Jesdanum 2005).

The federal response to this method of marketing was the pre-emption of many more restrictive state laws with the Can Spam Act of 2003. This law allows marketers to send unsolicited commercial e-mail, but require that it not have misleading headers or subject lines, that it must identify itself as a commercial message and it must give consumers a method for opting out of receiving e-mail messages from the same source. The law also prohibits e-mail address harvesting from websites (typically using robot crawlers), relaying commercial e-mails through other computers without permission, and using programs to generate possible e-mail addresses by combining popular names with e-mail locations. Since this law legalizes commercial e-mail, it is not surprising that it led to an increase in volume and boost of the sale of filtering software (MacMillan 2004).

In contrast to U.S. efforts to legalize spam with minor restrictions, Australia is effectively discouraging spam with a tough anti-spam law (effective April 2004) that imposes penalties of up to $1.1 million per day for spamming. Reports indicate that Australian spammers have virtually ceased activities and at least one has left the country (Spamhaus 2004). Similarly the E.U. and Canada regulate both the collection of personal information and the use of it to target electronic messages requiring prior explicit consent (opt in).

WAM or wireless advertising messaging is a much anticipated problem (Petty 2003) that has occurred in Japan and Europe, but has been slow to develop in the U.S., perhaps because the U.S. lacks a single cell phone system. In *Satterfield v. Simon & Schuster, Inc.* (2009) the court held that text messages are "calls" under the Telephone Consumer Protection Act (TCPA) of 1991 (47 U.S.C. § 227) which prohibits calls to cellphones from any machine capable of random number dialing (which included the machine being used in that situation and presumably for most if not all text message spamming again without prior consent).

Recent Federal Communications Commission rules under the TCPA that became effective in October 2013 require unambiguous written consent from consumers before businesses may contact them by automated telemarketing phone call, text, e-mail or fax (47 C.F.R. § 64.1200). This law also requires identification of the message as being commercial, a clear opt out mechanism and accurate electronic and snail mail return addresses for the sender. It is enforced by either government or private lawsuits with the latter authorized for damages between $500 and $1500 for each non-complying automated message. As more U.S. households give up landlines in favor of only using a cell phone (about 40% of U.S. households in 2014), telemarketing to cell phones has increased dramatically.

TCPA lawsuits also have increased dramatically. In 2007, there were only 14 TCPA lawsuits filed, but five years later over 1000 were filed and in 2015, 3,710 cases were filed. This dramatic increase has been fueled not only by increased cellphone voice and text marketing but also by equally dramatic class action settlements –some exceeding $30 million. Current FCC rules are under appeal but marketers who fail to obtain clear and in many cases written consent or exceed the number of messages that was authorized, may face lawsuits seeking at least $500 per unapproved contact (Mayer-Brown 2016).

Telemarketing began as a way to have personal sales agent engagement with potential consumers without the expense of door-to-door sales agents. Early telemarketers also sought to take advantage of the personal feeling of phone calls that used to be primarily from family and friends. However, when enacting the Federal TCPA in 1991, Congress estimated that over 300,000 telephone solicitors contacted more than 18 million Americans every day (cited in *Van Bergen v. Minnesota* 1995).

In 2003, the U.S. telephone marketing industry spent $79.7 billion in order to achieve $764.9 billion in sales (Direct Marketing Association 2005). This is over ten thousand times the $72 million estimated telephone solicitation sales in 1982 (Kertz & Burnette 1992). But seventy percent of all telemarketing revenues are generated from consumer initiated calls, not from marketer initiated calls. Telemarketers must make 50 or more calls to make one sale (Jacobson & Mazur 1995, p. 129.) A 1990 poll found that 70% of consumers surveyed agreed that telemarketing is a "major annoyance" (Jacobson & Mazur 1995, p. 127).

Despite consumer annoyance and recent lawsuits, U.S. law treats telemarketing calls as less intrusive than door to door sales. Consumers may hang up to be rid of the solicitation. However, disconnecting from what sounds like a friendly person may be difficult for some people, particularly elderly "shut-ins." Nevertheless, no automatic cooling off period is provided for telephone solicitations under federal law. A number of U.S. states have "get-to-the-point" laws requiring callers to identify their purpose within a short period of time. A few states even have "cooling off" periods for telephone-solicited sales as in Europe (Cain 1994).

Under federal law, non-consensual telephone solicitations may occur if made with equipment that lacks automatic dialing capacity, but these live calls only may occur between the hours of 8:00 a.m. and 9:00 p.m. and may not be harassing by repeat calls or the use of obscene or intimidating language. Repeat calling is defined nebulously as a pattern of calling "repeatedly or continuously with intent to annoy, abuse, or harass." Furthermore, many states and now the FTC offer a do-not-call list which marketers are required to check before making telemarketing calls, unless they have a pre-existing relationship with the customer (16 C.F.R. § 310).

In *Van Bergen v. Minnesota* (1995), the Eight Circuit Court of Appeals found that automatic telephone dialing announcement devices were uniquely intrusive because, once answered, the machines would not terminate the call until the message was completed. It therefor held that a ban on such machines was constitutional, given that they could still be used with prior consent of the party being contacted or if a live operator was used to see if the consumer consented to hear the message.

Solicitations to telephone fax machines and cellular phones without prior consent are prohibited because of the consumer costs of receiving these messages (47 C.F.R. § 64; Cain 1996). Consumers must buy paper for fax machines and typically pay for incoming calls on a cellular phone. Similarly, 900 number calls where consumers are billed a specified price for placing the call must have their fees clearly disclosed and cannot be marketed to children under 12 except for educational products with parental consent (16 C.F.R. § 308). Presumably under this regulation, most 900 number services are used by or under the authority of informed and consenting adults.

In sum, there are a few U.S. restrictions on marketing solicitations by direct mail, e-mail and landline telephone (after checking do-not-call lists). Specific laws suggest general guidance for marketers of being honest that the call is a marketing call, limit the number of solicitations and give consumers an opportunity not to receive future solicitations. Solicitations by fax and cell phone face greater restrictions—generally requiring explicit permission. In the past few years, class action lawsuits have become increasing popular for challenging marketing programs where consumers either have not clearly consented or they agree to receive a certain number of solicitations per month to their cell phones but then the marketing program exceeds that number.

F. AD-WARE

Ad-ware is software that, when loaded on consumers' computers, displays advertisements. Ads are often displayed frequently and may be targeted from tracking consumers' web viewing. When installed with full understanding and consent of consumers, ad-ware is generally consider legal unless it does something coercive (e.g., making itself hard to remove) as noted in the chapter introduction. However, ad-ware sometimes appears to be installed surreptitiously without consumer consent when the consumer is visiting particular websites or when it is bundled to "free-ware" software that consumers want to install "for free" as an alternative to purchasing software. Again if the ad-ware features are clearly disclosed as part of the free-ware bargain, there is no legal problem, but too often, it is alleged that consumers did not know they also were receiving ad-ware.

For this reason, ad-ware is often used synonymously with the term "spyware" because consumers don't realize it is on their computer. A 2004 AOL survey found that 80% of those surveyed had spyware on their computers and over 90% of those consumers said they did not realize this fact and had not given permission for the software to be installed (Roberts 2004).

The U.S. Computer Fraud and Abuse Act criminalizes the act of gaining access to someone else's computer without permission. However because there is often a question of consumer consent, this act has only been used against worms and viruses. Iowa and

Washington have established criminal laws making it illegal for anyone other than the computer owner to install software that changes web-browser settings, monitors keystrokes or disables security software. Ad-ware marketers must be careful to avoid violating these provisions.

The FTC has consistently taken action against deceptive ad-ware marketers, but not against brands that use ad-ware to advertise. However, some brand marketers have fired advertising agencies for contracting with ad-ware firms without the client's knowledge. The FTC often requires "disgorgement" of ill-gotten gains to consumers and imposes an injunctive order. Companies that later violate an order against them are liable for civil penalties payable to the U.S. Treasury. The table below summarizes FTC adware actions.

Table Two		
FTC Ad-Ware Actions		
Name	**Allegations**	**Remedy**
Various Inc. Dec. 2007	Displays sexually explicit ads on affiliate-installed adware.	Agreed to stop these practices without explicit consent.
Direct Revenue Feb. 2007	Undisclosed adware allegedly installed with freeware or installed through security vulnerabilities. Also adware was made difficult to remove.	Agreed to stop these practices and give up $1.5m. ill-gotten gains.
Enternet Media & several individuals Sept. 2006 & Feb. 2007	Promises of free music and ringtones and browser updates led consumers to install adware, which was difficult to remove.	Agreed to stop these practices, not to misrepresent software and not to install software that tracked internet usage, changed browser settings or included adware. Company and four individuals agreed to disgorge over $2m.
Zango, Inc. Nov. 2006	Adware distributed by third parties with freeware without disclosure. Pop-up ads and files not identified and difficult to remove.	Agreed to give up $3m and to verify consumer consent. It will label ads and files and maintain mechanisms for complaints and easily de-installation.

Seismic Entertainment & Sanford Wallace May 2006	Exploited MS Internet Explorer vulnerability to download adware offering anti-spyware products.	Default judgment prohibits downloading software without consent and orders disgorgement of $4m.
Odysseus Marketing & Walter Rines May 2006	Offered file sharing software that reformatted search engine results putting clients first.	Preliminary injunction bars these practices until trial.
Trustsoft, Inc. & Danilo Ladendorf Jan. 2006	E-mail and pop-up messages claiming a remote scan found spyware, offers free scan. Consumers then purchase removal that did little.	Stipulated injunction with $1.9m consumer redress.
MaxTheater, Inc. and Thomas L. Delanoy Jan. 2006	Similar to Trustsoft.	Similar to Trustsoft with $76k consumer redress.
Advertising.com & John Ferber Aug. 2005	Free security software included undisclosed adware.	Agreed not to misrepresent security software without disclosing that adware included.
Vulcan, Inc. Feb. 2016.	Replaced browser extension game cellphone app with adware avoiding Android permission processes.	Agreed to disclose information that will be accessed and how it will be used and obtain permission before installation.

Canada's new anti-spam law explicitly addresses the loading of software on someone else's computer and requires that the computer owner give informed and explicit consent. The program installer must clearly and simply describe (separately from any licensing agreement), the function and purpose of the computer program and any material elements about the program and its foreseeable impact on the computer system in which it is installed.

G. CONCLUSION

Consumer brand managers should realize that attempts to mislead or coerce consumers not only entail high legal risks, and the risk of political pressure for new laws, but also risks disenfranchising the consumers that they often seek to interest in a long term relationship with the brand. While it is possible that a favorable brand experience will overshadow any negative consumer feelings resulting from the brand marketing practices, it is obvious that brand marketers should strive to avoid negative brand experiences whenever possible. Overdoing cajolery practices is one likely way of providing a negative brand experience even if U.S. laws expect that consumers should be able to resist the cajolery.

CHAPTER 10

The 3 Cs of Attracting Brand Interest: Compensation

"No Price is Too High to Pay for a Bargain"

—Ross Petty

A. INTRODUCTION

Often the goal of brand marketing is to persuade consumers that your brand is uniquely suited for them and therefore they should not pay attention to competition from other brands. Many caution that to offer a price reduction on your brand diminishes brand value because it teaches consumers to pay attention to price and price reductions rather than simply being loyal because of the quality and fit of a brand even though it is priced at a premium.

Nevertheless, many brand marketers find it beneficial to offer various forms of promotion that essentially partially compensate the consumer for purchasing the brand. This may be particularly true with a new or newly redesigned branded product or during a recession. Compensation promotions might also be used to stimulate interest in a pre-existing brand, particularly one that is facing new entry. Merely reducing the price without promotion could work if consumers already are price sensitive, but it seems more common to promote the price reduction or other form of compensation in order to at least inform consumers and hopefully excite them about the "bargain." Consumers appreciate a bargain and like to be assured that a particular offering is a bargain (Lindsey-Mullikin and Petty 2011).

In this chapter we broaden the concept of price promotion to include any sort of bargain assurance under the broad category of Compensation—one of the 3Cs of attracting brand interest. Such tactics include simple price discounts presented in various ways or rebates (post purchase discounts that require consumer effort to obtain); additional product (either more of the same or another complementary product) provided either with a purchase or as a premium to be received later; contests that have a probability, but no guarantee, of winning and loyalty reward programs where each purchase earns credit toward prizes, rewards, or discounts on future purchases. While the FTC used to obtain consent agreements in this area, states and class action lawyers are filing suits and obtaining damages so this area continues to be important to the brand marketer.

These forms of compensation can offer benefits as part of the sale transaction (e.g., a price reduction or presentation of a simultaneous discount coupon) or after the sale transaction (e.g., a rebate or coupon for use with next purchase), often with additional effort by the consumer. They also differ from each other across five dimensions as illustrated in the chart opposite: operation, duration, scope, magnitude and specificity. When developing a compensation promotional plan, the brand manager will want to carefully consider options across these five dimensions to assure that each dimension is covered. This chapter discusses the specific details and legal requirements of various forms of Compensation tactics along these dimensions.

Table One		
Examples of Variations Across Compensation Practices		
Dimension	**Benefit is part of purchase transaction**	**Post-purchase benefit such as rebates or rewards**
Operation	Reduction in price, coupon or discount at check-out; pre-packaged product bundle	Rebate submission requirements; Rebate gift card disclosure; Reward program rules
Duration	Ongoing or Limited Time	Ongoing or Limited Time
Scope	All Inventory or Select Items	Sweepstakes conditions
Magnitude	Vague (must be significant); Price Comparison to what referent price and products	Size of product Value of points
Specificity	Amount off; Referent price identity; Calculate net price; range of price reduction, e.g., "up to __"; products covered. EDLP or price guarantee	Odds for each prize; Limitations gift card fees & limitations; points; specific products. Disclose prize probabilities and conditions on gifts or prizes.

B. PRICE PROMOTIONS

Price discounts are the simplest form of compensation. They generate the excitement of getting a bargain, but little other intrinsic excitement about the brand. This may be fine for retail brands seeking a low price image or brands that are already well known and liked by consumers. Marketing research suggests that consumers who are price sensitive brand switchers become more price sensitive over time requiring greater price discounts to switch. In contrast, traditional brand building advertising decreases price sensitivity of this group (Mela, Gupta and Lehman 1997). This suggests that price promotions to stimulate brand interest may be more effective in building brand loyalty if they are in a form such as a discount coupon that includes a brand advertising message.

An important legal issue in such price discounts is whether they are honored according to their terms. It is very clear that the advertiser must not mislead consumers regarding what is covered in its price advertisements (e.g., CA Codes bpc: 7507 2005). For example, a California case required a carpet advertiser to clearly identify the merchandise to which an advertised price applied, rather than advertising a low price but showing a large variety of carpet styles and quality levels (*People v. Custom Craft Carpets, Inc.* 1984).

When Verizon advertised that for $39.99 or higher calling plans, customers would receive unlimited free calls to other subscribers "anytime and anywhere" within the "IN" network area, the NAD felt consumers would interpret that message to include subscribers anywhere in the U.S., the NAD requested that it clearly disclosure the "IN" network was a limited area of subscribers (*Verizon Wireless* 2004). Similarly, DirecTV was asked to clarify that its ad proclaiming programming "starting at $21.99 per month" and "that 210 channels were available including local stations" should disclose that the local channels were available only for an extra charge (*DirecTV and Prime TV* 2001). Lastly, the NAD asked Nextel to clarify its advertising that for $49.99 per month customers would receive unlimited push to talk walkie-talkie calls. Although Nextel argued unlimited meant such calls were always available, the NAD believed that consumers would believe they could place or receive any number of such calls without paying additional charges. This latter message was false and Nextel agreed to make its fine print disclosures to that effect more conspicuous (*Nextel Communications Inc.* 2004).

I. Sale Proclamations

Designating prices as a sale may stimulate sales by suggesting that special low price(s) will be in effect for a limited time period. The effectiveness of this easily executed price promotion is surprising. While ultimately the effectiveness of a sale declaration depends on numerous factors including how many competing products are being offered at "sale" prices and how often these products are featured with "sale" prices, adding a sale sign can have a demand effect exceeding 50% without changing the price (Anderson and Simester 1998;

Anderson and Simester 2001, p. 139). The primary legal question is whether the sale is genuine or simply being proclaimed to mislead consumers. The law focuses on three issues for general sale proclamations. First, is the price reduction significant? Second, is the price reduction for a limited period of time or is it the regular selling price? Third, if a reason is given for the sale, is the reason genuine?

The Council of Better Business Bureaus (BBB) Code section 1(g) advises that price reductions advertised as a sale be significant compared to the advertiser's customary and reasonable price and that sellers comply with any stated expiration period. If the sale exceeds 30 days, the seller should be able to substantiate that the prices really are special reductions rather than regular prices. (Better Business Bureau 2005). The FTC (16 C.F.R. § 233.5) simply advises that bargain offers be "genuine and truthful." While FTC guides are not legally binding, courts have held that such guides are entitled to deference by the courts because of the FTC's expertise in regulating deceptive advertising (*B. Sanfield, Inc. v. Finlay Fine Jewelry Corp.* 1999).

Most state regulation tends to focus on the amount of the alleged price reduction for general sales announcements and the duration of the sale price, particularly when compared to former prices. The latter issue is discussed in the following section. Some states designate that certain percentage price reductions are sufficient to be advertised as a sale. Illinois and Missouri recognize a rebuttable presumption that a price reduction of 5% or more is sufficient for a sale (14 Ill. Adm. Code 470.290 (2005); 15 CSR 60–7.050 (Mo. 2005)). Massachusetts requires that sale price be at least 10% below the former price or 5% if the price is more than $200. Vermont also requires a minimum 10% reduction in price or the disclosure of the actual former price or the percentage price reduction (Vt. Att'y Gen. Cons. Fraud Rule CF 110.02(b) (2005)). Other states simply require that the price reduction be meaningful or material to consumers.

Even without comparison to former prices, it is clear that sales must be special events not continuous. A number of firms in older FTC cases have been challenged for advertising the same "sale" prices more or less continuously (*Royal Construction Co.* 1967; *Joseph Mill Trading* 1966; *Simmonds Upholstery Co.* 1953). More recently, the New York Attorney General settled with Jos. A. Bank Clothiers for offering some suits on sale almost continuously for an 18 month period (New York Attorney General 2004). Ohio requires that sales terminate within the stated or implied period of time unless the advertiser in good faith extends the period of time and clearly discloses the extension (OAC Ann. 109:4–3–12(D)(1) (Anderson 2005). Massachusetts limits sale advertising to 21 days except for comparative price claims and clearance sales that continue until inventory is depleted (940 CMR 604(4) (2005)).

The BBB section 1(h) also advises that if a reason is given for the sale e.g., clearance, liquidation, or going-out-of-business, that reason should be accurate (Better Business Bureau 2005). Michigan regulations go so far as to distinguish "clearance" sales where the seller will sell off its current stock, but then re-order the next season's versions of the same products, from "close out" sales where the seller also intends to sell all of its current inventory, but will not re-order that type of merchandise (Mich. Admin. Code R. 14.201). Iowa and South Dakota limit going out of business sales to 120 days (Iowa Code § 714.16 (2004); S.D. Codified Laws Ann. § 37–24–6(3) (2005)). Alaska and Connecticut simply prohibit sales for special circumstances (e.g., going out of business) unless the price reduction is permanent to clear the merchandise (9 Alaska Admin. Code 05.020 (2005); Regs. Conn. State Agencies § 42–110b–12a (2005)). About half of the states take a broader approach of generally prohibiting misleading statements of fact concerning the reasons for price reductions without worrying about defining various types of sales.

An FTC rule requires that grocery stores honor the sale prices they advertise and have sufficient stock to satisfy reasonably anticipated demand. Alternatively, they may issue rain checks so that consumers may purchase the item at the sale price when more stock is obtained (16 C.F.R. § 424). About half the states have specific rules that apply to any seller and require that the seller have sufficient stock, offer rain checks, or disclose that quantities are limited. Otherwise sellers might be accused of bait and switch as discussed in the preceding chapter.

II. Comparisons to Former (and Future) Prices

Brand managers have shown great creativity in promoting price comparisons. A concern in the marketing literature is that by including a high reference or regular price compared to the lower "sale" price in advertisements increases consumer's internal reference price for the item thereby increasing their perception of value and intent to purchase while decreasing their intention to conduct further price search (Compeau & Grewal 1998). If the perception of value communicated by such advertisements is misleading, then consumers are deceived concerning the actual value of the offering.

The first step in regulating price comparisons is requiring that the reference price be identified. The default position with several states is that if the basis for comparison is not disclosed, it must be to the seller's own former prices. The comparison of a current special price with a higher "former" or "regular" price is essentially the announcement of a sale. For this reason, both the BBB and FTC (16 C.F.R. § 233.1) advise that the former price be bona fide and in effect for a reasonably substantial time period in the regular course of business. FTC "Free" Guides (16 C.F.R. § 251.1(b)(2)) further note that in cases where the price fluctuates, the regular price is the lowest price at which any substantial sales were made during the previous 30 days.

Lanham Act precedent agrees with these guides (*B. Sanfield, Inc. v. Finlay Fine Jewelry Corp.* 1999). The NAD has a tougher standard. When Kmart argued its regular prices for jewelry were in effect for a substantial period of time, 183 days, the NAD still requested that Kmart show its prices were bona fide by showing substantial sales at those "regular" prices (*Kmart* Corp. 2001). State laws and regulations of comparisons to former prices agree in overall policy, but vary in details. Some follow the vague good faith approach while many have elaborate regulations. Recently, Kaufman Department Stores settled a complaint with the New York Attorney General for deceptive regular prices at which no products were sold (New York Attorney General 2005).

Comparisons with future prices also essentially announce that the current price is an introductory sale and that future prices will be higher. The FTC Guides request the advertiser to expect in "good faith" to increase the price in the future (16 C.F.R. § 233.5). In contrast, some states focus on the time period allowed for low introductory prices. Some only allow the introductory price for a "reasonable period of time" while others specify a time period (Komensky & Wegener 1991). The BBB Code, section 1(g) only addresses comparisons with future prices under its guidelines for sale advertising. The Code states that the sale should be for a limited time and expire at the stated time. If advertisers announce a future price increase, they should in fact follow the announcement and sustain the price increase for a reasonable time after its effective date (Better Business Bureau 2005).

III. "Up to," Savings and Percentage-Off Claims

"Up to" savings claims include statements such as "Save up to 50%," and "As low as $5." This category also includes range of savings claims such as "Save from 10% to 50% Off." The maximum amount of savings or the minimum price provide a specific factual component but ambiguity exists as to the selection of products whose price or savings actually will match the maximum savings or the lowest level of price. The ads suggest that not all prices and/or savings will be offered at the threshold. Not surprisingly, customers are skeptical about the proportion of goods to which the maximum savings apply (Mobley, Bearden, and Teel 1988).

It should be obvious that advertisers must be able to substantiate their savings claims. For example, when IDT advertised that subscribing to its "America Unlimited" telephone service would save customers $180 a year or more, AT&T challenged the advertising in front of the NAD by showing that the advertised level of savings was only true for one out of six states where the advertisement was run. The NAD cited a joint FCC-FTC Policy Statement for advertising long distance telephone services to decide that such comparisons must be substantiated and include any additional charges consumers would see on their phone bills. The NAD also noted that advertisers who choose to make price savings comparisons are obligated to monitor rival prices to make sure the advertising is accurate when it runs (*IDT Corp.* 2005). Similarly, a recent NAD case held that AT&T had to clearly indicate which customers would save the at least $250 per year (as claimed in advertising) by subscribing to its internet telephone service instead of traditional telephone service. It had to disclose that only those customers who already were subscribing to and paying for broadband internet service could achieve this amount of savings (*AT&T Corp.* 2005).

Advertising law also requires that the maximum amount of savings must be obtainable by an appreciable number of consumers under normally expected circumstances (*Plaskolite, Inc.* 1983). The BBB Code, section 1(i) requires that the number of items available for the maximum savings comprise a significant percentage, typically 10%. The Code further suggests that advertisers include both a minimum and maximum amount off without undue emphasis on the latter (Better Business Bureau 2005). Specifically, the provision says:

> Savings or price reduction claims covering a group of items with a range of savings should state both the minimum and maximum savings without undue or misleading display of the maximum. The number of items available at the maximum savings should comprise a significant percentage, typically

10% of all the items in the offering, unless local or state law requires otherwise.

Several states have similar requirements (Komensky and Wegener 1991).

IV. Price Comparisons Between Different Products

Avoiding consumer deception is even more complex in two ways when price savings claims are made comparing non-identical products. First, price savings claims may be made for different quantities of identical products. For example, the NAD supported a consumer complaint that Friendly's Restaurant menus advertised the lower priced Senior Classic Dinners but failed to disclose that the main entrée also was smaller. The NAD recommended that Friendly's disclose any size differences between regular entrees and the senior versions (*Friendly Ice Cream Corp.* 1997). Similarly, the BBB's *Dos and Don'ts in Advertising* recommends in section 19.227 that advertisers should indicate when savings comparisons are made between the price of a large package, such as a complete set of dishes, and the prices of individual items when sold separately (BBB 1996).

The second issue in price savings comparisons here is between products of different qualities—so called "apples to oranges" comparisons (which are generally illegal in the E.U.). In *The Home Depot, Inc.* (1998), the NAD wrestled with advertising that compared price and quality simultaneously. The NAD recognized that comparisons between dissimilar products could be made but the products being compared must be clearly identified with no implication that the rival does not carry a comparable quality product, if that is not the case, and no implication that the rival's products are generally inferior unless that can be substantiated as true.

The NAD also has allowed synthetic motor oil to be compared to conventional motor oil as long as the advertiser clearly discloses that the advertised product is a synthetic and it is being compared to rival brands' conventional products rather than their synthetic products (*Quaker State Corp.* 1995). Finally, in the world of online shopping, the NAD has allowed substantiated "save up to x%" claims as long as material differences between the online sites are disclosed (e.g., a bidding site on unspecified hotels in a particular city versus a shopping site with prices for specific hotels with particular amenities—*Priceline.com, Inc.* 2003). Similarly, an advertisement comparing prices for two computer systems must include the price of every component needed to compare the performance described in the ad (*Dell Computer Corp.* 2004).

V. Comparisons with Third-Party Prices

Brand managers and retailers often compare their prices to a higher priced brand in order to enhance the buyer's perceptions of value. Evidence indicates that comparative price advertising is a powerful advertising tool but with a strong opportunity for deception (Compeau and Grewal 1998; Grewal and Compeau 1992). Common reference points other than the seller's own price, discussed above, include (1) prices of sellers such a named competitor's price or the more vague "their price, our price,"; (2) prices obtained from the manufacturer or wholesaler such as wholesale price, the suggested list price, our cost or the invoice price and (3) vague references of comparable value.

Three deception issues arising from comparative price advertising have been examined in the marketing literature. First, as noted above, comparing to a high reference price might mislead consumers to believe that are receiving a better value than they are actually receiving, particularly if the referent is vague.

Second, consumers also may misunderstand the meaning of the reference price. Advertisers can compare their prices to other retailer's prices, their own former or regular price, their own future regular price, a manufacturer's suggested or list price or, as noted above, a "comparable value" price. Various studies suggest possible consumer misinterpretation of many of these options and several legal actions have sought to clarify their meanings (Grewal and Compeau 1992). For example, one study found that many consumers believed that Manufacturers Suggested List Price was a price the product was sold for in a majority of stores (Compeau, Lindsey-Mullikin, Grewal and Petty 2004). As discussed below, this would support requirements in some states that list prices be representative of sellers' actual prices (Komensky and Wegener 1991).

Third, Pechmann (1996) argues that when a marketer makes a single or small number of price comparisons, a halo effect might lead consumers to believe that all prices of the advertiser are lower. Similarly, advertisers compare attributes where their product is superior to rival offerings and consumers may believe the advertised product is superior on other attributes as well. Despite her concerns, advertising law clearly allows sales to cover only selected items and comparisons to other prices or products.

The FTC appears to have decided that the value of the specific comparison information to consumers generally exceeds the costs of consumer deception from the halo effect (16 C.F.R. § 14.15). It therefore encourages specific comparisons. For this reason, advertising specific price comparisons is allowed if they are accurate. Occasionally price comparison advertising does imply overall lower prices and when that occurs, it is condemned. This may be likely with so-called market basket comparisons that are discussed in the following section.

Perhaps the most specific and therefore credible tactic in comparative price advertising is a comparison to a named rival brand's price. From the consumer's perception, this tactic is most credible when it specifies the date when the rival's price was verified. Advertisers have been condemned if they do not change their price comparisons after the targeted rival changes its prices (*Lenscrafters, Inc.*

v. Vision World, 1996) or if the price surveys that support their comparative price claims are not recent (*Winn-Dixie Stores, Inc.* 1996; *Menard, Inc.* 2003; *Tops Markets, LLC* 2004).

State regulations consistently require that competitor reference prices be verified and in good faith. Furthermore, they sometimes require that the competitor price not exceed that of representative retailers in the area (Komensky and Wegener 1991).

VI. Everyday Low Prices and Price Matching Guarantees

The opposite tactic from promoting periodic sales is advertising everyday low prices (EDLP). This is the equivalent of announcing a "permanent sale"—a practice that advertising law does not allowed to be called "a sale." EDLP presumably eliminates the implication that prices are only low for a short period of time. Price matching guarantees are often very similar to EDLP but differ in the substantiation required to allow the advertiser to make such claims.

In a recent case, the NAD found that the claim "lowest prices guaranteed" communicated to consumers that the marketer always had the lowest prices and regularly conducted price surveys to substantiate the accuracy of that claim. In contrast, the claim "nobody beats our prices" communicated a price matching guarantee that any substantiated lower price would be matched. The NAD recommended the former be discontinued because the marketer did not have valid substantiation, but allowed the second claim because the marketer did offer a price matching guarantee (*The Home Depot* 2005).

This decision correctly suggests that EDLP claims are challenged when they can be proven inaccurate. In one case, where a grocery store attempted to bolster the credibility of its low prices claim by comparing a typical market basket of its goods with a market basket of the same items from a rival, the FTC challenged the comparison as biased and misleading. It included only dry goods, not meat or produce where the surveying store tended to perform less well on price and the items in the survey were selected by the managers who set local prices (*Kroger Co.* 1981). Similarly, when Tops compared savings on two grocery baskets full of goods, the NAD felt the ads did suggest store-wide lower prices and recommended the advertiser discontinue that unsubstantiated claim. The advertiser could only substantiate that the prices of its basket of goods, not store-wide prices, were lower than a named competitor's prices for the same basket of goods (*Tops Markets, LLC* 2004).

The NAD also has been active in considering overall claims of low prices. It has held that the boast of "better deals" could be a lower price claim in some contexts or a competitive price and better service claim in other contexts (*CIMO, Inc. d/b/a/ Hotwire* 2002). The NAD supported Wal-Mart's argument that its slogan "Always The Low Price. Always" was understood by consumers to mean it had a general policy of offering low prices, but did not mean it would always have the lowest prices on all items. The National Advertising Review Board, on appeal however, felt it might be misleading so Wal-Mart agreed to change its slogan to "Always Low Prices" (*Wal-Mart Stores, Inc.* 1994).

In contrast, Winn-Dixie's claim of "Everyday Lower Prices" in conjunction with specific price comparisons to Wal-Mart prices was thought to deceptively communicate that its prices generally were lower than those of Wal-Mart (*Winn-Dixie Stores, Inc.* 1996). Similarly, the NAD recommended that Menard, Inc. discontinue its "lowest prices" advertising campaign because its survey evidence was neither recent nor updated in a sufficiently timely way to support the claim (*Menard, Inc.* 2003).

Price-matching guarantees are offers by firms to match any lower prices found by customers to have been offered by competitors, although Jain & Srivastava (2000) argue that customers often believe businesses that advertise a price guarantee actually do offer lower prices. Of course firms offering such a guarantee must actually honor its terms (*Dick's Sporting Goods,* 2004). Missouri requires that price guarantee advertising clearly disclose all material conditions and limitations and that such guarantees not place an unrealistic or unreasonable burden on consumers (15 CSR 60–7.110 (Mo. 2005)). Section 1(k) of the BBB Code suggests the same requirements (Better Business Bureaus 2005).

The advertising of such guarantees is closely scrutinized to make sure EDLP is not being communicated to consumers. Both courts and the NAD have condemned the advertising of price guarantees as deceptively representing to consumers that the offering firm's prices are guaranteed to be the lowest available and they are not (*Lenscrafters, Inc. v. Vision World* 1996; *the Home Depot* 2005). However, a carefully crafted price guarantee may promise nothing about overall price levels, but simply promise to refund the difference if a lower price is found by consumers. Section 1(k) of the BBB Code suggests that price guarantees can create an implicit obligation to reduce all prices of a particular product once a lower competitive price has been found (Better Business Bureau 2005). While this does not suggest a duty to routinely survey rival prices and undercut them in order to have a reasonable basis for the low price guarantee, it is consistent with the suggestion that customers tend to believe that such guarantees indicate generally lower prices.

It is important to note that vague statements about price such as "We are the low cost commercial collection experts" have been held to be puffery (*Cooke, Perkiss and Liehe, Inc. v. Northern California Collection Service, Inc.* 1990). In contrast, superlative low pricing claims are often found not to be puffing. The NAD found the claim "The Best Price in Sight" to be a factual claim that the Eyeglass Factory offered the lowest prices. This interpretation was supported by the fact that most ads contained a smaller claim "We checked" (*The Eyeglass Factory* 1997). The NAD also challenged Kmart's statement "Lowest sale price every time" but Kmart had discontinued the claim by the time it was challenged (*Kmart Corp.* 2000). Similarly, in an early case, the FTC found the claim "World's Lowest Prices," for replacement windows and similar products also to be a factual claim rather than puffing (*Better Living, Inc.* 1957).

VII. Rebates—Post-Purchase Price Discounts

Rebates are post-purchase price discounts that are only paid to consumers who accurately complete and submit a rebate redemption form along with one or more forms of proof of purchase before the rebate expires. Firms prefer them to simple price discounts because, like coupons, not all consumers redeem rebates allowing the firm to sell to some consumers at a higher price. Furthermore, some consumers who intend to enjoy the rebate do not for one reason or another such as forgetting to apply in time or failing to save all the required documentation. However, brands run the risk of consumer dissatisfaction if rebate redemption requirements or time delays in the getting the rebate are too onerous (Pechmann and Silk 2015).

Rebate marketers potentially face four sets of legal issues involving: (1) advertising the product price, (2) disclosing the rebate and its redemption requirements/forms, (3) processing redemption requests and (4) paying the rebate (Pechmann and Silk 2015, p. 257). Concerning price advertising, while marketers prefer to promote the post-rebate lower price, the law generally requires that the before-rebate price be advertised since that is the price actually paid by purchasers. Connecticut and Rhode Island have an explicit exception allowing the advertising of the post-rebate price for rebates that are paid instantly. Rhode Island has gone the furthest in this direction by requiring that retailers/dealers who advertise the net (post rebate) price must grant the rebate upon purchase to consumers and apply for it themselves (R.I. Gen. Law. § 6–13.1–1). This law seems intended to inhibit dealer advertising of post-rebate prices. Two FTC consent agreements allow the after-rebate price to be advertised if the fact of the rebate and the amount of rebate savings also are conspicuously disclosed (Pechmann and Silk 2015, p. 258).

In addition to requiring disclosure that any reduced price is based on a rebate, the law also generally requires disclosure of all material conditions for obtaining the rebate before purchase. This includes providing ready access to any redemption form and disclosing any fees or other unusual or unduly restrictive requirements. New York requires that forms be included with the product or available at the point of purchase. One material condition that should be disclosed is the amount of time before the rebate expires. A few states require a minimum period (typically 30 days) that must be given to consumers to complete the rebate form (Pechmann and Silk 2015, pp. 261–265). A recent court decision refused to dismiss a complaint that challenged another undisclosed fact—that the rebate was not cash or a check but rather would be a VISA Reward card (*Faigman v. AT&T Mobility LLC*, 2007).

One of the most common complaints about rebates are onerous and repetitive requirements such as requiring a cash register or credit card receipt, transcribing a rebate code and cutting the UPC off the product package. Consumers feel such requirements are intended to deter rebate requests while marketers argue they are trying to minimize the probably of fraud—consumers buying one product but seeking multiple rebates from that single purchase. Other than North Dakota's requirement that post office boxes must be considered acceptable addresses for rebate checks, regulatory authorities have yet to act on the onerousness of some requirements.

Finally, the FTC requires that rebates be paid within thirty days or when promised. In one case, rebates were promised within 12 weeks, but less than 5% of rebates were issued within that time frame (Federal Trade Commission 2007b). In situations where both the manufacturer and dealers advertise rebates, the FTC has required that both be responsible for paying the rebates when promised or within 30 days of the purchase (Federal Trade Commission 2005). New York law requires rebates be mailed within 60 days (Gen. Bus. L. 391–p). The state of Washington requires that rebate checks be clearly identified on their mailers so they are less likely to be accidentally disposed of as "junk mail" (Pechmann and Silk 2015, p. 266).

C. "FREE" PRODUCTS: SAMPLING, BUNDLING AND PREMIUMS

Everyone likes to get something free. Samples are given to consumers in stores or through a mail-in offers that might include handling/shipping charges. Marketers invest over $15 billion annually to distribute brand-related gifts such as t-shirts and desk accessories. Studies show that 40% of recipients can remember the name of the gift giver as long as six months after receipt and 31% use the gift at least one year after receipt (Levinson n.d.). However, studies also suggest that consumers discount the value of a product that is given away for free unless they also have information suggesting the value or regular price of the product is high (Raghubir 2004).

It is not surprising that when marketers promise "free" gifts, they should actually be "free." As with post purchase rebates, any material conditions imposed on the "free" gift must be clearly disclosed. The FTC recently settled with Adteractive, Inc. for not disclosing that consumers had to wade through pages of ads and optional offers as well as participate in programs that required purchase before receiving the "free" gift that was promised in e-mail. Since this case involved violations of the CAN-SPAM act (deceptive subject lines promising "free" gifts), the FTC obtained a $650,000 civil penalty (FTC 2007a). Unscrupulous marketers sometimes send products and then bill the recipient as though the recipient had not ordered the goods. Under federal postal service law, this is considered fraudulent and the recipient is free to keep the unordered goods as though they were a gift or free sample (39 U.S.C. § 3009).

One common condition for receipt of a "free" product is the purchase of another product. Not surprisingly, the FTC Guides Concerning Use of the Word "Free" (16 C.F.R. § 251.1(b)) recommend that in cases where the "free" good is bundled with another item that the price of the other item should not be increased. The BBB Code, section 2, also suggests that the conditions of additional purchase be clearly and conspicuously disclosed and that the normal price or quality of the conditioned merchandise not be changed (Better Business Bureau 2005). The Code further recommends that the "free" offer be temporary.

In a classic case, the Supreme Court affirmed the FTC's holding that a paint seller's promotion of "Buy one can, get a second for free" was deceptive. The seller's promotion was continuous and it did not sell single cans. It deceptively described the price for two cans as the single can price (*FTC v. Mary Carter Paint Co.,* 1965). Recent NAD decisions follow the same policy of condemning continuous "buy one, get the second one for free or x% off" tactics (*NBTY, Inc.* 2005).

Selling two (or more) products or two units of the same product for a single price is typically called bundling in the marketing literature. Stremersch and Tellis (2002) define price bundling as two or more products that are packaged together but also available separately and pure bundling as when at least one product is only available as part of a bundle. Bundling may occur as a temporary tactic or as a long term decision that two products are best sold as a single unit (e.g., epoxy glue and hardener or shoes with shoe laces). Bundling is typically a pro-competitive tactic to offer consumers a preferred combination of components, but can be used by a firm with market dominance for one component to shut out rivals from offering a related separate component by bundling the second component with the first (Stremersch & Tellis 2002).

Temporary or promotional bundling may be a good opportunity to introduce consumers to a brand extension or a brand complement that may have the same or different brand name (e.g., shampoo and separate hair conditioner). Bundling may be an opportunity to offer a premium or prize, such as the free toy in the children's fast food meal or breakfast cereal. Consumers evaluate bundles based on the item sold in the bundle that is perceived to be most important (Yadav 1994). Parents may look at the food while children evaluate the prize. Studies suggest that price bundling often can decrease price sensitivity for the bundle compared to the individual products and increase purchase likelihood (Soman and Gourville 2001).

Generally, there are few consumer protection issues with bundling goods together so long as there is no deception about the quality or value of the goods. For example, TracFone advertised it cell phone service plans would now provide unlimited data, but it throttled or suspended data service when customers reached a preset data limit. This purported "bundling" of data service was challenged by four class action lawsuits and then by the FTC. TracFone recently settled with the FTC agreeing to pay $40 million into a consumer fund and it further agreed to pay class counsel another $5 million in attorneys' fees (Federal Trade Commission 2015).

D. PRICE PROMOTIONS AND ANTITRUST

Most antitrust issues of concern to brand managers, including bundling issues, are discussed in Chapter Eighteen. However, here it is worth noting that for brands enjoying a dominant market position, price discounts could be considered a form of price discrimination that lessens competition—also called predatory pricing. The focus of antitrust analysis is almost always the amount of the price discount rather than its promotion or the means by which it is granted. The major challenge in such cases is to prove that the price discounter has at least a dangerous probability of obtaining market power to be able to eventually raise it price and recoup its losses and that the reduced price was below some appropriate level of product cost (*Brooke Group, Ltd. v. Brown & Williamson Tobacco Corp.* 1993).

Courts recognize that even market dominating firms may use ordinary price promotions so long as the promotions are not so extensive that the retailer is losing money in order to drive other retailers out of business (*Wal-Mart v. American Drugs, et al.*, 1995). Similarly, although an antitrust challenge for predatory pricing is theoretically possible based on free samples i.e., pricing the product at zero, such a case seems very unlikely (c.f. *Wallace v. IBM* 2006). Sampling is seldom performed to such an extent that it might injure competition or force rival firms to go out of business.

The Attorney General of New York challenged a group of firms for eliminating coupons in favor of slightly lower prices. However, this action was settled without admission of wrong-doing, nor proof that the various firms, including Proctor & Gamble and Wegmans, a large retail chain, agreed with each other to eliminate coupons (Schultz 1997). Under the antitrust laws a conspiracy would have to be proven to make this illegal since any single firm is free to decide by itself whether or not to use coupons.

E. SWEEPSTAKES AND PRIZE PROMOTIONS

One set of compensation tactics of both growing importance and continuing controversy are sweepstakes and prize promotions. Over one billion sweepstakes solicitations are mailed annually in the U.S. Some people may receive over 100 such mailings in a year. Sweepstakes are used by 95% of all marketers that use any form of promotion. These promotions also appear to be of growing interest to internet marketers as well. In contrast to sweepstakes, contests are promotions where prizes are awarded primarily on the basis of skill or merit rather than primarily by chance. However, if entries are judged by public vote and entrants are free to encourage others to vote for their entry, than a court could find this contest was primarily of chance rather than merit.

The most important law for marketers in this area is the Federal Criminal Lottery Act, which makes it a crime for private parties to conduct a lottery in interstate commerce. The belief at the time of enactment was the promotion of gambling was bad public policy. To be an illegal lottery, a contest must offer a prize of value in a game (primarily) of chance (not skill or judgment) in exchange for consideration such as purchasing a product.

To avoid this consideration element, sweepstakes marketers typically offer an alternative form of entry that is free as opposed to sending in a coupon from the product package that requires purchase. While all states recognize monetary consideration such as buying the product as problematic, many also condemn non-monetary consideration such as consumer expenditure of substantial time and effort in order to participate (e.g., completing a substantial survey or visiting a store multiple times or perhaps a paying a premium to send a text message or assembling a collection of images on a social media site).

For example, a Boston area furniture store offered money back on purchases made during a specified time period if the Boston Red Sox won the World Series, which they did. While the state attorney general refused to challenge these promotions as illegal lotteries, Massachusetts law allows private parties to sue and one did. However, the court of appeals affirmed dismissal of the case because the complaining party failed to prove that some part of the purchase price was actually paid for the chance to win the rebate. In other words since consumers paid the full price for furniture, they did not pay any additional consideration for the chance of obtaining a refund. Note this is contrary to the typical analysis that simply asks whether product purchase is required to enter the sweepstakes.

In addition to federal criminal sanctions, most states have requirements for sweepstakes and prize promotions. Some require the game be registered with the state attorney general (AG) and may require a bond be posted or trust account established equal to the total amount of prizes. Others require that a list of winners be sent to the state AG and/or that rigorous internal procedures be established to avoid making mistakes. The purpose of these requirements appears to be to insure fairness to consumers.

Sweepstakes and prize promotions also are policed to avoid deception. In the late 1990s, Publishers Clearing House (PCH) and American Family Publishers (AFP) faced a number of state AG and private class action lawsuits alleging deception. AFP settled with 33 state attorneys general agreeing to tone down its language and eliminating such claims as "Its Down to a 2-Person Race for $11,000,000. You and one other person . . . " It also agreed to pay $50,000 to each state to cover the costs of the state investigation. By March 1999, AFP's sales were down 30%. PCH filed for Chapter 11 Bankruptcy protection and also has settled agreeing to careful use of the terms finalist and winner (Cyr 1999). The FTC has promulgated a set of rules for games of chance in gasoline and grocery stores requiring disclosure of the odds of winning, the number of prizes in each category, the length of the contest and other important information (16 C.F.R. § 419). Most states have similar laws of full disclosure of the rules and odds of winning.

Finally other laws may have an impact of sweepstakes, particularly those on social media. First, the terms of use of the social media may restrict promotions. For example, Facebook no longer allows firms to require a page be "liked" in order to enter a contest. The site says this is to ensure the integrity of consumer expression, but the FTC also has suggested that such a liking might be considered a misleading endorsement unless the material connection of liking to enter the contest is disclosed in each case. Social media promotions also tend to rely to electronic messages and therefore marketers need to consider the requirements of so-called "anti-spam" rules discussed in Chapter Nine. Finally, social media sweepstakes probably will collect personal information and they must comply with various privacy laws as well as their own stated privacy protection policies.

F. CONSUMER LOYALTY/FREQUENCY REWARD PROGRAMS

Loyalty programs date back at least to trading stamps and probably to informal discounts and rewards given by retailers to loyal customers. Kivetz and Simonson (2002) suggest that modern frequency programs began with American Airlines in 1981. Such programs are now used in a wide range of consumer and business-to-business companies. Some, such as retailer cards, offer select discounts not available to other consumers. Others, such as most airline programs, offer free or reduced prices on future purchases from the company or partner companies after so many "points" are earned by making purchases. These programs provide the perception of added value to consumers and are designed to make consumers less sensitive to rival price promotions and more likely to purchase the products associated with the loyalty program.

Loyalty programs can certainly attract consumer interest. The goal of loyalty programs is to increase the purchases of existing consumers and reduce brand switching (Kivetz and Simonson 2002). Under high consumer involvement situations, these loyalty programs increase brand loyalty both directly and indirectly (Yi and Jeon 2003). The long-term effect of loyalty programs when used with other marketing tactics is that consumers increase annual purchasing amounts (Lewis 2004).

Loyalty programs may shift consumer preferences toward luxury rewards in programs that have high requirements. The higher effort is thought to reduce the guilt associated with acquiring luxury items especially for those individuals who experience guilt about luxury consumption (Kivetz and Simonson 2002). For example, consumers may use airline programs to occasionally upgrade to first class when they otherwise would not spend the extra money to directly purchase such a luxury.

In contrast, lower quality tangible incentives can undermine post-program loyalty. For example, a retailer card that only gives discounts on store brand products will not be effective if consumers perceive the store brands to be of low quality (Roehm, Pullins, and Roehm 2002). Similarly, if consumers have a negative experience with a reward program itself, they will not be loyal to it. One current credit card advertisement pokes fun at the difficulties of redeeming reward mileages with an unnamed airline program. If the perception of difficulty becomes wide spread, the reward programs will be less effective in maintaining loyalty. For this reason, loyalty programs are only effective if consumers value them over the long term.

These programs are relatively new so there are not many court decisions. It is clear that a loyalty reward program that is not readily honored could be condemned as false advertising or breach of contract (except for airline programs where state law has been pre-empted). Kim, Shi & Srinivasan (2001) also suggest that adoption of loyalty programs by most industry members might be a tacit agreement to avoid price-cutting. Challenging loyalty programs on such antitrust grounds would be difficult because the existence of the agreement to adopt similar programs must be proven.

Lastly, because post purchase rebates and premiums as well as sweepstakes and loyalty programs all allow marketers to collect consumer information, these tactics raise privacy issues. In the U.S., the FTC has taken action against firms who disclose a privacy policy and then violate it. In the E.U., the Data Protection Directive (95/46/EC) requires that consumers be informed and consent when providing information to a marketing database, have the right to correct or erase inaccurate data, and have the right to object to its use for marketing purposes. Europe is currently considering updates to this Directive and transforming it from a Directive which member states must adopt to a

Regulation that will have direct legal effect throughout the E.U. if enacted.

G. CONCLUSION

Compensation tactics "buy" interest in the brand but often the price is considerably higher than a short term reduction in profitability. Consumers learn to expect periodic price reductions and become reluctant to buy at full price. In this way, premium price brands may be unintentionally converted to brands that compete on price. Of course, in addition to these marketing risks, brand marketers should be aware of the legal risks of violating detailed rules from pursuing these tactics.

The most common legal risk identified here is consumer deception. The law requires that all aspects of a sales offering be accurately described including salient details of the proposed sales contract. In contrast to the broad risk of deception, the legal risks of privacy law violations are relatively minor for compensation practices, but more significant for data collection practices that enable connection practices and even more significant for cajolery practices where the law restricts how and when consumers may be solicited. The most extreme legal sanctions are invoked under criminal law, which for practices that stimulate brand interest is most notable in the prohibition of lotteries and intentional fraud.

At any given time, there may be a lapse of enforcement against particular brand involvement practices. For example, The FTC interest in price promotion has fluctuated over time. However, we are now seeing both state attorneys general and private class action lawyers jumping into this area and unlike the FTC, they are seeking monetary relief. So what might have appeared as diminished regulation ends up being shifted regulation with increased sanctions! Given this expansion, it is crucial for the marketer to understand that while there are some general principles, there are numerous detailed state laws and regulations (and some for specific cities) and some of these apply just to particular industries. Marketers must make sure they comply with rules for all locations in which they offer price promotion or other compensation tactics.

CHAPTER 11

Connection (and Masked Marketing)

This chapter begins our examination of the third C of attracting brand interest—Connection. For centuries, merchants as neighbors and community members have been acquainted with the tastes and desires of their recurring customers and been able to connect with them by offering individualized recommendations. Today, technology allows distant merchants to make similar personal connections by personalizing solicitations with individual customer names and by collecting information about the browsing and purchase information of large numbers of consumers and offering specific recommendations to each. A basic tenet of Customer Relationship Management is that customers be kept satisfied to maximize lifetime purchases. Marketers attempt to establish a personal connection with each customer. Of course such connections might include compensation tactics, discussed in the preceding chapter. Customers enjoy feeling special—that they were singled out for special compensation that was not offered to everyone.

This chapter examines Connection tactics through two sets of tactics: Personalized Recommendations and Masked Marketing where the marketer seeks to establish a personal connection by disguising the identity of marketing agents and marketing messages. The chapter delves into greater depth on the various forms of Masked Marketing. Chapter Twelve then examines Secondary Brand Associations that includes various associations including endorsements by celebrities and experts. Chapter Thirteen finishes this topic by examining celebrities and how they can limit the ability of marketers to use their persona without their permission.

A. PERSONALIZED RECOMMENDATIONS

Perhaps the first formalized marketing program to offer personalized recommendations was the Book of the Month and similar buying clubs. These clubs contract with members to send them monthly recommendations unless the member contacts the club to notify it that they don't want this month's selection. Members agree to receive monthly promotions and pay for the selection of the month or its return expenses if they don't notify the club of their denial in a specified timely manner. The earliest clubs paid for return postage but that became too expensive so the option of notice and the option to "pre-refuse" selections was developed (Bowal 1999; Spriggs and Nevin 1996). Since the book or other product comes unless the consumer affirmatively refuses it, these clubs are called negative option plans. They are regulated under an FTC rule to make sure consumers are informed concerning their obligations and given the chance to refuse each month's selection before it is sent (16 C.F.R. § 425). Recently, the FTC enforced the provisions of this rule against Scholastic, Inc. (Federal Trade Commission 2005b).

Today customer loyalty cards and visits on the internet allow marketers to collect information about customer purchases and, in the case of the internet, browsing interests. In the U.S., there are a few limits on how marketers can collect and sell information about consumers that make personalized recommendations possible. Internal collection and use of shopping and browsing information is legal and the sale of such information to third parties is legal in the U.S., unless it violates the marketer's stated privacy policy. The FTC recently challenged a company's acquisition of eBay user names that it then used to send personalized deceptive e-mails to scores of eBay users. However, two Commissioners dissented from the settlement, arguing that merely sending e-mail solicitations does not cause substantial injury and therefore is not unfair (*ReverseAuction.com* 2000).

The Children's On-Line Privacy Protection Act of 1998 (15 U.S.C. § 6501 et seq.) prohibits operators from commercial websites or online services directed to children under the age of 13 to collect personal information from a child without notice and parental consent. In contrast E.U. Directive requires that all consumers be informed and consent when providing information to a marketing database, have the right to correct or erase inaccurate data, and have the right to object to its use for marketing purposes.

A similar practice involves the "you have won" type of solicitation. This suggests that a particular customer has been selected for a special deal that is not available to the general public. Consumers may be selected to be a model home in a particular town for a siding company. Businesses may be selected as one of a smaller number of companies given the opportunity to participate in a marketing program.

Initially some of these tactics may mislead the customer into thinking that they have actually won a prize or special deal. This would qualify as masked marketing described in the next section because the consumer does not initially recognize this as a marketing solicitation. The fact that this is actually a sales situation usually becomes clear in the details, although the consumer may still be led to believe he or she won the right to a special deal. This could still be considered deceptive advertising. In addition, some companies have offered what sound like great prizes that will be delivered once a delivery fee is paid. In some cases, the prize in never delivered—that would be criminally fraudulent. In other cases, the prize is delivered, but the motorboat turns out to be an inflatable raft with a small electric motor—not the larger motorboat most consumers would imagine. Such a situation could be pursued as deception.

B. MASKED MARKETING

Recent estimates suggest that consumers are exposed to some 5000 brand communications daily, but are so accustomed to such messages that they consciously perceive only 1–2% of them (Pringle 2004, pp. 60–61). Consumer surveys indicate that, in general, most consumers are skeptical of marketing messages (Calfee and Ringold 1994; Obermiller and Spangenberg 2000; Obermiller, Spangenberg, and MacLaughlin 2005). Most adult consumers have developed methods to cope with *overt* attempts at persuasion (e.g., "schemer schemas," Friestad and Wright 1994).

Masked marketers hope to avoid both consumer skepticism of marketing communications and consumer disinterest in such messages due to clutter (Kaikati and Kaikati 2004; Petty and Andrews 2008). The key is that the communication, at least initially, appears to come from a third party rather than the marketer. This approach appears sound under traditional marketing theory. In general, most consumers are skeptical of advertising, but are less skeptical about information from apparently independent sources (Balasubramanian 1994).

One technique that is similar (but not identical) to masked marketing is the practice of large multinational corporations posing as small businesses in marketing communications. Perhaps the classic example is Bartles & Jaymes wine coolers promoted by E & J Gallo Winery using two folksy advertising spokespeople who purportedly owned the company. At the end of each ad, they would thank consumers for their support. More recently, Philip Morris began selling Dave's discount cigarettes purportedly made by an entrepreneur named Dave who drives a yellow 1957 pickup truck and promises that if you don't like his cigarettes, he will eat them (Hwang 1995). This practice has not attracted recent legal action, although older FTC cases have condemned misrepresentations of a sole proprietorship that was a corporation (*Kodize Process Corp.* 1945) or that a company was a non-profit organization (*Consumer Products of America, Inc. v. FTC* 1968).

Masked marketing essentially is deception about the message being an advertising message as opposed to deception about product performance or attributes in a message that consumers would recognize as paid-for advertising. Both are likely to communicate a false message to consumers that is likely to cause some to purchase the product when they otherwise would not. In the case of masked marketing, the deception concerns the message appearing to be from an unbiased third party rather than the product seller andconsumers letting down their skepticism defenses to become more likely to believe the message. Such conduct satisfies the definition of deception even though it is pursued less often than product-based deception.

C. MASKED MARKETING PRACTICES

Masked marketing—the art of marketing without (appearing to be) marketing includes numerous practices that are proliferating everyday (Petty and Andrews 2008). The practices appear dividable into two broad categories: people that appear unconnected to brand marketing and information presented in a format that appears unconnected to brand marketing. Table Onr suggests that masked marketing techniques can be conceptualized into several *non*-mutually exclusive categories. For example, "posers" can be viewed as a subset of buzz marketing techniques if such fake actors or salespeople promote products before they are available and offer advice to consumers. Likewise, product placement may involve paid "experts" appearing on programs to suggest products or services. Buzz marketing practices via the internet or through e-mail may constitute viral marketing.

Table One	
Masked Marketing Techniques	
Practice	**Description**
Posers	Paid actors or salespeople who pretend to be ordinary people or researchers conducting a survey in order to explain product benefits and give potential consumers the chance to examine, sample or use a product.
Buzz marketing	Recruiting apparently ordinary people to talk about products through free samples or discounts before the product is available to the general public. Often the marketer provides suggestions on what to say and how to approach people about the product.
Viral marketing	Use of e-mail, the internet and text messaging encouraging consumers to talk to or pass on an ad to friends.
Advertainment	Product and advertising placement in television shows, sporting events and video games.
Advertorials; Native Advertising	Advertisements that appear in the same format as media content thereby appearing to be from an independent source. These include commercially prepared television news stories, infomercials that appear to be consumer television shows and print advertisements that appear to factual reports in a magazine or on a website.
Urgent ad-formation	Advertisements that appear in the form of important account information from firm with an existing business relationship, government notices, sweepstakes prize notices or checks that in fact are discount coupons.
Ad-sults from a search engine or other query	Use of invisible metatags by a marketer or the sale of priority by a search engine of the results from a particular query when the results are not identified as biased.
This table and discussion is based on Petty and Andrews (2008).	

I. Posers

Those buzz marketing campaigns that use unidentified agents to talk about products are very similar to campaigns that use paid actors or agents who are instructed to pretend to be ordinary product users and not disclose that they are paid agents. Such actors or agents may be called posers. Vespa scooters hired models to cruise night clubs and cafes on their trendy machines and "talk up" the product when they could. Perhaps the most infamous example is Sony Ericsson's use of 120 actors at popular tourist locations posing as tourists and asking people to take their picture using the phone and taking that opportunity to explain how the camera aspect works and its features (Dobele et al. 2005). This particular incident as well as similar practices were featured on the CBS news show *60 Minutes* ("Undercover Marketing Uncovered" 2004).

Posers also may be celebrities who are paid to promote a product and do so in the course of interviews—a routine situation for celebrities. Kaikati and Kaikati (2004, p. 12) describe three morning talk show interviews with celebrities where they each described medical problems and the product that helped them without disclosing they were paid to promote the product. They note that the talk shows have tightened their screening of interview candidates for such commercial connections. As noted in the next chapter, FTC guidelines suggest that any unexpected commercial connection between an endorser and the company marketing the endorser be disclosed to prevent deception. Otherwise the common implication is that the person speaking is expressing a purely personal (uncompensated) opinion.

Some marketers believe that agent honesty is critical to long term success and paid-for posers are disingenuous (Walker 2004). The FTC has taken occasional action against this sort of practice. For example, Georgetown Publishing mounted a direct mail campaign that appeared to be a personal mailing. Inside was what appeared to be an independent book review torn from a magazine with a small adhesive yellow note attached that appeared handwritten: "Try this. It works! (signed) J." In a consent agreement, Georgetown agreed not to misrepresent that future advertisements are not ads (*Georgetown Publishing House LP, Inc.* 1996). "J" essentially was a poser, albeit one that did not really exist. This also looks like a personalized recommendation, but of course it also is not really personalized at all.

A recent marketing study of the effectiveness of this technique found that it increased response rates when attached to ads making strong claims about the product. Response rates also increased for consumers who believed they could identify the sender (Howard and Kerin 2004).

Traditionally door-to-door salespeople might start off posing as non-sales people, but then reveal their true purpose once they had gained access. The FTC condemned such practices as posers misrepresenting the purpose of the contact, such as only delivering a free prize or booklet (*FTC v. Standard Education Society* 1937) or the pretext of conducting a survey (*Encyclopedia Britannica, Inc. v. FTC* 1979). The FTC also has condemned misrepresentations by sales agents about the organization that employs them (*Goodman v. FTC* 1957). To correct such misrepresentations, the FTC ordered salespeople of offending companies to announce the purpose of their call at initial contact and present the perspective purchaser with a business card identifying them as a sales representative (*Encyclopedia Britannica, Inc. v. FTC* 1979).

The FTC Telemarketing Rule (16 C.F.R. § 310.4(d)(2)) (but not the FTC's Door-to-Door Sales Rule) similarly requires such sellers to promptly identify themselves and that the purpose of the call is to sell goods or services. Moreover, the Can Spam Act of 2003 prohibits deceptive subject lines in commercial e-mail that mislead recipients about the contents of subject matter of the e-mail. However, some state laws, now pre-empted by the federal act, as well as other countries would have required an "ADV" prefix or other notation in the subject line to notify consumers that the message was a commercial message.

As discussed in Chapter Nine, an egregious case of posers involved furnace repair companies whose agents would offer free furnace inspections. The catch was that the "inspectors" would then refuse to re-assemble the furnaces until a service contract was purchased. Consumers were misled into believing these agents were inspectors rather than salespeople. Needless to say the FTC condemned this practice (*Davis Furnace Co.* 1961; *Holland Furnace Co.* 1958).

II. Buzz and Viral Marketing

Buzz and viral marketing include techniques designed to encourage word of mouth promotion by consumers. Dobele et al. (2005) define viral marketing in a similar fashion but limit it to electronic technology such as e-mail, chat rooms, blogs and text messaging. Kaikati and Kaikati (2004, p. 9) provide an even simpler definition of viral marketing: "word of mouth via a digital platform." In either case, the goal is to encourage conversation about the product. Estimates place the amount of money being spent on buzz marketing at $40 to $60 million in 2004 up 100% from the prior year (Creamer 2005). *Advertising Age* estimates industry size to be between $100 and $150 million (Horowitz 2005).

These practices range from simply offering a trendy product, such as Chrysler's PT Cruiser to Miami rental car companies to get consumers to rent and hopefully talk to others about their experience to practices that encourage such talking, perhaps through rewards, and/or provide "talking points." One advantage of viral marketing is that video or audio files can be sent to opinion leaders hoping they will resend them to others. Lee Jeans sent 200,000 male Web surfers amateurish video clips from three purportedly amateur film makers who turned out to be characters in an upcoming video game. But to be admitted, players had to get product codes from Lee products. Over 100,000 people responded to the website opening and Lee sales increased 20% (Khermouch and Green 2001). A second advantage of technology in viral marketing is that agents can appear in more places virtually. They can be in chat rooms, on bulletin boards and blogs, sending e-mail or text messages to friends.

When buzz agents are involved, these programs typically provide suggestions to agents about product selling points and general communication to consumers. However, they typically don't require adherence to a script or particular program. Agents enjoy being part of an elite group so that they are among the first to try new products. They also appreciate receiving the product or a discount on it. They enjoy being the first to tell others about a new product and believe they are giving their honest opinion. Programs encourage them to provide feedback to the company (Walker 2004).

More organized programs recruit a large continuing group of thought leaders. These programs become controversial when they offer rewards to agents, but don't require that they disclose this commercial connection. Procter & Gamble's group, Tremor, was featured in a recent complaint to the Federal Trade Commission (FTC) by Commercial Alert (2005) for inadequate disclosure to parents involving buzz marketing activities using teens and children. In contrast, BzzAgent found their campaigns were more effective when agents revealed that they were working for a particular client (Creamer 2005). The Word of Mouth Marketing Association (WOMMA) recommends disclosure in its new draft code of ethics available at https://womma.org/ethics/womma-code-of-ethics/. In addition, a recent study notes that important outcome measures, such as credibility, inquiry, use, purchase, and pass-along communication, were not negatively affected by a buzz agent disclosing their affiliation (Carl 2006).

III. Advertainment

Advertainment involves the inclusion of products or advertising in various forms of entertainment. In the case of products, consumers may not realize they are included in order to achieve a marketing effect. In the case of advertising, consumers may recognize the advertisements as such but believe they are included for realism or some other non-marketing purpose. For example, in November 2005, Shockwave.com is believed to be among the first companies to announce programs for advertisers who wish to insert ads into online video games. Shockwave.com hosts more than 200 games and claims over 20 million visitors monthly to its website. It advertising program will measure impressions for each ad. The ads will be incorporated into the game format such as billboard ads around a virtual skate park in a skateboarding game. Players will be aware that the video ads are mimicking real world ads but involvement in the game should prevent their direct involvement with the ads and actively processing them as advertisements. Video game advertising was estimated at $186 million in 2005 and was expected to reach $875 million by 2008 (Vranica 2005). An empirical study found that game players remember 25–30% of the brands immediately after playing and still remembered 10–15% of the brands five months later (Nelson 2002).

Similarly, celebrities appear on interview programs and tout particular products but don't disclose they are paid for doing so are not only posers but inserting a commercial message into that particular entertainment vehicle. "Experts" who also are paid to pitch products on TV news and interview shows introduce a paid-for selling message into what is supposed to be an objective news or interview show (Bandler 2005).

The traditional product placement involves the placement of products without an explicit selling message rather than ads in television shows. The use of Reese's Pieces in the movie "ET—the Extraterrestrial" is a classic example where (particularly younger) viewers may recognize the brand but not the selling intent behind the placement.

More recently, products do more than simply appear in a show or movie. The TV show "Extreme Makeover" always uses Sears appliances, mentioned by name, in its re-built houses. The character Gabrielle got a job promoting Buick automobiles on "Desperate Housewives." Sponsors of "The Apprentice" develop episode-long challenges featuring their brands and products. In 2004, the value of product or brand name placements increased by 46% over 2003 to $1.88 billion (Moore 2005). Nielsen Media Research reports that in the first quarter of 2005, the ten TV programs with the most product placements accounted for nearly 13,000 placements—more than half of the total placements in 2004 (Enright 2005). Product placements are expected to be used in about 75% of price time network television shows and have become part of the marketing mix for over 1000 U.S. brands (Russell and Stern 2006).

Similarly, for decades, occasional popular songs have mentioned brand names in the lyrics. However, rap music tends to do so with greater frequency. In 2003, Mercedes was the most popular brand with 112 musical mentions. This led to advertisers either seeking to pay for mention in a song or sponsoring a group after it had developed a song that included a brand mention (Kaikati and Kaikati 2004, p. 15). Concert sponsorship and brand advertising on a CD are obviously advertising, but being paid to include a brand name in lyrics or showing the branded product in the music video is typically not disclosed. So like product placements in movies and television programming, consumers recognize the brands but can't distinguish purely artistic mentions from paid-for commercial mentions. Live theater including the Radio City Christmas Spectacular also is looking for paid product placements to subsidize the costs of production, estimated between $10–$15 million per show (Petrecca 2006).

One recent study compared the effectiveness of product mention by a character within the storyline of a television program versus a celebrity product "plug" within a talk show (Roehm, Roehm and Boone 2004). The study results suggested that that the two types of product mentions were stored differently in memory with the celebrity plug being remembered by product category but the storyline use being stored with memory about the television show. The authors conclude that for marketers wishing to stimulate future purchases of their brand, the celebrity plug may be more useful than the character mention of the brand. Another study suggests that a product's connection to characters in a television show and the viewer's relationship with the characters also influence viewers' attitudes toward products placed in situation comedy television shows (Russell and Stern 2006). A third study in Brazil, suggests that viewers may not even assign promotional meanings to products placed in television soap operas (La Pastina 2001).

The Federal Communications Commission regulates disclosure of product placements in television and radio. In a 2005 speech, FCC Commissioner Adelstein (2005, p. 7) noted that current FCC regulations require disclosure of paid product placements. Indeed the FCC has been considering modifying the rules which some suggest do not reflect marketplace reality. For example, Jacobson and Mazur (1993, p. 72) point out that placement agencies typically donate merchandise to TV shows free of charge (so it is not paid product placement) and make money from payments by the marketers. Adelstein argued for a clear and prominent disclosure of paid product placements.

General research on televised ad disclosures indicates that although one-fourth of all national television commercials contain disclosures, none adhered to all of the clear and conspicuous standards (CCS) for such disclosures (Hoy and Andrews 2004). They also found that adherence to most of the CCS elements (dual modality, type size, contrast, etc.) has declined or remained unchanged over time. Aside from the coverage of CCS elements, Commissioner Adelstein's idea is to require a clearer and more prominent placement at the end of programs that would carry sponsorship information on-screen for at least four seconds and for 4% of the screen height—similar to that for current political ad disclosures (Teinowitz 2005a).

IV. Advertorials and Native Advertising

Native advertising and advertorials are efforts by marketers to make advertising look like some other form of communication/ entertainment. For example, Mercedes Benz produced what appeared to be a preview for an action movie that was shown with coming attractions in British movie theaters. The movie trailer ended, as many do, with the suggestion to visit a particular website. Only when visiting the website did consumers learn there was no movie, but the trailer was an advertisement for Mercedes Benz (Kaikati and Kaikati 2004, p. 13).

A more traditional example of blurring the line between media content and promotion is the two related struggles of magazine publishers. First, for over a century, advertisers have sought to place "Reading Notices" that look like magazine content rather than or in addition to regular advertisements (Petty 2013). Second, advertisers would try to get magazines to write (favorable) articles about their products in exchange for purchasing advertising in the magazine, ideally seeking placement next to the article.

The American Society of Magazine Editors has guidelines that recommend against placing ads next to related editorial material in any way that suggests endorsement. These guidelines also state that ads that look like editorial content should be avoided and yet, some ads deliberately mimic editorial content of particular magazines (Steinberg and Bandler 2004). Perhaps the most extreme example of blending editorial content and advertising are the some 116,000 custom "magazines" now published by marketers to tout their wares such as B magazine published by Bloomingdales (Collins 2004).

A similar practice with a long history is direct mail solicitations designed to look like personal mail. These may appear as greeting cards or other personal content with an apparent handwritten address and a postage stamp rather than postal meter cancellation (Abelson 2005). The hope is that potential consumers will open the mail and some will be interested in the advertising content. As discussed below, direct marketers also may try to make direct mail advertising look like an important message or a check from the government or an important private party.

Perhaps the most controversial examples of advertainment involve products and media directed at children. In the 1941, an early

Superman comic book included a story where Superman created the "Krypto Ray Gun"—essentially an advertisement for a recently created toy (Gordon 1998). Similarly in the 1960s, Captain Kangaroo was paid to use a portion of his children's show to explain the features of the latest Schwinn bicycles. He also appears as the Schwinn spokesperson in print advertising. Today, children's entertainment is often created in conjunction with merchandise (Anson 1984), so it is difficult to distinguish between the two.

Modern guidelines for advertising to children under 12 years old discourage the use of entertainment characters in advertising immediately adjacent to the entertainment content (http://www.caru.org/guidelines/guidelines.pdf). The Children's Advertising Review Unit (CARU) of the National Advertising Review Council is currently reviewing these guidelines and considering revisions in such areas as product placement (especially of food products) within children's programming, cartoon characters on food packages, buzz marketing, and "advergaming" (advertising-based video games) aimed at children (Menin 2005; Teinowitz 2005b). Such efforts aimed at children could also come under the scrutiny of the FTC's unfairness policy, although such actions are rarer than those brought under deception.

In the case of advertainment or advertorials directed at adults, the FTC pursued several early television infomercials that did not disclose their commercial nature and often appeared to be interrupted by advertising messages so as to appear to be a program rather than a marketing message (Jacobson and Mazur 1995, pp. 59–62). In 2004, the FTC again took action against two infomercials that appeared as independent TV programs with only brief disclosures at the beginning and end that this was a "paid advertisement" (Harbour 2005). These infomercials also included "guest" doctors who were principals in the marketing firm, apparently independent "viewer" questions and asked viewers to mention the name of the show to receive a discount when calling to order. These guests and viewers qualify as posers as discussed above.

In addition as discussed under posers, the FTC has condemned ads that appear to be independent magazine articles (*Georgetown Publishing House LP, Inc.* 1996). In *Braswell et al.* (2006), the FTC found false and misleading dietary supplement claims touting medical and scientific "breakthroughs" targeting the elderly and made through the "Journal of Longevity," a direct mail ad purporting to be a health information magazine. Similarly, the FCC has required disclosure for the source of video news releases. The FTC seems mostly likely to pursue native advertising and advertorials for being in a misleading format when the product-related advertising claims also are deceptive.

The most current iteration of this practice is called Native Advertising. In December 2015, the FTC issued its Enforcement Policy Statement on Deceptive Formatted Advertisements that also includes references to its other statements including its Endorsement Guides. The statement re-affirms the FTC's position that whether a message is an advertisement is material to consumers and it will examine the overall net impression of a message when deciding whether its format is deceptive. To avoid deceiving consumers, advertising should clearly and conspicuously disclose itself as such at the beginning of the message.

The FTC statement claims it's involvement with disguised advertising dates back to 1967, but as noted above, the FTC's involvement with same issue involving disguised salespeople dates back even earlier. Indeed, this issue dates back over a century to newspapers, magazines and the U.S. Postal Service (Petty 2013).

V. Urgent Ad-Formation

Advertising that looks like important or urgent information can take several forms: an important notice about the consumer's financial or service account, a notice from what appears to be an official government source, a notice of winning a sweepstakes prize or what appears to be a check, but is in reality is a discount coupon. One approach that seems currently popular with credit card companies is to send notices with "important information about your account" that are nothing more than "checks" that may be used to access the line of credit. Similar practices are used in telemarketing and e-mail (Direct Marketing Association 2005). With the advent of internet use, some advertisers have tried to make pop-up advertising look like an official system warning. All of these approaches attempt to disguise advertising or sales messages as another form of communication likely to appear important to consumers.

The NAD condemns the use of ads disguised as system warnings and has stated broadly that advertisers have an obligation to present their product claims in a form that consumers will recognize as advertising (*Bonzi.com Software* 2001). Early FTC cases also have condemned deceptive notices that appear to be checks (*United States v. Reader's Digest Association* 1981) or prize awards (*National Housewares, Inc.* 1977). One ambitious company made its checks appear to be Government issued with a return address of "Office of the Treasurer, Accounting Division" (*A.A. Friedman Co.,* 1968).

VI. Ad-Sults from a Query

The internet approximation of urgent information is search results. Sellers on the internet can adopt at least two tactics to improve their search rankings. First, they can include metatags—language such as a rival brand name that is repeatedly placed on websites. Metatags may be invisible to users but still read by search engines and the repeated use on a website allows the internet seller to improve its rank ordering in the search results. It might even be ranked above the brand owner thereby misdirecting consumers. Search engines try to design their search algorithms to avoid much emphasis on repeated metatags.

Lawsuits, particularly in the U.S. have examined the use of someone else's trademark as a metatag. Most courts found that invisible metatags did not cause consumer confusion because they could not been seen by potential customers. In addition, even if customers mistakenly went to the wrong site, they could quickly return to the search results page and select a different result. Internet users are used to not getting the correct search result on the first try. The Ninth Circuit, however, recognizes a particular form of confusion called initial interest confusion that could amount to actionable trademark infringement even if no long term source confusion resulted. Once directed to the incorrect website, the consumer may decide to use it instead of the one it was originally seeking thereby injuring the trademark owner (*Brookfield Communications v. West Coast Entertainment Corporation* 1999). This issue is discussed in Chapter Seventeen under a form of Judo Brand Diversion called misdirection.

Second, most search engines allow advertisers to bid for the right to have particular triggering words, called keywords by Google, trigger an advertisement on the search result page. Internet users seldom go beyond the first page of search results so appearing on that page can have a positive impact on sales. Since search engines make money on each key word they sell, they encourage this practice.

To avoid consumer confusion regarding search results and search-triggered paid for advertising, the FTC warned search engine firms that they should clearly distinguish results that are compensated from the uncompensated natural search results (Kopytoff 2002). Google does this by identifying paid for search results as "sponsored links" and listing them separately from search results.

D. GENERAL LEGAL AND REGULATORY ISSUES

Covert marketing is criticized by consumer groups and various industries are considering greater self-regulation (Kaikati and Kaikati 2004). However, as this chapter demonstrates, legal precedent on many of these practices already exists. This legal authority suggests two fundamental legal issues that must be considered by managers of masked marketing campaigns. First, when does the commercial connection between the messenger and the message sponsor become sufficiently significant that is would be misleading to consumers not to disclose the connection? Second, when does the commercial connection lead to questions about whether the messenger's statement is genuine? Masked marketers also must be concerned not to violate regulatory requirements for particular modes of communication. Each of these issues is discussed in turn.

I. Disclosure of the Commercial Connection

Every marketer's dream is to have a product or advertising campaign of such interest to consumers that everyone is talking about it. Of course, substantial sales also are desired. While motivating people to talk about a product is the goal of buzz marketing, and some other forms of covert marketing, that goal is not sufficient to raise legal concerns. At the lowest level of encouragement, the marketer merely sells or advertises the product and word-of-mouth spontaneously develops. There is not any legal issue since other consumers would expect to hear from their friends about products their friends found exciting.

Similarly, if marketers only encourage word-of-mouth advertising, a commercial connection (beyond the product sale) between enthusiastic consumers and the marketer does not exist. So asking consumers who like the product to tell their friends or encouraging everyone to sing the jingle does not raise the issue of an unexpected commercial connection.

In contrast, situations where people are hired to act as promotion agents but appear as ordinary consumers are likely to be deceptive under various cases that condemn the disguise of paid for marketing messages discussed above. Although Sony-Ericsson was not pursued for its phony tourist campaign (other than by *60 Minutes*), the law appears to require identification of paid marketing agents as such. The

FTC Guides "Concerning the Use of Endorsements and Testimonials in Advertising" clearly state that endorsements represented directly or by implication to be actual consumers should be from actual consumers. Otherwise the marketer should disclose the people are not actual consumers (16 C.F.R. § 255.2(b)). Similarly, case law has condemned the use of endorsements by apparently independent expert organizations, when the organization is not actually independent (*Gynex Corp. v. Dilex Inst. of Feminine Hygiene* 1936).

While FTC Guides are not binding statements of law like statutes or regulations, there is no reason why this principle should not apply to personal interactions with purported consumers as well as testimonials in advertising. This is particularly true because testimonials are contained within identified marketing communications and interactions with purported consumers may occur in a context that suggests the interaction is spontaneous and not sponsored by a marketer making deception more likely.

The question in the middle of these two extremes is the case of relatively small payments or rewards—when must the commercial connection be disclosed? In 1932, the Second Circuit Court of Appeals held that consumers expect that celebrities are paid for testimonials that appear in advertising so that no disclosure of that commercial connection is required (*Northam Warren Corp. v. FTC* 1932). The FTC Guides recommend that material connections between endorsers and sellers be disclosed if not reasonably expected as in the case of celebrity endorsements. The Better Business Bureau Code of Advertising similarly recommends that endorsers with a pecuniary interest in the company should be disclosed (Better Business Bureaus 2005, sec. 15). As noted above, the FTC has recently challenged infomercials that don't disclose that an expert endorser was a company officer and that "consumers" were friends or family members (*Buckingham Productions, Inc.* 1986).

This suggests that small rewards such as discounts and early product trial may not be sufficiently significant to buzz agents to require disclosure of the commercial connection. In contrast, company ownership or a commission on sales presumably would require disclosure of the agent's interest. The question of where to draw the line between small and significant commercial interests depends on the point at which consumers would believe the agent might be biased in his or her recommendations. The safest course is that advocated by BzzAgent, WOMMA, and Carl (2006)—disclosure of sponsorship by the marketer.

II. Genuineness of Statements

As noted in Chapter 7, the FTC Guides (16 C.F.R. § 255.1(a)) request that the opinions or statements made in the ad reflect the honest opinions and beliefs of the endorser. For example, endorsers who claim that they have used the product must have used the product (16 C.F.R. § 255.1(b)). FTC consent agreements have required endorsers to make a reasonable inquiry into the truth of the claims and occasional private lawsuits have held celebrities financially liable for negligence in making misleading claims when the advertiser can't be located or is in bankruptcy (Kertz and Ohanian 1991). However, ordinary consumers have not been held to similar requirements.

FTC Guides also suggest that advertisers should not use endorsements out of context and may not create an advertisement out of consumer endorsements that communicates statements of fact about product attributes or performance in order to avoid the requirement to have substantiation to support such claims. Advertisers must still have a reasonable basis to support factual claims they make in advertising (16 C.F.R. § 255.2) or any form of marketing communication.

The question raised by masked marketing is the reverse—rather than marketers creating ads from testimonials, for masked marketing marketers create testimonials that appear not to be ads. Since these efforts are not clearly marketing communications, the requirement of genuineness of the belief if the statements made by marketing agents should be even more compelling in this context.

Thus, prudent stealth marketers should caution their agents to state genuinely-held opinions. If they are encouraged to repeat marketer-based factual product claims, then the agent should identify those facts as coming from the marketer. Obviously, masked marketers, like any other marketer, should be held liable for any deceptive or unsubstantiated factual claims that it caused to be used in its covert marketing activities.

Marketers of durable products that have sales agents prone to exaggeration often include a clause in the sales contract limiting product representations and warranties to those expressed in the contract and disavowing any contrary statements made by sales agents. In the U.S. such contract provisions, if clear and conspicuous, are typically enforced. However in Europe, they are considered unfair in consumer contracts and therefore are unenforceable (Petty and Hamilton 2004). This contractual technique would be advisable for U.S. covert marketers who fear their marketing efforts may communicate messages that are untrue or unsubstantiated.

III. Regulation of Particular Marketing Methods

Stealth marketers need to be aware of regulations upon particular communication methods (discussed in Chapter Nine) they may use in their covert marketing campaigns. For example, the FTC Door-to-Door Sales Cooling Off Rule (16 C.F.R.§ 429) requires that sellers provide a three day cooling off period for sales made outside the ordinary place of business and that their sales agents inform consumers about the period and how to exercise their right to cancel the transaction.

At first glance, this would not appear to apply to buzz marketing because the agents don't consummate the sales; that is, they merely suggest consumers "check out" the product. Since most products may be searched for and purchased using the internet, it is less necessary that agents close the sale as it once might have been. However, in the case where a buzz agent shows the consumer how to order the product on the consumer's computer, the requirements of the rule would appear to be satisfied. Thus, the marketer would be liable for financial penalties for failing to provide information on how to use the three day cancellation period.

Similarly, a buzz agent who telephoned a friend to "talk up" a product would have to follow the telemarketing laws just as one who e-mailed friends would have to follow the rules on commercial e-mailing. For telemarketing, a number of U.S. states have "get-to-the-point" laws requiring callers to identify their purpose within a short period of time. A few states even have "cooling off" periods for telephone-solicited sales as in Europe (Cain 1994). As noted above, the FTC Telemarketing Rule (16 C.F.R. § 310.4(d)(2)) requires that sales calls be identified. However, if it is not clear whether these rules would apply to calls that merely "talk up" a product without seeking to close the sale.

Under federal law, telephone solicitations only may occur between the hours of 8:00 a.m. and 9:00 p.m. and may not be harassing by repeat calls (16 C.F.R. § 310). Solicitations to cellular phones are prohibited without permission (47 C.F.R. § 64; Cain 1996). Activities of buzz agents might easily violate these provisions. Furthermore, many states and now the FTC offer a do-not-call list which marketers are required to check before making telemarketing calls, unless they have a pre-existing relationship with the customer. Perhaps buzz agents who call their friends will be able to claim a pre-existing relationship even if they violate other telemarketing rules.

A court of appeals in Arizona has held that the use of an automatic dialing system to send commercial text messages to cell phones violates the Telephone Consumer Protection Act (*Joffe v. Acacia Mortgage Corp.* 2005). The court noted that the Can Spam Act of 2003 may also apply to cell phone text messaging (Petty 2003). The Can Spam Act allows marketers to send unsolicited commercial e-mail, but requires that it not have misleading header or subject lines, must identify itself as a commercial message and must give consumers a method for opting out of receiving e-mail messages from the same source. The law also prohibits e-mail address harvesting from websites (typically using robot crawlers), relaying commercial e-mails through other computers without permission, and using programs to generate possible e-mail addresses by combining popular names with e-mail locations (15 U.S.C. § 7701). Viral marketers that rely on e-mail communications need to make sure their agents don't run afoul of these laws. Use of a misleading subject line and lack of notification on how to stop future commercial e-mails are two requirements that agents are likely to violate.

Most European countries, including Austria, Belgium, Czech Republic, Denmark, Estonia, Finland, Germany, Greece, Hungary, Italy, Latvia, Lithuania, Luxembourg, Poland, Portugal, Slovakia, Spain, and Sweden have general prohibitions against disguising advertising as some other form of communication. Several of these such as Austria, Denmark, Finland, Greece, Hungary, Italy, also have media-specific rules on such practices. For example, Denmark has condemned contractual offers that appear to be invoices and newspaper advertising that conceals the marketer's location by using a Post Office box. France requires newspaper ads be identified as such if they might be mistaken for content. Italy prohibited a newspaper subscription contract from appearing as an "official letter" (Henning-Bodeweg 2006).

E. CONCLUSION

Of the many methods of connecting with consumers, masked marketing may be the most troubling. Although buzz and viral marketing currently are touted as the latest methods for addressing the twin problems of consumer skepticism and consumer overload with marketing communications (e.g., clutter), this chapter makes it evident that masked marketing has been practiced for most of the 20th century, if not longer. In some cases, legal and regulatory requirements are clear. Marketing messages must not be disguised as third-party opinion or information and those promoting products must make it clear if they are getting paid to do so (or own the marketing company), if these facts are not well understood by consumers.

Unfortunately, the practice of marketing advances at a pace far faster than that of marketing regulation. For this reason, brand marketers must rely upon existing laws concerning testimonials, personal selling, telemarketing and commercial e-mail to address modern practices that while similar are also somewhat different. Careful analysis of the principles expressed in these laws provides reasonable guidance at this point for modern masked marketing practices.

CHAPTER 12

Connection: Secondary Brand Associations and Endorsements

A. INTRODUCTION

Kevin Lane Keller (2005) identifies three drivers of brand equity. The most important is the product or service itself and related marketing activities and programs. The second driver is the portfolio of brand elements or identifiers such as names, logos, slogans, packaging, etc. These are created and typically controlled by the brand owner and are discussed in the first seven chapters of this book. The third driver according to Keller is what he calls secondary brand associations (SBAs). SBAs are links between brands and other entities that have pre-existing perceived qualities or attributes in the minds of consumers such as geographic regions, celebrity endorsers, sporting events and links with other brands—ingredients, channels, etc. SBAs are one of several methods for establishing a connection between the brand and the customer.

Keller (2005) suggests three factors that determine how much leverage will result from SBAs: (1) consumer knowledge of the linked-to entity or association, (2) the meaningfulness of consumer knowledge of the association and, (3) the transferability of consumer knowledge of the associational target to the particular brand. An entity with congruent associations might easily transfer them to a brand, but an entity with incongruent associations would probably not transfer those associations as readily. Nonetheless, he argues that sometimes a brand might want to accept the struggle of a more difficult association transfer because the association will be important to future brand equity once the association is established.

Table One

Examples of Secondary Brand Associations of Increasing Strength

→

Type/Strength	Vague	Descriptive	Endorse/Cert.	Identity
People	Spokespeople	Identify celebrity users	People/experts who recommend brand	Celebrity branded product lines
Other Brands (Judo Brand Diversion, Chs. 14–17)	Vague comparison, e.g., "Compare with"	"Made with" Specific comparison	"Certified by" "Recommended or approved by"	Licensed brand extension
Product	Non-specific product name similarity	Comparison	Performance certified	Satisfies government or industry standard
Places	Regional suggestion, e.g., Häagen-Dazs, or Bermuda shorts	Country of origin or design	Certified location, e.g., Florida oranges	Government owned or operated
Causes/Events	Advertising related to cause or event	One of many sponsors	Official sponsor	Purchase of naming rights

Petty (2006) proposes a fourth leverage factor: the strength of the association. A well-known company/brand merely listed as a client/customer or a celebrity who is an advertising spokesperson presumably should transfer less of his or her perceived qualities to the advertised brand than a company/brand or celebrity who affirmatively endorses the advertised brand. Associational strength can be roughly divided into four categories from weak to strong: vague associations, descriptive associations, endorsement or certification associations, and at least in some cases identity associations. The latter category allows a brand to claim congruency with an SBA even beyond certification. Examples of Keller's types of SBAs categorized by strength are illustrated in Table One.

Marketing managers must be able to manage the legal issues concerning SBAs. These legal issues are discussed generally in the next section and then discussed more specifically while examining each level of association strength in more detail.

B. LEGAL BACKGROUND

As discussed in Chapter Two, trademark law generally disallows protection of generic or purely descriptive terms. Such words must be available for everyone to use in commerce. For example the Trademark Trial and Appeal Board, denied Remington Products registration as an ordinary trademark for its slogan "Proudly Made in the U.S.A." for electric shavers because the slogan only described the products, but did not identify the company source of the products to consumers (*In re Remington Products, Inc.* 1987). Of course denying registration doesn't mean Remington can't continue using the slogan, it just means that others may use it as well so it has no exclusive right.

In addition, as noted in Chapter Five and discussed further in Chapter Fifteen, even valid descriptive trademarks are limited in their protection from unauthorized imitation by the concept of descriptive fair use. Other firms may use wording somewhat similar to the descriptive trademark if that language fairly describes the other product and if the description is not used as a trademark, merely as a descriptive promotion. For example, firms other than Remington could still indicate that were proud their products were produced in the U.S.

Thus, the first question when examining potential SBAs is whether any sort of permission or authorization is needed for an association. For example, permission to use the product category name to accurately describe a product is generally not needed, unless somehow protected as discussed in Chapter Six. Similarly, permission to say the product satisfied a particular product or industry standard or the producer is a member of a particular trade association may be needed if the standard or association name is trademarked such as REALTOR® which is the registered trademark of the NATIONAL ASSOCIATION OF REALTORS® (the generic term is real estate agent).

While brand marketers cannot prevent all others from using generic or descriptive terms, to some degree they can limit the use of some terms by establishing a collective or certification trademark as noted for product category labels in Chapter Six. Both types of marks must be available for use on qualified goods and services, but to some degree both also may be used to limit which firms may use descriptive terms beyond category labels.

To review from Chapter Six, collective marks require membership in the mark-owning organization which may only require production of a particular product, perhaps in a particular location (e.g., Florida Oranges) and certification marks must be licensed for use to qualifying third parties. Certification marks may certify material content or mode of manufacture as well as quality, accuracy or other characteristics (15 U.S.C. § 1127). If a certifying organization is not able to legitimately exercise control over a descriptive mark or indiscriminately refuses to certify goods or services that satisfy the certification standard, the mark may be cancelled (15 U.S.C. § 1064(5)). Because they may certify a certain level of quality, certification marks may provide a stronger association than a mere "membership" (collective) mark. However, membership marks establishing production by firms with union workers for example may still be quite compelling to large numbers of consumers.

Collective and certification marks are important for a new brand seeking to establish an SBA for two reasons. A brand will likely want to use collective and certification marks to establish associations different from those created by its brand name. Since purely descriptive brand names are usually not available for protection as a trademark, descriptive collective or certification marks can provide the desired association.

The use of descriptive terms may be authorized by collective or certification marks or as noted in Chapter Six by government regulation. For example, until 2002, the term "organic" was largely unregulated in the U.S. (Petty 2015). Since that time U.S. Department of Agriculture regulations allow the use of three terms: "100 percent organic" (for foods containing only organically produced ingredients other than water and salt), "Organic" or "USDA Organic" (for foods with at least 95% organically produced ingredients) and "Made with organic ingredients" (for foods containing at least 70% organically produced ingredients).

Similarly, the U.S. Food and Drug Administration (FDA) recommends that "fresh" not be used to describe any food that has been subject to hear or chemical processing. In the early 1990s, it pursued several food advertisers for using the term in violation of its guideline (Chen 1992). The Food and Drug Administration is currently seeking comments on whether it should establish some sort of regulation or guidance defining how the term "natural" should apply to food products.

Such government regulations simultaneously authorize some uses of the regulated term while denying other uses. In essence, the regulations are declaring that disallowed uses are deceptive. This is the second legal issue brand marketers must consider—is the use of a particular term generally deceptive or misdescriptive of the product or service under trademark law? For example AMERICAN GIRL was registered as a trademark for shoes because the name indicated the target market rather than the country of origin for the shoes. However, "American Beauty" was not allowed registration for sewing machines from Japan because that name would indicate country of origin to consumers. Of course, if a product is advertised it was "Made in

America," it would have to satisfy the FTC Enforcement Policy Statement on U.S. Origin Claims (Federal Trade Commission 1997).

C. VAGUE ASSOCIATIONS

The simplest association is one that suggests nothing more than a vague association with the brand. For example, a brand may sponsor a sporting or charitable event or a celebrity may agree to be an advertising spokesperson who appears in advertising but is not identified by name. While some consumers may perceive a stronger association such as an endorsement, consumers also are used to seeing an explicit endorsement if one is intended.

The primary legal issue for vague associations is determining whether anyone's permission is needed and obtaining needed permission (through a licensing contract) to use the name and other brand identifiers of the associational target. For example, a retailer can accurately promote the brands that it carries and the seller of refurbished or used goods can identify the original brand of those goods without the brand owner's permission. However, dealers should be careful not to falsely imply they are official or authorized dealers. Some case law suggests that the use of the logo rather than just the name may imply that a dealer is official or authorized.

Similarly, a firm can truthfully identify its clients or customers by name so long as use of the client/customer name doesn't imply "origin, sponsorship or approval or affiliation, connection or association" under the trademark laws. A careful disclaimer of approval, affiliation or sponsorship might help ease concerns and the advertiser must be careful to be factually accurate. For example, a simple list of clients should not include firms that were merely solicited.

Traditionally in most countries, a business could use its location in its brand name and the business owner could use his or her own name in their business even if it was similar to someone else's name. In addition a product category such as Bermuda Shorts may evoke the country of Bermuda but not suggest that all Bermuda Shorts are produced in Bermuda (just like all Danish pastry is not made in Denmark). However, this traditional "right" has been reduced over time to exclude cases where the name use might cause consumer confusion about the source of the goods or whether they were endorsed or sponsored by a similarly named firm or celebrity.

This exception most often comes into play when a use is perceived as bad faith in the U.S. or contrary to honest business practices in the E.U. For example, a U.S. court did not allow the brother of Ernest and Julio Gallo to use the Gallo name on retail packages of cheese for fear that consumers would falsely associate the cheese with the winery because cheese is often served with wine (*E. & J. Gallo Winery v. Gallo Cattle Co.* 1992).

Similarly, as discussed in the next chapter in most countries the law recognizes the rights of celebrities to control the commercial use of their name or likeness and so people whose names happen to be identical to a celebrity's famous name, generally may not use that name in their business without permission or in some cases a clear disclaimer of association with the celebrity. One exception to this rule is the United Kingdom, which has been slower to recognize celebrity rights. The U.K. does protect celebrities that have registered their name or picture as a trademark and also protects celebrities from implied endorsements. Otherwise, however, U.K. law is not sympathetic to the argument that using a celebrity's name in advertising or even as part of a product name suggests to consumers that the celebrity or his estate has approved of the use (Alcock et al. 2003).

Finally, as discussed in Chapter Sixteen, marketers often make vague mention of other products, sponsorship opportunities or brands hoping to avoid a false suggestion of an actual association. One well-known example is ambush marketing where marketers tie their brand to a sports event, e.g., "the big game" (or perhaps a charity or trade show) without explicitly identifying the target or claiming any sort of formal relationship with it.

D. DESCRIPTIONS

Descriptive terms are not available for trademark protection so that such terms are available for use by all the brands for which the description is accurate. As noted in Chapter Three, deceptively descriptive names may not be registered under U.S. law (15 U.S.C. § 1052(e)). This includes geographically descriptive names that falsely suggest a particular geographic origin. For example, Durango chewing tobacco, Manhattan cookies and Rodeo Drive perfume all were denied registration because consumers might falsely believe the marks were geographically descriptive (Bendekgey and Mead 1992).

In contrast, some names with geographic terms do not falsely suggest geographic origin and may therefore be registered such as Nantucket men's wear, Tapatio hot sauce and Venice Maid canned food. None of these locations are known for these products, so the names are arbitrary in the minds of consumers like Apple computers or Camel cigarettes. One of the more curious cases involves Häagen-Dazs suing Frusen Glädjé for copying its "unique Scandinavian marketing theme." The court refused to order a preliminary injunction. It noted that both products were made in the U.S., so that the first had "unclean hands" and therefore could not complain about the second being deceptive (*Häagen-Dazs, Inc. v. Frusen Glädjé, Ltd.* 1980).

As noted in Chapter Six, U.S. law considers some names that sound geographically descriptive to be generic—describing a category of goods rather than goods from a specific source. However Europe is more protective of what it calls geographical indications (GIs). The issue of geographic descriptions is important because numerous marketing studies suggest that country of origin cues generally have a positive effect on consumer perceptions of product quality/reliability and a smaller but still positive effect on purchase intentions (Peterson and Jolibert 1995). It is therefore not surprising that the U.S. and many other countries require imported products to disclose the secondary brand association of their country of origin somewhere on the product or package. U.S. law further requires that U.S. and foreign content must be disclosed on automobiles, textile, wool and fur products and that imported goods be marked with their foreign country of origin.

As noted above, products may proclaim "Made in the USA" only if all or virtually all of their parts and processing are of U.S. origin (Federal Trade Commission 1997). In one court decision, a Louisiana statute that prohibited use of the term "Cajun" on food that was not produced in Louisiana was held to violate the First Amendment in part because the country of origin for imported seafood was clearly disclosed thereby making deception unlikely (*Piazza's Seafood World, LLC v. Odom* 2006).

Geographically descriptive terms are not the only terms whose use is regulated by the government. As discussed above, "organic" and "fresh" are regulated for food and "natural" is the subject of several class action lawsuits and may soon be regulated by the FDA (Petty 2015). Outside the area of food, the U.S. Indian Arts and Crafts Act (25 U.S.C. § 305) prohibits the sale of goods in a manner that falsely suggests the goods are Indian products. At a minimum, this statute requires that goods that appear to be Native American, such as some forms of jewelry, or are sold with indicia of Native American origin such as tribal names or symbols must disclaim any Native American origin or association (*Native American Arts, Inc. v. Waldron Corp.* 2005).

Another form of descriptive association is the use of ingredient brands such as TIDE with DOWNY, CREST with SCOPE and PUFFS with VICKS (Sewell 2007). Studies suggest that using a well-known ingredient brand can be more effective than developing a new brand for an ingredient, particularly when the host brand is seeking to create a brand extension that has a new product attribute as opposed to simply replacing an existing product attribute with a branded ingredient (Kalpesh & Keller 2002). Again obtaining permission from the ingredient brand owner is the safest approach, but truthful identification of a branded ingredient without permission is often allowed if there is no suggestion of authorization as discussed in Chapters Fifteen and Sixteen. Licensing agreements often contain both restrictions and mandates on how the ingredient brand should be promoted as discussed at the end of this chapter.

E. ENDORSEMENTS AND CERTIFICATIONS

The line between descriptive associations and those that endorse or certify a particular level of quality or performance is hazy. Ingredient brands often appear to be as much an endorsement or certification as a description. Similarly, the use of government regulated descriptive terms such as "organic" or "fresh" would appear to be certification that the foods making this association have met the standards. Finally technology standards such as DOLBY and JAVA are often protected by a trademark or certification mark. As discussed in Chapter Six, Fuji Film was able to trademark DPOF (Digital Print Order Format) for digital cameras and printers because it would distinguish goods using the format from those that did not and that such goods were from Fuji or licensed by it to use the mark (*Fuji Film Co.* 2006).

Endorsement/certification SBAs are stronger than vague associations and descriptions because they promise to consumers that a product or service has met certain standards or will perform in a specific way. Celebrity or expert endorsers and consumer testimonials may make these promises explicitly. A brand also may use a certification mark or claim that it has received an award or high rating from a third party. Membership in some professional organizations would suggest that a professional brand has met the minimum standards of that organization.

Charitable sales promotions ("Buy our product and a portion of the price will go to a specified charity") are becoming increasingly popular and are best placed in the endorsement category because the marketer is clearly trying to associate itself with the charity and suggest the charity approves of the brand being marketed. This is what American Express did with the Statue of Liberty Restoration Project back in 1983. Since then, more than half the states have developed commercial co-venture (CCV) laws to regulate this practice in order to avoid consumer deception.

While state requirements vary, they often include the signing and filing of a written contract between the marketer and charity defining the obligations of each party and requiring specific mandatory terms such as the temporal and geographic scope of the program and the dollar amount or percent per unit of goods to be donated to the charity.

From the consumer perspective, the required disclosures are important. They typically include clear identification of the charity, the beginning and ending dates of the campaign, the dollar or percentage of sales amount that will do to the charity and any guaranteed minimum or maximum donation amount that has been promised. A few states require registration and some require the posting of a bond before the campaign begins. Lastly, some states require the filing of a closing statement at the end of the campaign and many require the retention of records, typically for three years (Brody and Shah 2015).

The first legal issue concerning an endorsement or certification is whether one is being made. An anonymous actor/actress who appears in an advertisement or is the company spokesperson in the advertisement is generally not held liable as an endorser for any false or misleading statements that they may make in the advertisement. If consumers are likely to recognize the advertising spokesperson, then the question arises whether the celebrity is just functioning as an advertising spokesperson or intentionally lending his or her good name to persuade consumers to buy the product and more likely to be considered an endorser. Actor Dennis Haysbert has been the spokesperson and voiceover in ALLSTATE ads since 2003, but has never been identified by name so he would appear to be a spokesperson rather than endorser.

Marketing studies generally don't differentiate between celebrity spokespeople and celebrity endorsers, but often find that using celebrities is a profitable strategy and can enhance message recall, believability and recognition of the brand name as well as create a positive attitude for the brand (Agawal & Kamakura 1995). Practitioners argue that a campaign can be two to three times more effective if it includes a celebrity (Hanas 2006). Use of celebrities is further discussed in the next chapter.

Endorsements and testimonials must be authorized by the alleged endorser. As discussed in the next chapter, early U.S. case law held that celebrities (and ordinary people) could not protect themselves from the unauthorized commercial use of their name or likeness because they waived their right to privacy by seeking fame. This is similar to the current U.K. approach. But in the second half of the twentieth century, courts and some state legislatures began to recognize the right of publicity—the right of celebrities to control when their name or likeness is used in advertising (*Haelan Laboratories v. Topps Chewing Gum* 1953).

Today roughly half the states recognize this right. It has been extended from name and likeness to include nicknames, slogans associated with celebrities, sound-a-likes, and even robots that usurp a celebrity's identity. Thus, today brand owners typically need an endorsement contract similar to trademark licensing agreements to make endorsement SBAs with celebrities. In many U.S. states and other countries such as France and Germany, the right to control the use of a celebrity's name or likeness extends beyond the death of the celebrity and may be exercised by the celebrity's heirs or assignees.

Endorsements also must not be deceptive. FTC Guides also suggest that brand owners should not use endorsements (by celebrities, experts, organizations or ordinary consumers) out of context and may not create an advertisement out of consumer testimonials that communicates statements of fact about product attributes or performance in order to avoid the requirement to have substantiation to support such claims. Advertisers must still have a reasonable basis to support factual claims they make in advertising including those made by endorsers (16 C.F.R. § 255.2). The FTC also recommends that when marketers use consumer testimonials about results, they also disclose the average or typical result achieved by consumers.

Endorsements and certifications face the additional burdens of being both genuine and honest. When a consumer, celebrity, individual expert or expert organization endorses a product, consumers generally presume they are offering their independent opinion about the product. For this reason, Federal Trade Commission Guides (16 C.F.R. § 255.1(a)) require the opinions or statements made in the endorsement reflect the honest opinions and beliefs of the endorser. For example, endorsers who claim that they have used the product must have used the product (16 C.F.R. § 255.1(b)). FTC consent agreements have required endorsers to make a reasonable inquiry into the truth of the claims and occasional private lawsuits have held celebrities financially liable for negligence in making misleading claims when the advertiser can't be located or is in bankruptcy (Kertz and Ohanian 1991).

Endorsements made by use of a certification trademark suggest to consumers that the endorsed product satisfies certification standards. However, courts disagree as to whether such an endorsement creates an express warranty that the product meets certification standards. Two cases involving Whirlpool illustrate this issue. An Ohio court dismissed the complaint because it found that the ENERGY STAR logo was not an affirmation of fact or promise (*Savett v. Whirlpool* 2013). In contrast a DC court refused to dismiss an express warranty claim against Whirlpool for use of the same ENERGY STAR certification holding that the mark certified the product met Energy Star standards, i.e., refrigerators must be at least 20% more efficient than minimum standard models (*Del Rossi v. Whirlpool Corp.* 2013). While some certification marks may not have any sort of technical or factual certification upon which to base an express warranty in the sales contract, most probably do. Collective trademarks on the other hand are more likely to represents membership or qualifications (often geographical) that may not create an express warranty.

Organizational endorsements must be from bona fide independent entities, not organizations set up by the advertiser to sound independent. Expert endorsements both from individuals and organizational experts must be based on the endorser's expertise and the endorser must have appropriate expertise to make the endorsement (16 C.F.R. § 255.3). As noted above, organizations that own certification marks must license those marks to anyone who satisfies the certification standard. Otherwise, the organization risks losing its certification mark altogether.

While consumers expect that celebrity endorsers are paid to appear in advertising, any unexpected material connection between endorser and marketer, such as company ownership, should be disclosed. For example, the FTC obtained a settlement with a doctor who endorsed a pain relief device in an infomercial as an apparently independent expert without disclosing that he was a vice president in the company selling the product (Federal Trade Commission 1993). Similarly, if endorsers who appear to be ordinary independent consumers have an unexpected connection to the marketer, such as friend or family member, that should be disclosed as well (16 C.F.R. § 255.5).

Brand owners may not use trademarks that falsely suggest an endorsement. In a recent case, the Canadian Trademarks Opposition Board refused to register "Physician's Choice" as a trademark for skin care products. The Canadian Medical Association successfully argued that mark was too similar to its official mark "Physician" and would deceive the public into thinking the medical community had endorsed the product line.

F. IDENTITY ASSOCIATIONS

The strongest secondary brand association is the identity association that tells consumers that the advertised brand is a particular type of product or satisfies a particular product category label. For example, there is a standard of identity for maple syrup (21 C.F.R. § 168.140) and the Vermont Maple Sugar Makers Association has recently spearheaded a petition to ask the FDA to enforce the standard against bogus "maple" products. As discussed in Chapter Six, in some cases, there is little formal enforcement of such regulations, but in others such as Europe there is strong interest in protecting traditional regional industries and products. In still other cases there may be relevant collective or certification marks covering a particular term such as REALTOR.

In the examples discussed above, the party seeking to establish an SBA through the use another's trademark, collective trademark or certification mark typically will need to obtain a license from the trademark owner for that use. In some cases, such as cooperative advertising, dealers are paid to feature brands in their advertising. For example, Intel paid and persuaded PC makers to use the "Intel Inside" motto. Other methods of co-branding include sponsoring sporting or cultural events, using endorsers or licensed characters, identifying the company or country of origin for the brand, third-party awards and carefully selected channel strategies to leverage retail brands. The increasing popularity of these types of strategies may be the reason why a recent study found that in most product categories, brands are perceived by consumers as less distinct then in the past (Clancy and Trout 2002).

The additional use of previously developed brand assets is obviously dependent on either owning those brand assets or having access to them. Even when a license is granted, things don't always go smoothly and the parties can end up in expensive litigation over licensing terms (e.g., *DC Comics v. Kryptonite Corp.* 2004; Agin and Quick 2001). While a detailed discussion of trademark licensing is beyond the scope of this book, the common REQUIRE-ments of trademark licensing agreements (after identifying the parties to the license and compensation) are outlined in the table on the next page.

It is important to note that franchising involves trademark licensing with strict quality control, but also is regulated to avoid deception or other unfairness to potential franchisees. With franchising, the brand owner typically develops a model for successful retail operations and then licenses both trademarks and the models to independent businesses that run the retail operations.

In essence the franchise licensed retail business lacks its own brand and is entirely subsumed by the "secondary" association of the franchise brand. The association becomes primary. Federal and many state laws require numerous disclosures within franchise offerings to avoid deceiving perspective franchisees. In addition, some state laws recognize the investment of the franchisees and limit the ability to terminate them without cause and notice, at least for particular industries.

Table Two	
Legal Issues for Trademark Licenses	
Issue	**Comments**
Rights in Trademark	Both parties acknowledge the ownership of the trademark being licensed. The licensee typically promises to use the appropriate trademark notice (e.g., ®, ™) when using the mark and often to disclose ownership by the licensor and that use is under license. The licensee also typically promises not to dispute ownership nor apply to register the mark itself.
Enforcement	The licensee typically agrees to assist in protecting the mark by informing the owner of any unauthorized uses that it may discover.
Quality Control	Some assurances of quality control are required to preserve the owner's right to the trademark. Typical provisions include specifications, consistency with owner's image, non-disparaging use, right of the owner to inspect samples, actual products, marketing materials and monitor advertising or website use. The licensee is typically required to correct any deficiencies within a short time after notification.
Use permitted to the licensee	The scope of use should be specified as precisely as possible—what goods, what locations, in what manner must the mark be used, whether the license is exclusive for particular goods, whether the license can be sub-assigned (typically not except for manufacturing).
Indemnification from IP claims	The owner typically indemnifies the licensee in case of a challenge to the validity of the mark or the licensee's use of it.
Resolution of disputes	The law governing the license should be specified as well as method or venue for resolving any disputes between the parties.
End of the license	The term of the license should be specified including the possibility of renewal for additional periods if desired. Conduct that is considered breach of the license and therefore would cause termination should be specified.

G. CONCLUSION

Secondary brand associations often may be an important means for creating brand equity (Keller 2005). SBAs may be developed with the product category label, other brands, professional associations, certifying or membership organizations, geographic locations, celebrities and even ordinary consumers. SBAs also can have varying strengths from relatively weak vague associations to strong associations of endorsement or certification (and even identity associations in some industries).

SBAs should be available to everyone so long as their use does not deceive consumers or take unfair advantage of competitors. For this reason, many descriptive terms are freely available for non-deceptive use as an SBA. However as discussed in Chapter Six, this general availability principle can be overruled by domain names, collective and certification trademarks that limit the use of the trademarked term to members of an organization or those who satisfy specified standards and standards of identity. Furthermore, brands that wish to associate with other brands can either seek permission from those brands or must carefully follow the rules of trademark fair use that are discussion in Chapters Fifteen and Sixteen under the concept of Judo Brand Diversion.

CHAPTER 13

Connection: Using Celebrities to Connect with Consumers

A. INTRODUCTION

The current fascination and interest of society in celebrities undoubtedly has contributed to the increasing use of celebrities in marketing (Pringle 2004). Celebrities are used in marketing in two fundamental ways. First, it is clear that today many celebrities are brands in and of themselves. They are promoted and protected just like branded products and services. In 2005, retail sales of licensed celebrity merchandise totaled over $3 billion (Bury 2006).

Second, as discussed briefly in the preceding chapter, celebrities are often used to advertise other branded products. In this function, they serve as Secondary Brand Associations. Advertising appearances by movie stars can earn them as much as $10 million and in 1998, the three sport stars Michael Jordan, Tiger Woods, and Dale Earnhardt earned more than $100 million in product endorsements (Stone, Joseph and Jones 2003). Experts estimate that U.S. companies paid more than $1 billion in 1996 just to athletes for endorsements and that 25% of all U.S. advertising uses celebrities (Erdogan 1999). In addition to the use of current celebrities, there is growing use of deceased celebrities in both advertising and merchandising (Petty & D'Rozario 2008). The dead celebrity licensing industry started about 25 years ago and now earns estimated revenues of $300 million annually (Brott 2004).

Brand marketers who seek to describe celebrities as brand users or perhaps imply an endorsement must be aware of the "right of publicity." This legal concept has developed both at common law through court decisions as well as through statutory law. It essentially gives people the right to control the use of various indicia of their persona such as name, image, etc. in advertising. If brand marketers want to use a celebrity in advertising, they typically must negotiate and pay for a license. In a sense the "right of publicity" is similar to trademark rights. Because this law is still evolving, this chapter first presents a historical overview and then examines the current state of the law and compares it to similar laws.

B. HISTORICAL DEVELOPMENT

Celebrities have been used in advertising in America since the eighteenth century. In those earliest uses, they were reportedly used to endorse everything from artificial teeth to patent medicine and by the early twentieth century, royalty had been supplanted by entertainers and sports figures as favorite celebrities (Goodrum and Dalrymple 1990). Queen Victoria endorsed Cadbury Cocoa (Erdogan 1999) and actress Lillie Langtry appeared on the package of Pears soap in 1893 (Mistry 2006). Pepsi has used celebrities fairly consistently since recruiting race car driver Barney Oldfield to appear in a 1909 newspaper ad. It also has used actress Lucille Ball and musical performers such as Johnny Cash, the Four Tops, Michael Jackson and Brittney Spears (Dubrow 2006).

Celebrity merchandise licensing also has nearly a century long history. The practice may have started in 1913 with Teddy Roosevelt licensing his name to the Teddy Bear and using the proceeds to establish a network of National Parks. By the 1930s, six million licensed Shirley Temple dolls had been sold. Cowboy actors Tom Mix and Hopalong Cassidy (http://www.hopalong.com/home.asp) followed Shirley Temple's (http://www.shirleytemple.com/) success with toys, premiums and endorsements in the 1940s (Anson 1984).

In 1960, four years after the death of actor Bela Lugosi, Universal Pictures started a highly successful merchandise licensing program featuring the likenesses of the late actor as Count Dracula and other actors as famous horror characters. By 1966, Universal had completed approximately 50 licensing agreements for such products as model figures, t-shirts and other apparel, card games, puzzles, masks, kites, and even soap and detergent products and earned over a quarter of a million dollars. While the trial court awarded damages of $70,000, the California Supreme Court disagreed holding that the right of publicity expired with the death of the subject person. (*Lugosi v. Universal Pictures* 1979).

These celebrities, when living, generally participated willingly in these licensing deals and advertising endorsements for appropriate compensation. However, there probably are many more examples where the celebrity did not authorize the use and received no compensation. For example, Benjamin Franklin when visiting France in 1776 noted his picture on all sorts of memorabilia (Klink 2003).

In the early years, the law was uncertain whether permission of the celebrity was needed to include his or her likeness of name on merchandise or in advertising (Petty and D'Rozario 2009). Cautious marketers appear to have sought permission in exchange for royalties. They could truthfully claim an authentic license to use a celebrity's name or likeness. However, those who simply used the images or names they wanted without permission generally enjoyed lower costs and may still have benefited from the celebrity connection.

C. EARLY LEGAL DEVELOPMENTS

As the use of celebrities in marketing increased, there was increasing pressure on the legal system to consider whether some regulation was appropriate. The fundamental question was whether or not people and celebrities were entitled to control these commercial uses of their names and likenesses or whether marketers could use anyone's name or likeness without fear of legal repercussion.

Perhaps the earliest court decision to wrestle with this issue involved an ordinary citizen, Mrs. Roberson, who sued the Rochester Folding Box Company for the unauthorized use of her likeness for the sale of bags of flour (*Roberson v. Rochester Folding Box Co.* 1902). The advertisement in question is pictured first below. The New York Court of Appeals rejected her request for an injunction and damages for mental distress noting that it was up to the legislature to define the right to privacy and determine whether it should include the use of a person's photograph in advertising without their consent. Given significant public disapproval of this decision, the New York legislature took up the challenge issued by the court and responded the following year with a statute that prohibited the "use of name, portrait, picture or voice of a living person for advertising or purposes of trade without written consent" (N.Y. Civ. Rights Law §§ 50–52).

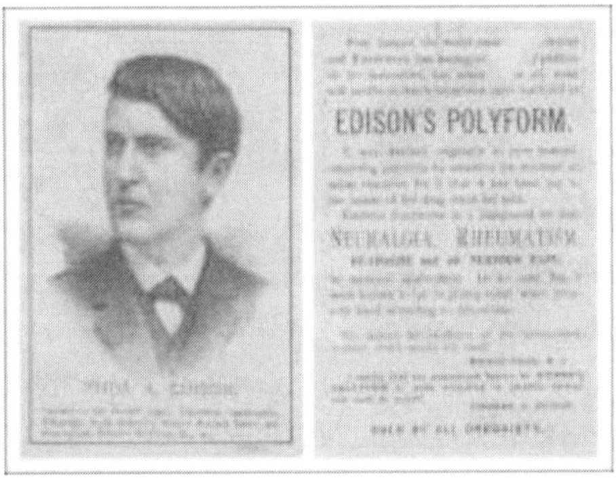

Courts in other states condemned similar uses of an unauthorized photograph in an advertisement starting with the Supreme Court of Georgia in a 1905 decision (*Pavesich v. New England Life Insurance Co.* 1905). Pavesich is the man pictured to the left of the middle advertisement above. In both of these early cases, the image but not name of a relatively unknown person was used. Like the Roberson case, the legal theory was trespass on the person's right to privacy citing what became an influential *Harvard Law Review* article by Warren and Brandeis published in 1890.

Two years later a court first considered a case involving the name and image of a celebrity, famed inventor Thomas Edison. The New Jersey Court of Chancery found for the first time that a person had a property right (rather than a personal right of privacy) in the commercial use of their name and likeliness and enjoined further unauthorized use of Edison's name and image by Edison Polyform

(*Edison v. Edison Polyform Mfg. Co.* 1907). The property right argument was indirectly confirmed ten years later in a contract case when a New York court found a contract to be valid that authorized an agent to find commercial licensing opportunities for Lady Duff-Gordon (*Wood v. Lady Duff-Gordon* 1917).

However, many courts were less sympathetic to similar claims made by entertainment and sports celebrities. Since celebrities sought out fame and publicity, many decisions held they were not damaged when their images were used in advertising without their permission. This was found to be true even for a professional football player who opposed the use of alcohol by young people and whose picture was used in a beer company's annual sports calendar (*O'Brien v. Pabst Sales* 1941).

Over fifty years after the *Roberson* decision, Judge Jerome Frank coined the term "right of publicity." While determining which of two chewing gum companies had the right to use the image of a baseball player on their trading cards, he stated: "[I]n addition to and independent of that right of privacy . . . a man has a right in the publicity value of his photograph, i.e., the right to grant the exclusive privilege of publishing his picture . . . This right might be called a 'right of publicity' "(*Haelan Labs, Inc. v. Topps Chewing Gum, Inc.* 1953). This decision cited *Wood v. Lady Duff-Gordon* to hold that the right of publicity could be transferred by contract. This *Haelan* decision was highlighted the following year in an influential law review article entitled "The Right of Publicity" (Nimmer 1954).

That very same year, a New York court decided that the right of publicity in New York did not survive the celebrity to whom the right attaches because the statute only granted rights to "living persons." Furthermore, the *Roberson* decision held there was no common law right of publicity in New York (*Schumann v. Loew's Inc.* 1954). Five years later, California courts also ruled that the right of publicity did not survive death (*James v. Screen Gems, Inc.* 1959).

In 1977, the U.S. Supreme Court finally addressed the right of publicity in a case where a "human cannonball" circus act was broadcast in its entirety as part of the television news, despite the performer's request not to do so. The Court recognized the state of Ohio's recognition of the right of publicity. It further held that this right was misappropriated by the television station, despite First Amendment protection of news broadcasts (*Zacchini v. Scripps-Howard Broadcasting Co.* 1977).

D. THE DEVELOPMENT OF POST-MORTEM RIGHTS

No sooner had Elvis died then a marketer produced a poster with the title "In Memory" printed over a photograph of Elvis performing. The New York federal court hearing the lawsuit brought by the assignee to Presley's publicity rights rejected both First Amendment—newsworthy event and copyright pre-emption defenses to order a permanent injunction against the marketer and an awarding of all the profits from past sales to the assignee. However this decision was reversed by the Second Circuit Court of Appeals that suggested that Tennessee law would not recognize a descendible right of publicity (*Factors Etc., Inc. v. Pro Arts, Inc.* 1980). In contrast in 1981, the Federal District Court of New Jersey announced that it believed New Jersey court made law would recognize a right to publicity that was descendible to the celebrity's heirs (*Estate of Elvis Presley v. Russen* 1981).

Since courts seemed reluctant to recognize a descendible right of publicity, dead celebrity heirs and their lawyers took their case to state legislatures. In 1984, the California legislature, prodded in hearings by the sons of John Wayne, Harpo Marx and Abbott and Costello passed the 'California Celebrity Rights Act', which amended its 1972 statute to forbid unauthorized use of a celebrity's image, including the name, voice, signature, photograph or likeness without the permission of the family for 50 years after the celebrity's death (Glionna 1997). Until that point in time, most states held that publicity was a personal right, not a property right and therefore could not be handed down to anyone after death (Haas 2003). Soon, other states would follow with similar legislation.

In 1988, the Trademark Law Revision Act was enacted making it illegal under Section 43(a) of the Lanham Act to "deceive as . . . to affiliation, . . . sponsorship or approval" (15 U.S.C. § 1025(a)). Although prior language condemning "false designation of origin" had been used to challenge unauthorized uses of a celebrity's name or likeness (e.g., *Estate of Elvis Presley v. Russen* 1981), this change to federal law provides another specific basis for celebrities to challenge unauthorized uses of their personae since most such uses suggest some sort of affiliation, sponsorship or approval.

E. CURRENT LEGAL ANALYSIS

As noted in the preceding section, the development of the right of publicity has been the principal method for celebrities and eventually their heirs to control the unauthorized use of their names and likenesses in marketing in the United States during the second half of the twentieth century. This right also has developed in most of civil law Europe, Australia (Carty 2004), Jamaica and several Canadian provinces. Even English law, perhaps the most reluctant in the world to recognize anything similar to the right of publicity, recognizes false (unauthorized) celebrity endorsements as a form of passing off (Carty 2004). However, other laws including trademark, copyright and unfair competition also can come into play. This section examines these laws and the interplay among them.

I. Right of Publicity

Currently, eighteen states have statutes that establish the right of publicity. Experts disagree about the states that recognize the right to publicity by judicial decision (16 according to Bryer and Simensky 2003, but 35 states according to Solomon 2004). Eight to eleven states overlap having both statutes and recognition of the common law right of publicity (Bryer and Simensky 2003; Solomon 2004). In these states, courts considering right to publicity cases must consider both the statute (and judicial decisions interpreting the statute) as well as the common law right as defined by judicial decisions within the state.

When interpreting common law rights, courts may also consider judicial decisions from other jurisdictions and expert opinion such as the Restatement (Third) of Unfair Competition. The Restatement was developed by legal expects to summarize and clarify the "common law" that arises from judicial decisions. Chapter 4 of the Restatement recognizes the propriety of liability for those who appropriate the commercial value of a person's identity under the general title of the Right to Publicity.

The right of publicity is not consistent across states. All states with statutes cover at least the celebrity's name and likeness (e.g., Ky. Rev. Stat. Ann. § 391.170). Some states—California, Florida, Nevada, Oklahoma, Tennessee and Texas, specifically include photographs within their statutory coverage. Others—California, New York, Nevada, Oklahoma, and Texas, statutorily include the right to a person's voice (Coats, Lerner and Hsu 2006). Indiana has one of the broadest statutes that specifically covers one's name, voice, signature, photograph, likeness, image and distinctive appearance, gestures, and mannerisms (Ind. Code § 32–13–7).

A person's likeness has been broadly defined to include celebrity look-alikes (*Allen v. Nat'l Video, Inc.* 1985; *Onassis v. Christian Dior, Inc.,* 1984). Even the distinctive stance of a baseball pitcher was found to be a possible basis for appropriating that athlete's identity (*Newcombe v. Adolf Coors, Co.* 1998). Judicial decisions in some jurisdictions also have included vocal impersonations of a singer's distinctive voice and style. For example, both Tom Waits and Bette Midler have successfully challenged the use of sound-a-likes in commercial advertising. In both cases, the Ninth Circuit Court of Appeals found both false endorsement under the Lanham Act and misappropriation of the celebrities persona under California state law (*Waits v. Frito-Lay, Inc.*, 1992; *Midler v. Ford Motor Co.* 1988).

However, because New York does not recognize common law rights and its statute only applies to names, images and likeness, a court dismissed a similar case involving the use of a "Fat Boys" sound-a-like (*Tin Pan Apple, Inc. v. Miller Brewing Co.* 1990). Furthermore, courts have consistently held that the mere use of a "signature song" in advertising without sounding like the singer for whom it is a "signature song" is not a violation of the singer's right to publicity (*Oliveira a/k/a/ Gilberto v. Frito Lay, Inc.* 2001; *Sinatra v. Goodyear Tire & Rubber Co.* 1970).

In addition to aspects of the person, courts have expanded the right of publicity to cover well known celebrity associations. Such associations include nicknames (*Hirsch v. S.C. Johnson & Son, Inc.* 1979; *Lombardo v. Doyle, Dane & Bernbach, Inc.* 1977), the "signature" introduction of a talk show host (*Carson v. Here's Johnny Portable Toilets Inc.* 1983) and a racer's distinctive car even with the number changed (*Motschenbacher v. R.J. Reynolds Tob. Co.* 1974).

In contrast to the lack of protection for signature songs (absent a vocal impersonation), a couple of judicial decisions do recognize the celebrity's right to "signature roles." The Third Circuit court of Appeals recognized that the actor who played Spanky in the "Spanky and Our Gang" movies series had a right to protect the name Spanky from use by others in a restaurant name (*McFarland v. Miller*, 1994). Similarly, a court allowed two actors from the television show *Cheers* to challenge the depiction of their characters, based on a license from the producer and copyright owner of *Cheer's* by robots placed in airport bars (*Wendt v. Host International, Inc.* 1997). The project was eventually abandoned.

The furthest extension of this concept to date occurred when the Ninth Circuit overturned a summary dismissal of a lawsuit brought by Vanna White of *Wheel of Fortune* fame. She sued Samsung for an advertisement that showed a robot with a blond wig in an evening gown on the "longest running game show" (*White v. Samsung Electronics, Inc.* 1992). Vanna White and her robot doppelganger are pictured below.

In contrast to these imitations where liability has been suggested, courts find that use of an actual musical or film recording is governed solely by copyright law and if proper permission from the copyright owner is obtained, and the celebrity has no additional rights under the Right of Publicity (*Laws v. Song Music Entertainment, Inc.* 2006; *Comedy III Productions, Inc. v. New Line Cinema*, 2000).

Because rights of publicity are based on state law, an important question is who has the right to sue under the laws of any particular state. For example, the trust established by the estate of Princess Diana sued the Franklin Mint for making an unauthorized commemorative plate claiming this violated California state law. The court held that because Princess Diana was not a resident of California when she died, California law would not apply. Rather the court had to look to the laws of Great Britain, which provided no publicity rights to celebrities after death (*Cairns v. Franklin Mint Co.* 1998).

This and other events led the California Legislature to adopt the Astaire Celebrity Image Protection Act in 1999. This new act would allow anyone to sue and apply California law so long as the commercial use of the celebrity's persona took place in California. This act also extended the period of protection from 50 to 70 years and did so retroactively to cover celebrities who died between 1930 and 1950 whose publicity rights had expired under the fifty year time period (Laurens 2001). Since most commercial uses of celebrities are national in scope, this change allows almost any celebrity (or celebrity heir) to sue in California.

A major difference among the states is the recognition and definition of the descendibility of the right of publicity. Baby-boomers appear to be attracted by celebrities they knew doing childhood and dead celebrities are easier to control and less expensive than living celebrities (Petty and D'Rozario 2009). Hyman (1997) provides one example of the cost difference for advertisers: "for the use of (Babe) Ruth photos in three newspaper ads, investment bank Alex Brown & Sons Inc. paid $15,000, chicken feed compared with the fees commanded by some of today's superstars." This price difference is substantial despite the licensing agency's cut of 20% of the profits which is double the rate of a living celebrity endorsement (Glaister 2005).

The trend of allowing celebrity publicity rights to continue after death is increasing. Courts in France, Germany and Italy have suggested that such celebrity rights should continue after death (Carty 2004). In fourteen states, the right of publicity statute defines it as transferable and descendible to heirs or estate as summarized in the following table.

Table One				
Statutes Providing Post-Mortem Right of Publicity				
State	**Scope**	**Remedies***	**Post-Mortem Duration**	**Citation**
Cal.	Commercial use within state of any person's name, voice signature, photograph or likeness	Not less than $750; attorney's fees & costs	70 years; registration required for transfer	Cal. Civ. Code Ann. § 3344
Fla.	Commercial use of name, portrait, photograph or other likeness	none	40 years	Fla. Stat. Ann. § 540.08
Ill.	Commercial use of name, signature, photograph, image, likeness, or voice	Not less than $1000	50 years	765 Ill. Comp. Stat. Ann. § 1075
Ind.	Commercial use within the state of any personality's name, voice, signature, photograph, likeness, image and distinctive appearance, gestures, or mannerisms if they have commercial value	Not less than $1000; attorney's fees and costs; seizure	100 years	Ind. Code Ann. § 32–36–1–1 et seq.
Ken.	Commercial use of name or likeness of public figure	none	50 years	Ky. Rev. Stat. Ann. § 391.170
Neb.	Commercial use of name, picture, portrait or personality	none	Right survives death (without apparent limit), but is personal and non-assignable (?)	Neb. Rev. Stat. § 20–201
Nev.	Commercial use within state of person's name, voice, signature, photograph or likeness regardless of person's domicile	Not less than $750	50 years; registration required for transfer	Nev. Rev. Stat. § 597.810

Ohio	Commercial use of resident's name, voice, signature, photograph, image, likeness, or distinctive appearance if they have commercial value	Attorney's fees & costs; 3x damages for knowing violations; seizure	60 years	Ohio Rev. Code Ann. § 2741
Okl.	Commercial use of name, voice, signature, photograph, or likeness	Attorney's fees & costs	100 years; registration required for transfer	Okla. Stat. Ann. Title 12 1449.
Penn.	Commercial use of name or likeness with commercial value of natural person	none	30 years	42 Pa.C.S. § 8316
Tenn.	Commercial use of name, photograph or likeness	Seizure; misdemeanor	Not less than 10 years, expires there after 2 years of non-use	Tenn. Code Ann. § 47–25–1101 et seq.
Tex.	Commercial use of name, voice, signature, photograph, or likeness with commercial value	none	50 years, registration allowed	Tex. Prop. Code Ann. § 26.001
Va.	Commercial use of name, portrait, or picture	none	20 years	Va. Code Ann. § 8.01–40
Wash.	Commercial use of name, voice, signature, photograph, or likeness	Not less than $1500; attorneys' fees & costs; seizure	10 years for individuals; 75 years for personalities with commercial value	Wash. Rev. Code Ann. § 63.60.040–070
* All states explicitly or implicitly provide for injunctions, damages and profits as remedies.				

As mentioned in the preceding section, a federal court decided that the New Jersey common law right of publicity is descendible. Federal courts also have decided that the common law right of publicity is descendible in Connecticut (*Jim Henson Prods. v. John T. Brady & Assocs.*, 1994) as well as Georgia (*Martin Luther King Ctr. for Social Change v. American Heritage Prods.* 1983). A Tennessee court of appeals held that it also would recognize that the common law right of publicity was descendible without any time limitation and this would cover rights that pre-existed before the enactment of the Tennessee statute (*Elvis Presley Int'l Memorial Found v. Crowell* 1987). In contrast, federal courts have suggested that Ohio common law would not recognize a descendible right of publicity (*Reeves v. United Artists Corp.* 1985). Thus, the trend seems to establish descendibility either by statute or judicial interpretation of the common law right of publicity.

Between the two extremes of descendible or not descendible rights of publicity lies the third option suggested by the *Lugosi* decision that the right may be descendible only if exploited by the celebrity when the celebrity was alive. Federal courts have asserted that this approach would be followed in Arizona (*Sinkler v. Goldsmith* 1985), Utah (*Nature's Way Prods., Inc. v. Nature-Pharma, Inc.* 1990) and New York (*Factors Etc., Inc. v. Pro Arts, Inc.* 1980). However, the New York Court of Appeals has repeatedly stated that the New York right of publicity law is governed exclusively by statute, not by common law, and the statute on its terms only applies to living persons (*Stephano v. News Group Pub. Inc.,* 1984).

II. Other Laws

Trademark, unfair competition, and copyright law all provide alternative methods for celebrities to protect their right of publicity to some degree. Trademarks identify the source of goods so that celebrities (or their estates) who can show that consumers identify a particular celebrity name or likeness as being a source of goods can sue for trademark infringement or dilution, even if the trademark is unregistered. However, courts are clear that achieving celebrity fame does not equate to trademark protection. For the latter to occur, the public must identify the celebrity name or likeness not just with the celebrity, but also with a business enterprise. For example, Paul Newman uses a particular likeness of himself and his name to identify his well-known line of salad dressings and other food products. In contrast, the use of a picture of Babe Ruth in a baseball calendar or the likeness of Princess Diana on collectable plates has been found not to signify the origin of such goods and therefore not to violate trademark law (Solomon 2004).

The trademark law rule that disallows registration of names that are primarily merely a surname may be loosening a bit. In October 2007, the TTAB allowed well known NASCAR driver J.J. Yeley to register his name as a trademark for entertainment services. Similarly, the TTAB allowed registration of the mark M.C. Escher by his estate noting that that the proposed mark was not primarily merely a surname, but rather a "personal name that identified a specific person of considerable renown."

The Board distinguished earlier decisions that held adding initials to a surname reinforces the surname significance noting that those earlier decisions contained no evidence of secondary meaning. Thus many celebrities have already registered their names as trademarks and this will probably become an increasingly common practice. Trademark law would not only continue as long as there is use of the mark, but would protect not only against the unlicensed use of the exact mark, but also confusingly similar marks, such as slightly different images and similar marks that are likely to dilute (impair the distinctiveness or reputation)the original mark.

Trademark law also prohibits the use of the name, portrait or signature of living individuals and particularly living U.S. Presidents as a trademark without their written permission. The name, portrait or signature of a deceased President whose spouse is still living also is protected without written permission of the spouse (15 U.S.C. § 1052(c)). If this section is interpreted to implicitly allow registration of deceased Presidents' names, likenesses or signatures as trademarks after the death of their spouse then it might pre-empt state laws on right of publicity for those deceased Presidents. However, this seems an unlikely overly broad interpretation of the statutory prohibition.

Lastly, the Federal trademark statute prohibits the registration of immoral or scandalous trademarks (15 U.S.C. § 1052(a)), such as "Old Glory" as the brand name for condoms. This provision was used as a basis for litigation that eventually was settled with an agreement to stop the selling of Crazy Horse brand malt liquor. Descendants and members of the Sioux tribe found the name offensive on this product because the revered Sioux leader, Crazy Horse, was opposed to alcohol consumption (Associated Press 2001). This provision would be effective only in situations involving extremely tasteless exploitation of a celebrity unless it is declared unconstitutional as contrary to the first amendment guarantee of freedom of speech.

Unfair competition law is closely related to trademark law. In fact, section 43(a) of the federal trademark law (Lanham Act 15 U.S.C. § 1125(a)), condemns various forms of unfair competition including false descriptions, false statements and false representations of sponsorship or endorsement. Many states also recognize a tort of misappropriation which has been applied to various aspects of celebrity identity. These unfair competition legal theories have been used in conjunction with right of publicity to protect the commercial use of various aspects of the personae of living celebrities.

However, it is not clear whether or not consumers would perceive a false endorsement or sponsorship by a deceased celebrity. Similarly, it is unclear whether some aspect of a deceased celebrity's persona could be misappropriated, particularly if the public generally understood the celebrity was deceased. If the descendible right of publicity became generally well understood by the public, then a claim for false sponsorship or misappropriation would become more viable.

Copyright law (Chapter Five) provided the earliest protection for celebrities, but the protection was limited to copyrighted works. For example, if an advertiser wanted to use a musical performance of a deceased performer, the copyright on that performance provides protection that now (after a recent extension) will often be life of the performer plus seventy years. Similar protection would accrue to a particular photograph or painting of a celebrity, but in such cases the photographer or artist typically controls the copyright. If permission was obtained from the celebrity to do the portrait, the contract could include restrictions on the display of the work such as prohibiting its use in advertising or licensing. A smart celebrity could even seek assignment of the copyright to better control the uses of the image.

Television and motion picture images and sounds are similarly protected, but are more likely subject to the fair use defense of copyright law that allows for relatively small amounts of a copyright work to be used without permission (17 U.S.C. § 107). However, the four part fair use test provides greater protection for artistic works rather than factual reproductions (i.e., a caricature might receive more protection than an accurate portrait) and provides less fair use for commercial uses of copyrighted works such as advertising and merchandising.

III. Defenses

It should be noted that all of the legal theories would be limited by a general freedom of speech or fair use type of defense that would allow use of a celebrity's name, likeness or personae for news reporting and for general biography purposes. Right of publicity statutes often specifically permit such uses. Of course the challenge is distinguishing allowable free speech from forbidden commercial uses. The Ninth Circuit did not allow Dustin Hoffman to recover for the use of his image from the movie *Tootsie* altered to show a new evening gown published by a magazine next to an article about fashion (*Hoffman v. Capital Cities/ABC Inc.,* 2001), but did allow surfers to recover for the use of their images near an article on the history of surfing that appeared in the *Abercrombie & Fitch Quarterly,* a publication of the retail chain store (*Downing v. Abercrombie & Fitch,* 2001).

So called "transformative" uses also may be allowed. For example, an artist's painting commemorating Tiger Woods' victory at the Masters Tournament in 1997 that included three images of Mr. Woods as well as images of other famous golfers was permitted by the Sixth Circuit. The court held that his picture alone did not function as a trademark and then balanced Mr. Woods' right to publicity against the right of the artist and the right of public to enjoy the art (*ETW Corp. v. Jireh Publishing,* 2003). In contrast, the Supreme Court of California found that a charcoal drawing of the *Three Stooges* that was reproduced on t-shirts and lithographs was a straightforward depiction of their likenesses and sales of the t-shirts and lithographs were based primarily of the *Stooges'* fame and popularity rather than the talent and imagination of the artist. The Court found these works were not transformative works of art that deserved protection under the First Amendment and upheld an award of $75,000 in damages as well as an injunction (*Comedy III Productions, Inc. v. Gary Saderup, Inc.* 2002).

This analysis is similar to that of the court considering "The Big El Show," an Elvis Presley impersonation show. Ultimately, the court decided that the show primarily imitated Presley thereby exploiting his celebrity rather than providing a novel artistic impersonation of Presley (*Estate of Elvis Presley v. Russen* 1981). For example, a parody impersonation of Elvis Presley likely would have been found to be transformative (cf. *Cardtoons v. Major League Baseball Players Association* 1996). However, as discussed previously, an arguable parody of Vanna

White's role as letter turner on Wheel of Fortune by a robot with blond wig and evening gown was still found to violate White's right of publicity (*White v. Samsung Elecs. Am. Inc.* 1992).

Occasionally marketers will argue that an alleged advertisement referencing a celebrity is not commercial speech in the sense of a proposal of a commercial transaction. For example, as famed basketball star Michael Jordan was about to be inducted into the Hall of Fame, *Sports Illustrated* solicited advertising for a special issue. Two Chicago-based retailers elected to run the ads pictured below. The Jewel-Osco insert on the left initially led to a finding by the trial court that the ad did not propose a commercial transaction and therefore was not commercial speech to which the right to publicity would apply. However, the Seventh Circuit Court of Appeals reversed finding that the ad was a form of image advertising promoting goodwill for the advertiser by associating it with the popular Michael Jordan. This case was settled in December 2015 and Jordan will donate his winnings to charity. Dominick's conceded that its ad (pictured to the right below) was commercial speech. Based on Michael Jordan's testimony that he

didn't do deals below $10 million, a jury awarded him $8.9 million in damages (Brenner and Becker 2015).

One last proposed defense that also was not been successful is abandonment. College basketball player Lew Alcindor converted to Islam and legally changed his name to Kareem Abdul-Jabbar. More than twenty years later, Oldsmobile ran ads during the NCAA men's basketball tournament asking who held the record for being voted the most outstanding player of the tournament. The ad then revealed the answer of Lew Alcindor for 1967–69 and compared that feat to the fact that the Oldsmobile '88 had been selected as a best buy more than once. Although the trial court found that Abdul-Jabbar had abandoned his prior name, the appellate court reversed holding that it was not possible for a person to abandon rights in name or image through non-use (*Abdul-Jabbar v. General Motors Corp.* 1996).

F. CONCLUSION

While brand marketers are prone to think of legal concepts as coming from a single source and being internally consistent, this chapter demonstrates the diversity of approaches at the state level for the right of publicity. Therefore, it is crucial in this area that marketers pay attention to all jurisdictions in which their promotional efforts are experienced. Statutes in California and Indiana clearly provide jurisdiction once the marketing effort reaches consumers in that state. For these two states, it no longer matters where the celebrity lives or where the celebrity's estate was processed. Generally speaking any use of a celebrity identifier is subject to legal risk because most celebrities or their heirs can afford legal challenges and want to control the commercial market for their brand.

The concept of trademark fair use discussed in the next chapters allows certain unauthorized third-party trademark uses such as identifying a specific brand (perhaps in comparison advertising) or descriptive use of words in a descriptive trademark. For the right of publicity, there is no similarly recognized fair use beyond biographic or news reporting non-commercial use. A brand marketer that simply wants to list celebrity users—a descriptive association runs a high legal risk that this will violate right of publicity laws. Celebrities also will argue that such a descriptive list implies some sort of endorsement or takes away the opportunity for them to get paid to associate with the brand. Moreover, obtaining a license from the celebrity or his/her estate doesn't completely resolve issues because the picture or other indicia of celebrity personae used in advertising likely will have copyright protection, so a separate license is needed from the creator of the celebrity image or sound recording.

PART 3

Judo Brand Diversion—The Legal Issues of Using Another's Brand to Your Advantage

---

This part suggests that if a license or purchase of an existing brand is not available under affordable terms, several tactics, primarily based on the concept of trademark fair use, offer the advantage of associating with someone else's well-known brand identity without obtaining a license. Even when carefully executed, these tactics will engender some legal risk, but in many cases the expected costs of legal challenge may be outweighed by the increased effectiveness and the savings of permission costs. In other cases such as Interruption and Misdirection tactics discussed in Chapter Seventeen there are higher legal risks. This set of tactics is collectively identified as Judo Brand Diversion (JBD) and is summarized in the table on the following page (Petty 2010).

Table One				
Judo Brand Diversion Tactics				
Neutralization (Ch. 14)	**Comparison (Ch. 15)**	**Unauthorized Extensions (Ch. 16)**	**Interruption (Ch. 17)**	**Misdirection (Ch. 18)**
Pre-emption	Copycat products	Resellers	Recommendation of a different brand	E-mail and domain name "spoofing"
Abandonment	Comparative advertising	Compatible products	Trigger pop-ups on search engine site	Typosquatting
Genericide	Descriptive fair use	Vague Associations: Ornamental Products, Parodies & Ambush Marketing	Trigger pop-ups on rival website	Metatag use to bias search results

Judo Brand Diversion as conceptualized here, encompasses what used to be considered a variety of seemingly unrelated marketing tactics. The JBD framework shows that these tactics all have similar goals, may have similar levels of effectiveness, and share similar legal risks. While the risks of legal challenge and liability are not negligible in any JBD situation, they are manageable. The factual details of the actual execution of any particular tactic and the likelihood of consumer confusion in that situation are key determinants of legal risk.

If JBD is more effective than other forms of brand promotion for any particular level of budget, than some of the marketing budget could be devoted to obtaining legal advice and perhaps a quick consumer study of the practice to determine levels of consumer confusion and select the least risky execution of the practice. Since the likely costs of litigation may be significantly less than 1% of a typical marketing budget, there may be latitude to develop a litigation reserve fund at the beginning of brand launch that could be redirected toward additional promotion, if no legal challenge appears.

CHAPTER 14

Introduction to Judo Brand Diversion and Neutralization Tactics

A. INTRODUCTION TO JUDO BRAND DIVERSION

The plethora of brand management books and articles all recommend that marketers develop distinctive and strong brand identities for their products and services in the minds of consumers in order to avoid the harsh price competition of undifferentiated commodity products. Such recommendations are easier said than done. Not only is developing a distinctive brand difficult and subject to erosion over time, but 90% of new brand introductions fail (Landler *et al.* 1991). Furthermore, advertising is less effective for unfamiliar compared with familiar brands (Campbell and Keller 2003). For these reasons, launching a new brand has been estimated to cost about $150 million in some consumer markets (Aaker and Keller 1990). Branding guru Kevin Lane Keller summarizes:

> Today's challenging and unforgiving marketplace makes brand building difficult. Fickle consumers, intense competition, demanding retailers, constrained resources, and impatient investors put unparalleled pressure on marketers to skillfully design and execute their programs. As a result,

marketers welcome any means toward helping them build brand equity and value (Keller 2005, p. 19).

One alternative to decrease the risk and expense of a new brand introduction is to acquire rights to an existing brand name trademark either by license or outright purchase. The Selsun Blue dandruff shampoo trademark, other intellectual property, and some manufacturing equipment were sold for $75 million (Ruder 2003). Another possible strategy to enhance the probability of a successful product launch is to use a co-branding strategy such as the use of the MAYTAG repairman for CHEEZ-ITs in a Superbowl ad or his use by CHEVROLET in 2002 (Baar 2005). Rao and Ruekert (1994, p. 87) assert: "perhaps because brand names are valuable assets, they may be combined with other brand names to form a synergistic alliance in which the sum is greater than the parts." Chapter Twelve discusses the use of ingredient brands such as PUFFS tissues containing VAPORUB to enhance consumer interest in a product.

This chapter begins with background on judo business and imitation strategies. The various tactics of JBD are then introduced. This chapter then examines the Neutralization tactics. Chapter Fifteen examines Comparison tactics, Chapter Sixteen examines Unauthorized Extensions, and Chapter Seventeen examines Interruption and Misdirection Tactics as well as offering some conclusions about JBD strategies.

B. STRATEGY BACKGROUND

The strongest brands are not necessarily associated with the first introduction of a new product. While first mover advantages are often touted as a justification for pursuing innovation strategies, it also is true that being the "second mover" i.e., an imitator, can be an effective strategy as well. The imitator faces costs that may be only 65% or lower from those of the innovator since the imitator does not have to engage in as much research and development and does not have to explain the product to customers. These cost savings allow some imitators to follow a low price strategy. Others find improvements to the initial product and follow an "imitate and improve" strategy. Often it is not the first brand that becomes the leading brand in a category, but an improved imitator that more correctly targets what consumers want (Schnaars 1994).

A recent empirical study of market pioneers confirms the historical weakness of those brands that are first to the market. Nearly two thirds of the first movers in sixty-six industries had failed by the year 2000 and the average market share for survivors was only 6%. Only 9% of those first movers studied actually maintained their market leadership in the year 2000 (Tellis & Golder 2006).

Brand imitation is a relatively simple but also legally risky strategy. As explained in Chapter Two some marketers copy popular brands very closely while still hoping to avoid the strong civil and criminal penalties for counterfeiting. Others try to develop similar brands that are sufficiently distinctive to at least avoid counterfeiting and perhaps any other liability for imitation. Unfortunately, predicting with much certainty how to avoid liability for copying is difficult.

For example just in considering brand names, Bonamine was found to be phonetically similar to Dramamine, Listogen to Listerine and Sarnoff to Smirnoff. In contrast, Surge was not found phonetically similar to Surf nor was Hour to Hour phonetically similar to Shower to Shower. Awake was found to be too close in meaning to Arise, Beauty Sleep to Beauty-Rest and Mister Stain to Mister Clean, but Daylight was not confusingly similar in meaning to Dawn nor Ivy Hall to Ivy League (Shilling 2002, pp. 141–42).

Imitation is more permissible in situations where it has already occurred. For example, having allowed a multitude of similar sounding names for chlorophyll based chewing gums, marketers of CLORETS could not prevent a rival from using the name CLOR-AIDS but the rival was prohibited from copying the CLORETS package (*American Chicle Co. v. Topps Chewing Gum, Inc.* 1954).

JBD is more sophisticated brand association strategy compared with simple brand imitation. JBD could be described as a form of judo business strategy made popular in a book by David Yoffie and Mary Kwak (2001). They cite the *Columbia Encyclopedia* definition of judo: "[Judo] depends for success upon the skill of using an opponent's own weight and strength against him, thus enabling a weak or light individual to overcome a physically superior opponent (p. 1)." *Inter alia*, Yoffie and Kwak argue that judo strategy may leverage an opponent's assets to be used against the opponent. The opponent finds it difficult to respond without diminishing the value of its own assets (Yoffie and Kwak 2001, p. 68).

In the case of JBD, a small or new seller with limited consumer brand recognition uses an imitation of a strong brand's brand identifiers to generate interest in the new brand. This strategy can decrease the risk and expense of independently attempting to develop a strong brand. In fact, many well-known brands have been accused of using their fame and large advertising budgets to overwhelm the introduction of new rival brands. We might call this Sumo Brand Confrontation after the famously large sumo wrestlers of Japan who seek to defeat their rivals by simply charging at them and overwhelming them. Such tactics undoubtedly are responsible for some of the high risk and expense of new brand introductions.

JBD marketers essentially free ride to some degree on the previous development efforts of the brand owners. When executed carefully, however, the costs associated with the legal challenge are modest, typically in the tens of thousands of dollars, and also may be associated with spontaneous publicity unfavorable to the well-known brand (Goliath) and favorable to the small business (David) facing legal challenge.

If the tactic proves effective in attracting consumer interest, then a smaller brand introduction budget may be used, or better response should be expected from the budget that is used. Lastly, if a well-known brand attempts to overwhelm the introduction of a new brand with Sumo Brand Confrontation, JBD, if done effectively, might remind consumers of the new brand, each time the established brand is advertised thereby reducing the established brand's advantage.

Despite the legal risks, firms do employ JBD tactics. For example, Parfum de Coeur offered a line of Designer Imposter® perfumes that it advertises using the slogan: "If you like (a particular brand of designer perfume), you'll love (our imitation brand)". Similarly, a copycat cosmetic firm offers an entire line of generic cosmetics under its trademark, Generic Brand. It used the same bottle shape as Sykes Perfect Nail for its nail hardener and conditioner and labeled it "Generic Brand Version of Sykes Perfect Nail." The court dismissed the trademark infringement claim asserting there was no likelihood of confusion, but allowed the state dilution claim to proceed to trial. The court held Sykes could win at trial if it could show by the imitator's use of the Sykes trademarks within its name, would likely render the Sykes trademarks generic (*Sykes Laboratory, Inc. v. Kalvin* 1985).

The differences between JBD, traditional brand marketing and commodity marketing are summarized in Table One.

Table One		
Forms of Marketing Compared		
Commodity Marketing	**Brand Marketing**	**Judo Brand Marketing**
Undifferentiated products	Products differentiated by unique brands	Weak or new brand associates with another's strong brand
Competition based on low prices	Competition based on expensive brand promotion to develop consumer brand loyalty	Competition based on promotion of association with strong brand and often price difference
Low cost producers are most successful. They avoid large promotional expenditures because their low prices attract customers.	Success depends on a quality product, quality branding and an expensive launch	Salient and creative association leads to notice by consumers and media enhancing the effectiveness of promotional efforts.
Risk of lower cost producer	Many brands compete for consumer attention.	Possible legal challenge by strong brand. Question of long term distinctive brand identity.

The federal trademark statute contains several provisions related to JBD. As already noted in prior chapters, trademark registration is prohibited when the proposed mark is (1) geographically misdescriptive, (2) incorporates the flag or insignia of any nation, state or municipality, (3) includes the name, signature or portrait of any living individual (without consent) or a deceased President with a living widow, (4) falsely suggests association with persons, institutions, beliefs or national symbols or (5) is likely to be confusingly similar to existing marks (15 U.S.C. § 1052). Under appropriate circumstances, a firm being challenged for using a similar trademark can argue the prior trademark is not entitled to trademark protection. However, that likely means that the new similar trademark also may not be protect-able. The statute also allows for fair use of a trademark term provided that the term is not used as a trademark and is used in good faith by the user to describe its goods (15 U.S.C. § 1115(b)(4)). This provision is an important basis for several JBD tactics.

Despite or perhaps because of the century long expansion of trademark protection described in Chapter One, the U.S. Supreme Court in the past fifteen years has been careful to recognize the pro-competitive advantages of imitation and to preserve the right to imitate consistent with the laws of intellectual property. Interestingly, this trend of cases began with a copyright decision where the Court held that "originality, not 'sweat of the brow' is the touchstone of copyright protection" thereby rejecting protection based on the "free riding" upon someone else's efforts and allowing the facts in telephone directories to be copied by competitors (*Feist Publications Inc. v. Rural Telephone Service Co. Inc.* 1991, at 359–60). Richard Posner, a respected jurist of the Seventh Circuit Court of Appeals wrote an opinion where he suggested the possibility of a similar anti-free riding justification for the Federal Trademark Dilution Act, but then noted that "the validity of the rationale may be doubted" (*Ty, Inc. v. Perryman* 2002, p. 512).

The six Supreme Court trademark decisions that continue and build upon this trend are summarized in Table Two. The first three decisions clarify that functional aspects of product designs may not be protected under trademark law and because product designs are inherently functional to some degree, they may not be considered inherently distinctive. The most recent two decisions provide for the imitation of trademarked brand names under appropriate circumstances. The *Dastar* decision simply notes that consumers often appreciate imitative brands and so these should not be prohibited by trademark law.

Table Two	
Recent Supreme Court Trademark Opinions Favoring Imitation	
Case	**Supreme Court Discussion of Imitation**
Qualitex Co. v. Jacobson Products Co., Inc. 514 U.S. 159, 169 (1995)	"The functionality doctrine [that prohibits functional aspects of product design from being protected as a trademark] thus protects competitors against . . . their inability reasonably to replicate important non-reputation-related product features."
Wal-Mart Stores, Inc. v. Samara Bros., Inc. 529 U.S. 205, 213 (2000)	"Consumers should not be deprived of the benefits of competition with regard to the utilitarian and esthetic purposes that product design ordinarily serves by a rule of law that facilitates plausible threats of suit against new entrants based upon alleged inherent distinctiveness."
TrafFix Devices, Inc. v. Marketing Displays, Inc. 532 U.S. 23, 29 (2001)	"Trade dress protection must subsist with the recognition that in many instances there is no prohibition against copying goods and products. In general, unless an intellectual property right such as a patent or copyright protects an item, it will be subject to copying. . . . [C]opying is not always discouraged or disfavored by the laws which preserve our competitive economy."
Dastar Corp. v. Twentieth Century Fox Film Corp. 539 U.S. 23, 32–33 (2003)	"The consumer who buys a branded product does not automatically assume that the brand-name company is the same entity that came up with the idea for the product, or designed the product—and typically does not care whether it is. The words of the Lanham Act should not be stretched to cover matters that are typically of no consequence to purchasers."
Moseley v. V. Secret Catalogue, Inc. 537 U.S. 418, 433 (2003)	" . . . [A]t least where the marks at issue are not identical, the mere fact that consumers mentally associate the junior user's mark with a famous mark is not sufficient to establish actionable dilution. . . . [S]uch mental association will not necessarily reduce the capacity of the famous mark to identify the goods of its owner . . . "
KP Permanent Make-Up, Inc. v. Lasting Impression I, Inc. 125 S.Ct. 542, 550 (2004)	" . . . [I]t follows . . . that some possibility of consumer confusion must be compatible with fair use, and so it is. The common law's tolerance of a certain degree of confusion on the part of consumers followed from the very fact that in cases like this one an originally descriptive term was selected to be used as a mark, not to mention the undesirability of allowing anyone to obtain a complete monopoly on use of a descriptive term simply by grabbing it first."

C. NEUTRALIZATION TACTICS

As illustrated in Table One of the Part 3 introduction, Neutralization Strategies include three tactics: trademark pre-emption, adopting an abandoned trademark and asserting genericide over another's trademark.

I. Trademark Preemption

This business tactic may be used against newly proposed trademarks that are not inherently distinctive. Inherently distinctive marks are entitled to protection from the moment of first use in the U.S. or the moment an Intent-to-Use application for registration is filed. However, the Supreme Court has indicated that product color (*Qualitex Co. v. Jacobson Products Co., Inc.*, 1995) and product configuration (*TrafFix Devices, Inc. v. Marketing Displays, Inc.* 2001) may never be considered inherently distinctive. Furthermore, descriptive proposed marks are not inherently distinctive and must be used and promoted to indicate a particular brand (secondary meaning) in the minds of consumers before they will be protected.

When RC 1000 was introduced in 1980 as the first caffeine-free cola, Pepsi in 1982 and Coca-Cola in 1983 also adopted the caffeine-free description making sure the phrase became commonly descriptive rather than suggestive of one particular brand. A similar imitation strategy was adopted toward the end of the decade when the major brands all adopted gold color packaging for their caffeine-free colas (both regular and diet). Similarly, "Lite" beer (*Miller Brewing Co. v. G. Heileman Brewing Co.* 1977) and "Gold" credit cards (*American Express Co v. Mastercard International, Inc.* 1988) are good examples where competitors quickly imitated the use of descriptive words and successfully had the terms declared generic descriptions of a product category ineligible for trademark protection.

A recent case demonstrating trademark preemption by a competitor involved amphibious city tours, typically conducted in boats called "duck" boats. Ride the Ducks started such tours in Philadelphia in May 2003 and as part of the experience distributed duck call noise makers to its patrons. In July 2004, Super Ducks started providing similar tours and also gave patrons duck call devices. Although Ride the Ducks registered the quacking noise made by patrons and tour guides as a service mark, the court denied it a preliminary injunction against its rival.

The court found that the quacking sound was not inherently distinctive but rather commonplace It further found that the sound had not yet developed secondary meaning to identify a particular tour operator in the minds of consumers because it had only been used exclusively for one full tourist season. Finally the court noted that Ride the Ducks advertising, while it did promote the distribution of duck call noisemakers, did not promote the sound of the duck calls as indicative of the Ride the Ducks brand (*Ride the Ducks. L.L.C. v. Duck Boat Tours, Inc.,* 2005). By denying the preliminary injunction, the court essentially allowed Super Ducks to use a quick imitation strategy to preempt the ability of its rival to obtain trademark protection for the sound.

II. Adopting an Abandoned Trademark

Alternatively, a firm may seek to revive an abandoned brand hoping the brand still has some interest with consumers. After three years of non-use with no intent to resume use, trademark abandonment is presumed. Proctor & Gamble discontinued its White Cloud brand of toilet paper in 1992 after 58 years of use, in order to concentrate marketing efforts on its Charmin brand. After litigation, Paper Partners won the right to use the brand name on toilet paper in 1996. White Cloud has become a very successful store brand exclusively at Wal-Mart (Ruder 2003). Similarly, the company that made and sold STRATOTONE brand guitars went out of business in the 1970s. The first company to file for intent to use the trademark is entitled to register it even if a later applicant claims it acquired all the assets of the original company (*Agler v. Westheimer Corp.* 2015). However, trademarks are often updated, called "tacking" in Chapter Two, and tacking continues the original mark so it is not considered abandoned (*Jack Wolfskin Ausrustung Fur Draussen GmbH & Co. KGAA v. New Millennium Sports, S.L.U.* 2015).

III. Genericide

As noted in Chapters Two and Six, generic terms are generally not entitled to trademark protection. For this reason "generic" is often considered the lowest level of trademark strength. However, genericide occurs when a well-known mark is so commonly used that it becomes the de facto name for the product category. In essence a very strong mark loses its ability to distinguish one brand from another. When this occurs, competitors become able to use the former trademark to describe goods within that category. Brand managers who select and promote enforce-able identifiers are often thrilled when the brand name becomes a short hand term for the product itself, such as COKE, XEROX, KLEENEX, BAND-AID in the U.S. and HOOVER in the United Kingdom. In fact Ries and Ries (2000, p. 41) declare this to be the ultimate sign of brand success.

However, despite the marketing advantages of "owning the category," brands with this level of ubiquity run the risk of being declared generic even though when first used they were not generic. For example, in recognition of the leading position of Q-TIP brand, Johnson & Johnson began marketing its Johnson's "Cotton-Tipped Applicators." When it later changed to Johnson's Cotton Tips, Q-Tips sued claiming infringement. Johnson & Johnson argued first that Q-Tips had become generic for the category and alternatively that Cotton Tips was intended to be a generic description of the product rather than a trademark. The trial and appellate courts rejected both arguments and enjoined further use of the name Cotton Tips (*Q-Tips, Inc. v. Johnson & Johnson* 1953).

In some cases, it is difficult to tell if a proposed trademark is pre-empted or has always been considered generic. In 1994, Genesee introduced "JW Dundee's Honey Brown Lager" and sought trademark protection for the entire name without disclaiming rights to the phrase "Honey Brown" which was the popular name for the brand. Two years later Stroh Brewing introduced "Red River Valley Honey Brown Ale." The following year, an appeals court affirmed the denial of a preliminary injunction against the second product, holding that brown ale was a generic product category and honey brown ale would be descriptive of a product in that category that was flavored with honey (*Genesee Brewing Co., Inc. v Stroh Brewing Co.* 1997). It is important to note that if a competitor waits for a descriptive name (e.g., WATERMAN fountain pens) to acquire substantial strength and fame through use, and then tries to imitate what has become a strong mark, the courts will prevent him from doing so unless the brand name has become the generic category label (e.g., *L.E. Waterman Co. v. Modern Pen Co.* 1914).

To avoid genericide, the first step should be to select a brand name that is not the name for the product category. Inventors of new types of products should not only select a distinctive brand name, but also name the product category. Dupont failed to do this for cellophane. As a result, when its patents on cellophane expired, a court allowed other companies to call their product cellophane since there was no other name for that type of plastic (*Dupont Cellophane Co. v. Waxed Products Co.* 1936). For this reason, brands often carefully distinguish their name from that of the product category such as KLEENEX brand **facial tissues**. They also clearly identify their brand name as a brand name as in the jingle "I am stuck on BAND-AID **brand** (adhesive bandages), and BAND-AID is stuck on me." They should promote the brand name as a brand name (Hagan 2004).

Trademark attorneys typically advise brand managers to make sure the brand name is used as an adjective describing a generic noun. They suggest that trademarks should never be used as nouns (including plurals or possessives) or verbs. But this view is too simplistic. In fact verbal trademarks have been registered such as DO YOU YAHOO? and DON'T WORRY THERE IS A FEDEX FOR THAT.

The key to preventing "genericide" is not how the brand name is used but what it means to consumers. As long as it means a particular product source, the trademark is not generic. For this reason, brand managers must try to police and correct both their rivals and the media for use of their brand name as a generic. They must also police their own use to make sure the purported brand identifier is not used descriptively in advertising such as water that is "Bottled at the Source." Although one firm was allowed to register "Bottled at the Source" as a trademark, descriptive use of the phrase by competitors, the media and the company itself recently caused a court to declare the registration invalid and the phrase generic (*Fiji Water Co. LLC v. Paramount Int'l Export Ltd.* 2008).

Without these efforts, the general public may come to believe the word identifies a product category rather than a particular marketer's product. This is what happened to Thermos brand vacuum bottles (*King-Seeley Thermos Co v. Aladdin Industries*, 1963) and Murphy beds that fold into a wall enclosure (*Murphy Door Bed Co., Inc. v. Interior Sleep Systems, Inc.* 1989). Other products that were declared generic are illustrated by a famous advertisement by XEROX that is partially reprinted on the following page.

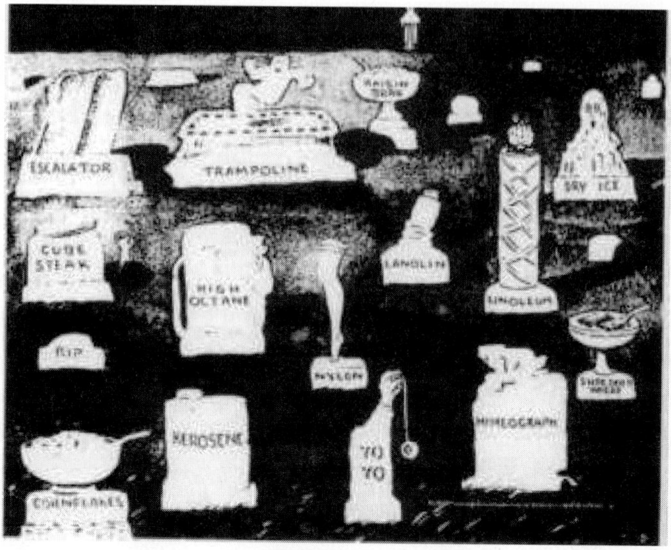

It is important to note that genericide occurs on a country-by-country basis. THERMOS is still a trademark in the U.K., YO-YO is still a trademark in Canada and XEROX is reportedly generic in parts of Eastern Europe. Despite the age of many of these examples, genericide is a very real risk to the modern brand manager. Below is a table of terms declared generic in the U.S. in this century.

Table Four		
Terms Declared Generic in the United States (21st Century)		
Phrase Declared Generic	**Year**	**Citation**
Crab House for restaurants	2001	*Hunt Masters, Inc. v. Landrey's Seafood Restaurant, Inc.*, 240 F.3d 251 (4th Cir.)
You've Got Mail for internet services	2001	*America Online, Inc. v. AT&T Corp.*, 243 F.3d 872 (4th Cir.)
Yellow Cab for taxicabs	2003	*Yellow Cab Co. of Sacramento v. Yellow Cab Co. of Elk Grove*, 266 F. Supp. 2d 1199 (E.D. Cal.)
Freebies for magazines	2004	*Retail Services Inc. v. Freebies Pub.*, 364 F.3d 535 (4th Cir.)
Brick Oven for pizza	2006	*Schwan's IP, LLC v. Kraft Pizza Co.*, 460 F.3d 971 (8th Cir.)

Kettle for potato chips	2007	*Classic Foods, Int'l Corp. v. Kettle Foods, Inc.*, 468 F. Supp.2d 1181 (C.D. Cal.)
Disinfectable for nail files	2007	*Rudolph Int'l, Inc. v. Realys, Inc.*, 482 F.3d 1195 (9th Cir.)
M4 for firearms	2007	*Colt Defense LLC v. Bushmaster Firearms, Inc.*, 486 F.3d 701 (1st Cir.)
Duck Tours for amphibious tours	2008	*Boston Duck Tours, LP v. Super Duck Tours, LLC*, 531 F.3d 1 (1st Cir.)
Bottled at the Source for bottled water	2008	*Fiji Water Co. LLC v. Paramount Int'l Export, Ltd.*, 2008 WL 2782745 (N.D. Cal.)
Christmas Ale	2012	*Great Lakes Brewing*, TTAB Jan. 9, 2012

If a purported brand name is declared generic, it is possible, albeit unlikely, that through promotion a brand could reclaim exclusive use of the name by showing that it once again identifies a single source of product rather than an entire category of product. Despite an earlier ruling that "Lite" was a generic term for beer (*Miller Brewing Co. v. G. Heileman Brewing Co.* 1977), a district court in 1980 was persuaded that Miller had successfully reclaimed the term as its brand name in the minds of consumers. However, the court of appeals disagreed arguing that once a term has become generic, all brands in that product category are entitled to use the term and it cannot be reclaimed (*Miller Brewing Co. v. Falstaff Brewing Corp.* 1981).

Examples of successfully reclaiming a generic name are rare but do exist. Both SINGER and GOODYEAR were declared generic prior to 1900, but were recaptured as brand names after 1950. More recently, MATCHBOX toy cars, OPRY for country music performances and SOFTSOAP have regained their trademark status as well, the latter after only six years of generic status. Despite the *Miller Brewing* decision, it appears as though the U.S. trend is to allow trademark recapture, but to do so only if the generic use of the term is "practically obsolete" with the public.

Courts recognize that brand marketers invest heavily to distinguish brand names to help consumers identify the brand they wish to purchase and set a high level of proof in order to declare a trademark generic. On the other side, once a word is generic, many brand marketers become accustomed to using the term, and the legal system is equally reluctant to then take the term out of the public domain (Levy 2005). In Europe, a term that is descriptive may be registered as a trademark if proven to have acquired secondary meaning, but proving such a case appears to be at least as difficult as in the U.S. Marketers should not rely upon possible recapture of a generic term, but rather follow the suggestions above for preserving the trademark status of their brand names.

If a name is declared generic, brand marketers need not give up all control of it. They still have at least four possible strategies for restricting to some degree the use of the term by other firms as discussed in Chapter Six.

D. CONCLUSION

This chapter focuses on the simple concept that one way to imitate another's brand identifiers is to make such that those brand identifiers are not protected by trademark law. When a rival starts to use a new potential brand identifier that is descriptive, competitors may also use the same descriptor to prevent it from being associated with a single brand in the minds of consumers. It never becomes a brand identifier.

On the other side of trademark life, a trademark may be abandoned for valid marketing reasons but still have value in the minds of consumers. Alert competitors may adopt the abandoned trademark as their own with the first new adopter generally entitled to trademark protection. This is the only Neutralization tactic that provides the Judo Brand marketer with exclusive rights.

Trademarks also may "die" if they have become the generic product category label in the minds of consumers. When a rival brand marketer's research shows that this has occurred, the rival may petition to have the mark declared generic or simply start using the mark, e.g.,

ALLADIN brand thermos, and wait to be challenged by the competitor. Proving the mark to be generic is a defense to trademark counterfeiting, infringement and dilution.

The successful use of any of these tactics voids any benefits from past brand building to the original brand marketer, but enhances brand competition by opening up descriptive terms for use by others.

CHAPTER 15

Judo Brand Diversion Comparison Tactics

A. INTRODUCTION

Comparison JBD tactics have long been recognized as beneficial to consumers provided the comparison is clear and the source of the JBD brand is clearly distinguished as not being the same as the brand that is the point of comparison. By using comparison tactics, the judo brand marketer is deliberately comparing its offering (either explicitly or implicitly) with a well-known brand, sometimes to highlight similarities and sometimes to emphasize differences such as superior attributes or performance or lower price. The next chapter on unauthorized brand extension also addresses tactics that are somewhat comparative such as compatible and parody products that can be used with a well-known brand or make fun of it, respectively. This chapter examines copycat products (such as store brands), comparative advertising and descriptive fair use where the judo brand describes itself in ways similar to a trademark of a well-known brand.

B. COPYCAT PRODUCTS

Imitation is often said to be the sincerest form of flattery. Imitating the packaging of a famous brand sends a clear message to consumers that the copycat product should be considered comparable to the famous brand but typically is priced significantly lower (Warlop and Alba 2004). Packaging can help build brand identity both as a form of advertising, particularly at the point of purchase, and as part of brand use experience after purchase (Underwood 2003).

While many marketers believe consumers are skeptical of copycat store brands, marketing studies suggest that this is not always the case. Consumers often evaluate copycat store brands favorably unless there is little price difference with national brands (Warlop and Alba 2004). Harvey et al (1998) reports that copycat store brands are an effective way to develop consumer interest and are probably more profitable than non-copycat store brands that need a larger price differential over the national brand to attract as much attention. Collins-Dodd and Zaichkowsky (1999) note that national brands appear more likely to sue imitative competitors than retailers. Eighty percent of those surveyed took action against manufacturers, but only 42% sued retailers.

As mentioned in Chapter Four, most recent court decisions have allowed imitative packaging so long as the brand name is distinctive. For example, in *Yankee Candle Company, Inc. v. Bridgewater Candle Company, LLC* (2001), distinctive brand names were held to prevent confusion, despite similarities of the candles, containers, in-store displays, and catalogs. Similarly in *Nora Beverages, Inc. v. the Perrier Group of America, Inc.* (2001), the use of identical bottles for bottled spring water was allowed when distinctive labels and brand names are used and in *Conopco, Inc. v. May Department Stores Co.* (1994), the court allowed a retailer to copy the trade dress of a national brand as long as the product name was distinctive. Such blatant copying of trade dress is allowed even when done intentionally (*Bristol-Myers Squibb Co. v. McNeil-P.P.C., Inc.* 1994).

The packaging in *Nora Beverages* and *Conopco*

Recently, however, the Third Circuit Court of Appeal took a step backwards from this approach. It held that the use of a prominent well known store brand name could overwhelm overall package similarity, but that the display of a store name anywhere on the package was not an automatic defense to likely confusion. Rather it held courts had to carefully consider the overall impression of the imitative package including the name to determine if it was sufficiently similar to cause confusion with a well-known brand. It reversed the denial of a preliminary injunction of the package on the right below finding that the store brand GIANT was not sufficiently prominent to dispel likely consumer confusion (*McNeil Nutritionals, LLC v. Heartland Sweeteners LLC* 2007).

While the defense that a distinctive trade name prevents confusion seems viable with a number of courts, a JBD marketer might also argue that particular trade dress was merely descriptive and therefore generic to the product category. For example, in the sweetener example above, the color yellow communicates the specific sweetener, sucralose, in the package. Saccharin-based sweeteners such as SWEET N LOW are typically sold in pink packages and aspartame sweeteners such as EQUAL are sold in blue packages. The colors are used both by the national brands and by store brands.

This defense was successful for Mars when it introduced peanut butter M & Ms with colors (tan, orange and brown) and packaging similar to those used by Reece's Pieces. The court found that such colors and packaging were descriptive of peanut butter candy and not distinctive to Reese's Pieces (*Hershey Foods Corp. v. Mars, Inc.* 1998). Such a defense also may work when a brand is slow to challenge the package color of its imitators thereby allowing imitators to pre-empt color as an identifier of a particular brand as noted in the previous chapter. As noted in Chapter Four, color also may be functional in that a maker of tractor accessories may want to offer items in "John Deere green" because consumers want accessories that match their tractors.

Trademark misdescription may also serve as a defense in some cases. When Frusen Glädjé was marketed to compete with Häagen-Dazs in the super premium ice cream market, the names were dissimilar but both evoked a Scandinavian marketing theme. Häagen-Dazs also complained of packaging similarities including the phraseology used to list ingredients, the recitation of artificial ingredients not included in the product, a map of Scandinavia on the package and the Germanic-sounding names.

In denying a preliminary injunction, the court noted that Frusen Glädjé was no more misleading as to Scandinavian origin than Häagen-Dazs and that the latter was not entitled to exclusive rights to the use of such a theme (*Häagen-Dazs, Inc. v. Frusen Glädjé, Ltd.* 1980). Imitation of the marketing theme was allowed here because both name and package were distinctive. In contrast, the makers of GUNSMOKE cigarettes were found to have imitated not just MARLBORO's cowboy/western theme but also its red packaging and cowboy picture.

The confusingly similar GUNSMOKE packaging was enjoined (*Philip Morris Inc. v. Star Tobacco Corp.* 1995).

Copycat products entail legal risks. A court might find either or both the name and packaging to be confusingly similar. For example, Keebler obtained a preliminary injunction when rival Nabisco introduced Pecan Supremes with similar trade dress to Keebler's Pecan Sandies (*Keebler Co. v. Nabisco Brands, Inc.*, 1992). Similarly, the name basique was found distinctive from Clinique when used with similar packaging in part because many beauty products end with "ique." However, when basique was used with the single letter "b" similar to the way Clinique is used with the single letter "C," the court found that use with very similar trade dress to be trademark infringement (*Clinique Labs., Inc. v. Dep Corp.* 1996).

Most of these trade dress cases require the imitated brand to prove that its trade dress has secondary meaning and therefore identifies the brand in the minds of consumers. However, at least one court has disallowed copycat brand packaging disagreeing with the decisions above and noting that a 1992 Supreme Court decision holding that trade dress could be inherently distinctive and therefore protected under trademark law without a showing of secondary meaning in the minds of consumers (*McNeil—PPC, Inc. v. Guardian Drug Co.,* 1997). In that Supreme Court decision, the Court held the imitation of distinctive trade dress to be trademark infringement despite the non-confusing nature of the restaurant names. It noted that the Lanham Act applies with equal force to trademark and trade dress infringement (*Two Pesos, Inc. v. Taco Cabana, Inc.* 1992).

The Supreme Court recently clarified that only product packaging trade dress (as opposed to product design) can be inherently distinctive (*Wal-Mart Stores, Inc. v. Samara Brothers Inc.* 2000). For example, the shape of Pepperidge Farm's goldfish snack crackers can be protected as trade dress because it has nothing to do with the function of cheese crackers. However, because it is the product rather than the package,

Pepperidge Farm must be able to prove the shape is a distinctive indicator of the source of the crackers in the minds of consumers. Not surprisingly, it was able to do this.

What may be surprising is that a court granted it product shape trade dress protection over a product that was a mixture of different shaped crackers, including fish. The court found trademark infringement liability even though any possible confusion would occur after purchase, only by non-purchasers, and would likely be temporary because the fish shape was mixed in with other shapes (*Nabisco, Inc. v. PF Brands, Inc.* 1999).

C. COMPARATIVE ADVERTISING

As long ago as 1910, Justice Holmes acknowledged the fair use of another's trademark in comparative advertising: "They have a right to tell the public what they are doing and to get whatever share they can in the popularity of the [trademarked product] . . . by advertising they are trying to make the same article, and think they succeed" (*Saxlehner v. Wagner* 1910, p. 380). The Ninth Circuit has added that comparative advertising is permissible even if the advertiser reaps the benefit of "the product recognition engendered by the owner's popularization, through expensive advertising, or the mark" (*Anti-Monopoly Inc. v. Gen. Mills Fun Group* 1979, p. 301, n.2).

Some courts refer to this as nominal fair use because the other party's trademark is being used to correctly name its products. A 1992 court of appeals decision created a three part test for nominative fair use: (1) the product or service must not be readily identifiable without use of the trademark, (2) only as much of the trademark may be used as needed to reasonably identify the referent product or service, and (3) the user of the referent trademark must do nothing to suggest sponsorship or endorsement by the trademark owner (*New Kids on the Block v. News America Publishing, Inc.* 1992).

However, legal tradition suggested that another party's trademarked name could not be used in advertising without permission. Therefore, comparative advertising was typically vague referring only to "Brand X" or "another leading brand." In the 1970s, the Federal Trade Commission began supporting explicit comparative advertising as an incentive to stimulate product improvement and the provision of information to help consumers choose among alternative products (16 C.F.R. § 14.15). Today it is well recognized in the United States that another company's trademarks may be used to identify that particular brand in comparative advertising (15 U.S.C. § 1125(c)(4)(A)).

Despite FTC endorsement of the concept of comparative advertising, it is frequently the subject of deceptive advertising challenges as discussed in Chapter Eight. This has led some marketers to create brand doppelgangers to compare with. The most famous example is Apple's Mac vs. PC campaign. In that series of ads the cool Mac brand character continually demonstrates his superiority over the PC character as both emulate behaviors of their respective computers. Legal risk is lower because Apple did not challenge any particular brand of PC or even Microsoft directly so those brands had less incentive to challenge the Apple ads for possibly being misleading.

Other countries have shown greater reluctance that the U.S. in allowing explicit comparative advertising. Europe adopted a Directive amending a prior Directive on misleading advertising to permit comparative advertising in 1997. Prior to that time some European countries prohibited or greatly restrictive explicit comparative advertising. The current 2006 European Directive on Misleading and Comparative Advertising still requires member states to permit explicit comparative advertising under specified circumstances:

(a) it is not misleading;

(b) it compares goods or services meeting the same needs or intended for the same purpose;

(c) it objectively compares one or more material, relevant, verifiable and representative features of those goods and services, which may include price;

(d) it does not discredit or denigrate the trade marks, trade names, other distinguishing marks, goods, services, activities or circumstances of a competitor;

(e) for products with designation of origin, it relates in each case to products with the same designation;

(f) it does not take unfair advantage of the reputation of a trade mark, trade name or other distinguishing marks of a competitor or of the designation of origin of competing products;

(g) it does not present goods or services as imitations or replicas of goods or services bearing a protected trade mark or trade name;

(h) it does not create confusion among traders, between the advertiser and a competitor or between the advertiser's trade marks, trade names, other distinguishing marks, goods or services and those of a competitor.

The Directive has been interpreted as a defense to trademark infringement. In a recent U.K. case involving comparative price advertising, the advertiser used a bubbles motif when discussing the higher priced competitor and these bubbles were found to infringe upon the rival's trademark. However, the Court of Appeal affirmed dismissal of the lawsuit because the comparative advertising was legal under the Directive and therefore should be allowed despite the trade mark infringement. This decision was supported by the European Court of Justice that held if comparative advertising fully satisfied the Comparative Advertising Directive it should be allowed unless there was trademark confusion, which in this case, according to the court of appeals on remand, there was not (*O2 Holdings Ltd v. Hutchinson 3G Ltd.*

2006). In the U.S., the likely result would be to allow the comparisons but enjoin similar imitations of the rival's trademark if there was any confusion between the two brands.

This Directive may continue some of the differences in the treatment of comparative advertising both within Europe and between the E.U. and U.S. While legal violations such as trademark infringement, disparagement, and passing off are recognized in both the U.S. and E.U., they are typically more broadly construed in the latter. Furthermore, the particular E.U. requirements that comparisons: (b) only compare goods meeting the same needs, (d) does not discredit or denigrate the trademarks of a competitor, and (f) does not take unfair advantage of the reputation of a trademark also appear inevitably to lead to differences in the treatment of comparative advertising across the Atlantic and allow the continuation of much of the intra-European differences until the European Court is called upon to resolve them.

Recently the ECJ allowed a beer to compare itself to Champagne holding that the E.U. Directive and Regulation must be interpreted permissively and that this comparison did not take unfair advantage of the reputation of Champagne (*De Landtsheer Emmanuel SA v Comité Interprofessionnel du Vin de Champagne* 2007). Another interesting example of JBD by comparison across categories of goods was the advertising assertion by a U.S. leather furniture store that "only Revlon has more colors." This example is noteworthy because it positions Revlon quite positively as the pinnacle of color selection. Nonetheless, this statement was challenged by Revlon but allowed by the court since consumers would not be confused that the cosmetic company was now selling furniture (*Revlon Consumer Products Corporation v. Jennifer Leather Broadway* 1994). In Europe, because cosmetics and furniture don't meet the same needs, this ad may not have been allowed as taking unfair advantage of Revlon's reputation.

Numerous marketing studies have shown comparative advertising to be effective. A meta-analysis of these studies found that comparative advertising generated higher levels of brand interest, stronger purchase intentions and more purchases than non-comparative advertising. The authors also found that past studies showed new brands comparing themselves to established brands benefited most from comparative advertising (Grewal et al. 1997). Pechmann (1996) argues that when a marketer makes a narrow or small number of comparisons, a halo effect might lead consumers to believe that the advertised product is superior on other attributes as well. As discussed in Chapter Eight, one common comparative claim, "No product is better than ours" has been shown to mean to a majority of consumers the advertised product is better than rival products rather than merely as good as them as literal interpretation would suggest (Wyckham 1987; Buchanan and Smithies 1989).

It is important to note that comparisons may be made without using another's trademark. The target of the comparison is implicit and not identified by name. This reduces the legal risk of trademark infringement or dilution since another's trademark is not used. A classic example is Avis' slogan "We're Number Two. We Try Harder." Market leader Hertz is not explicitly identified, but the value of its market leadership position is used against it by the portrayal of Avis as an eager-to-please upstart company with sufficient size to provide good service.

While there is still the potential that such implicit comparisons may be found illegal, U.S. courts appear to treat such comparisons favorably. For example, the Fifth Circuit dismissed a case of false advertising against Papa John's pizza for its slogan "Better ingredients. Better Pizza." The appellate court found the slogan to be puffery rather than a statement of fact and held that challenger Pizza Hut failed to prove the slogan was material to consumers in the context of advertising that made specific factual claims about specific ingredients such as sauce and dough (*Pizza Hut, Inc. v. Papa John's Int'l, Inc.* 2000).

Similarly, when Norelco compared itself to a razor that appeared as a fire breathing dragon, a snake and a razor with metal jaws (pictured below) and other equally unpleasant parody products, the challenge to the advertising for being deceptive was dismissed when the challenger failed to prove the meaning of the ads to consumers (*Gillette Co. v. Norelco Consumer Prods. Co.* 1999).

When rivals use competitors' trademarks in advertising, they run the risk of trademark infringement. The trademark owner must prove there is likely consumer confusion over the source of the ads or the advertised products. For example, the package of a board game called Sixth Sense repeatedly referred to the inventor of the game as the same person who invented the game MASTERMIND. These repeated references, made in large type, were held to likely confuse consumers as to the origin of the new game and whether it was from the same company that sold MASTERMIND (*Invicta Plastics (U.S.A.) Ltd. v. Mego Corp.* 1981). Rival trademarks are used in parody advertising to poke fun at a rival brand (such as the Norelco ad illustrated above), often creating at least an implied comparison. Parody advertising is discussed in the next chapter.

The tort of disparagement (Chapter Five) may be applied to comparisons under limited circumstances. Gillette alleged that the visual images of wet shaving were disparaging. However, the court found the images were puffing—obvious exaggerations rather than factual statements. In the U.S, this tort requires proof that intentionally false statements about a product were made. However, it is difficult to prove intent and most U.S. advertisers are sufficiently sophisticated to avoid making obviously false statements.

The most obvious risk of comparative advertising is that it may be challenged for being false, misleading or unsubstantiated. This is particularly true in the U.S., where most Lanham Act advertising cases and most industry self-regulation challenges are brought by competitors. For example, a copycat perfume marketer was allowed to compare its fragrance, 2d Chance, to Chanel No. 5 using Chanel trademarks (*Smith v. Chanel, Inc.* 1968), but was held liable for making false statements within those comparisons (*Chanel, Inc. v. Smith* 1973).

D. DESCRIPTIVE USE

Use of common or descriptive trademarked words to describe another brand is typically allowed even though consumers might be reminded of the famous brand. For example, a lipstick company did not infringe another's "Sealed with a Kiss" trademark when it distributed promotional cards for mailing with instructions to place a lipstick imprint on the cards and the statement "Seal it with a Kiss!" (*Cosmetically Sealed Industry, Inc. v. Chesebrough-Pond's USA Co.*1997). Similarly, "fish fry" may be used descriptively by competitors despite registration of the trademark "Fish-Fri" (*Zatarain's Inc. v. Oak Grove Smokehouse, Inc.* 1983).

More recently, courts allowed a cranberry juice brand to describe its product as "sweet-tart" despite the trademarked brand name SWEETARTS (*Sunmark, Inc. v. Ocean Spray Cranberries, Inc.* 1995). Similarly, a court allowed CREST brand toothpaste to advertise that it was "The Dentist's Choice for Fighting Cavities," despite protests from DENTIST'S CHOICE brand toothbrushes (*Wonderlabs, Inc. v. P & G Co.* 1990). Most recently, the Supreme Court decided that the words "micro color" could be used to by a tattoo ink marketer to describe its products, despite a rival owning the trademark MICRO COLORS. The Court stated that some consumer confusion might exist but the judo marketer has no burden to disprove consumer confusion when using descriptive words (*KP Permanent Make-Up, Inc. v. Lasting Impression I, Inc.* 2004).

The rationale of these decisions is often twofold. First, the descriptive use is not use as a trademark and therefore, the use can't constitute trademark infringement. Second, because the original trademark is descriptive in nature, the brand owner in selecting the mark obtains only narrow protection from infringement. Descriptive use of the same common word(s) is not likely to cause confusion because the words are so common.

Often the descriptive use constitutes a product or product category description rather than a trademark indicating a single source of goods. So the trademark owner of WORLD BOOK encyclopedia could not complain of the publication of an "Illustrated World Encyclopedia" (*Field Enterprises Educ. Corp. v. Cove Indus., Inc.* 1969). Similarly, despite the similarity of meanings, the use of the phrase "Lip Repair Cream" did not infringe the trademark LIP-FIX (*Eli Lilly & Co. v. Revlon, Inc.* 1983). Often courts also note the prominence of a distinctive brand name such as REVLON in the lip repair case that clarifies the origin of the product making consumer confusion less likely. Of course descriptive use does not excuse the use of an infringing trademark. When MOBILE MECHANICS essentially adopted that name as their unregistered trademark, the court found it was confusing similar to and therefore infringed MOBIL OIL (*Mobil Oil Corp. v. Mobile Mechanics, Inc.* 1976).

Under current case law, trademarks normally may not be used in domain names of commercial websites without ownership or permission (*Brookfield Communications v. West Coast Entertainment Corp.* 1999). Fair use of a common term such as "Clue" in a domain name (common terms may be included in many different trademarks) is legal absent a showing of likelihood of consumer confusion (*Hasbro Inc. v. Clue Computing Inc.* 2000). However, courts generally are not sympathetic to the use of common terms in domain names by pornographers and have generally found such uses to constitute dilution by tarnishing (*Ford Motor Co. v. Lapertosa*, 2000; *Toys "R" Us v. Akkaoui*, 1996). Infringement/consumer confusion also has been used to enjoin domain names that include trademarks with other language, such as Playboyxxx.com and Playmatelive.com (*Playboy Enterprises. Inc. v. Calvin Designer Label* 1997).

E. CONCLUSION

Because comparison advertising has been long recognized as legal in the U.S. and other comparisons such as copycat brands also have been allowed under many circumstances, this category of JBD offers relatively low legal risk with some significant short term benefits in terms of inducing trial of the new brand.

CHAPTER 16

Judo Brand Diversion Unauthorized Extensions

Launching an extension of an existing brand rather than an entirely new brand is a well-known risk-decreasing alternative for brand marketers. Recent estimates suggest that as many as 80% of new product introductions are brand extensions. Aaker and Keller (1990) note that extending a well-known brand name may make promotional expenditures more effective and possibly allowing a reduced brand launch budget. According to one report, well over half of the new brands introduced in the 1980s were brand extensions. Success factors for brand extensions include fit between the parent and the extension, marketing support and retailer acceptance of the extension, and consumer experience with and conviction to the parent brand (Volckner and Sattler 2006).

Unfortunately, research suggests that while flagship brand products may be relatively immune to brand equity dilution by incompatible or disappointing brand extensions, the overall parent brand may suffer reduced equity from multiple low quality extensions (John et al. 1998; Loken and John 1993). In addition, about 80% of brand extensions in many fast moving consumer goods categories fail which is only slightly better than the 90% new brand failure rate cited previously (Volckner and Sattler 2006).

Some JBD tactics are similar to brand extensions, but of course are neither authorized nor licensed by the brand being "extended." For the small business that lacks an established brand obtaining permission to market an extension of someone else's brand may be impossible or expensive. However, the entrepreneur may adopt JBD tactics that get some of the benefit of being an apparent brand extension but without the necessity of negotiating a license.

As with all JBD tactics, the precise execution of the tactic will determine the legal risk. These unauthorized brand extension tactics can be placed into three categories: Reselling, Compatible products or services and Vague Associations. The first two categories are fairly straightforward with few surprises, but the last group includes ornamental products, ambush marketing and parody products—all of which are controversial.

One point is clear. Rivals cannot simply provide a comparable product when a customer asks for a particular brand of product. Coca-Cola was famous for policing restaurants that did not serve its brand with undercover agents posing as customers and ordering a COKE. If they were served a cola beverage without explanation that the restaurant did not serve COKE, the restaurant received a cease and desist letter (Petty 2012). Similarly, when the general counsel of In-N-Out Burgers ordered a meal at a rival restaurant using names trademarked by In-N-Out and received his order without comment, he filed a judicial complaint and obtained a temporary restraining order prohibiting the practice and requiring the rival to informed other consumers placing similar orders that the restaurant does not offer that style of hamburger (*In-N-Out Burgers v. Chadders Restaurant* 2007).

A. RESELLERS

Parties that sell a particular brand of goods are entitled to use the brand name to advertise that fact. For example, an independent dealer of new and used vacuum cleaners can advertise the brands it sells as long as it does not suggest affiliation or endorsement (*Scott Fetzer Co. v. House of Vacuums, Inc.* 2004). In fact, the E.U. Trade Marks Directive specifically allows non-trademark owners to use the mark to indicate the kind or quality of goods being offered in the course of trade as long as this is done in accordance with honest practices (Art. 6). In *Parfums Christian Dior SA v. Evora* BV (1997), the ECJ held that even an unauthorized reseller could use the brand name unless the particular situation of use seriously damaged the reputation of the brand.

Similarly, sellers of "re-" goods may use the trademark of the brand of the goods provided that they also disclose the changed condition of the goods, the identity of the party marketing the goods in that particular form, and disclaim or at least do not imply any association or connection with the brand marketer. "Re-" goods include those that have been recycled, reconditioned (*Champion Spark Plug Co. v. Sanders* 1947), refurbished (*NitroLeisure Prods. LLC v. Acushnet Co.* 2003: Schumacher 2006), refilled, recharged or repackaged (*Prestonettes, Inc. v. Coty* 1924; *Farouk Systems, Inc. v. Target Corp., Inc.* 2008).

In Europe, advertising the original brand in repackaging and reselling situations falls under the concept of the exhaustion of trademark rights after the first sale and serves the important purpose of allowing the free flow of goods within the union. Europe imposes an additional requirement that the reseller give prior notice to the trademark owner and at least in the case of pharmaceutical goods a specimen of the new package so that the trademark owner can check to see if the repackaging might damage the trademark and to ensure the repackager is clearly identified (*Hoffman-La Roche* 1978).

One unusual example of a "product" being resold is the website of Terri Welles, former PLAYMATE OF THE YEAR. The Ninth Circuit allowed her to use this trademark and to accurately describe herself as a former Playmate of the Year on her website, provided she disclaim any current association with Playboy Enterprises (*Playboy Enterprises, Inc. v. Welles* 1998). In essence, she was reselling her status as a PLAYMATE OF THE YEAR.

Another usual example that might best fit within the category of resellers is the broadcast of a local sporting event. Interested spectators could view the event in person or watch its broadcast (analogous to reselling) on local television. A Boston area television station was allowed to use the trademark BOSTON MARATHON to advertise its broadcast of the event (*WCVB-TV v. Boston Athletic Association* 1991). Alternatively, the broadcast of this event might be viewed as a service compatible with the event.

B. COMPATIBLE PRODUCTS AND SERVICES

Not only can resellers advertise the brand they offer but those who service particular brands of products may advertise that fact as well as long as they don't imply specific affiliation with or authorization by the brand owner. This is permitted both under U.S. and E.U. law (*Volkswagenwerk A.G. v. Church* 1969; *Bayerische Motorenwerke AG (BMW) v. Deenik* 1999).

Repair services often sell spare parts and the European Trade Marks Directive specifically allows sellers of accessories or spare parts to use the trademark of the main product provided such use is in accordance with honest practices (Art. 6). In a case involving razor handles that were compatible with GILLETTE SENSOR blade cartridges, the ECJ held that the blade cartridges were the principle products rather than accessories or spare parts. Nonetheless, it held the GILLETTE trademarks could be used if necessary to indicate the intended purpose of the product (as opposed to a generic designation such as uses all razor cartridges) and if the use was in accordance with honest commercial practices (*Gillette Co. v. LA Labs. Ltd. Oy* 2005). U.S. law also allows the seller of a compatible or accessory product to use the brand name to advertise the compatibility as long as the advertisement does not imply approval or an association between the two (*Polyglycoat Corp. v. Environmental Chems. Co.* 1980). Advertising compatible goods also could be considered a form of comparison with branded accessories.

Two recent decisions of the European Court of Justice also allow competitors of compatible components to copy most of the product part reference numbers of the primary brand of equipment and parts as comparative advertising to claim their parts were compatible. For example the Siemens part number 6ES5–928–3UB21 could be copied by its rival VIPA as VIPA–928–3UB21 (*Siemens AG v. CIPA Gesellschaft fur Visualisierung und Prozessautomatisierurng mbH* 2006; *Toshiba Europe GmbH v. Katun Germany GmbH* 2002). Similarly in the U.S., Lean Cuisine was allowed to truthfully advertise how its products could be used by those following a Weight Watchers program that used Weight Watchers exchange points as long as approval by and affiliation with Weight Watchers were clearly disclaimed (*Weight Watchers Int'l Inc. v. Stouffer Foods Corp.* 1990).

C. VAGUE ASSOCIATIONS

In Chapter Twelve, vague associations were described as the least strong association that a brand could make with another brand, celebrity or other association. In this chapter, the focus is on the vague nature of the association rather than its relative strength. A vague association can be vague in at least one of two ways. First, it can be vague regarding the nature of the association. For example, some ornamental products such as team logo clothing are proudly labeled as officially licensed by the appropriate brand owner whereas others may display a team logo but say nothing about being licensed.

The second method an association can be vague involves the exact identity of the party to which an association is being asserted. The classic example of this is ambush marketing where brand advertising makes vague reference to the Olympic Games or another large sporting event, but without using the protected word "Olympics." Rather advertising refers to the location of the games, or the national team that is competing. Of course some associations such as parodies are vague along both dimensions. They do not use another brand's exact trademark, but some are sufficiently close that consumers may wonder if they are licensed or not by the trademark owner.

Sometimes advertising is used to create a vague association that does not fit neatly into one of these categories. One example is Showtime's advertisement proclaiming "Showtime & HBO. It's Not Either/Or Anymore." HBO sought and obtained a preliminary injunction arguing consumers would be confused into falsely thinking HBO had formed an alliance with Showtime or was co-sponsoring or endorsing the ad. The court held that a disclaimer denying HBO's sponsorship of the ad, if proven effective by Showtime, could allow for this campaign to continue (*Home Box Office, Inc. v. Showtime/The Movie Channel, Inc.* 1987).

I. Ornamental Products

What if a "compatible" product is not functionally compatible but rather simply emotionally compatible such as automobile floor mats that proudly display a particular automobile brand logo? Ornamental use occurs when a trademark is used on a product not to designate the product's source but to nominally identify and celebrate the product owner's affection for the brand. To escape liability for counterfeiting, the product used for ornamental purposes such as a t-shirt must not be the primary product offered by the trademark owner. For example, the Ford logo appears on all its cars and trucks as a trademark, but when it appears on a t-shirt, hat, or jacket, it is not necessarily being used to identify the source of those products since Ford is not normally thought to be a marketer of clothing. When possible, the product should clearly disclose that it is not authorized or licensed by the brand owner.

Earlier court decisions tended to allow unlicensed ornamental products, particularly when labeling or packaging disclaimed any license or authorization. For example, a case involving aftermarket automobile floor mats with unauthorized automobile company logos on them allowed the ornamental use, particularly noting there was a clear disclaimer on the package and the back of the mats that they were not made by nor authorized by the automobile company (*Plasticolor Molded Prods. v. Ford Motor Co.* 1989).

Such disclaimers can be crucial in determining legality. In a case involving sportswear that mimicked NFL colors and stripes, but without logos, the court enjoined the sale of the clothes unless a disclaimer was included (*National Football League Properties, Inc. v. Wichita Falls Sportswear* 1982). In a later case, the Eleventh Circuit court of appeals enjoined "Battlin Bulldog Beer" from using a bulldog similar to the University of Georgia mascot (it wore a red sweater with a black "G" and carried a football) on a can that also used the school colors because the disclaimer of sponsorship on the cans was too small to be effective (*University of Georgia Athletic Ass'n v. Laite* 1985).

Ornamental use cases in the U.S. and E.U. also have condemned unlicensed replica toy cars that use distinctive hood ornaments or grilles of real cars without permission (*GMC v. Lanard Toys, Inc.* 2007; *Adam Opel AG v. Autec AG* 2007). While the ECJ left open the possibility that consumers might not perceive a toy replica car's use of a trademarked hood ornament as functioning like a trademark to indicate origin (particularly when the toy is marketed under its own trademark), the German Supreme Court on remand found trademark infringement liability.

Another recent U.S. decision also makes it clear that the ornamental use has to be clearly distinguished from an authorized brand extension or accessory. Companion Products developed a whimsical ornamental product called Stretch Pets that consisted of a stuffed animal head on an elastic body that could stretch around a computer monitor. The original embodiment of this idea was a black and white spotted cow, which was offered as a possible licensed accessory to Gateway. Gateway used black and white cows and cow spots as its trademarks. When Gateway refused to license this product, Companion Products produced it and other animals, but the cow was its best seller since it reminded consumers of the Gateway brand. The court enjoined further sales of the cow Stretch Pet because a survey showed nearly 40% of respondents believed it was made or sponsored by Gateway (*Gateway, Inc. v. Companion Products, Inc.* 2004).

In terms of professional sports, some early court decisions allowed unlicensed ornamental products, but later decisions tend not to allow such products (compare *Boston Professional Hockey Ass'n, Inc. v. Dallas Cap & Emblem Mfg., Inc.*, 1975 with *University of Pittsburgh v. Champion Prods., Inc.*, 1983). While logo jewelry makers have had good luck with the ornamental use defense, professional sports teams have had better luck defeating the defense in recent decisions by using consumer survey evidence to show a large proportion of consumers believe logo merchandise is (and must be) licensed.

The ECJ has also found that the use of sport team trademarks on ornamental clothing likely would jeopardize the guarantee of origin—the essential function of a trademark. Therefore, the trademark owner can prevent such uses even if they are also a badge or loyalty, support or affection for the team (*Arsenal Football Club plc v. Reed* 2002). For this reason, marketers of unlicensed ornamental products concerning professional sports teams often choose to offer less risky vague references as illustrated by products from Red Seat.

II. Ambush (Suggested Affiliation) Marketing

Vague references are the normal *modus operandi* for ambush marketing campaigns aimed at major sporting events. Instead of naming the event a vague reference is made to it. This can occur in at least three ways. **Proximity:** Ambush marketers may run advertising during the broadcast of an event or set up advertising within the event such as the Nike balloon that flew over the 1994 Goodwill Games, despite Reebok's official sponsorship of the games. **Partial sponsorship:** Rather than sponsor the entire sporting event or a national team, ambush marketers may sponsor the broadcast, a single sport team or a single athlete. For example, in the 1984 Los Angeles Olympics when Fuji film paid a large amount of money to become a worldwide sponsor of the Olympics, Kodak paid a more modest fee to "sponsor" the ABC telecast of the games and to become the official film of the U.S. Track team. **Promotional theme:** Without suggesting sponsorship, ambush marketers link their advertising to the ambushed event. For example, Seagram's developed a campaign to send the families of U.S. Olympic athletes to the 1988 Seoul Games thereby appearing to support the U.S. Olympic Teams without paying to become any sort of official sponsor.

Ambush marketers also have distributed unofficial programs (often for free) as well as conducted prize promotions with ticket events as prizes. Below are two ads clearly denying official sponsorship while at the same time attempting to benefit from consumer interest in the World Cup.

The classic judicial analysis of this tactic occurred in Canada when Pepsi sponsored a "Pro Playoff Hockey Pool" contest during the 1990 NHL Stanley Cup Play-offs when Coca-Cola was the official sponsoring soft drink of the NHL. Pepsi sponsored Hockey Night on Canadian television and its advertisements included a former NHL hockey coach sitting in a locker room. But Pepsi carefully avoided use of any NHL trademarks, identifying teams by location (e.g., Boston rather than the Boston Bruins) and included disclaimers of NHL sponsorship in advertising, on playing pieces and packages.

The Supreme Court of British Columbia dismissed the NHL's lawsuit holding that Pepsi had not unfairly interfered with NHL business, nor infringed its trademarks and felt the disclaimers effectively communicated non-affiliation between Pepsi and the NHL (*National Hockey League v. Pepsi-Cola Canada Ltd* 1992). Note that this decision would appear to allow ornamental products such as shirts and jerseys as long as location, but not trademark logo, is the only indication of the team.

When the modern Olympic Games started in 1896, they were funded largely through private donations. In contrast, one third of the revenue of the 1996 Atlanta Olympic Games is estimated to have been generated by sponsorship contracts. In the U.S., sponsorship marketing expenditures have risen from $850 million in 1985 to an estimated $5.4 billion in 1996 (Meenaghan 1996).

While Mastercard successfully enjoined Sprint from using the Olympic symbols on its properly licensed telephone cards because it had an exclusive contract for payment cards (*Mastercard International Inc. v. Sprint Communication Company* 1994), most cases of ambush marketing don't involve clear cut sponsorship violations that lead to court decisions. During the 1996 Atlanta Olympics, the game sponsors sent over 1000 "cease and desist" letters to local businesses warning them not to use the Olympics name or symbols without permission (Frank 1995). The Amateur Sports Act of 1978 grants the U.S. Olympic Committee exclusive rights over Olympic symbols and trademarks (36 U.S.C. § 380). Other major sporting events are not so fortunate and must attempt to rely upon trademark law with its fair use provision.

Ambush marketing appears to be effective in establishing the association between the brand and the event. When Converse was the official shoe of the Olympics, Nike ran an attention-getting advertising campaign featuring Nike track and field athletes. After the games in a national poll, 42% felt Nike was the official shoe of the Olympics compared to only 15% for Converse (Meenaghan 1994, p. 83). Similarly, during the 1992 Olympics, Wendy's ads featured U.S. Olympic skater Kristie Yamaguchi. A consumer survey found that 57% of those surveyed thought Wendy's was the official fast food sponsor of the Olympics with only 37% of consumers correctly identifying McDonalds (Meenaghan 1996, p. 108).

It often seems that each time the Olympics occurs, event organizers try to develop more effective regulations. The British Parliament adopted new protections for the London 2012 Olympics. The law established a presumption of infringements if any of the words: games, two thousand and twelve, 2012, or twenty twelve are used with another of those words or with any of the following words: gold, silver, bronze, London, medals, sponsor, and summer. This would make it risky for hotels to advertise "book now for summer 2012" (Collett and Johnson 2006).

Sometimes, courts allow the use of the trademarked name in situations similar to ambush marketing. For example, a newspaper was allowed to use the NEW KIDS ON THE BLOCK trademark without permission when conducting a poll of their readers concerning which "kid" was most popular (*New Kids on the Block v. News America Publishing, Inc.* 1992). Clearly the newspaper was taking advantage of the group's popularity at the time.

This decision created a three part test for nominative fair use discussed in the preceding chapter: (1) the product or service must not be readily identifiable without use of the trademark, (2) only as much of the trademark may be used as needed to reasonably identify the referent product or service, and (3) the user of the referent trademark must do nothing to suggest sponsorship or endorsement by the trademark owner.

Nominative fair use, whether in comparisons or suggested connections, supports freedom of speech. Sometimes courts explicitly recognize free speech interests. When a boxer displayed a temporary body tattoo promoting a health club in violation of the Nevada Athletic Commission rules, he was able to enjoin the Commission from enforcing its ban on free speech grounds (McKelvey 2003).

While ambush marketing is most often described around major sporting events, there is no reason why the tactic of association without suggesting sponsorship should be limited to such venues. A tradeshow participant who purchases a small booth may use other marketing techniques (e.g., an appearance by a well-known celebrity) to enlarge its impact beyond the impact of sponsoring a larger booth or display. The participant may give away free t-shirts or other items that immediately attract attention, or have a character circulate within the show. Similarly, a non-sponsor may be able to advertise or give away promotional items outside the venue or use something creative like sky-writing above the venue.

III. Brand Parody Products

In contrast to the other unauthorized brand extension JBD tactics that attempt a serious association with a famous brand, brand parodies attract consumer interest by making fun of a well-known brand. However, parodies run the risk of either confusing consumers into thinking they are authorized by the target brand or being accused of trademark dilution. The key seems to be to avoid confusion with sufficient distinctiveness while still having enough imitation that consumers "get the joke" but aren't confused about sponsorship. Parody products for social commentary targeted at the trademark or its owner are often allowed with many courts (and the U.S. dilution statute) recognizing a free speech interest in social commentary.

Parody products are most likely to be considered trademark infringement when the product is the same type as that sold by the trademark owner. For example, a diaper bag marketer was not allowed to use the name Gucchi Goo while imitating the trade dress of the Gucci brand handbags and totes. The court found that the similarities made it likely some consumers would think the diaper bag was an extension from other Gucci bags (*Gucci Shops, Inc. v. R.H. Macy & Co.* 1977).

A similar example with the opposite result is Just Did It's parody of NIKE shirts with its line of "Mike" shirts. The parody shirts offered a "swoosh" design identical to Nike's and the script and style of lettering for Nike and Mike also were identical. The idea was to poke fun at people who paid money to become a walking billboard for Nike. A federal appellate court reversed summary judgment in favor of Nike finding that it was not a clear matter of law that consumers were confused when making the purchase (Lans 1994: *Nike Corp. v. Just Did It Enterprises* 1993).

When the parody is obvious and confusion is unlikely, the courts allow product parodies for the same type of product. A court allowed a maker of designer jeans for larger women to use the trade name Lardashe as a parody of Jordache jeans (*Jordache Enterprise Inc. v. Hogg Wyld, Ltd.* 1987). The court found that consumers were not likely to be confused that Jordache made or sponsored the Lardashe jeans. It may have helped that the larger jeans arguably were offering social commentary on the limited size offerings of Jordache.

Similarly after eight years of litigation, a court allowed a small coffee roaster to continue selling "Charbucks Blend" for a dark roast playing on the consumer perception that Starbucks roasts its products more darkly than other brewers. "Charbucks Blend" was sold in distinctive packaging with a different logo so that consumer confusion was found to be unlikely (*Starbucks Corp. v. Wolfe's Borough Coffee, Inc.*, 20135).

When the parody product is distinctively different from the target brand product, it is even more likely the parody will be allowed. A coffee shop and espresso machine seller was allowed to use the name Federal Espresso, despite the objections of the well-known shipping company with a similar name (*Federal Express Corp. v. Federal Espresso Inc.* 2000). The name was reportedly selected not so much to parody Federal Express, but rather to indicate the location was across from the Federal building in Syracuse, New York.

Offensive or tasteless parody products may be condemned for trademark tarnishment. When a condom maker decided to package its product in a card that precisely duplicated the well-known American Express credit card and the condom package inside the card stated "Never Leave Home Without It" imitating American Express's well known slogan, the court found dilution by tarnishing. The court also found no infringement since consumers would not think American Express endorsed the practice. (*American Express Co. v. Vibra Approved Laboratories Corp.* 1989). Similarly, Anheuser-Busch stopped a company from producing a "Buttwiser" t-shirt because it would tarnish the BUDWEISER trademark (*Anheuser-Busch, Inc. v. Andy's Sportswear, Inc.* 1996).

Recently, the Fourth Circuit allowed a parody dog toy called "Chewy Vuiton" despite the protests of handbag marketer LOUIS VUITTON. The court found this to be a valid parody because it conveyed just enough of the original trademark to be recognized by consumers, it communicated an element of satire or amusement and it was sufficiently different to communicate it was not the original product. In one of the first appellate decisions interpreting the Trademark Dilution Revision Act of 2006, the court also found no dilution by blurring because strong famous marks are less likely to have their distinctiveness impaired by a parody. The differences between the parody and original also help preserve the distinctiveness of the original. Lastly, the court also affirmed dismissal of the argument that this parody might tarnish the original trademark because a dog might choke on the chew toy (*Louis Vuitton Malletier, S.A. v. Haute Diggity Dog, LLC* 2007).

Lower courts have also allowed pet-related parody t-shirts (e.g., "Bone Cold Steve Pawstin") and perfumes (e.g., "Timmy Holedigger") (*World Wrestling Federation. Entertainment, Inc. v. Big Dog Holdings, Inc.* 2003 and *Tommy Hilfiger Licensing, Inc. v. Nature Labs. LLC* 2002). However, the parodist must make sure the parody is recognized as such. A court did not allow "Dogiva" pet treats, wrapped in gold foil just like GODIVA chocolates because it was persuaded consumers would actually think the pet treat was licensed by the chocolatier (*Grey v. Campbell Soup Co.* 1986).

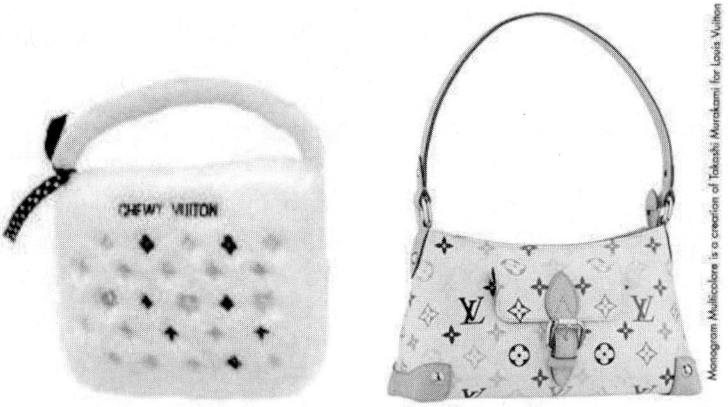

The parody and original handbag at issue in *Louis Vuitton*

IV. Parody Advertising

Another example of a vague association is parody advertising primarily of non-competing unrelated products. In many cases, the parodies are not challenged and may even remind consumers of the original brand advertising. After all, imitation is said to be the sincerest form of flattery (Steinberg 2004). When such parodies are challenged, they are often allowed by the courts.

For example as discussed in Chapter Five, a court allowed a Coors beer commercial to spoof the Energizer Bunny under both trademark and copyright fair use as long the parody was noticeably different from real Energizer Bunny commercials (*Eveready Battery Co., Inc. v. Adolph Coors Co.* 1991). In the parody, actor Leslie Nielson interrupted a fake advertisement, dressed in a business suit but wearing bunny ears and bunny feet and playing a drum. The ad ended with the tagline: "Coors Beer, it just keeps growing and growing" imitating the battery company's slogan that it keeps going and going. Apparently in challenging this parody, Eveready forgot that its original Energizer Bunny advertisement was a parody of a Duracell advertisement featuring a room full of toy drummer bunnies powered by batteries with all but the Duracell powered toy eventually stopping. Similarly, a florist association was allowed to advertise "This Bud's for you and 11 More Rosebuds"—a play on the trademarked slogan THIS BUD'S FOR YOU (*Anheuser-Busch, Inc. v. Florists Association of Greater Cleveland, Inc.*, 1984).

In some cases, parody advertising can be confusing about the sponsor. When the small hamburger chain, Big Bite, used close copies of competing burger restaurant icons and slogans, it was condemned for infringement (*Wendy's Int'l Inc. v. Big Bite Inc.* 1983). Similarly, in the U.K., Burger King was enjoined from passing off for using the slogan "It's Not Just Big, Mac" in print ads displaying the Burger King Whopper sandwich and logo. McDonald's, marketers of the Big Mac sandwich, conducted a poll that showed 55% thought the ad was for McDonald's and another 10% thought the Big Mac could be obtained from Burger King (*McDonald's Hamburgers Ltd. v. Burger King Ltd.* 1985).

Parody advertising does run the risk of trademark dilution. Dilution by blurring may occur by advertising for products unrelated to the original. For example as noted in Chapter Seven, Ringling

Brother's Circus won a dilution by blurring case against a firm proclaiming "The Greatest Used Car Show on Earth" (*Ringling Bros.-Barnum & Bailey Combined Shows, Inc. v. Celozzi-Ettleson Chevrolet, Inc.* 1988) More recently, the Circus lost its efforts to stop "The Greatest Bar on Earth" and "The Greatest Snow on Earth" and "The Greatest Show on Earth Isn't" because courts found the slogan largely descriptive and allowed the use of similar descriptive words.

Parody advertising may also be condemned for trademark tarnishment or unfair competition by disparagement. Had Gillette been specifically identified as the harsh metal-toothed razor in the Norelco ads discussed in the previous chapter, the court might have believed the Gillette brand was being injured. Yardmaster was condemned for tarnishment dilution because its ads depicting one of its tractors chasing an animated John Deere logo that appeared to be running in fear. The ad also poked fun at John Deere's slogan, "Nothing Runs Like a Deere" (*Deere & Co. v. MTD Products Inc.* 1994).

V. Parody as Social Commentary

Parodies for social commentary purposes overlay parody products and parody advertising. The key difference is that parody products and advertising are used to sell products whereas social commentary seeks to make a point while selling a commentary product such as a poster. Given the First Amendment guarantees of free speech, it is not surprising that U.S. courts generally are permissive of social commentary parodies. Even somewhat unwholesome parodies that otherwise might be found tarnishing to the brand have been allowed. For example an adult products parody of the LL Bean catalog and a parody of the Girl Scout slogan "Be Prepared" used on a post depicting a pregnant girl in a scouting uniform have been allowed (*L.L. Bean, Inc. v. Drake Publishers, Inc.*, 1987; *Girl Scouts of U.S.A. v. Bantam Doubleday Dell Publishing Group*, 1993).

These parodies arguably communicated social commentary on the wholesome image of these two organizations. However, the L.L. Bean catalog parody (which was not a real catalog for adult sex products) in particular arguably might have been a copy of the style of the catalog rather than a parody of the company itself. This argument, rejected in L.L Bean, worked to condemn the story of OJ Simpson's murder trial written in the style of Dr. Seuss for the cat not in the hat.

In contrast to these cases allowing parodies that offer social commentary about the target brand or its owner, courts have disallowed parody products that tarnish a brand through an unsavory association, but offer only a play on words rather than social commentary (Shaughnessy 1986). For example, courts disallowed parody products such as a poster imitating the General Electric trademark but stating Genital Electric and an entire line of Mutant of Omaha items because the parody did not comment on the trademark or company (*General Electric Co v. Alumpa Coal Co.* 1979, *Mutual of Omaha Insurance Co. v. Novak* 1987).

In close cases, such as a poster imitating the graphics of the slogan "Enjoy Coca-Cola" but saying "Enjoy Cocaine" and the adult movie Debbie Does Dallas that imitated the uniforms of the Dallas Cowboy cheerleaders, courts seem to favor protecting the trademark from tarnishment, even though parody arguments could be made concerning Coca-Cola's original ingredient of cocaine and sex in professional football (*Coca-Cola Co. v. Gemini Rising, Inc.* 1972; *Dallas Cowboys Cheerleaders, Inc. v. Pussycat Cinema, Ltd.* 1979).

D. CONCLUSION

Successful brands are the envy of other marketers. Suggesting some sort of relationship to the successful brand can stimulate interest and sales but the law is clear that the relationship must not falsely suggest the same origin as the famous brand or sponsorship by it. In other words, the JBD marketer can't suggest its product is actually a brand extension authorized by the famous brand. This caveat suggests that one way to minimize legal risk is to include a clear disclaimer of origin, affiliation or sponsorship.

CHAPTER 17

Interruption and Misdirection Judo Brand Diversion

A. INTRODUCTION

Until recently most lawsuits involving brand names involved the use of the same or similar name on another product. However, the internet has raised new questions. Can a brand name trademark be used as a metatag (invisible to consumers) on the website of non-owners to bias internet search results? Can a marketing firm sell the use of one firm's trademarked brand name to another firm, typically a competitor, for use as a trigger of pop up advertising or sponsored search results? This chapter examines Judo Brand Diversion interruption and misdirection techniques particularly within the context of internet marketing.

B. INTERRUPTION

Interruption occurs when the judo marketer notices a consumer's interest in a well-known brand and suggests the consumer consider its brand instead. This set of tactics is similar to the comparison tactics discussed in Chapter Thirteen but a bit bolder. For example, copycat retailer brands positioned next to the national brand on the shelf could be characterized as an attempt to interrupt the shopping of national brand shoppers and get them to consider the less expensive retailer brand. When a customer asks for assistance in locating a branded product in a store, the same type of interruption might occur when the clerk suggests the cheaper store brand alternative (with higher profit margins for the store). Although Coke used to pursue restaurants that served another brand when the customer ordered a Coke, no one has suggested that a sales clerk suggestion of an alternative brand is illegal.

On the internet, two forms of advertising serve the same interruption purpose. In the first, adware notices that a consumer is searching for a particular type of product or brand name and posts a pop-up ad on the consumer's computer. One important issue with adware is whether it had been placed on an individual's computer with that person's knowledge and consent.

The second type of interruption occurs when a consumer's internet search is interrupted by ads for brands different from those sought by the consumers. This used to occur by pop-up ads over the search engine page, but now thanks to pop-up blocking technology and guidance by the Federal Trade Commission, search engines feature "sponsored results" next to actual search results. Brand owners most often pursue the advertising enabler—the adware firm or search engine but they also may pursue the rival brand that purchases the advertising.

I. Pop-Up Ads/Sponsored Results

Pop-up advertising is enabled by software called adware connected to particular websites such as search engines or connected to particular computers. Adware is not illegal, although as discussed in Chapter Nine, the FTC has pursued several cases where adware was surreptitiously implanted in consumer computers and designed to be difficult to identify and difficult to remove. The FTC insists that consumers be given notice that adware will be downloaded to their machine and consent to that download.

The use of pop-up ads on the web leads to two questions. First, can search engines and others sell the use of a trademarked word to a competitor of the brand that registered the trademark? Second, are the resulting pop-up ads ever confusing or misleading to consumers and if so who is responsible, the advertiser, the company that operates the adware system or both?

Most U.S. courts that have ruled on the issue of whether the sale of trademarked keywords is trademark use in commerce have ruled in the affirmative because use of the trademark is being sold. However, one court found that the trademark owners had not proven secondary meaning for AMERICAN BLINDS (*Google, Inc. v. Am. Blind & Wallpaper Factory, Inc.*, 2007). Another court suggested that advertisers don't buy particular keywords, but rather buy a proprietary system that displays ads based on consumer search behavior. Since the trademark words themselves are not sold, there is no trademark use in commerce even if the trademarked words are part of the software program. This use does not seek to identify the source of goods, but only trigger ads after a computer user searches for the trademark.

In *1-800 Contacts, Inc. v. WhenU.com* (2005), the Second Circuit likened the internal use of trademarked words by an adware firm to an individual's private thoughts about a trademark because the internal use did not communicate the trademarks to the public. Despite these attempts to avoid trademark use, most U.S. jurisdictions now agree that sale of keyword words is use in commerce, but the real question is whether or not the subsequent advertising leads to trademark infringement or dilution (*Rescuecom Corp. v. Google Inc.*, 2009).

This U.S. decision was followed by a European Court of Justice decision that agreed the sale of trademarked words as advertising triggers did constitute "in the course of trade," the Court also noted that Google did not use the trademarks as trademarks and therefore could not be liable for direct infringement. The Court found that Google qualified as a hosting service under the E-commerce Directive (2000/31/EC) and could only be liable for an advertiser's infringing use of a trademark if Google had actual knowledge of that use and did not act expeditiously to stop the infringement (*Google France v. Louis Vuitton Malletier* 2010).

Earlier U.S. court decisions foretold this result. One court held that use of the GEICO trademark did occur when sold by Google for advertising purposes to third parties but found no likelihood of confusion unless the GEICO trademark also appeared in the third-party advertisement (*Government Employees Insurance Co. v. Google, Inc.* 2005). Another found that the sale of trademarked words for key word advertising would not be direct infringement but rather could be a form of contributory trademark infringement. However, it held the case needed to go to trial to determine if infringement was likely and whether a fair use defense would apply (*800-JR Cigar, Inc. v Goto.com, Inc.* 2006).

Most of the court decisions considering the legality of this practice focus on the legality of search engines selling advertising keywords that are trademarked words that typically belong to a competitor of keyword purchaser. However, two decisions considered the legality not of a search engine selling trademarked keywords for advertising, but rather of a competitor buying such keywords from the search engine. One decision allowed this complaint to proceed to trial for trademark infringement (*Edina Realty, Inc. v. TheMLSonline.com* 2006). The other found the practice of buying trademarked brand names to trigger sponsored links not to be trademark use all and to be analogous to the practice of retailers placing generic brands next to the national brand product to capitalize on the latter's name recognition (*Merck & Co. Inc. v. Mediplan Health Consulting, Inc.* 2006).

Now courts generally agree that the correct focus is not on the purchase or sale of keywords, but rather whether the sponsored result advertisement is confusing as to the message sponsor. One decision ruled that if the plaintiff's trademark is not used in the text of the ad, then the ad cannot be confusing (*JG Wentworth v. Settlement Funding* 2009). However an earlier case included evidence that over 60% of people surveyed did not understand sponsored links (*Edina Realty v. TheMLSOnline.com* 2006). It remains to be seen how future cases will be decided, but it is clear that challengers will want to present evidence based on the message and perhaps consumer surveys that consumers are likely confused about the message origin or sponsorship.

As noted in previous chapters, comparative and reseller advertising may use another's trademark if it is clear there is no claimed affiliation or authorization. Many pop-up ads, while triggered by a trademarked keyword, do not mention the trademarked keyword and presumably thereby avoid any consumer confusion. Other trademarked words also may be fairly common words such as "playboy" so that the trademark registrant may find it difficult to prove that selling the common word as an advertising keyword involved the trademark at all.

Pop-up ads are more likely to confuse consumers when they appear over a competitor's website during a consumer visit—a form of interruption JBD that comes perilously close to misdirection discussed below. For example, Weight Watchers received a consumer complaint about pop-up advertising for a diet pill when visiting the Weight Watcher's website. For this to occur, the consumer must have previously downloaded adware that notices he or she is visiting a specific webpage such as WeightWatches.com and this triggers advertising that had been previously sold to a rival weight control product. The consumer's computer shows a pop up advertisement over the Weight Watchers website even though Weight Watchers did not authorize the ad.

Weight Watchers settled this case with an injunction suggesting that at least in this instance consumers could be reasonably confused about whether WeightWatchers sponsored the ad and whether the advertised pill was approved or endorsed by WeightWatchers (Stansky, 2003). Other cases found that the ads did not modify the trademark owner's website so there was no copyright violation based on the website copyright (*U-Haul International, Inc. v. WhenU.com* 2003; *Wells Fargo & Co. v. WhenU.com* 2003).

II. Offering Similar Products

These pop-up advertising internet practices are somewhat analogous to pop-up coupons offered by some retailers at the cash register. However, the coupons don't interrupt the shopping experience since they are awarded after the current purchase transaction is completed. They attempt to interrupt brand use by attempting to persuade the consumer to try a similar product to those purchased either from the same company or a rival for the next purchase.

Like pop-up advertising on a search engine web page, this practice at least offers the coupons in neutral territory, the checkout counter. Furthermore, pop-up coupons are triggered not by the trademarked product name but by the UPC bar code of the rival product. Pop-up coupons have not been condemned by the courts, but in a decision finding passing off based on product and packaging similarities, the pop-up coupon practice was cited as evidence of intent to confuse consumers (*Keebler Co. v. Nabisco Brands*, Inc. 1992).

There is still great legal uncertainty regarding online interruption tactics. Since several decisions have held that the sale of a specific trademark term is questionable, JBD may wish to avoid the purchase of keywords that are only trademarks such as KODAK. Interruption tactics may be better suited for marketers who can limit their purchases to more ambiguous words that are descriptive or even arbitrary trademarks (apple as in APPLE computer). Most importantly, those who employ these tactics should make sure the sponsored result or banner ad does not imply any association with the brand whose trademarked name has been purchased.

C. MISDIRECTION

Search engine users did not like pop-up ads that interfered with their search and soon pop-up blocking technology became widely adopted, so search engines switched their word-triggered advertising to some sort of listed results. Ads listed along with search results could be viewed as interrupting the search results by recommending purchase or misdirecting consumers if the listed ads do not clearly indicate that they are for a brand different from the subject of the search. The FTC has insisted that search engines distinguish actual search algorithm results from the paid-for results and Google started identifying the latter as "sponsored results."

Misdirection JBD tactics are those that initially mislead consumers interested in a particular brand into thinking about a competing brand. If consumers are confused into mistakenly purchasing the second brand, trademark infringement has occurred. But if consumers are simply misdirected toward a second brand, but can readily perceive the correct identity of the second brand and decide to pursue it or not, this may not constitute trademark infringement if the misdirection is fleeting. However, as noted above, some U.S. courts do recognize the concept of initial interest confusion and could find even brief misdirection to be actionable. Since it is not clear how long consumers might be confused, misdirection tactics generally are more risky than other JBD tactics.

Despite the substantial legal risks, the misdirection category is included here because the law is not settled as to what sort of brief initial confusion is sufficient for trademark infringement liability. Thus in some cases, misdirection has been allowed. In addition, by examining the most difficult cases, the issues become clearer for other forms of JBD with lower legal risk. Brand owners are likely to argue that even the most brief period of confusion should not be tolerated because that free rides on their branding efforts. In contrast, consumer advocates might argue (as the FTC argued in favor of comparative advertising) that initial confusion, as long as it is dispelled before purchase and it does not delay the shopping experience significantly, should be allowed because the use of such tactics encourages consumer choice. Until the law is settled on misdirection tactics, they should be considered for use by judo marketers only with great care.

There is recent hope that some misdirection tactics may be consider legal under some circumstances. Online retailer Amazon.com allows potential buyers to search its website and if it does not offer a particular brand, the search engine will identify other similar products and brands that it does sell. A watch manufacturer sued arguing that consumers might be misdirected because the Amazon search result page listed its brand name at least three times and showed pictures of watches similar in style to the ones it marketed. However, the Ninth Circuit affirmed the trial court grant of summary judgment for Amazon finding that consumers for this project were reasonably sophisticated and experienced with online shopping and each alternative product recommended by Amazon was clearly labeled with its own brand name and model number. So Amazon is not forced to simply announce "No Results Found" but may display similar results so long as it is clear to most consumers that the similar results are a different brand (*Multi Time Machine, Inc. v. Amazon.com, Inc.* 2015).

Three current internet practices fit into the category of misdirection: e-mail and web page spoofing, typosquatting, and metatag use of well-known brand names by judo marketers to tip search engine results in their favor. Of these three practices, only e-mail and web page spoofing have yet to be analyzed by the courts, although e-mail spoofing has been challenged by many large firms.

Spoofing occurs when a judo marketer sends out consumer e-mail that appears to be from a well-known brand marketer. The e-mail often links to a "spoofed" web page. This is analogous to covert marketing direct mail pieces that appeared to be from a government agency. A key difference is that most of the direct mail practices involved the imitation of a fictitious government agency, but most spoofing seems to involve exact duplication of well-known brands. Since such spoofing would probably be declared illegal as trademark counterfeiting or infringement, it is unlikely that any spoofer will defend the practice in court.

This practice is typically used to secure consumer credit card numbers for fraudulent purposes. While several brand owners with similar brand names might have an equal right to a domain name consisting of the word or words they share, unique arbitrary/made up brand names cannot be claimed by another marketer, since they mean nothing other than a particular brand. However, this practice could evolve to become more legitimate if done to sell legitimate products or services and the brand association is quickly dispelled.

Similarly, typosquatting, discussed in Chapter Six, is readily challenged when the domain name contains another party's trademark in a confusing way such as "buybrand.com" rather than "brandsucks.com. Court decisions on the dealer use of domain names that contain another's brand without authorization are mixed. The E.U. Trade Marks Directive specifically allows non-trademark owners to use the mark to indicate the kind or quality of goods being offered in the course of trade as long as this is done in accordance with honest practices (Art. 6). In *Parfums Christian Dior SA v. Evora* BV (1997), the ECJ held that even an unauthorized reseller could use the brand name unless the particular situation of use seriously damaged the reputation of the brand.

Some U.S. court decisions allow use of the trademark in advertising as trademark fair use unless authorization was implied by the domain name or website such as use of a logo trademark (*Toyota Motor Sales USA v. Tabari,* 2010; Roberts and Brody 2010). On the one hand, Audi successfully sued the registrant of audisport.com for cybersquatting based on the unauthorized sale of AUDI-branded merchandise (*Audi AG v. D'Amato* 2005). Similarly, a district court granted Volvo's motion for summary judgment granting its rights to "volvospares.com" despite internet dispute resolution previously finding no bad faith intent to profit and allowing the spare parts seller to use its website (*Volvo Trademark Holdings AB v. volvospares.com* 2010).

Metatags are words placed on websites that are invisible to users but read by search engines. Unlike domain names that are listed once, metatags may be repeated many times on a website and may be used by multiple websites. By repeated use of a trademark in metatags, a seller can improve its rank ordering in search results for that trademark and even may be ranked above the brand owner potentially misdirecting consumers. Modern search engines claim their algorithms will not be fooled by metatag use alone. A site that uses a trademark metatag but has no related content within the site will probably be eliminated from search results altogether. For that reason, a website may want to include a product comparison which might also make the use of the target brand's trademark as a metatag more appropriate.

Most court decisions hold that the use of a trademark as a metatag by someone other than the brand owner constitutes infringement or, in the case of pornographers, tarnishing. Early decisions enjoined metatag use along with domain name use (*Playboy Enterprises, Inc. v. Calvin Designer Label*, 1997) or by itself with little analysis (*Oppedahl & Larson v. Advanced Concepts* 1997). However, as noted in the prior discussion of domain names, trademark fair use allows trademark use for resellers and comparison purposes. Presumably such purposes would allow for use of someone else's trademark as a metatag.

A Ninth Circuit decision did present careful analysis of metatag use. It that found trademark infringement from domain name use (moviebuff.com), but in separate analysis of metatag (moviebuff) use, rejected traditional trademark infringement likelihood of confusion for metatag use. The court reasoned that search engines provide a list of results and consumers are used to trying several before finding the specific one they were seeking. If the domain name is distinctive, consumers are not confused by incorrect results. Nevertheless, the court found likelihood of initial interest confusion from metatag use and issued an injunction. It argued that initial interest confusion was actionable under trademark law even if no long term source confusion resulted. Once directed to the incorrect website, the consumer may decide to use it instead of the one it was originally seeking thereby injuring the trademark owner (*Brookfield Communications v. West Coast Entertainment Corporation* 1999).

The court provided what may become a classic analogy in such cases of a highway sign for West Coast Video that says use Exit 7, when in fact West Coast is located at Exit 8. Its rival, Blockbuster, had put up the sign and is located at Exit 7. Some consumers, once they take Exit 7 will decide not to continue looking for West Coast and will shop at Blockbuster. The court felt this deception of consumers to divert trade is condemned by trademark law even though consumers realize they are shopping at Blockbuster not West Coast Video. The court was clear that that metatags could still be used descriptively to describe another's products, e.g., movie buff, but not just "moviebuff."

In situations where consumers have been diverted from the proper path to the trademarked product and "getting back on track" is difficult, misdirection away from the searched-for brand name toward another is similar to bait and switch advertising (Chapter Nine) and should be condemned (*Dorr-Oliver, Inc. v. Fluid-Quip, Inc.* 1996; *Checkpoint Sys. v. Check Point Software Technologies., Inc.* 2001). In one case, a court condemned a typosquatter because it required consumers to click through several advertisements before leaving its website (*Shields v. Zuccarini* 2001). The Federal Trade Commission later obtained a default judgment for disgorgement of profits and a permanent injunction of the practice (*FTC v. Zuccarini* 2002).

However, in cases where getting back on track is as easy as hitting the screen back button to return to search results, there is a reasonable argument that metatag use in a descriptive sense or to identify a brand that is the subject of a parody or comparison should be allowed. The Ninth Circuit in one of many cases involving Playboy Enterprises agreed that initial confusion was likely with such pop up ads because their sponsor was not clearly identified. It also decided without discussion that selling competitors the right to ads triggered by popular trademarks such as PLAYBOY was "use" of the trademark in commerce. This decision overturned the lower court denial of a preliminary injunction based on the argument that when search engine users entered the term playboy, they were using the descriptive term not the trademark (*Playboy Enterprises. v. Netscape Communications* 2004).

D. CONCLUSION

The future legal viability of many of these tactics is uncertain but should become more certain as case law evolves and as policy makers decide how permissive or restrictive to be. Responsible use of JBD tactics can help make these tactics more acceptable, while irresponsible uses, such as to promote pornography and fraud, will likely lead to greater restrictions.

There also is legal uncertainty over certain attempts to expand trademark law that would restrict JBD. Some courts have accepted a concept called initial interest confusion and used it to condemn short-lived consumer confusion concerning the source of goods. Similarly, courts occasionally condemn post purchase confusion by non-purchasers such as the case involving gold fish crackers. While the concept of JBD would disagree at least to some degree with both initial interest and post purchase confusion, it remains to be seen whether the law will recognize the communication value of JBD for consumers, particularly in the online context where correcting is quick and easy. Alternatively, brand owners may persuade legal policy makers that their "property rights" in their brands should be zealously protected.

The use of misdirection JBD tactics have the highest legal risk because consumers are necessarily initially confused about the sponsorship of the tactic. This is sufficient for initial interest confusion according to the few courts that have recognized this concept. Brand marketers who decide to use this high risk tactic should clearly disclaim sponsorship by the targeted brand as soon as possible. In addition, they should endeavor to have their misdirection tactic also qualify as a tactic with lower legal risk such as descriptive use of the words claimed as trademarks by the well-known brand or parody or comparison.

E. PRACTICAL ADVICE FOR JUDO BRAND DIVERSION

If challenged, the JBD marketer has several low cost options. First, particularly for non-rival brands, a quick apology and promise to stop may end the legal challenge with minimal cost (and probably minimal effectiveness of the JBD tactic, unfortunately). Second, the JBD marketer can attempt to negotiate a license or other settlement. This could drag on for months until the JBD tactic is no longer fresh and should be discarded for marketing reasons anyway. Third and finally, litigation itself can delay any sanctions and allow the JBD tactic to continue for some period of time.

Of course, there is a risk of a preliminary injunction before trial that would switch the advantage of delay over to the target brand. However, such injunctions are only issued if there is a likelihood of success for the overall case and with proper execution of JBD, the marketer should be able to avoid such a clear cut legal violation. In close cases, the likelihood of any monetary award such as damages to the target brand or disgorgement of ill-gotten profits by the JBD marketer, is greatly reduced, so little more is risked in litigating than an order to stop the JBD practice.

The above analysis demonstrates six simple rules that should be followed to reduce the legal risk of using JBD.

1. The JBD marketer should avoid using someone else's brand identifiers as trademarks if possible. This is particularly true for brand names.
2. Certain types of trademarks, such as descriptive words and slogans, product design trade dress and colors, must gain secondary meaning in the minds of consumers before they can be protected. JBD marketers should strive to imitate these types of marks quickly before consumers identify them with just one brand.
3. If possible, the JBD marketer should target a non-competing brand.
4. Unless using another's brand identifiers to identify the other brand or as descriptive words, the JBD marketer should use brand identifiers that while similar enough to be recognized, are not identical to those of the target brand.
5. The JBD should avoid unwholesome connotations for the target brand and seek connotations that are humorous or supportive of the target brand.
6. To avoid confusion, the JBD marketer should include a clear disclaimer of any sponsorship or approval by the targeted brand.

The other strategic concern for JBD is the question of how well it builds brand equity. By associating with a well-known brand, the JBD marketer risks reminding the consumer about the target brand rather than communicating its own brand attributes and developing interest and loyalty for the JBD brand. This suggests that in many cases, JBD may be viable only as a short term tactic. On the other hand, some copycat store brands have developed brand equity over the years (Harvey et al 1998). Clearly, more research concerning the long term effectiveness of JBD tactics is needed. It could be that JBD may be effective initially or when used only occasionally to attract new attention and should always be considered in conjunction with other forms of brand promotion.

It should be noted that licensing is always a possible alternative for JBD. The worse that happens is the license is refused, but often other brands might consent to co-promotion. For Superbowl 2005, Mastercard unveiled advertising that used ten famous brands icons sharing a family style meal. The usual Mastercard "Priceless" format was used: "Broccoli—$1.79 on debit card, tuna—$3.59, crescent rolls—$1.99, getting everyone together for dinner, priceless." JBD when done carefully to minimize legal risk, could break through brand clutter and also prove "priceless" particularly for new or smaller brands.

PART 4

Big Brands Beware

Up to this point, this book has focused on legal tactics for protecting and promoting new brands. With a strong brand development strategy, a brand may become the dominant brand in a market and develop a global brand identity. Brand managers need to be aware that being a "big" brand adds complexity to the legal aspects of brand management.

CHAPTER 18

Issues for Growing Within and Across Markets

A. INTRODUCTION

With a strong brand development strategy, a brand may succeed. It may become the dominant brand in a market. It also may seek to "go global" if it has not already. Brand managers need to be aware that such success adds complexity to the legal aspects of brand management. This chapter examines three legal risks associated with successful brands: reverse confusion, antitrust issues and global control of trademarks.

B. REVERSE CONFUSION

Reverse confusion involves the question of trademark infringement when a large firm essentially usurps a pre-existing trademark of a small firm. This differs from the preemption of a descriptive term before it identifies a single brand discussed in Chapter Fourteen because the small firm suffering reverse confusion has a well-established trademark that identifies its brand, but the trademark isn't well known to the general public. Small firms dislike reverse confusion because consumers who discover the small firm's product are likely to be confused into thinking the product originates or is licensed by the large, usurping firm. Alternatively, consumers might think the small firm is copying the larger firm's trademark when in fact the large firm is the imitator. Typically the large firm substantially outspends the original firm in marketing and its use of the trademark becomes better known to most consumers than the use by the smaller firm.

The concept of reverse confusion appears to have originated when the makers of MUSTANG brand camper tops for pick-up trucks tried to stop Ford from using the same name for its new sports car. The court in that case held that the company's rather weak mark would not extend from campers to automobiles and rejected the theory of reverse confusion (*Westward Coach Mfg. Co. v. Ford Motor Co.* 1968).

The next case involved a group of independent tire dealers in 14 states who began selling tires in April 1974 using the unregistered brand name BIG FOOT. Goodyear, the largest U.S. tire maker started selling its BIG FOOT brand of tires five months later, advertising them nationally on Monday Night Football. The Tenth Circuit Court of Appeals affirmed a jury verdict that this constituted trademark infringement based on reverse confusion, but reduced the amount of damages from $19.6 million to $4.7 million (*Big O Tire Dealers, Inc. v. Goodyear Tire & Rubber Co.* 1977). Shortly after this, the Trademark Trial and Appeal Board implicitly seemed to adopt this theory when rejecting General Motor's application to register STARFIRE as a trademark for a new OLDSMOBILE model based on the previous registration of STARFIRE as the trademark of a small shock absorber company (*In re General Motors Corp.* 1977).

Today, the concept of reverse confusion is well accepted, although large damage awards for it are not. When GATORADE adopted its slogan "GATORADE is Thirst-Aid" an appellate court upheld the trial court that the slogan infringed a small competitor's trademarked name of THIRST-AID, but remanded for a re-determination of the amount of damages originally calculated at $24 million that the appellate court found to be inequitable (*Sands, Taylor & Wood Co. v. The Quaker Oats Co.* 1992). After additional expensive appeals, the defendant was ordered to pay just over $10 million.

Courts recognize that the traditional trademark infringement factors should be modified for reverse confusion. Strength of the mark is likely to focus on inherent distinctiveness since the original user is small and has likely developed relatively little acquired distinctiveness for its mark. Actual confusion and degree of customer care when shopping should be analyzed for customers of the original trademark user rather than customers of the newer user. Intent of the second user is probably irrelevant because the second user will seldom if ever be trying to create confusion between its goods and those of the original user (Fletcher 2005).

However, if the intent of the second user can be proven to be the elimination of the first, this would make a compelling case for punitive damages for trademark infringement and the possible basis for an antitrust lawsuit if market conditions were such that there was a reasonably probability of monopolizing the market once the competitor was eliminated. Thus, although the number of reverse confusion cases finding liability is small, this is still an area of concern for large brand marketers. Ultimately, trademark law condemns infringement regardless of the size of the firms involved.

C. MONOPOLIZING CONDUCT BY MARKET DOMINATING BRAND MARKETERS

Antitrust law is concerned with the restriction of competition by one or more firms to the detriment of consumers. Consumers may suffer from higher prices or less innovation and product selection or both. In order to restrict competition, a single firm or a cartel of firms colluding together typically enjoy a large share of the market and high barriers to entry to the market prevent other firms from entering to compete. But it is important to note that antitrust law does not condemn success per se. If a brand grows in popularity to dominate the market—that is not an antitrust violation.

Rather than condemning success, antitrust law looks at the conduct of market dominating firm(s) to see if they are using deliberate unfair tactics to exclude rivals or otherwise exploiting their market power to the detriment of consumers. For example since at least 1871, courts have expressed concern that granting a monopoly to one firm over a particular word could under certain circumstances reduce competition and hurt the public. In *Canal Co v. Clark* 1871, the Supreme Court did not allow the original producer of Lackawanna coal to enjoin later firms from using the same designation when it accurately described the origin of their coal from the Lackawanna valley in Pennsylvania. However, modern courts are less concerned with this word-monopoly because trademark law only grants limited rights against imitation and would allow descriptive fair use of coal from Lackawanna.

As discussed below, brand marketers should have only slight concerns regarding monopolizing conduct by marketing dominating brand marketers, but should pay closer attention to horizontal collusion that might occur in trademark licensing and distribution antitrust issues.

As noted in Chapters Two and Fourteen, successful brands risk having their brand names declared generic for all to use. They walk a fine line between enjoying being the *de facto* name for the product category while enforcing their trademark rights to avoid becoming the *de jure* name for the product category. Section 14 of the Lanham Act allows the FTC to petition the trademark office to declare a particular trademark generic.

Between 1950 and 1961, the FTC exercised this authority five times. The only other petition filed by the FTC was against Formica in 1978 (Shipley 1978). The earlier petitions sought cancellation based on abandonment or fraud, but the Formica petition was more controversial arguing that the FORMICA trademark had become generic. In 1980 in its appropriation bill, Congress forbid the FTC from pursuing any trademark cancellations.

Additionally, in late 1970s, the Federal Trade Commission considered requiring Borden to license its REALEMON trademark to other lemon juice marketers as a remedy for its monopolization by predatory pricing campaigns against its competitors. Although the Commission decided against the compulsory licensing remedy, the Commission majority and the Sixth Court of Appeals felt that Borden's highly successful brand name and product differentiation enhanced Borden's ability to conduct successful predatory pricing campaigns.

Fortunately for brand marketers who aspire to similar success, the Reagan FTC persuaded the Supreme Court to vacate the FTC's original decision and then negotiated a settlement favorable to Borden (*Borden Inc. v. FTC* 1982). The FTC's statement upon accepting the settlement acknowledged that brand differentiation served important competitive functions and stated that it could no longer support the condemnation of successful dominant brands in its original opinion (McClure 1996). The E.U. also does not view a trademark "monopoly" by itself as a source of market power or market dominance (Mandly 2003). While successful brands have avoided antitrust challenge based solely on their dominance since that time, brand marketers of market dominating brands have to be careful that their marketing conduct is within the boundaries of the law.

Trademark misuse is a concept shared by trademark and antitrust law. Trademark misuse involves "inequitable" conduct with a trademark including antitrust violations. Trademark misuse may be alleged as a defense to infringement of a trademark even if the mark has been registered for five years and achieved incontestable status. Early misuse defenses included trademark deceptiveness. However, modern cases tend to downplay trademark misuse and suggest that it should only apply in situations where the trademark itself is the prime and effective instrument of the alleged misuse (Geraldi 1992). For example, as discussed below, exclusive dealing—a brand selects one or a few distributors as its only distributors—may be illegal under appropriate market circumstances. However, even in cases of liability, the antitrust violation would probably not excuse a rival who was using an infringing trademark.

One case where misuse was allowed as a defense to infringement involved the Jaycees who sued a local chapter for using their trademark after canceling the chapter's license because the chapter admitted women as members in violation of the national organization's rules. The national Jaycees changed its rules to allow women members but continued to pursue the past violation of the local chapter. The court held such vindictive pursuit of the outdated lawsuit was inequitable and therefore trademark misuse (*United States Jaycees v. Cedar Rapids Jaycees* 1986). There are no recent examples of antitrust misuse being found as a defense to trademark infringement. Modern courts generally find trademarks to be pro-competitive.

I. Brand Extensions and Proliferation

During the same time period as the REALEMON case, the FTC filed a complaint accusing the four major ready-to-eat cereal marketers of maintaining a shared monopoly by proliferating brands and promoting trademarks through intensive advertising. The industry was highly concentrated with three firms, Kellogg, General Mills, and General Foods, collectively controlled 83% of all sales. The Administrative Law Judge dismissed the complaint being unable to find evidence of coordinated action. He also found brand proliferation to be rigorous competition rather than evidence of a conspiracy to restrict competition. The Reagan FTC affirmed the dismissal (*Kellogg Co.* 1982).

A principle weakness of the FTC case was that there was no evidence of a tacit agreement. New brands were introduced often, but there was no evidence that the manufacturers agreed to only compete through this method, that they were coordinating introductions or that they were doing these things to exclude other companies from entering the ready-to-eat cereal market.

A third case brought by the FTC at this time challenged several types of conduct including the use of a "fighting brand" by General Foods to preserve the East coast dominance of its MAXWELL HOUSE brand of coffee against the entry of Proctor & Gamble's FOLGERS brand. Just as FOLGERS entered a particular geographic market, General Foods would introduce its HORIZON brand coffee in that same market. HORIZON had been previously test-marketed and withdrawn as a failure, but was resurrected and packaged very similarly to FOLGERS to confuse consumers in order to take half of FOLGERS initial market share. General Foods hoped that limiting FOLGERS initial sales would persuade P & G not to continue its East coast expansion.

Although the ALJ found that HORIZON was indeed an anticompetitive fighting brand, the Commission itself dismissed the complaint believing that the smaller General Foods could not monopolize coffee over the larger P & G. The Commission further noted that the use of HORIZON had no apparent competitive impact (*General Foods Corp.* 1984).

The use of fighting brands was condemned in several of the big monopolization cases in the early part of the 20th century, but seldom since then. The Supreme Court affirmed in 1993 that Brown & Williamson was not liable for illegal price discrimination or monopolization when it copied Liggett's black 7 white generic cigarettes but offered more lucrative wholesale discounts (*Brooke Group Ltd. v. Brown & Williamson Tob. Corp.* 1993). Since all the major tobacco companies soon entered the fast growing generic cigarette category, these new products were deemed legitimate rather than short term fighting brands to drive Liggett out of the market and then disappear.

The use of "fighting brands" now often is considered a legitimate strategy by brand marketers. For example, when Heublein faced low price competition for its market leading brand SMIRNOFF in the U.S. vodka market from new entrant WOLFSCHMIDT, it launched a low priced brand RELSKA to compete with WOLFSCHMIDT. For good measure it also introduced an even lower priced brand. POPOV (Kotler & Keller 2006, p. 354).

Similarly, In 1975, when Proctor & Gamble (P & G), maker of Scope mouthwash, test marketed an amber mouthwash called Extend, Warner Lambert, the maker of Listerine—the leading amber mouthwash—responded in several ways, including the introduction of three new products: Depend, an amber mouthwash with advertising copy similar to Extend, in one test market, Listermint, a green mouthwash like Scope was introduced nationally and later a second green mouthwash, Signal, was test marketed and then introduced nationally. Both Signal and Listermint appear to be "cross parry" fighting brands attacking P & G's main mouthwash Scope. This signal might have proposed a market division—if P & G specializes in green mouthwashes and withdraws Extend, Warner Lambert will limit its offerings to amber mouthwashes and withdraw the alleged fighting brands. Ultimately, P & G withdrew Extend and Warner Lambert withdrew Depend, but kept Listermint and Signal.

The key from the legal perspective to determining whether such "countermoves" against a new brand should be deemed pro-competitive or anti-competitive is the intent of the brand marketer and the likely market effect. If the goal is to drive out the new entrant brand, monopolize the market, and then abandon the "fighting brand," an antitrust violation should be found if the market structure is conducive to monopolization. If, on the other hand, the responding brand marketer's intent is to recognize a previously unrecognized market segment and at least attempt to offer a legitimate new brand to serve that new segment, then the new brand introduction is legitimate.

The selling of private label or store brand products is somewhat similar to the concept of "fighting brands," except that such offerings appear to be legitimate, long term competitively priced offerings. The legal issue related to private labels that are sold at lower prices than national brands is that it might be illegal price discrimination to offer a private label at a low price to some distributors but only the national brand at a higher price to competing distributors. Price discrimination law would only apply to situations where the private label is of "like grade and quality" with the national brand so one easy way around this issue is to make the two products different (*FTC v. Borden Co.* 1966).

The party claiming illegal price discrimination also would have to prove a likelihood of a lessening of competition because of the sales at different prices. This could be alleviated by brand marketers who offer comparable store brand production at the same low price to everyone who wishes to buy store brands. This gives marketers some leverage to refuse exclusive production contracts for store brands with just one retailer, but still allows each retailer to have their own store brand and related trademarks.

A second practice related to fighting brands is the preannouncement of a new product or brand introduction at some point in the future that "freezes" the market in the short term but then the new product fails to meet its announced launch date. For example, in April 1964, IBM announced its intention to market a "supercomputer" to compete in the sophisticated scientific market, primarily against the products of Control Data Corporation (CDC). In August 1964, IBM announced that its 360/90 would out-perform CDC's 6600. IBM had difficulties developing this machine and in late 1967 abandoned the series only filling the 17 orders that had been placed to date. IBM lost $126 million on the project. In contrast, CDC eventually sold nearly 100 machines.

CDC believed that IBM had announced a computer for which it did not even have a prototype and that IBM salesmen talked up this "paper machine" to delay CDC sales of its 6600. After complaining to the Department of Justice, which stated it did not intend to sue IBM,

CDC filed suit in December 1968. In 1971, IBM filed counterclaims accusing CDC of reciprocal marketing practices. IBM purportedly was nervous about this suit because it was aware that CDC was cooperating with Justice. It initiated settlement negotiations in January 1972 and settlement was announced one year later.

IBM agreed to pay CDC $101 million and sold its subsidiary, Service Bureau Corp., to CDC for $16 million. Industry experts believed the subsidiary was worth $45 to $50 million. CDC agreed to destroy its computerized index to 75,000 IBM internal memoranda. This index was an important asset to Justice's case against IBM. Nine years later when Justice dismissed its monopolization case against IBM, a memorandum by Abbot Lipsky, Jr., on behalf of William Baxter, Assistant Attorney General in charge of the Antitrust Division referred to this story as "the most convincing episode" Unfortunately, from the perspective of antitrust analysis, this case was never tried on the merits.

Similar allegations for preannouncements of "vaporware" were leveled against Microsoft. In rejecting a proposed consent decree, Judge Stanley Sporkin condemned the preannouncement of products that do not exist and may never come into existence in the described time period of form as "a practice that is deceitful on its face and everybody in the business community knows it" (*U.S. v. Microsoft Corp.* 1995, p. 337). However, his rejection of the consent decree was overturned and the Department of Justice never pursued vaporware allegations against Microsoft.

One case has found liability for a premature product announcement as a tort of unfair competition rather than an antitrust violation. In that case, Greenlee, an established manufacturer of electrical equipment announced in 1971 that would soon market a conduit bender that was better and cheaper than the innovative product introduced in 1970 by Manufacturing Research Corporation (MRC). Greenlee's product was in the early development stage in 1971 and was not introduced until 1975. There was some evidence that a customer and investor terminated relationships with MRC at least in part because of this announcement.

A court of appeals affirmed both liability and the damage award holding that this action constituted intentional interference with business relationships (*Manufacturing Research Corp. v. Greenlee Tool Co.* 1982). Antitrust cases that have considered similar conduct have refused to find liability requiring the difficult burden of proof that the preannouncement was knowingly false (*ILC Peripherals Leasing Corp. v. IMB Corp.* 1978; *MCI Communications v. American Tel. & Tel. Co.* 1983).

A final issue related to brand proliferation is the introduction of a brand "innovation" that also limits interoperability with complementary rival products. In the 1970s, both IBM and Kodak survived multiple legal challenges that improved product introductions were predatory. Courts emphasized their reluctance to second guess product innovations.

One recent case did affirm a jury finding of liability when the maker of a biopsy "gun" that fired needles into body tissue to obtain a tissue sample for medical testing modified its gun so it no longer worked with replacement needles marketed by other companies. The majority of judges felt there was ample evidence that this was done to exclude competition from other brands of replacement needles rather to otherwise improve the gun or system in anyway (*C.R. Bard, Inc. v. M3 Systems* 1998). Similarly in Europe, the manufacturer of aseptic packaging machines was held liable for slight "innovations" that prevented others from making compatible cartons for use with the machines. Despite a proffered safety improvement justification for the changes, the Court of First Instance found liability noting that given the limited competition in the industry, it was crucial for the machine seller to publish clear standards and specifications so others could offer compatible cartons (*Tetra Pak v. Commission* 196).

II. Bundling and Tying

As noted in Chapter Ten, bundling one product with another can be a useful way to compensate consumers for trying a new product, e.g., a new sample of hair conditioner packaged with a bottle of shampoo. It also can be a longer term tactic to boost sales of the second product by requiring its purchase along with the first. For example, Microsoft bundled additional functionality within each successive version of Windows. While this may be more convenient for consumers, it has been accused of foreclosing competition from specialized software products such as those by Netscape.

When such longer term bundling is done by a firm with market power in one product, this not only locks-in customers to this single source for both products but also may lock-out other firms that want to sell the second product. Because purchasers buy the second product as part of the bundle, their switching costs to buy the second product separately are high. Barriers to entry for new competition are increased because rival firms now must sell the entire bundle in order to enter the market. This type of bundling is called tying under antitrust law.

The Supreme Court requires four elements be proved to win a tying case: (1) two separate products or services, (2) to get one product the other must also be purchased, (3) there must be market power in the tying product thereby compelling the consumer to buy the unwanted or tied product, and (4) the arrangement must affect a substantial volume of commerce (*Fortner Enterprises v. United States Steel Corp.* 1969, p. 503).

The issue of bundling/tying is confounded by the question of whether the offering is a combination of two separate products or a single product. The latter completely sidesteps any potential antitrust issues. For example, although a small minority of consumers might prefer to be able to buy left and right shoes separately, for most consumers whose feet are nearly the same size, buying a single pair is more efficient. It is therefore more efficient for marketers to sell the single pair of shoes and the pair is considered a single product (Hovenkamp 1994, p. 362).

In *Multistate Legal Studies Inc. v. Harcourt Brace Jovanovich Legal and Professional Publications, Inc.* (1995), the court found that a bar exam review course provider tied two separate products by bundling its multi-state bar exam course with its full service bar exam course. In other states such courses were often marketed separately and the defendant historically had marketed these courses separately. While new law school graduates typically take both review courses, out-of-state lawyers often have passed the multi-state and need only review for the state specific part of the bar exam. For these reasons, they were two separate products.

Tying is commonly referred to in the case law as per se illegal, meaning it is condemned without any structural analysis of market power. However to be liable under the antitrust laws for tying, courts require proof that the accused firm enjoys market power in the tying product. Otherwise, there is no coercion to purchase the package: customers could get each product from other sources.

Eastman Kodak Co. v. Image Technical Services, Inc. (1992) was successfully brought as a tying case where service was tied to spare parts. Kodak allegedly had market power in spare parts because customers were locked into a Kodak copier for a long period of time and therefore Kodak was a monopolist of its own brand. Although Kodak had less than 20% share of market for photocopiers, the Court found that because of customer lock-in, it had a virtual monopoly position in the market for Kodak copier parts (*Eastman Kodak Co. v. Image Technical Services, Inc.,* 1992). The Ninth Circuit later found Kodak liable because its motive for this change was to deny service firms access to the market rather than to protect its intellectual property (*Image Technical Services, Inc. v. Eastman Kodak Co.* 1997).

In contrast, the Federal Circuit Court of Appeals found that Xerox's longstanding similar policy of not selling parts to independent service organizations was legal because customers had opportunity to learn of this policy before lock-in. Consumers who were concerned about lifetime service costs could choose a copier brand based on spare parts availability to independent service firms if that was (*Independent Service Orgs. Antitrust Litigation* 2000).

Early tying cases pondered whether a well-known trademark could be sufficient to establish market power in the tying product. Thus, Kodak or Xerox could have market power because of their famous brand names. Despite some early decisions suggesting this possibility, more recent decisions reject this theory. Given the Supreme Court's recent decision that even patents should not be presumed to confer market power (*Illinois Tool Works, Inc. v. Independent Ink, Inc.* 2006), trademarks are less likely to be so presumed in the U.S. As this is being written, the European Commission appears to be pursuing antitrust penalties for Google improperly favoring its own websites in its search results to the detriment of competing websites. Google is alleged to have market power not because of its well-known trademark and brand, but rather because of its large market share in the internet search market.

As mentioned above, a well-known example of alleged technological tying occurred when Microsoft decided to include its Internet Explorer web browser within the Windows operating system. It stopped offering Windows without Internet Explorer so consumers had no choice but to buy the bundle. This provided little incentive for consumers or PC marketers to buy the rival browser. U.S. lawsuits involving this issue ultimately were settled (Hansell 2003) without requiring unbundling.

The E.U. took the opposite approach with the bundling of Media Player and required the sale of an unbundled product, Windows without Media Player while allowing the sale of the bundled product to continue. Since Windows is priced the same whether it contains Media Player or not, it seems unlikely consumers will be interested in the unbundled version. In contrast to Microsoft in Europe, when IBM bundled its memory units in with central processing units, the U.S. courts generally found IBM's intent was to reduce costs and improve performance and so the tie in was not illegal (Royall 2001).

Antitrust authorities also are unlikely to be concerned if bundling occurs as a short-term promotion. Such a promotion is unlikely to have a long-term exclusionary effect on the market and consumers often may still be able to buy the bundled products separately or may wait for the promotion to end.

III. Trademark Licensing and Cartels

The most straightforward antitrust cases are those involving agreements among competitors to restrict competition. Had the breakfast cereal companies agreed among themselves which firms would introduce new brands at any given time, liability would have been straightforward. Collusion cases also are straightforward because once an agreement is proven to exist and to unreasonably restrain trade it is condemned without any inquiry into market power.

For example, in *Timken Roller Bearing Co. v. United States* (1951), the Supreme Court held that an agreement that purported to license a common trademark among different companies was nothing more than a geographic division of markets among competitors and therefore violated the antitrust laws. Similarly, the Court more recently found that an agreement between the leading national brand of bar exam review materials and a company that sold bar exam review courses in Georgia that gave the exclusive right to use the national trademark and sell the national courses in Georgia in exchange for the Georgia company agree not to sell any bar exam review materials outside of Georgia to be illegal. The Court held that this agreement also was a straight forward division of markets among competitors (*Palmer v. BRG of Georgia, Inc.* 1990).

A more troubling ruling occurred some twenty years after *Timken* when the Court condemned an effort by about 25 small grocery store chains to jointly create the TOPCO store brand that each of them would then have the exclusive right to market within their assigned territory. Although the small chains averaged only 6% market share in their assigned markets, and entry was easy, the Court held that this was a cartel that prohibited competition in TOPCO brand products (*U.S. v. Topco Associates, Inc.* 1972).

Despite heavy criticism of this case and a decision five years later that recognized that a lessening of intra-brand competition might be acceptable if it enhanced inter-brand competition (*Continental T.V., Inc. v. GTE Sylvania, Inc.* 1977), this decision has not been overruled. Most recent lower court decisions allow joint ventures of small firms to share a brand to compete with larger national brands. For example, the D.C. Circuit allowed a brand promotion agreement among local moving van companies to include exclusive territories to enhance the incentives of the local firms to promote the national brand (*Rothery Storage and Van Co. v. Atlas Van Lines* 1986).

D. DISTRIBUTION ISSUES

Market dominating brands also occasionally are held liable under the antitrust laws for distributional restraints of trade. For example, a brand owner that requires dealers to sell at or below a specified price would be found liable for resale price maintenance (also called vertical price fixing) in the E.U. Until a 2007 U.S. Supreme Court decision, the same result would have occurred in the U.S. However, the Supreme Court decided that resale price maintenance should not be *per se* illegal, but rather should be judged under the rule of reason and only considered illegal if unreasonable under market circumstances (*Leegin Creative Leather Prods., Inc. v. Psks, Inc.* 2007).

In a market where there is robust competition among various brands, it is likely to be legal for each brand to establish a system of resale price maintenance as well as exclusive dealers. In a recent decision, the Sixth Circuit dismissed an antitrust case against 3M that alleged 3M offered retailers of automotive sandpaper a substantial upfront payment to adopt a multiyear exclusive dealing contract that excluded NicSand, the plaintiff in the lawsuit. The court held that the upfront payments did not lead to prices below cost and therefore were not predatory and in fact consumers enjoyed lower prices because of the price competition (*NicSand, Inc. v. 3M Co.* 2007). The dealers that enjoy an exclusive contract have strong incentives to support their only brand confident that it they invest in sales training and service that consumers will not be able to buy the brand for less elsewhere.

However, in situations where one large brand dominates the market, setting up exclusive dealers may foreclose other dealers from offering a competitive brand and setting retail prices essentially eliminates price competition. This reduces intra-brand competition with no corresponding increase in inter-brand competition. Under these circumstances, exclusive dealing contracts and resale price maintenance are found to be unreasonable and condemned (*U.S. v. Dentsply Int'l Inc.* 2005; *U.S. v. Microsoft Corp.* 2001; *U.S. v. Visa U.S.A., Inc.* 2003).

To avoid antitrust liability, some firms that offer dominant brands offer loyalty programs that encourage but do not mandate exclusivity. These programs may be legal if they still allow for effective competition. However, if the loyalty rebate payments are set sufficiently high so that dealers can only earn substantial rebates by buying all their requirements from the large firm, the effect is the same as an exclusive dealing contract. Smaller brands are foreclosed from effective distribution.

For example, 3M was held liable for its loyalty program that made it extremely difficult for smaller rival LePage's to find dealers willing to carry its brand of tape and other office supplies (*LePage's Inc. v. 3M* 2003). However, another appellate court recently rejected this vague standard of liability, holding instead that the challenger must prove the discounts resulted in prices that were below the incremental cost of producing the goods that competed with those of the plaintiff (*Cascade Health Solutions v. PeaceHealth et al.* 2007).

Earlier cases have held that if there are alternative distribution methods that do allow rivals to compete effectively, antitrust liability is avoided and the exclusive dealing arrangement is allowed because competitors are not foreclosed (*Omega Environmental, Inc. v. Gilbarco, Inc.* 1997; *PepsiCo., Inc. v. Coca-Cola, Co.* 2002). Similarly, short time periods of exclusive dealing allow rivals to frequently bid for their own privilege of exclusive dealing and are often found to be legal since competition for these rights is healthy (*Omega Environmental, Inc. v. Gilbarco, Inc.* 1997; *Roland Machine Co v. Dresser Industries, Inc.* 1984).

Bundling or tie-ins can also raise similar distributional antitrust issues. If a dominant brand requires dealers to carry all of its products or even just a second product by contract or by loyalty incentive program, then firms that sell only the second product or only a small number of products in the product line are at a disadvantage. In most markets, there is sufficient competition so that this is not a problem, but these practices may be condemned when practiced by a market dominating brand so that consumers don't get the benefit of intra-brand competition among dealers.

For example, in 2002 Georgia Pacific (GP) introduced its "enMotion" brand automated touchless paper towel dispenser designed to use GP's proprietary, "fabric-like" paper toweling. The dispensers bear marks "enMotion," "Georgia-Pacific" and a stylized "GP" and are leased to distributors who sublease them to end users. The leases and subleases expressly provide that only enMotion brand paper toweling may be used in the dispensers.

When rival Von Drehle began selling lower-quality paper towels designed for use in GP's enMotion dispenser in 2004, Georgia Pacific brought several suits, not against its own distributors for breaching lease provisions, but against Von Drehle and its distributors for contributory trademark infringement. GP argued that Von Drehle induced GP lessors to put non-GP towels in the GP dispensers. Consumers would then be confused thinking the lower quality towels were part of the GP brand thereby damaging the brand.

Two courts dismissed these cases finding little evidence that consumers thought the paper was the same brand as the dispenser. However, a third court held a jury trial and the jury ordered Von Drehle to pay its profits from the sale of its paper towels to GP. The court also enjoined the practice within its circuit (Coultas 2015).

In the U.S., a rule of reason analysis would apply to a brand owner that assigned each of its dealers to an exclusive territory. In most cases this would be allowable because of competition among competing brands. However, in Europe, competition laws intend to establish a single European market so that exclusive territories, particularly by country, would not be allowed. It probably would be permitted to assign dealers to a particular address or territories of primary responsibility.

E. GRAY MARKET IMPORTS

One method of limiting a trademark owner's feared monopoly in olden days was to emphasize the first sale or exhaustion doctrine. Under that concept, once a firm sold its goods, it would lose control over those goods and they could be re-sold, even if originally sold in another country, to compete with sales by the trademark owner. Today goods that legitimately bear a trademark in one country but are imported into a second country where another firm owns the rights to that particular trademark are called gray market goods. This distinguishes them from black market (or counterfeit) goods that have no legitimate right to use a particular trademark.

Aaker and Joachimsthaler (2000) suggest that a brand's goal should not be to become a single global brand, but rather should be to exercise brand leadership throughout the globe. In other words a brand should be globally consistent, but not necessarily globally identical. They suggest that this means following key brand values throughout the globe, but adapting those values to local markets. This often means brands will share the same name and trade dress, but may have different qualities and relative prices for local markets.

These price and quality differences provide opportunities for arbitrageurs to buy the brand in the lower priced county and import it for sale in the higher priced country. This not only challenges a brand's ability to be profitable in some countries, but also may diminish brand equity if the less expensive gray market goods also are different in quality and consumers are surprised and disappointed by this difference.

In 1923, the Supreme Court first recognized that trademark law should protect the rights of brand owners in each particular country because consumers in any given country come to expect that the brand in their country comes from a particular source (*A. Bourgois & Co. v. Katzel* 1923). While this decision addresses the problem of a branded product made in another country by a separate company, it does not resolve the problem of products made in or for U.S. firms that are re-imported into the U.S. without authorization.

Today, there are several bases in U.S. law for dealing with gray market imports. Other countries have similar laws. While it is conceivable that anti-dumping laws could be applied where such goods are sold in the U.S. at a price below the home market price, the statutes more commonly used to regulate gray market imports are summarized in the table on the opposite page. Successful cases result in an exclusion order barring importation of the goods by any party and might include an order barring the sale of goods that have already been imported.

Table One		
Statutes Used to Regulate Gray Market Imports		
Statute	**Coverage**	**Standard of Proof**
Tariff Act § 526 (District Court)	Bars importation of goods bearing a registered TM owned by U.S. citizen or company	Must be no common ownership or control between the U.S. and foreign firm
Tariff Act § 337 (before the ITC)	Bars importation of goods that infringe registered or unregistered U.S. TMs	Must be a material difference between the imported goods bearing the TM and U.S. goods
TM Act § 42 (District Court)	Bars importation of "non-genuine" goods that copy or simulate a registered U.S. TM	Must be a material difference between the imported goods and U.S. goods
Customs Border Protection	Must record TM with CBP and should provide importation information	Same

A key question in two of these types of cases is whether the imported goods are different from the normal U.S. goods in a way that would be material to the consumer purchasing decision. This also is the standard that is applied to gray market goods in an ordinary infringement lawsuit or a lawsuit under section 43(a) of the trademark statute that prohibits false designations of origin, false descriptions and false representations. Thus it is not illegal to sell identical goods in the U.S. without permission of the U.S. trademark owner. It is only illegal if consumers may be confused about the source of the products and the U.S. trademark owner may suffer a reduction in brand equity because of differences in the unauthorized goods that consumers don't expect.

This material differences standard was first applied in a decision involving Cabbage Patch kids imported from Spain whose birth certificates and adoption papers were in Spanish and therefore could not be processed by the U.S. fulfillment house. The court held that even though the Spanish products bore genuine authorized trademarks, they were not "genuine goods" under U.S. law because U.S. consumers expected the birth certificate and adoption papers to be in English (*Original Appalachian Artworks, Inc. v. Granada Electronics, Inc.* 1987).

Other courts have found the following differences in the following to be material: ingredients, aesthetics, packaging, labeling, quality or quality control measures, warranties, manuals and other written material (Oswald 2006–07). Even the lack of Universal Product Codes that allowed consumers to participate in a merchandise redemption program was deemed to be a material difference (*Philip Morris, Inc. v. Allen Distributors, Inc.* 1999). In contrast, courts have found the color of otherwise identical circuit breakers and the careful removal of batch numbers without otherwise changing the packaging to be immaterial differences (Oswald 2006–07).

U.S. brand owners have two options for privately restricting gray market imports. First, as noted above, U.S. antitrust law often will allow brands that don't have market power to assign exclusive territories to wholesalers and dealers. If a brand owner finds a reseller that violates its contractual assignment, it could terminate the firm or sue for breach of contract. Unfortunately, it is often easier to find the goods that are imported without permission then to find out which distributor breached its contract by selling to the importing company.

A second strategy would be to insure that branded goods either shipped abroad or manufactured elsewhere have material differences from the branded goods intended for the U.S. market. If branded goods intended for other markets appear in the U.S., the brand owner can prevent their importation and sale because of the material differences between the goods.

E.U. law allows similar restriction of the sale of branded goods from outside Europe without permission of the European trademark owner, but to further the single market concept, E.U. allows gray market imports from any European country into another (Reed 2002). In *Silhouette Int'l Schmied GmbH & Co.KG v. Hartlauer Handelsgesellschaft mbH* (1998), the European Court of Justice clarified that provisions in the European Trademark Directive dealing with exhaustion of rights through the first sale of a trademarked product do not apply to products sold outside the E.U. As a result, firms can prevent such products from being re-imported into the E.U.

In contrast, trademarked items sold within the E.U. do exhaust the rights of the trademark owner and such items can be resold anywhere in the E.U. without the consent of the E.U. trademark owner. As noted above, prohibiting such shipments by contract probably would violate E.U. competition law, although some encouragement of exclusive territories is permissible. In *Levi Strauss Co., Inc. v. Tesco PLC* (2001), the ECJ clarified that the E.U. trademark owner must give explicit permission for goods bearing that trademark to be imported into the E.U. Silence on this issue does not constitute consent. Thus, E.U. law generally prohibits gray market imports from outside Europe. U.S. law may do so only if there are material differences in the goods or no common control of the companies that have registered the U.S. and foreign trademarks.

F. INTERNATIONAL TRADEMARK PRE-EMPTION

In many developing countries, it is common for local firms to adopt brand names and identifiers that are similar to internationally famous brands. Indeed, if possible local firms may seek trademark registration of the famous brand name or its translation before the famous brand is sold in that particular country. Since trademark law and registration are national in scope, this would appear at first glance to be a viable strategy.

This is particularly true because many countries do not protect trademarks until they are registered in that country. The local mark registrant could try to sell products under the brand name or could simply wait and try to sell the local rights to the name to the brand marketer when requested. This is similar to cybersquatting where parties register domain names in the hope of selling the domain name to a trademark owner. Cybersquatting is only outlawed by a specific statute in the U.S.

The good news for global brand owners is that the Paris Convention, originally agreed to by some countries in 1883, requires that signatory countries not require trade names be registered as trademarks in order to be protected. The TRIPS (Trade Related Aspects of Intellectual Property Rights) agreement incorporates these aspects of the Paris Convention. Both the Convention and TRIPS encourage countries to protect "well known" trademarks from other countries. The only requirement is that the mark be well known to consumers in the country where trademark protection is sought. To the extent courts in various countries enforce this doctrine; marketers can be less concerned about trademark preemption in a country where their trademarks are not yet registered if the marks are nonetheless well known.

G. CONCLUSION

Big brands enjoy their own special set of legal issues. While dominating a market by itself is usually not a legal issue, reverse confusion as well as antitrust collusion and distribution issues should be carefully avoided. In addition, when a brand goes global, it frequently faces gray market import issues that are only partially addressed by existing law. The careful brand manager can develop strategies for using existing laws to protect itself from this problem.

APPENDIX A

References

"Undercover Marketing Exposed," (2004), *60 Minutes*, July 25, available at http://www.cbsnews.com/stories/2003/10/23/60minutes/printable579657.shtml, accessed 19 June 2006.

Aaker, David A. (1996), *Building Strong Brands*, New York: The Free Press.

Aaker, David A. and Erich Joachimsthaler (2000), *Brand Leadership*, New York: The Free Press.

Aaker, David A. and Kevin Lane Keller (1990), "Consumer Evaluations of Brand Extensions," *Journal of Marketing*, 54(1), 27–41.

Abelson, Jenn (2005), "The Offer's in the Mail," *Boston Sunday Globe*, (June 12) A1, A25.

Acheson, Arthur (1917), *Trade-Mark Advertising as an Investment*, New York: New York Evening Post.

Adelstein, Jonathan S. (2005), " 'Fresh is not as Fresh as Frozen': A Response to the Commercialization of American Media," remarks before the American Media Institute (May 25), available at http://hraunfoss.fcc.gov/edocs_public/attachmatch/DOC–258962A1.pdf.

Advertising Self-Regulatory Council (2015), "NAD Recommends Splintek Discontinue '#1 Brand Prescribed' Claim" available at http://www.asrcreviews.org/nad-recommends-splintek-discontinue-1-brand-prescribed-claim-bitepad-strength-claim-for -dental-guards/, accessed 23 March 2015.

Advertising Self-Regulatory Council (2015), "NAD Recommends Vogue Change Product Names for Certain Shampoos, Conditioners" available at http://www.asrcreviews.org/nad-recommends-vogue-change-product-names-for-certain-shampoos-conditioners/, accessed 4 April 2016.

Agins, Teri and Rebecca Quick (2001), "Calvin Klein, Warnaco Settle Their Bitter Feud," *Wall Street Journal*, (Jan. 21), B1.

Agrawal, Jagdish and Wagner A. Kamakua (1995), "The Economic Worth of Celebrity Endorsers: An Event Study Analysis," *Journal of Marketing*, 59(July), 56–62.

Aide, Christopher M. (2003), "The Community Design: European Union-Wide Protection for Your Design Portfolio," *Northwestern Journal of Technology and Intellectual Property*, 1(1), 35–46.

Alcock, Lucy et al. (2003), "Image Rights—Are They Worth the Contract They're Written On?" *Brand Management*, 11(2), 119–123.

Alcock, Lucy, Paul Chen, Hui Min Ch'ng and Sarah Hodson (2003), "Using Other Intellectual Property Rights to Enhance Brand Value," *Brand Management*, 11(2) 109–110.

Aleck, Pamela L. and Robert B. Settle (1999), "Strategies for Building Consumer Brand Preference," *Journal of Product & Brand Management*, 8(2), 130–144.

American Law Institute (1993), *Restatement of the Law Third, Unfair Competition*, St. Paul: American Law Institute Publishers.

Anderson, Eric T. and Duncan I. Simester (1998), "The Role of Sale Signs," *Marketing Science*, 17 (2), 139–155.

Anderson, Eric T. and Duncan I. Simester (2001), "Are Sale Signs Less Effective When More Products Have Them?" *Marketing Science*, 20 (2), 121–142.

Anson, Weston (1984), "A Licensing Retrospective and Glimpse into the Future," *The Merchandising Reporter*, 3(5), 4–5.

Associated Press (2001), "Brewery Settles Crazy Horse Beverage Suit," New York Times, (April 27), A14.

Baar, Aaron (2005), "Burnett Recycles Maytag Repairmen for Cheez-It," available at http://www.adweek.com/news/advertising/burnett-recycles-maytag-repairmen-cheez-it-77266, accessed 4 April 2016.

Balasubramanian, Siva K. (1994), "Beyond Advertising and Publicity: Hybrid Messages and Public Policy Issues," *Journal of Advertising*, 23(4), 29–46.

Bandler, James (2005), "Advice for Sale: How Companies Pay TV Experts for On-Air Product Mentions," *Wall Street Journal*, (April 19), A1.

Battersby, Gregory J. and Charles W. Grimes (1986), "Merchandise Revisited," *The Trademark Reporter*, 76(3), 271–307.

Bayerische Motorenwerke AG (BMW) v. Deenik (1999), ECJ Case C63–97, 1999 ETMR 339.

Baz, Luis (2015), "European Union General Court: The Time has Come to Limit the Scope of Protection for the Watch Brand SWATCH," *INTA Bulletin*, 70(14), (August 1).

Beales, Howard J. (1991), What State Regulators Should Learn From FTC Experience in Regulating Advertising, *Journal of Public Policy & Marketing* 10(1) 101–117.

Beales, Howard J. III and Timothy J. Muris (2015), "FTC Consumer Protection at 100: 1970s Redux or Protecting Markets to Protect Consumers," *George Washington Law Review*, 83(6), 2157–2229.

Beebe, Barton (2006), "An Empirical Study of the Multifactor Tests for Trademark Infringement," *California Law Review*, 94 (Dec.), 1581–1654.

Bendekgey, Lee and Caroline H. Mead (1992), "International Protection of Appellations of Origin and Other Geographic Indications," *The Trademark Reporter*, 82(Sept.–Oct.) 765–792.

Berkens, M. (2013), "ICANN Opens Comment Period on Closed Generic New GTLD's," *The Domains*, (Feb. 6), http://www.thedomains.com/2013/02/06/icann-opens-comment-period-on-closed-generic-new-gtlds/, accessed 4 April 2016.

Better Business Bureau (2005), "BBB Code of Advertising" available at www.bbb.org/membership/codeofad.asp, accessed 3 November 2015.

Better Business Bureau (2009), "Self-Regulatory Program for Children's Advertising," available at http://www.caru.org/guidelines/guidelines.pdf, accessed 4 April 2016.

Birkner, C. (2012), "Master of your Domain," *Marketing News*, (Feb. 29), 20–24.

Birkner, Christine (2015), "What's Your Type?" *Marketing News*, (July), 10–11, available at https://www.ama.org/publications/MarketingNews/Pages/whats-your-type.aspx, accessed 10 July 2015.

Black, Vaughn (1988), "A Brief Word about Advertising," 20 *Ottawa Law Review* 20(3), 509–557.

Boddewyn, J.J. (1985), "The Swedish Consumer Ombudsman System of Advertising Self-Regulation," *Journal of Consumer Affairs* 19(1) 140–162.

Boddewyn, J.J. (1988), *Advertising, Self-Regulation and Outside Participation*, Westport, CT: Quorum Books.

Bollier, David (2005), *Brand Names Bullies*, Hoboken: John Wiley & Sons.

Bone, Paula Fitzgerald and Swati Jantrania (1992), "Olfaction as a Cue for Product Quality," *Marketing Letters*, 3(3), 289–296.

Branfman, David & Randy Broberg (2006), "Invasion of the Pod Snatcher," *IP Law & Business*, (Nov.), 24–25.

Brenner, Lee and Andreas Becker (2015), "Do Not Mess with Michael Jordan and his Right of Publicity," *Drye Wit* (Aug. 26), available at http://www.dryewit.com/2015/08/do-not-mess-with-michael-jordan-and-his-right-of-publicity/, accessed 1 September 2015.

Brody, Jess M. and Shah, Suemyra A. (2015), "No Cause for Concern," *Marketing News*, (May 15), 28–31.

Brody, Peter M. (2005), "What's In a Nickname? Or Can Public Use Create Private Rights?" *The Trademark Reporter*, 95(6), 1123–1164.

Brooke, Zach (2016), "More Brands Getting a #Trademark on Hashtags," *Marketing News Weekly,* (March 23), available at https://www.ama.org/publications/eNewsletters/Marketing-News-Weekly/Pages/More-Brands-Getting-a-Trademark-on-Hashtags.aspx, accessed 29 March 2016.

Brott, Tamar (2004), "Grateful Dead," *Los Angeles Magazine*, 49(12), 93–99.

Bryer, Lanning and Melvin Simensky (2003), "Acquisition and Licensing of Famous Name Trademarks and Rights of Publicity in the United States," in *Intellectual Property Assets in Mergers & Acquisitions*, (Lanning and Simensky eds.), New York: John Wiley & Sons.

Buchanan, Bruce and Ronald H. Smithies (1989), "Substantiating a Parity Position," *Journal of Advertising Research* 29(5), 509–20.

Buck, Glen (1916), *Trademark Power*, Chicago: Munroe & Southworth Publishers.

Bury, Martine (2006), "A Cause Celeb—As Celebrity Licensed Products Boom, Consumers Demand More Authenticity," *Women's Wear Daily*, (June 7), 12.

Byrne, Joanne (2006), "Legal Update: Feta Cheese and Pork Pies: PDOs and PGIs," *Brand Management*, 13(4/5), 363–368.

Byrt, Sarah (2003), "Legal Pitfalls in Protecting Advertising Slogans in the European Union," *Brand Management*, 11(2), 99–108.

Cain, Rita Marie (1994), "Call Up Someone and Just Say Buy—Telemarketing and the Regulatory Environment" *American Business Law Journal*, 31(4), 641–698.

Cain, Rita Marie (1996), "Recent Developments in Telemarketing Regulation," *Journal of Public Policy & Marketing*, 15(1) 135–141.

Calfee John and Debra Ringold (1994), "The Seventy Percent Majority: Enduring Consumer Beliefs about Advertising," *Journal of Public Policy & Marketing*, 13(Fall), 228–38.

California Attorney General (2002), "Attorney General Lockyear Praises $20 Million Fine against R.J. Reynolds for Targeting Minors with Ads," available at https://oag.ca.gov/news/press-releases/attorney-general-lockyer-praises-20-million-fine-against-rj-reynolds-targeting, accessed 4 April 2016.

Callcott, Margaret F. and Barbara J. Phillips (1996), "Observations: Elves Make Good Cookies," *Journal of Advertising Research*, 36(Sept./Oct.), 73–79.

Calvaruso, Andrea L., Nancy H. Lutz and Yasmin Tavakoli (2012), "gTLDs in the Running: Take a Look at the Line-up and What it means for your Organization," *Lexology.com* (June 14), available at http://www.lexology.com/library/detail.aspx?g=078d39ff-e8df–47de–8ded–19692a8ef208, accessed 19 June 2012.

Campbell, L. and Z. Yaqub (1999), *The European Handbook on Advertising Law*. London: Cavendish Publishing, Ltd.

Campbell, Margaret C. and Kevin Lane Keller (2003), "Brand Familiarity and Advertising Repetition Effects," *Journal of Consumer Research*, 30(Sept.), 292–304.

Carl, Walter J., Jr. (2006), "To Tell of Not to Tell? Assessing the Practical Effects of Disclosure for Word-of-Mouth Marketing Agents and Their Conversational Partners," summary report, Boston, MA: Northeastern University, January, 1–23 available at http://papers.ssrn.com/sol3/papers.cfm?abstract_id=877760, accessed 4 April 2016.

Carty, Hazel (2004), "Advertising, Publicity Rights and English Law," *Intellectual Property Quarterly*, 2004(3), 209–258.

Chamberlin, Edward H. (1933), *A Theory of Monopolistic Competition*, (Cambridge, MA: Harvard University Press).

Chen, Christopher (1992), "Food and Drug Administration Food Standards of Identity: Consumer Protection through the Regulation of Product Information," *Food and drug Law Journal*, 47, 185–206.

Children's Advertising Review Unit (2009), *Self-Regulatory Program for Children's Advertising*, available at http://www.caru.org/guidelines/guidelines.pdf, accessed 23 July 2015.

Clancy, Kevin J. and Trout, Jack (2002), "Brand Confusion," *Harvard Business Review*, 80(3), 22

Coats, William Sloan, Julieta Lerner and Alvina Hsu (2006), "Fame Dahling: Rights of Publicity and Entertainment Licensing," *The Licensing Newsletter*, (April), 1–10.

Coca-Cola Co. (1923), *Opinions, Orders, Injunctions and Decrees Relating to Unfair Competition and Infringement of Trademark, Vol. 1*, Atlanta: Coca-Cola Co.

Coca-Cola Co. (1939), *Opinions, Orders, Injunctions and Decrees Relating to Unfair Competition and Infringement of Trademark, Vol. 2*, Atlanta: Coca-Cola Co.

Cohen, Dorothy (1986), "Trademark Strategy," *Journal of Marketing*, 50(January), 61–74.

Collett, Pippa and Nick Johnson (2006), "Don't Be Ambushed in 2012," *Brand Strategy*, (Feb. 1—issue 199), pp. 34–35.

Collins, Clayton (2004), "Lines Blue Between Ads and Articles," *Christian Science Monitor*, (May 27) available at www.csmonitor.com/2004/0527/p11s02–ussc.htm, accessed 19 October 2004.

Collins- Dodd, Colleen and Judith Lynne Zaichkowsky (1999) "National brand responses to brand imitation: retailers versus other manufacturers", *Journal of Product & Brand Management*, 8(2), 96–105.

Commercial Alert (2005), "Request for Investigation of Companies That Engage in "Buzz Marketing"," submitted to the Federal Trade Commission, October 18, 1–6.

Commissioner of Patents (1870), Annual Report of the Commissioner of Patents, Washington, D.C.: Government Printing Office, Washington, DC.

Compeau, Larry D. and Dhruv Grewal (1998), "Comparative Price Advertising: An Integrative Review," *Journal of Public Policy and Marketing*, 17 (Fall), 257–273.

Compeau, Larry D., Joan Lindsey-Mullikin, Dhruv Grewal and Ross Petty (2004), "An Analysis of Consumers' Interpretations of the Semantic Phrases Found in Reference Price Advertisements." *Journal of Consumer Affairs*, 38 (summer), 178–187.

Coultas, Jody (2015), "Appeals Court Cleans Up Faulty Ruling in Dispute Between Paper Towel Makers," *Intellectual Property Law Daily*, (March 31), available at http://www.dailyreportingsuite.com/ip/news/appeals_court_cleans_up_faulty_ruling_in_dispute_between_paper_towel_makers, accessed 3 April 2016.

Creamer, Matthew (2005), "Foul Mouth: Stealth Marketers Flirt with Law," *Advertising Age*, 76(Oct. 3), 6.

Cunningham, Ross M. (1956), "Brand Loyalty—What, Where How Much?" *Harvard Business Review*, 34(1), 116–128.

Cyr, Diane (1999), "Sweeps Saga: PCH and AFP Plan for Future in the Wake of Public Uproar," *Direct* (Sept. 30), available at www.directmag.com/mag/marketing_sweeps_saga_pch/, accessed 21 April 2005.

Dawar, Niraj (2004), "What are Brands Good for?" *MIT Sloan Management Review*, 46(1), 31–37.

Desai, D. R. (2012), "From Trademarks to Brands," *Florida Law Review*, 64(4), 981–1044.

Direct Marketing Association (2005), "Economic Impact: U.S. Direct Marketing Today," available at http://www.the-dma.org/cgi/registered/research/libres-ecoimp2003.shtml.

Dobele, Angela, David Toleman and Michael Beverland (2005), "Controlled Infection! Spreading the Brand Message through Viral Marketing," *Business Horizons*, (48), 143–49.

Dogan, Stacey L. and Mark A. Lemley (2005), "The Merchandising Right: Fragile Theory or Fait Accompli?" *Emory Law Journal*, 54(Winter), 461–506.

Dommering, Egbert (1992), Unlawful Publication under Dutch and European law—defamation, libel, and advertising. *Media law and Practice* 13(4) 262–270.

Drescher, Thomas D. (1992), "The Transformation and Evolution of Trademarks—From Signals to Symbols," *The Trademark Reporter*, 82(May–June), 301–340.

Dubrow, Larry (2006), "Pepsi Stays in Sync with hot Celebrity Hand," *Advertising Age*, (Feb. 20), S4.

Duguid, Paul (2013), "California Marketing & Collective Amnesia", *University of California Davis Law Review*, 47(2), 581–600.

Duguid, Paul (2009), "French Connections: The International Propagation of Trademarks in the Nineteenth Century," *Enterprise & Society*, 10(1), 3–37.

Economist (1988), "The Year of the Brand," *The Economist*, 309(7582), 95–6.

Enrich, David (2006), "Credit Card Mail Pitches on Decline," *The Metrowest Daily News Sunday*, E3.

Enright, Allison (2005a), "Stats: To Your Places Everyone," *Marketing News*, (July 15), 4.

Entis, Laura (2015), "No Eggs, No Mayo: FDA Goes After Hampton Creek for Naming Its Vegan Spread 'Just Mayo' ", *Entrepreneur.com* (Aug. 26), http://www.entrepreneur.com/article/249992, accessed 20 November 2015.

Erdogan, B. Zafer (1999), "Celebrity Endorsement: A Literature Review," *Journal of Marketing Management*, 15(2), 291–314.

FairWinds Partners (2008a), "Combosquatting: The Business of Cybersquatting, Part 3 of 3," *Perspectives*, 3(9), http://www.fairwindspartners.com/en/newsroom/perspectives/vol–3–issue–9/forward, accessed 26 January 2009.

FairWinds Partners (2008b), "Typosquatting: The Business of Cybersquatting, Part 2 of 3" *Perspectives*, 3(8), available at http://www.fairwindspartners.com/en/newsroom/perspectives/vol–3–issue–8/forward, accessed 26 January 2009.

Federal Trade Commission (1983), *FTC Policy Statement Regarding Advertising Substantiation,* available at https://www.ftc.gov/public-statements/1983/03/ftc-policy-statement-regarding-advertising-substantiation, accessed 24 March 2015.

Federal Trade Commission (1993), "California Infomercial Marketer Settles FTC Charges of False and unsubstantiated Claims for Purported Pain-Relieving Device," *FTC Press Release*, May 25.

Federal Trade Commission (1997), "Enforcement Policy Statement on U.S. Origin Claims," available at https://www.ftc.gov/public-statements/1997/12/enforcement-policy-statement-us-origin-claims, accessed 20 November 2015.

Federal Trade Commission (2005a), "The Rebate Debate: Why were They Late? FTC Settles Charges Against CompUSA." *FTC News Release* (March 11), available at www.ftc.gov/opa/2005/03/compusa.htm.

Federal Trade Commission (2005b), "Children's Book Publisher to Pay $710,000 to Settle Charges it Violated Commission's Negative Option and Telemarketing Sales Rule, *FTC Press Release,* (June 21), available at https://www.ftc.gov/news-events/press-releases/2005/06/childrens-book-publisher-pay-710000-settle-charges-it-violated, accessed 29 March 2016.

Federal Trade Commission (2007a), "Major Online Advertiser Settles FTC Charges. Free Gifts Weren't Free; Settlement Calls for $650,000 Civil Penalty," *FTC News Release*, (Nov. 28), available at www.ftc.gov/opa/2007/11/free.shtm.

Federal Trade Commission (2007b), "FTC Settles Two Complaints Charging Rebate-Fulfillment Violations," *FTC News Release*, (April 27), available at www.ftc.gov/opa/2007/04/soyoinphonic.shtm.

Federal Trade Commission (2010), "FTC Settlement Prohibits Marketers of Children's Vitamins from Making Deceptive Health Claims about Brain and Eye Development," available at https://www.ftc.gov/news-events/press-releases/2010/12/ftc-settlement-prohibits-marketers-childrens-vitamins-making, accessed 23 July 2015.

Federal Trade Commission (2015), "Prepaid Mobile Provider TracFone to Pay $40 Million to Settle FTC Charges It Deceived Consumers About 'Unlimited' Data Plans," available at https://www.ftc.gov/news-events/press-releases/2015/01/prepaid-mobile-provider-tracfone-pay-40-million-settle-ftc, accessed 29 March 2016.

Fletcher, Anthony L. (2005), "The Curious Doctrine of Reverse Confusion—Getting It Right in Reverse," *The Trademark Reporter*, 95(Nov.-Dec.), 1273–1307.

Folsom, R.H. and Teply, L.L. (1980), "Trademarked Generic Words," *The Yale Law Journal*, 89(7): 1323–1359.

Frank, Robert (1995), "Olympic Flame Singes Some Atlanta Businesses," *The Wall Street Journal*, (Mar. 22), at B1.

Friestad, Marian and Peter Wright (1994), "The Persuasion Knowledge Model: How People Cope with Persuasion Attempts," *Journal of Consumer Research*, 21 (1), 1–31.

Fry, Joseph N. (1967), "Family Branding and Consumer Brand Choice," *Journal of Marketing Research*, 4(Aug.), 237–47.

Galloway, Chester S., Herbert Jack Rotfield and Jef I. Richards (2005), "Holding Media Responsible for Deceptive Weight-Loss Advertising," *West Virginia Law Review,* 107(Winter) 353–384.

Gao, Z. (2005), Harmonious Regional Advertising Regulation? A Comparative Examination of Government Advertising Regulation in China, Hong Kong, and Taiwan, *Journal of Advertising*, 34(3), 75–87.

Gardner, Burleigh B. and Sidney J. Levy (1955), "The Product and the Brand," *Harvard Business Review*, 33(March–April), 33–39.

Garretson, Judith A. and Scot Burton (2005), "The Role of Spokescharacters as Advertisement and Package Cues in Integrated Marketing Communications," *Journal of Marketing*, 69 (Oct.), 118–132.

Geissler, L.R. (1917), "Association-Reactions Applied to Ideas of Commercial Brands of Familiar Articles," *Journal of Applied Psychology*, 1(Sept.), 275–290.

Geraldi, Alan R. (1992), "Misuse: An Equitable Defense to Intellectual Property Infringement Actions," *Hastings Communication and Entertainment Law Journal*, 14(Winter), 235–260.

Gershman, Jacob (2015), "Eau de Fracking? Companies Try to Trademark Scents," *The Wall Street Journal*, (April 14), available at http://www.wsj.com/articles/should-companies-trademark-scents–1428965455, accessed 7 July 2015.

Gilson, Jerome and Anne Gilson LaLonde (2005), "Cinnamon Buns, Marching Ducks and Cherry-Scented Racecar Exhaust: Protecting Nontraditional Trademarks," *The Trademark Reporter*, 95 (July–Aug), 773–824.

Glaister, Dan (2005), "Dead Stars Who Rain Money on the Living: Sale of image rights agency focuses attention on lucrative after-life of deceased celebrities", *The Guardian*, (April 9), available at http://www.theguardian.com/world/2005/apr/09/arts.film, accessed 4 April 2016.

Glionna, John M. (1997), "Protecting the Dead; The Celebrity Rights Act vs. John Wayne Toilet Tissue and Other Atrocities", *Los Angeles Times*, October 25.

Gobé, Marc (2001), *Emotional Branding: The New Paradigm for Connecting Brands to People*, New York: Allworth Press.

Goebel, Burkhart (2003), "Geographical Indications and Trademarks—the Road from Doha," *The Trademark Reporter*, 93(July–Aug.), 964–995.

Goodrum, Charles and Helen Dalrymple (1990), *Advertising in America: The First 200 Years*, New York: Harry N. Abrams, Inc.

Gordon, Ian (1998), *Comic Strips and Consumer Culture 1890–1945*, Washington: Smithsonian.

Gordon, Richard L. (1988), Networks Hit for Ad Clearance Cuts. *Advertising Age*, 59(37) 6.

Greene, Timothy Denny and Jeff Wilkerson (2013), "Understanding Trademark Strength," *Stanford Technology Law Review*, 16(3), 535–582.

Grewal, Dhruv and Larry D. Compeau (1992), "Comparative Price Advertising: Informative or Deceptive?" *Journal of Public Policy and Marketing*, 11(Spring), 52–62.

Grewal, Dhruv, Sukumar Kavanoor, Edward F. Fern, Carolyn Costley and James Barnes (1997), "Comparative versus Noncomparative Advertising: A Meta-Analysis," *Journal of Marketing*, 61(Oct.), 1–15.

Grover, Evynne (1991), "The Trademark Protection of Advertising Slogans: A Modern Perspective," *Fordham Entertainment, Media and Intellectual Property Law Forum*, 1(2), 213–229.

Hagan, Rose A. (2004), "The Myths of Genericide", *Intellectual Property Law Newsletter,* 22(2), 13–14, available at http://www.abanet.org/intelprop/bulletin/winter_04.pdf.

Haigh, David and J Knowles (2004), *How to Define Your Brand and Determine its Value*, Marketing Management, May/June 23–28.

Hammond, Kate and Jason K. Schmitz (2003), "How to Protect Slogans in the E.U. and U.S.," *Managing Intellectual Property* (Oct.), available at http://www.managingip.com/IssueArticle/1255572/Archive/How-to-protect-slogans-in-the-EU-and-the-US.html, accessed 4 April 2016.

Hanas, Jim (2006), "Star Power: Celebrity Endorsements in this wide-ranging 24/7 Media Circus are Amplified like Never Before," *Advertising Age*, (Feb. 20), S1.

Handler, Milton and Charles Pickett (1930), "Trade-marks and Trade Names—An Analysis and Synthesis I," *Columbia Law Review*, 30(2), 168–201.

Hanson, Karl G. (1999), "Intellectual Property Strategies for Protecting the Looks of a New Product," *Journal of the Patent and Trademark Office Society*, 81(Dec.), 887–922.

Harbour, Pamela Jones (2005), "Advertising and Unfair Competition: Federal and State Enforcement," available at http://www.ftc.gov/speeches/harbour/050318advertisingandunfaircomp.pdf, accessed 25 April 2016.

Harvey, Michael, James T. Rothe and Laurie A. Lucas (1998), "The 'Trade Dress' Controversy: A Case of Strategic Cross-Brand Cannibalization," *Journal of Marketing Theory and Practice*, 6(2), 1–18.

Hass, Nancy (2003), "I Seek Dead People", *The New York Times*, Section 6, Part 2, Column 1, (Oct. 12), p. 36, available at http://www.nytimes.com/2003/10/12/magazine/i-seek-dead-people.html?pagewanted=all, accessed 25 April 2016.

Hastak, Manoj and Michael B. Mazis (2011), "Deception by Implication: A Typology of Truthful but Misleading Advertising and Labeling Claims," *Journal of Public Policy & Marketing*, 30(2), 157–167.

Headden, Susan (1997), "The Junk Mail Deluge," *U.S. News and World Reports* (Dec. 8), 42–44.

Hemnes, Thomas M.S. (1985), "How Can You Find a Safe Trademark?" *Harvard Business Review*, 63(March/April), 36–49.

Henderson, Pamela W. and Joseph A. Cote (1998), "Guidelines for Selecting or Modifying Logos," *Journal of Marketing*, 62(April), 14–30.

Henning-Bodeweg, Frauke (2006), *Unfair Competition Law: European Union and Member States*, The Hague: Kluwer Law International.

Herman, Mario L. (2003), "A Brief History of Franchising," available at http://www.franchise-law.com/Franchise-Law-Overview/A-Brief-History-of-Franchising.shtml, accessed 6 December 2006.

Hess, J.D. and E. Gerstner (1998), "Yes, "bait and switch" really benefits consumers," *Marketing Science*, 17(3), 283–89.

Hoeffler, S. and K.L. Keller (2003), "The Marketing Advantages of Strong Brands, *Journal of Brand Management,* 10(6), 421–45.

Horn, Norbert, Hein Kotz and Hans G. Leser (1982), *German Private and Commercial Law: An Introduction.* Oxford: Clarendon Press.

Horowitz, Bruce, "P & G Buzz Marketing Unit Hit with Complaint," *USA Today*, (Oct. 19), 1B.

Hotchkiss, George B. and Richard B. Franken (1923), *The Leadership of Advertised Brands*, New York: Doubleday.

Hovenkamp, Herbert (1994), *Federal Antitrust Policy: The Law of Competition and Its Practice*, St. Paul: West Publishing.

Howard, Daniel J., Roger A. Kerin and Charles Gengler (2000), "The Effects of Brand Name Similarity on Brand Source Confusion: Implications for Trademark Infringement," *Journal of Public Policy & Marketing*, 19(Fall), 250–264.

Howard, Daniel J. and Roger A. Kerin (2004), "The Effects of Personalized Product Recommendations on Advertisement Response Rates: The "Try this. It Works!" Technique," *Journal of Consumer Psychology*, 14(3), 271–79.

Hoy, Mariea Grubbs and J. Craig Andrews (2004), "Adherence of Prime-Time Televised Advertising Disclosures to the "Clear and Conspicuous" Standard: 1990 versus 2002," *Journal of Public Policy & Marketing*, 23 (2), 170–182.

Hwang, Suein L. (1995), "Philip Morris makes Dave's—but sh. Don't Tell," *Wall Street Journal*, (March 2), B1.

Hyman, Mark (1997), "Dead Men Don't Screw Up Ad Campaigns", *Business Week*, (March 10), #3517, p.115.

INTA Internet Committee—Domain Disputes Subcommittee (2014), "Six Months of the New gTLD Uniform Rapid Suspension

System: What Brand Owners Need to Know," *INTA Bulletin*, 69(15), 1, 3–4.

Jackson, Traci S. (2004), "How Far is Too Far? The Extension of the Right of Publicity to a Form of Intellectual Property Comparable to Trademark/Copyright," *Tulane Journal of Technology and Intellectual Property*, 6, 181–197.

Jacobson, Michael F. and Laurie Ann Mazur (1995), *Marketing Madness*, Boulder: Westview Press.

Jacoby, Jacob and Wayne D. Hoyer (1990), "The Miscomprehension of Mass-Media Advertising Claims: A Re-Analysis of Benchmark Data," *Journal of Advertising Research*, 29(June/July), 9–16.

Jain, Sanjay and Joydeep Srivastava (2000), "An Experimental and Theoretical Analysis of Price-Matching Refund Policies," *Journal of Marketing Research*, 37(3), 351–362.

Jesdanun, Anick (2005), "Deleting Spam Costs Billions, Study Finds," *Associated Press*, (Feb. 2).

John, Deborah Roedder, Barbara Loken and Christopher Joiner (1998), "The Negative Impact of Extensions: Can Flagship Products Be Diluted?" *Journal of Marketing*, 62(January), 19–32.

Johnson, Roy W. (1926), "Why 7,000 Imitations of Coca-Cola Are in the Copy Cat's Graveyard," *Sales Management*, 9(Jan.), 27–28, 44.

Jones, John Philip (1986), *What's in a Name? Advertising and the Concept of Brands*, Lexington: Lexington Books.

Kaikati, Andrew M. and Jack G. Kaikati (2004), "Stealth Marketing: How to Reach Consumers Surreptitiously," *California Management Review*, 46(4), 6–22.

Kalpesh, Kaushik Desai and Kevin Lane Keller (2002), "The Effects of Ingredient Branding Strategies on Host Brand Extendibility," *Journal of Marketing*, 66(Jan.), 73–93.

Keller, Kevin Lane (2003), *Strategic Brand Management: Building, Measuring, and Managing Brand Equity*, Upper Saddle River, N.J.: Pearson Education, Inc.

Keller, Kevin Lane (2005), "Branding Shortcuts," *Marketing Management*, 14(5), 18–23.

Keller, Kevin Lane (2007), "Advertising and Brand Equity," in *Handbook of Advertising*, eds. Gerard J. Tellis and Tim Ambler, London: Sage Publications, 54–70.

Keller, Kevin Lane, Susan E. Heckler and Michael J. Houston (1998), "The Effects of Brand Name Suggestiveness on Advertising Recall," *Journal of Marketing*, 62(Jan.), 48–57.

Kertz, Consuelo Lauda and Lisa Boardman Burnette (1992), "Telemarketing Tug-of-War: Balancing Telephone Information Technology and the First Amendment with Consumer Protection and Privacy," *Syracuse Law Review*, 43, 1029–1072.

Kertz, Consuelo Lauda and Roobina Ohanian (1991), "Recent Trends in the Law of Endorsement Advertising: Infomercials, Celebrity Endorsers and Nontraditional Defendants in Deceptive Advertising Cases," *Hofstra Law Review*, 19(3), 603–656.

Khermouch, Gerry and Jeff Green (2001), "Buzz Marketing," *Business Week*, (July 30), 50–57.

Kiley, David (2004), *Can You Name That Slogan?* Business Week Online, 14 Oct 2004.

Kilmer, Paul F. (2013), "The Value Equation of Trademark Oppositions: A Multinational Comparisons of Costs and Perceived Benefits," *INTA Bulletin*, 68(5) available at http://www.inta.org/INTABulletin/Pages/TheValueEquationofTrademarkOppositionsAMultinationalComparisonofCostsandPerceivedBenefits.aspx.

Kim, Byung-Do, Mengse Shi and Kannan Srinivasan (2001), "Reward Programs and Tacit Collusion," *Marketing Science*, 20(2), 99–120.

Kim, W. Chan and Renee Mauborgne (2005), *Blue Ocean Strategy: How to Create Uncontested Market Space and Make Competition Irrelevant*, Cambridge: Harvard Business School Press.

Kivetz, Ran and Itamar Simonson (2002), "Earning the Right to Indulge: Effort as a Determinant of Customer Preferences Toward Frequency Program Rewards," *Journal of Marketing Research*, 39 (May), 155–170.

Klett, Alexander R. and Gleiss Lutz (2007), "Three-Dimensional Trademarks Before the European Court of Justice—A Lost Cause?" *INTA Bulletin*, 62(8), 8–9.

Klink, Jan (2003), "50 Years of Publicity Rights in the United States and the Never Ending Hassle with Intellectual Property Rights and Personality Rights in Europe," *Intellectual Property Quarterly*, 4, 363–387.

Kohli, Chiranjeev and Douglas W. LaBahn (1997), "Observations: Creating Effective Brand Names: A Study of the Naming Process," *Journal of Advertising Research*, 37(1), 67–75.

Kohli, Chiranjeev and Rajneesh Suri (2000), "Brand Names that Work: A Study of the Effectiveness of Different Types of Brand Names," *Marketing Management Journal*, 10(2), 112–20.

Kohli, Chiranjeev, Katrin R. Harich and Lance Leuthesser (2005), "Creating Brand Identity: a Study of New Brand Names," *Journal of Business Research*, 58, 1506–1515.

Kohli, Chiranjeev, Rajneesh Suri and Mrugank Thakor (2002), "Creating Effective Logos: Insights from Theory and Practice," *Business Horizons*, (May–June), 58–64.

Komensky, Alan M. and Mark D. Wegener (1991), "When is a Sale Not a Sale? State Regulation of Price Comparison Advertising," *Antitrust*, (summer), 28–33.

Kopytoff, Verne (2002), "Sites told to 'Fess Up'," *San Francisco Chronicle*, June 29, B1.

Kotler, Philip and Kevin Lane Keller (2006), *Marketing Management*, Upper Saddle River: Pearson/Prentice Hall (12th ed.).

La Pastina, Antonio C. (2001), "Product Placement in Brazilian Prime Time Television: The Case of the Reception of a *Telenovela*," *Journal of Broadcasting and Electronic Media*, 45(Fall), 541–557.

Lageat, Thierry, Sandor Czellar and Gilles Laurent (2003), "Engineering Hedonic Attributes to Generate Perceptions of Luxury: Consumer Perception of an Everyday Sound," *Marketing Letters*, 14(2), 97–109.

Laird, Pamela Walker (1998), *Advertising Progress: American Business and the Rise of Consumer Marketing*, Baltimore: John Hopkins University Press.

Landler, M., Z. Schiller and L. Therrien (1991), "What's in a Name? Less and Less," *Business Week*, (July), 66–67.

Lane, Wallace R. (1909), "Development of Secondary Rights in Trade Mark Cases," *Yale Law Journal*, 18(8), 571–582.

Lane, Vicki R. (2000), "The Impact of Ad Repetition and Ad Content on Consumer Perceptions of Incongruent Extensions," *Journal of Marketing*, 64(2), 80–91.

Laurens, Rhett H. (2001), "Year of the Living Dead: California Breathes New Life Into Celebrity Publicity Rights," *Hastings Communications and Entertainment Law Journal*, 24(Fall), 109–147.

Leibowitz, Wendy R. (1999), "Lawyers and Technology: Law Spanks Spammers," *National Law Journal*, (March 15), A18.

Lemley, Mark A. (1999), "The Modern Lanham Act and the Death of Common Sense," *Yale Law Journal*, 108(May), 1687–1715.

Leong, Susanna H.S. and May O. Lwin (2005), "Seeking Exclusivity over a Brand Naming System? The McDonald's Experience," *Journal of the Academy of Marketing Science*, 34(1), 84–85.

Levitt, Theodore (1960), "Marketing Myopia," *Harvard Business Review*, 38(July–Aug.), 45–56.

Levy, Marc C. (2005), "From Genericism to Trademark Significance: Deconstructing the De Facto Secondary Meaning Doctrine," *The Trademark Reporter*, 95(6), 1197–1220.

Lewis, Michael (2004), "The Influence of Loyalty Programs and Short-Term Promotions on Customer Retention," *Journal of Marketing Research*, 3(41), 281–292.

Lieb, Rebecca (July 26, 2002), "Make Spammers Pay Before You Do," *The ClickZ Network*, available at http://web.archive.org/web/20070807113021/http://www.clickz.com/showPage.html?page=1432751, accessed 23 July 2015.

Lindgren, Thomas B. (1985), "The Sanctity of the Design Patent: Illusion or Reality? Twenty Years of Design Patent Litigation Since Compco v. Day-Brite Lighting, Inc., and Sears, Roebuck & Co. v. Stiffel Co." *Oklahoma City University Law Review*, 10(summer), 195–261.

Lindsey-Mullikin, Joan and Ross D. Petty (2011), "Marketing Tactics Discouraging Price Search: Deception and Competition," *Journal of Business Research*, 64(1), 67–73.

Lindstrom, Martin (2005), *Brand Sense: Build Powerful Brands through Touch, Taste, Smell, Sight, and Sound*, New York: Free Press.

Loken, Barbara and Deborah Roedder John (1994), "Diluting Brand Beliefs: When do Brand Extensions Have a Negative Impact?" *Journal of Marketing*, 57(July), 71–84.

Long, Clarisa (2006), "Dilution," *Columbia Law Review*, 106(June), 1029–1076.

Longstreth, A. (2013), "Amazon's Play for Web Names Could Test Antitrust Law," *Thomson Reuters News & Insight*, (13 March), http://newsandinsight.thomsonreuters.com/Legal/News/2013/03_-_March/Amazon_s_play_for_Web_names_could_test_antitrust_law/, accessed 14 March 2013.

Low, George S. and Ronald A. Fullerton (1994), "Brands, Brand Management, and the Brand Manager System: A Critical-Historical Evaluation," *Journal of Marketing Research*, 31(May), 173–190.

Mack, Peter, Geoff McNutt, John Vasuta and Michael Song (2004), "Choosing Fame over Family," *Akron Law Review*, 37, 203–216.

MacMillan, Robert (2004), "Survey: Spam Driving Internet Users Away from E-mail," *Washingtonpost.com*, (March 17).

Mandly, Charles R., Jr. (2003), "Article 82 of the E.C. Treaty and Trademark Rights," *The Trademark Reporter*, 93(6), 1314–1353.

Masters, Greg (2008), "Victory for Enterprises in Typosquatting Case," *SC Magazine*, available at http://www.scmagazine.com/victory-for-enterprises-in-typosquatting-case/article/123369/ (posted 29 December 2008, accessed 23 January 2009).

Matheson, Julia Anne (2003), "The Sweet Smell of Successful Registration: An Update on Olfactory Marks," available at http://www.finnegan.com/resources/articles/articlesdetail.aspx?news=d28c44ca-6b7a-440b-a97d-ee09588e9c02, accessed 4 April 2016.

Mathur, Lynette K. and Ike Mathur (1995), "The Effect of Advertising Slogan Changes and the Market Value of Firms," *Journal of Advertising Research*, 35(1), 59–65.

Matty, Lesley (2006), "Rock, Paper, Scissors, Trademark? A Comparative Analysis of Motion as a Feature of Trademarks in the United States and Europe," *Cardozo Journal of International and Comparative Law*, 14(fall), 557–591.

Matyszczyk, C. (2012), "Is anyone actually going to .XXX domains?" *CNET* (2 May), http://www.cnet.com/news/is-anyone-actually-going-to-xxx-domains/, accessed 2 September 2014.

Maxeiner, James R. and Peter Schotthofer eds. (1992), *Advertising Law in Europe and North America*. Deventer, Netherlands: Kluwer Law and Taxation Publishers.

Mayer-Brown (2016), "Disconnected: The Telephone Consumer Protection Act at 25 Years Old," *Legal Update,* March 28, available at https://www.mayerbrown.com/files/Publication/42194571-165c-431f-be09-7248698fa60a/Presentation/PublicationAttachment/8ba4641c-3feb-4812-9bb0-853b2deb4f7b/160328-UPDATE-CLCA-TMT-Cybersecurity.pdf, accessed 30 March 2016.

McCauley, Lucy A. (1989), "The Face of Advertising," *Harvard Business Review*, 67(Nov./Dec.), 135–159.

McClure, Daniel M. (1979), "Trademarks and Unfair Competition: A Critical History of Legal Thought," *The Trademark Reporter*, 69(July–Aug.)305–356.

McClure, Daniel M. (1996), "Trademarks and Competition: The Recent History," *Law and Contemporary Problems*, 59(Spring), 13–43.

McCormick, Kevin K. (2006), " 'Ding' You are Now Free to Register that Sound," *The Trademark Reporter*, 96(5), 1101–1121.

McKelvey, Stephen M. (2003), "Commercial 'Branding": The Final Frontier or False start for Athletes' Use of Temporary Tattoos as Body Billboards," *Journal of Legal Aspects of Sport*, 13(Winter), 1–37.

McKendrick, N. Brewer, J. and Plumb, J.H. (1982), *The Birth of a Consumer Society: The Commercialization of Eighteenth-Century England*, Bloomington: Indiana University Press.

McKenna, Mark P. (2007), "The Normative Foundations of Trademark Law," *Notre Dame Law Review*, 82(June), 1839–1916.

McKinney, Luther C. and Dewey J. Caton (1990–91), What to do When the Attorney General Calls: State Regulation of National Advertising. *DePaul Business Law Journal*, 3(1), 119–165.

Meenaghan, Tony (1994), "Point of View: Ambush Marketing: Immoral or Imaginative Practice," *Journal of Advertising Research*, 34, 77–83.

Meenaghan, Tony (1996), "Ambush Marketing—A Threat to Corporate Sponsorship", *Sloan Management Review*, (Fall) 103–107.

Mela, Carl F., Sunil Gupta and Donald R. Lehman (1997), "The Long-Term Impact of Promotion and Advertising on Consumer Brand Choice," *Journal of Advertising Research*, (Spring), 248–261.

Micklitz, H., J. Stuyck and E. Terryn (Eds.) (2010), CASES, MATERIALS AND TEXT ON CONSUMER LAW. Oxford: Hart Publishing.

Mistry, Bhavna (2006), "Star Spotting," *Marketing*, (June 7), 33–34.

Mobley, Mary F, William O. Bearden and Jesse E. Teel (1988), "An Investigation of Individual Responses to Tensile Price Claims," *Journal of Consumer Research*, 15 (September), p. 273–279.

Moore, Frazier (2005), "Stealth Ads hit TV," *Metrowest Sunday News*, July 23, C4.

Morein, Joseph A. (1975), "Shift from Brand to Product Line Marketing," *Harvard Business Review*, 53(Sept–Oct.), 56–64.

Moskin, Jonathan E. (2002), "The Shape of Things to Come—Emerging Theories of Design Protection," 92 *Trademark Reporter* (92), 691.

Neeley, Sabrina M. and David W. Shumann (2004), "Using Animated Spokes-characters in Advertising to Young Children," *Journal of Advertising*, 33(3), 7–23.

Nelson, M.R. (2002), "Recall of Brand Placements in Computer/Video Games," *Journal of Advertising Research*, 42(2), 80–92.

New York State Attorney General (2004), "Clothing Chair Settles Misleading Ad Inquiry," (Sept 14), available at www.oag.state.ny.us/press/2004/sep/sep14a_04.html.

New York State Attorney General (2005), "Major Department Store Chain Agrees to End Fake Sales," (Jan. 24), available at www.oag.state.ny.us/press/2005/jan/jan24a_05.html.

Newell, Cora S. (1989), "Advertising Standards in Court," *New Law Journal,* (September), 1161–1162.

Nguyen, Xuan-Thao N. (2001), "Shifting the Paradigm in E-Commerce: Move Over Inherently Distinctive Trademarks—The E-Brand, IBrand and Generic Domain Names Ascending to Power?" *American University Law Review*, 50(4), 937–978.

Nimmer, Melville (1954), "The Right of Publicity," *Law & Contemporary Problems*, 19(spring), 203–223.

O'Reilly, Vincent (2004), "The Community Trademark System: A Brief Introduction and Overview," *Marquette Intellectual Property Review*, 8(winter), 93–117.

Obermiller, Carl and Eric R. Spangenberg (2000), "On the Origin and Distinctness of Skepticism toward Advertising," *Marketing Letters*, 11(4), 311–322.

Obermiller, Carl, Eric R. Spangenberg and Douglas L. MacLachlan (2005), "Ad Skepticism: The Consequences of Disbelief," *Journal of Advertising*, 34 (3), 7–18.

Oswald, Lynda J. (2006–07), "Statutory and Judicial Approaches to Gray Market Goods: The 'Material Differences' Standard," *Kentucky Law Journal*, (95), 107–144.

Pavia, Teresa M. and Janeen Arnold Costa (1983), "The Winning Number: Consumer Perceptions of Alpha-numeric Brand Names," *Journal of Marketing*, 57(July), 85–98.

Pechmann, Cornelia (1996), "Do Consumers Overgeneralize One-Sided Comparative Price Claims, and Are More Stringent Regulations Needed?" *Journal of Marketing Research*, 33 (May), 150–162.

Pechmann, Cornelia and Tim Silk (2013), "Policy and Research Related to Consumer Rebates: A Comprehensive Review," *Journal of Public Policy & Marketing*, 32(2), 255–270.

Peterson, Kim (2004), "Microsoft sues Lindows—then Pays $20 Million," *The Seattle Times*, (July 20), available at http://seattletimes.nwsource.com/html/businesstechnology/2001983512_lindows20.html.

Peterson, Robert A. and Alain J.P. Jolibert (1995), "A Meta-Analysis of Country-of-Origin Effects," *Journal of International Business Studies*, 26(4), 883–900.

Peterson, Robert A. and Ivan Ross (1972), "How to Name New Brands," *Journal of Advertising Research*, 12(6), 29–34.

Petrecca, Laura (2006), "There's No Business like Ad Business," *USA Today*, (June 9), 4B.

Petty, Ross D. (1993), "Joe Camel and the Commission: The Real Legal Issues," *Journal of Public Policy & Marketing*, 12(2), 276–279.

Petty, Ross D. (1997), "Advertising Law in the United States and European Union," *Journal of Public Policy & Marketing* 16(1), 1–13.

Petty, Ross D. (1999), "Tobacco Marketing Restrictions in the Multistate Attorneys General Settlement Is this Good Public Policy?" *Journal of Public Policy & Marketing*, 18(2), 249–257.

Petty, Ross D. (2000), "Marketing Without Consent: Consumer Choice and Costs, Privacy and Public Policy," *Journal of Public Policy & Marketing*, 19(1), 42–53.

Petty, Ross D. (2003), "Wireless Advertising Messaging: Legal Analysis and Public Policy Issues," *Journal of Public Policy & Marketing*, 22(1), 71–83.

Petty, Ross D. (2006), "Marketing Law: Hit of Mislead—Secondary Brand Associations," *Marketing Management*, 15(5), 44–48.

Petty, Ross D. (2010), "The Strategic Use of Legal Margins: How to Introduce an Extension of Someone Else's Brand" in LEGAL STRATEGIES: HOW CORPORATIONS USE LAW TO IMPROVE PERFORMANCE, Antoine Masson and Mary J Shariff, eds. Chapter 15, 317–334 (Springer Publishing 2010).

Petty, Ross D. (2011), "The Co-development of Trademark Law and the Concept of Brand Marketing in the U.S. before 1946," *Journal of Macromarketing*, 31(1), 85–99.

Petty, Ross D. (2012a), "From label to trademark: The legal origins of the concept of brand identity in nineteenth century America," *Journal of Historical Research in Marketing*, 4(1), 129–153.

Petty, Ross D. (2012b), "Coca-Cola Brand Protection before WWII—It's the Real Thing," *Journal of Historical Research in Marketing*, 4(2), 224–244.

Petty, Ross D. (2013) "From Puffery to Penalties: a Historical Analysis of U.S. Masked Marketing Public Policy Concerns," *Journal of Historical Research in Marketing*, 59(1), pp.10–26.

Petty, Ross D. (2014), "International Advertising Law and Regulation: A Research Review and Agenda—the Devil Is in the Details," in *The Handbook of International Advertising Research* (Hong Cheng, ed.), pp. 395–413, West Sussex: Wiley-Blackwell.

Petty, Ross D. (2015a), " 'Natural' Claims in Food Advertising: Policy Implications of Filling the Regulatory Void with Consumer Class Action Lawsuits," *Journal of Public Policy & Marketing*, 34(1), 131–141.

Petty, Ross, D. (2015b), "After the Dot: Marketing Policy Issues with the New Generic Top-Level Domain Names Program," *Marketing and Public Policy Proceedings*, Stacey Menzel Baker and Marlys Mason, eds., 38–42.

Petty, Ross D. (2016), "A History of Brand Identity Protection and Brand Marketing," in THE ROUTLEDGE COMPANION TO MARKETING HISTORY, D.G. Brian Jones and Mark Tadajewski, eds., Chapter Six, 97–114 (Routledge Publishing 2016).

Petty, Ross D. and J. Craig Andrews (2008), "Covert Marketing Unmasked: A Legal and Regulatory Guide for Practices that Mask Marketing Messages," *Journal of Public Policy & Marketing* 27(1), 7–18.

Petty, Ross D. and Denver D'Rosario (2009), "The Use of Dead Celebrities in Advertising and Marketing: Balancing Interests in the Right of Publicity," *Journal of Advertising* 38(4), 39–51.

Petty, Ross D. and Jennifer Hamilton (2004), "Seeking a Single Policy for Contractual Unfairness to Consumers: A Comparison of U.S. and E.U. Efforts," *Journal of Consumer Affairs* 38(1), 146–166.

Petty, Ross D. and Robert J. Kopp (1995), "Advertising Challenges: A Strategic Framework and Current Review," *Journal of Advertising Research* 35(2), 41–55.

Petty, Ross D., Susanna H.S. Leong and May O. Lwin (2010), "Slogans: U.S. and E.U. Legal Protection for Slogans that Identify and Promote the Brand," *International Journal of Advertising* 29(3), 473–500.

Petty, Ross D. and Joan Lindsey-Mullikin (2006), "The Regulation of Practices that Promote Brand Interest: A 3 Cs Guide for Brand Managers," *Journal of Product & Brand Management* 15(1), 23–36.

Pope, Daniel (1983), *The Making of Modern Advertising*, New York: Basic Books.

Posavac, Steven S., David M. Sanbonmatsu, Frank R. Kardes and Gavan J. Fitzsimons (2004), "The Brand Positivity Effect: When Evaluation Confers Preference," *Journal of Consumer Research*, 31(Dec.), 643–651.

Preston, Ivan L. (1990), "The Federal Trade Commission's Identification of Implications as Constituting Deceptive Advertising" *University of Cincinnati Law Review* 57(4), 1243–1310.

Preston, Ivan L. and Jef I. Richards (1986), Consumer Miscomprehension as a Challenge to FTC Prosecutions of Deceptive Advertising. *John Marshall Law Review*, 19, pp. 605–635.

Pridgen, Dee (1997), "How Will Consumers Be Protected on the Information Superhighway?," *Land & Water Law Review* 32(1), 237–255.

Pringle, Hammish (2004), *Celebrity Sells*, John Wiley & Sons, Chichester, U.K.

Raghubir, Priya (2004), "Free Gift with Purchase: Promoting or Discounting the Brand?" *Journal of Consumer Psychology*, 14(1 & 2), 181–86.

Rao, Akshay R. and Robert W. Ruekert (1994), "Brand Alliances as Signals of Product Quality," *MIT Sloan Management Review*, 36(Fall), 87–97.

Ratchford, Brian T. (1987), "Further insights about the FCB grid," *Journal of Advertising Research*, 27(5), 24–38.

Reed, Diane Martens (1989), "Use of 'Like/Love' Slogans in Advertising: Is the Trademark Owner Protected?" *San Diego Law Review*, 26 (Jan.), 101–136.

Reed, Kimberly (2002), "Levi Strauss v. Tesco and E.U. Trademark Exhaustion: A Proposal for Change," *Northwestern Journal of International Law and Business*, 23(fall), 139–186.

Reeves, Rosser (1961), *Reality in Advertising*, New York: Alfred A. Knopf.

Richards, Jef I. (1990), "A 'New and Improved' View of Puffery," *Journal of Public Policy and Marketing* 9, 73–84.

Richards, Jef I. and Ivan L. Preston (1992), Proving and Disproving Materiality of Deceptive Advertising Claims. *Journal of Public Policy & Marketing*, 11(2), 45–56.

Richards, Jef I. and Richard D. Zakia (1981), Pictures: An Advertiser's Expressway Through FTC Regulation. *Georgia Law Review, 16*, 77–134.

Ries, Al and Jack Trout (1981), *Positioning: The Battle for your Mind*, New York: McGraw-Hill.

Rijkens, Rein and Gordon E. Miracle (1986), *European Regulation of Advertising*. Amsterdam, North Holland Co.

Roberts, Paul (2004), "AOL Survey Finds Rampant Online Threats, Clueless Users," *Computerworld.com*, available at http://www.computerworld.com/article/2567556/security0/aol-survey-finds-rampant-online-threats—clueless-users.html, accessed 23 July 2015.

Roberts, Alexandra J. and Peter M. Brody (2010), "What's in a Domain Name? Nominative Fair Use Online after *Toyota v. Tabari*," *Trademark Reporter*, 100(6), 1290–1334.

Robertson, Kim (1989), "Strategically Desirable Brand Name Characteristics," *Journal of Consumer Marketing*, 6(4), 61–71.

Roehm, Michelle L., Ellen Bolman Pullins and Harper A. Roehm, Jr. (2002), "Designing Loyalty-Building Programs for Packaged Goods Brands," *Journal of Marketing Research*, 39 (May), 202–213.

Roehm, Michelle L., Harper A. Roehm, Jr. and Derrick S. Boone (2004), "Plugs versus Placements: A Comparison of Alternatives for Within Program Brand Exposure," *Psychology & Marketing*, 21(1), 17–28.

Room, Adrian (1998), "The History of Branding," in *Brands: The New Wealth Creators*, Susannah Hart and John Murphy, eds., 13–23, New York: New York University Press.

Rotfeld, Herbert J. and Patrick R. Parsons (1989), Self-Regulation and Magazine Advertising. *Journal of Advertising* 18(4) 33–40.

Rotfeld, Herbert J., Avery M. Abernathy and Patrick R. Parsons (1990), Self-Regulation and Television Advertising. *Journal of Advertising* 19(4) 18–26.

Royall, M. Sean (2001), "Coping with the Antitrust Risks of Technological Integration," *Antitrust Law Journal,* 68(3), 1023–1061.

Ruder, David S. (2003), "The Fallacy of Trademark Residual Goodwill," *IPL Newsletter*, 22(1), 1, 5–7, 42.

Russell, Cristel Antonia and Barbara B. Stern (2006), "Consumers, Characters, and Products: A Balance Model of Sitcom Product Placement Effects," *Journal of Advertising*, 35(1), 7–21.

Ryan, Patrick S. (2004), "Case C–191/01 P. Office for Harmonisation in the Internal Market (Trade Marks and Designs), v. Wm. Wrigley Jr. Co. (E.C.J. October 23, 2003)," *Columbia Journal of European Law*, 10(2), 392–402.

Sanders, Edmund (1999), "Credit Card Firms Face Backlash Over Some Questionable Tactics," (June 20), F7.

Schecter, Frank I. (1927), "The Rational Basis for Trademark Protection," *Harvard Law Review*, 40(6), 813–833.

Schnaars, Steven P. (1994), *Managing Imitation Strategies*, New York: The Free Press.

Schricker, Gerhard (1990), Law and Practice Relating to Misleading Advertising in the Member States of the EC. *International Review of Industrial Property and Copyright Law*, 21(5), 620–644.

Schultz, Randy (1997), "Coupon Issuers Get Clipped," *CNNMoney,* (10 Sept.), available at http://money.cnn.com/1997/09/10/companies/procter/, accessed 29 March 2016.

Schumacher, Christian (2006), "Use of Trade-Marks on Repackaged and Relabelled Pharmaceutical Goods," in *Trademarks at the Limit*, (Jeremy Phillips ed.), Cheltenham: Edward Elgar.

Sewell, Dan (2007), "Brands Double Up," *The Daily News Sunday*, (Nov. 18), E2.

Shalevich, Inessa (2008), "Essay: Protection of Trademarks and Geographical Indications," *Buffalo Intellectual Property Law Journal*, 6(Fall), 67–82.

Shaughnessy, Robert J. (1986), "Trademark Parody: A Fair Use and First Amendment Analysis," *Virginia Law Review*, 72, 1079–1117.

Shilling, Dana (2002), *Essentials of trademarks and Unfair Competition*, New York: John Wiley & Sons.

Shipley, David E. (1978), "Generic Trademarks, the FTC and the Lanham Act: Covering the Market with Formica," *William and Mary Law Review*, 20(1), 1–32.

Solomon, Barbara A. (2004), "Can the Lanham Act Protect Tiger Woods? An Analysis of Whether the Lanham Act is a Proper Substitute for a Federal Right of Publicity," *The Trademark Reporter*, 94(Nov.–Dec.), 1202–1228.

Soman, Dilip and John T. Gourville (2001), "Transaction Decoupling: How Price Bundling Affects the Decision to Consume," *Journal of Marketing Research*, 38 (February), 30–44.

Spamhaus (2004), "Follow Australia!" available at http://www.spamhaus.org/news.lasso?article=154, accessed 23 July 2015.

Spriggs, Mark T. and John R. Nevins (1996), "Negative Option Selling Plans: Current Forms Versus Existing Regulations," *Journal of Public Policy & Marketing*, 15(2), 227–237.

Spring, Tom (2004), "Spam Slayer," *PC World*, (May 24).

Stansky, Lisa (2003), "A Brand Everyone Knows", *National Law Journal*, (March 24), A9.

Steinberg, Brian and James Bandler (2004), "Blurring the Line? Magazines Face New Pressure as Marketers Seek to Blend Advertisers With Content," *Wall Street Journal*, (Aug. 9), B1.

Steinberg, Brian (1994), "Advertising: 'Spoofing' Ratchets Up the Ad Wars," *The Wall Street Journal*, (Nov. 30), B4.

Stim, Richard (2000), *Trademark Law*, Albany: West Legal Studies.

Stone, George, Mathew Joseph and Michael Jones (2003), "An Exploratory Study on the Use of Sports Celebrities in Advertising: A Content Analysis," *Sports Marketing Quarterly*, 12(2), 94–102.

Strasser, Susan (1989), *Satisfaction Guaranteed: The Making of the American Mass Market*, New York: Pantheon Books.

Stremersch, Stefan and Gerard J. Tellis (2002), "Strategic Bundling of Products and Prices: A New Synthesis for Marketing," *Journal of Marketing*, 66 (January), 55–72.

Suarez, F.F. and S. Grodal (2015), "Mastering the 'Name Your Product Category' Game," *MIT Sloan Management Review*, 56(2): 23–29

Swinyard, William R. (1979), "How Many Ad Exposures Is a Sales Call Worth?" *Journal of Advertising Research*, 19(1), 17–21.

Tauber, Edward M. (1981), "Brand Franchise Extension: New Product Benefits from Existing Brand Names," *Business Horizons*, 24(2), 36–41.

TechWeb News (2004), "U.S. Is Spam Superpower: 83 Percent of All Junk," *InternetnetWeek.com*, (May 25).

Tedlow, Richard S. (1990), *New and Improved: The Story of Mass Marketing in America*, New York: Basic Books.

Teinowitz, Ira (2005a), "FCC Commissioner Decries 'Commercialization of Media': Rails Against 'Fake News' and 'Relentless Marketing'," Advertising Age, May 25.

Teinowitz, Ira (2005b), "CARU Targets Product Placement and Cartoon Ads," Advertising Age, September 16.

Tellis, Gerald J. and Peter N. Golder (2006), *Will and Vision: How Latecomers Grow to Dominate Markets*, Los Angeles: Figueroa Press.

The Trademark Reporter (1992), "Trademark Timeline," *The Trademark Reporter*, 82 (Sept./Oct.), 1022–1040.

Thompson, J. Walter (1911), *Things to Know About Trade-marks*, New York: J. Walter Thompson Co.

Trademark Clearinghouse (2014), "The Deterrent Effect of the Clearinghouse," (25 March), http://www.trademark-clearinghouse.com/content/deterrent-effect-clearinghouse, accessed 2 September 2014.

Underwood, Robert L. (2003), "The Communicative Power of Product Packaging: Creating Brand Identity via Lived and Mediated Experience," *Journal of Marketing Theory and Practice*, 11(1), 62–76.

United States Patent and Trademark Office (n.d.), "Geographical Indication Protection in the United States," available at http://www.uspto.gov/sites/default/files/web/offices/dcom/olia/globalip/pdf/gi_system.pdf, accessed 4 April 2016.

Villafranco, John E. and Katherine E. Riley (2013), "So You Want to Self-Regulate? The National Advertising Division As Standard Bearer," *Antitrust,* 27(2), 79–84.

Volckner, Franziska and Henrik Sattler (2006), "Drivers of Brand Extension Success," *Journal of Marketing,* 70(April), 18–34.

Vranica, Suzanne (2005), "Trends: Advertising; Anywhere, Anytime," *Wall Street Journal,* (Nov. 21), R. 6.

Walker, Rob (2004), "The Hidden (In Plain Sight) Persuaders," *New York Times,* (Dec. 5), 69.

Warlop, Luk and Joseph W. Alba (2004), "Sincere Flattery: Trade-Dress Imitation and Consumer Choice," *Journal of Consumer Psychology,* 14(1 & 2), 21–27.

Wassom, Brian (2014), *Augmented Reality Law, Privacy and Ethics: Law, Society and Emerging AR Technologies,* Elsevier, Waltham, MA.

Weber, Thomas E. (1999), "E-World; The Spam King is Back, And His New Recipe Clicks on Changing Net," *The Wall Street Journal* (Dec. 13), B–1.

Whittaker, Keola R. (2006), "Trademark Dilution in a Global Age," *University of Pennsylvania Journal of International Law,* 27(3), 907–938.

Wilkie, William L., Carl F. Mela and Gregory T. Gundlach (1998), "Does 'Bait and Switch' Really Benefit Consumers?" *Marketing Science,* 17 (3), 272–282.

Wilkins, Mira (1992), "The Neglected Intangible Asset: The Influence of the Trade Mark on the Rise of the Modern Corporation," *Business History,* 34(1), 66–95.

WIPO Arbitration and Mediation Center (2013), *End Report on Legal Rights Objection Procedure 2013,* http://www.wipo.int/export/sites/www/amc/en/docs/lroreport.pdf, accessed 2 September 2014.

Wyckham Robert G. (1987), "Implied Superiority Claims," *Journal of Advertising Research,* 27(1), 54–64.

Yadav, Manjit S. (1994), "How Buyers Evaluate Product Bundles: A Model of Anchoring and Adjustment," *Journal of Consumer Research*, 21 (September), 342–353.

Yi, Youjae and Hoseong Jeon (2003), "Effects of Loyalty Programs on Value Perception, Program Loyalty, and Brand Loyalty," *Journal of the Academy of Marketing Science*, 31 (3), 229–240.

Yoffie, David B. and Mary Kwak (2001), *Judo Strategy: Turning Your Competitors' Strength to Your Advantage*, Cambridge, MA: Harvard Business School Press.

Zanot, Eric J. (1985), "Unseen But Effective Advertising Regulation: The Clearance Process," *Journal of Advertising* 14 (4), 44–51, 59, 68.

APPENDIX B

Table of Cases

1-800 Contacts, Inc. v. WhenU.com (2005), 414 F.3d 4000 (2d Cir.).

7–Eleven, Inc. v. Wechsler (2007), Opp. No. 91117739 (T.T.A.B. May 15).

800-JR Cigar, Inc. v. Goto.com, Inc. (2006), 437 F. Supp. 2d 273 (D. N.J.).

A. Bourgois & Co. v. Katzel (1923), 260 U.S. 689.

A.A. Friedman Co. (1968), 74 F.T.C. 1056.

A.J. Canfield Co. v. Honickman (1986), 808 F.2d 291 (3d Cir.).

Abdul-Jabbar v. General Motors Corp. (1996), 75 F.3d 1391 (9th Cir.).

Abercrombie & Fitch Co. v. Hunting World, Inc. (1976), 537 F.2d 4 (2d Cir.).

Academy of Motion Picture Arts and Sciences v. Network Solutions, Inc. (1997), 989 F. Supp. 1276 (C.D.Cal.).

Adam Opel AG v. Autec AG (2007), ECJ Case C–48–05.

Agler v. Westheimer Corp. (2015), 2015 U.S. LEXIS 145855 (N.D. Ind.).

Alberto-Culver Co. v. Andrea Dumon, Inc. (1972), 466 F.2d 707 (7th Cir.).

Allen v. Nat'l Video, Inc. (1985), 610 F. Supp. 612, 624 (S.D.N.Y.).

Aloe Crème Labs, Inc. v. Aloe99, Inc. (1975), 188 U.S.P.Q.2d 1835 (T.T.A.B.).

America Online, Inc. v. AT&T Corp. (2001), 243 F.3d 872 (4th Cir.).

American Airlines, Inc. v. A-1-800-A-M-E-R-I-C-A-N Corporation (1985), 622 F. Supp. 673 (N.D.Ill.).

American Aloe Corp. v. Aloe Crème Labs (1970), 420 F.2d 1248 (7th Cir.), *cert. denied*, 400 U.S. 820.

American Brands, Inc. v. R.J. Reynolds Tobacco Co. (1976), 413 F. Supp. 1352 (S.D.N.Y.).

American Chicle Co. v. Topps Chewing Gum Inc. (1954), 210 F.2d 680 (2d Cir.).

American Direct Marketing, Inc. v. Azad Int'l, Inc. (1992), 783 F. Supp. 84 (E.D.N.Y.).

American Express Co v. CFK, Inc. (1996), 947 F. Supp. 310 (S.D. Mich.).

American Express Co v. Mastercard International, Inc. (1988), 685 F. Supp. 76 (S.D.N.Y.).

American Express Co. v. Vibra Approved Laboratories Corp. (1989), 10 U.S.P.Q.2D 2d 2006 (S.D.N.Y.).

American Italian Pasta Co. v. New World Pasta Co. (2004), 371 F.3d 387 (8th Cir.).

American Pop Corn Co. (1979), NAD Case #1481 (April 15).

Amoskeag Mfg. Co. v. Spear (1837), 2 Sand. 599 (N.Y. Sup. Ct.).

Anheuser-Busch, Inc. v. Andy's Sportswear, Inc. (1996), 40 U.S.P.Q.2d 1542 (N.D. Cal.).

Anheuser-Busch, Inc. v. Customer Co., Inc. (1996), 947 F. Supp. 422 (N.D. Cal.).

*Anheuser-Busch, Inc. v. Florists Association of Greater Cleveland, Inc. (*1984), 603 F. Supp. 35 (N.D. Ohio).

*Anheuser-Busch, Inc. v. L & L Wings, Inc. (*1992), 962 F.2d 316 (4th Cir.), *cert. denied*, 506 U.S. 872.

Anti-Monopoly Inc. v. Gen. Mills Fun Group (1979), 611 F.2d 296 (9th Cir.).

Arrow Fastener Co. v. Stanley Works (1995), 59 F.3d 384 (2d Cir.).

Arsenal Football Club plc v. Reed (2002), ECJ Case C–206/01, 2002 ECR I–10273, 2003 ETMR 19.

Arthur Murray Studio of Washington (1971), 78 F.T.C. 401, *aff'd*, 458 F.2d 622 (5th Cir. 1972).

Asics Corp. v. Target Corp. (2003), 282 F. Supp. 2d 1020 (D. Minn.).

AT&T Corp. (2005), NAD Case Report #4338 (June 1).

Audi AG v. D'Amato (2005), 381 F. Supp. 2d 644 (E. D. Mich.), *aff'd*, 469 F.3d 534 (6th Cir. 2006).

Aunt Jemima Mills Co. v. Rigney & Co. (1917), 247 F. 407 (2d Cir.), *cert. denied*, 245 U.S. 672 (1918).

Avia Group Int'l v. L.A. Gear (1988), 853 F.2d 1557 (Fed. Cir.).

Avis Rent A Car System, Inc. v. Hertz Corp. (1986), 782 F.2d 381 (2d Cir.).

B. Sanfield, Inc. v. Finlay Fine Jewelry Corp. (1999), 168 F.3d 967 (7th Cir.).

B&B Hardware, Inc. v. Hargis Industries, Inc. (2015), 135 S. Ct. 1293.

Bandura v. Orkin Exterminating Co. (1987), 664 F. Supp. 1219 (N.D. Ill.).

Bayerische Motorenwerke AG (BMW) v. Deenik (1999), ECJ Case C63–97, 1999 ETMR 339.

Beatrice Foods (1972), 81 F.T.C. 830.

Beylen Telecom Ltd. (1997), FTC No. 972 3128, available at www.ftc.gov/opa/1997/11/audiot–2.htm, accessed 23 July 2015.

Big O Tire Dealers, Inc. v. Goodyear Tire & Rubber Co. (1977), 561 F.2d 1365 (10th Cir), *cert. denied*, 434 U.S. 1052 (1978).

Bleistein v. Donaldson Lithographing Co. (1903), 188 U.S. 239.

Bonzai.com Software (2001), NAD Case #3797C (Oct. 7).

Borden Inc. v. FTC (1982), 674 F.2d 498 (6th Cir.), *vacated*, 461 U.S. 940 (1983).

Bose Corp. v. Consumers Union (1982), 692 F.2d 189 (1st Cir.).

Boston Beer Co., In re (1999), 198 F.3d 1370 (Fed. Cir.).

Boston Duck Tours, LP v. Super Duck Tours, LLC (2008), 531 F.3d 1 (1st Cir.).

Boston Professional Hockey Ass'n, Inc. v. Dallas Cap & Emblem Mfg., Inc. (1975), 510 F.2d 1004 (5th Cir.), *cert. denied*, 423 U.S. 868.

Braswell, A. Glen et al. (2006) (U.S. District Court, Central District of California, Western Division) FTC settlement and final order, FTC Matter No. X030059, Civil Action No. CV 03–3700–DT (PJWx) (January 30).

Bristol-Myers Squibb Company v. McNeil-P.P.C., Inc. (1994), 973 F.2d 1556–1559 (Fed. Cir.).

Brooke Group, Ltd. v. Brown & Williamson Tobacco Corp. (1993), 509 U.S. 209.

Brookfield Communications v. West Coast Entertainment Corporation (1999), 174 F.3d 1036–1066 (9th Cir.).

Brooks Shoe Mfg. Co., Inc. v. Suave Shoe Corp. (1983), 716 F.2d 854 (11th Cir.).

Brunswick Corp. v. British Seagull Ltd. (1994), 35 F.2d 1527 (Fed. Cir.), *cert. denied*, 514 U.S. 1050 (1995).

Buckingham Productions, Inc. (1986), FTC Docket No. 9194, August 14.

C.R. Bard, Inc. v. M3 Systems (1998), 157 F.3d 1340 (Fed. Cir.).

Cairns v. Franklin Mint Co. (1998), 24 F. Supp. 2d 1013 (C.D. Cal.), *aff'd*, 292 F. 3d 1139 (9th Cir. 2002).

California Milk Producers Advisory Bd. (1979), 94 F.T.C. 429.

Caloric Appliance Corp. v. Knapp-Monarch Co. (1963), 137 U.S.P.Q. 477 (T.T.A.B.).

Campbell Soup Co. (1991), 1991 FTC LEXIS 303.

Canal Co. v. Clark (1871), 80 U.S. 311.

Canandaigua Wine Company (1991), FTC File No. 912–3008 (March 12).

Colt Defense LLC v. Bushmaster Firearms, Inc. (2007), 486 F.3d 701 (1st Cir.).

Comedy III Productions, Inc. v. Gary Saderup, Inc. (2002), 25 Cal. 4th 387, *cert. denied*, 534 U.S. 1078.

Comedy III Productions, Inc. v. New Line Cinema (2000), 200 F.3d 593 (9th Cir.).

Commerce Bank (2004), NAD Case #4134 (Jan. 23).

Communications Satellite Corp. v. Comcet, Inc. (1970), 429 F.2d 1245 (4th Cir.), *cert. denied*, 400 U.S. 942.

Conopco, Inc. v. May Department Stores Company (1994), 46 F.3d 1556 (Fed. Cir), *rehearing denied*, 1994 U.S. App. LEXIS 34513 (1994), *cert. denied*, 514 U.S. 1078 (1995).

Consumer Products of America, Inc. v. FTC (1968), 400 F.2d 930 (3d Cir.), *cert. denied*, 393 U.S. 1088 (1969).

Continental T.V. Inc. v. GTE Sylvania, Inc. (1977), 433 U.S. 36.

Cooke, Perkiss and Liehe, Inc. v. Northern California Collection Service, Inc. (1990), 911 F.2d 242 (9th Cir.).

Cosmetically Sealed Industry, Inc. v. Chesebrough-Pond's USA Company (1997), 125 F.3d 28.

Couture v. Playdom, Inc., 113 U.S.P.Q.2d 2042 (Fed. Cir. 2015).

Creative Beauty Innovations, Inc. (2000), 56 U.S.P.Q.2d 1203 (T.T.A.B.).

Cuisinarts, Inc. v. Robot-Coupe Int'l Corp. (1982), No. 81 Civ. 731–CSH, 1982 WL 121559 (S.D.N.Y. June 9).

Custom Craft Carpets, Inc., People v. (1984), 159 Cal. App.3d 676 (2d Dist., Div. 2).

DaimlerChrysler AG v. Bloom (2003), 315 F.3d 932 (8th Cir.).

*Dallas Cowboys Cheerleaders, Inc. v. Pussycat Cinema, Ltd. (*1979), 604 F.2d 200 (2d. Cir.).

Dannon Milk Products, Inc. (1962), 61 F.T.C. 840.

Dastar Corp. v. Twentieth Century Fox Film Corp. (2003), 539 U.S. 23.

Davis v. The Gap, Inc. (2001), 246 F.3d 152 (2d Cir.).

Davis Furnace Co. (1961), 59 F.T.C. 583.

DC Comics v. Kryptonite Corp. (2004), 336 F. Supp.2d 324 (S.D.N.Y.).

De Landtsheer Emmanuel SA v Comité Interprofessionnel du Vin de Champagne (2007), ECJ C–381/05 (April 19).

Deere & Co. v. Farmhand, Inc. (1983), 721 F.2d 253 (8th Cir.).

Deere & Co. v. MTD Products, Inc. (1994), 41 F.3d 39–45 (2d Cir.).

Dei Rossi v. Whirlpool Corp. (2015), 2015 U.S. Dist. LEXIS 55574 (E.D. Cal.).

Dell Computer Corp. (2004), NAD Case #4152 (March 2).

Dentsply Int'l Inc., United States v. (2005), 399 F.3d 181 (3d Cir.).

Deutsche SiSi-Werke GmbH & CO. Betriebs KG v. Office for Harmonization in the Internal Market (2006), Case C–173/04 P (E.C.J.).

Dial-A-Mattress Franchise Corporation v. Page (1989), 880 F.2d 675 (2d Cir.).

Dial-A-Mattress Operating Corp., In re (2001), 240 F.3d 1341 (Fed. Cir.).

Diana Packman v. Chicago Tribune Co. (2001), 267 F.3d 628 (7th Cir.).

Dick's Sporting Goods (2004), NAD Case #4179 (May 7).

DirecTV and Prime TV (2001), NAD Case #3799 (July 20).

Dorr-Oliver, Inc. v. Fluid-Quip, Inc. (1996), 94 F.3d 376–382. (7th Cir.).

Downing v. Abercrombie & Fitch (2001), 265 F.3d 994.

Dr. Pepper Co. v. Sambo's Restaurants, Inc. (1981), 517 F. Supp. 1202 (N.D. Texas).

Dranoff-Perlstein Association. v. Sklar (1992), 967 F. 2d 852 (3d Cir.).

DSquared Solutions, LLC (2004), FTC No. 032 3233, available at http://www.ftc.gov/opa/2004/08/dsquared.htm, accessed 23 July 2015.

Dual-Deck Video Cassette Recorder Antitrust Litigation (1993), 11 F.3d 1460 (9th Cir.).

Dupont Cellophane Co. v. Waxed Products Co. (1936), 85 F.2d 75 (2d Cir.).

Duraco Products, Inc. v. Joy Plastic Enterprises, Ltd (1994), 40 F.3d 1431 (3d Cir.).

E. & J. Gallo Winery v. Gallo Cattle Co. (1992), 967 F.2d 1280 (9th Cir.).

Eastern Airlines, Inc. (1982), NAD Case #1957 (July 15).

Eastman Kodak Co. v. Image Technical Services, Inc. (1992), 504 U.S. 451.

Eddie Z's Blinds and Drapery, Inc., In re (2005), 74 U.S.P.Q.2d 1037 (T.T.A.B.).

Eden SARL v. Office for Harmonization in the Internal Market (2005), Case T–305/04 (CFI).

Edina Realty, Inc. v. THEMLSONLINE.COM (2006), 2006 WL 737064 (D. Minn.).

Edison v. Edison Polyform Mfg. Co. (1907), 67 A. 392 (N.J. Ch.).

Eilberg, In re (1998), 49 U.S.P.Q.2d 1955 (T.T.A.B.).

Elgin National Watch Co. v. Illinois Watch Case Co. (1901), 179 U.S. 665.

Eli Lilly & Co. v. Revlon, Inc. (1983), 577 F. Supp. 477 (S.D.N.Y).

Eli Lilly & Co's Community Trade Mark Application (2004), E.T.M.R. 4 (OHIM 2nd Bd. App).

Elliot Knitwear, Inc. (1961), 59 F.T.C. 893.

Elvis Presley, Estate of v. Russen (1981), 513 F. Supp. 1339 (D. N.J.).

Elvis Presley Int'l Foundation v. Crowell (1987), 733 SW2d 89 (Tenn. Ct of App.).

Encyclopedia Britannica, Inc. v. FTC (1979), 605 F.2d 964 (7th Cir.), *cert. denied*, 445 U.S. 934 (1980).

ETW Corp. v. Jireh Publishing (2003), 332 F.3d 915 (6th Cir.).

Eveready Battery Co. v. Adolph Coors Co. (1991), 765 F. Supp. 440 (N.D. Ill.).

Express LLC v. Fettish Group, Inc. (2006), 424 F. Supp. 2d 1211 (C.D.Cal.).

Factors Etc., Inc. v. Pro Arts, Inc. (1980), 496 F. Supp. 1090 (S.D.N.Y.), *reversed*, 652 F.2d 278 (2d Cir. 1981), *cert. denied*, 456 U.S. 927 (1982).

Faigman v. AT&T Mobility LLC (2007), 2007 U.S. Dist. LEXIS 52192 (N.D. Cal.).

Farouk Systems, Inc. v. Target Corp., Inc. (2008), 86 U.S.P.Q.2D (BNA) 1221 (5th Cir.).

Federal Express Corp. v. Federal Espresso Inc. (2000), 201 F.3d 168 (2d. Cir.).

Feist Publications Inc. v. Rural Telephone Service Co. (1991), 499 U.S. 340.

Field Enterprises Educ. Corp. v. Cove Indus., Inc. (1969), 297 F. Supp. 989 (E.D.N.Y.).

Fiji Water Co. LLC v. Paramount Int'l Export, Ltd. (2008), 2008 WL 2782745 (N.D. Cal.).

Finchley, Inc. v. George Hess Co., Inc. (1938), 24 F. Supp. 94 (E.D.N.Y.).

Firestone Tire & Rubber Co. v. FTC (1973), 481 F.2d 246 (6th Cir.), *cert. denied*, 414 U.S. 1112.

Fleischman v. Shuckmann (1881), 62 How Prac. (N.Y.) 92.

Ford Motor Company. v. Lapertosa (2000), 126 F. Supp. 2d 463–67. (E.D. Michigan).

Fortner Enterprises v. United States Steel Corp. (1969), 394 U.S. 495.

Foxworthy v. Custom Tees, Inc. (1995), 879 F. Supp. 1200 (N.D. Ga.).

Fruit of the Loom, Inc. v. Sara Lee Corp. (1986), 674 F. Supp. 1020 (S.D.N.Y.).

FTC v. Borden Co. (1966), 383 U.S. 637.

FTC v. Keppel & Bro. (1934), 291 U.S. 304.

FTC v. Mary Carter Paint Co. (1965), 382 U.S. 46.

FTC v. Pharmtech Research, Inc. (1983), 576 F. Supp. 294, 299 (D.D.C. Cir.).

FTC v. Royal Milling Co. (1933), 288 U.S. 212.

FTC v. Sperry & Hutchinson Co. (1972), 405 U.S. 233.

FTC v. Standard Education Society (1937), 302 U.S. 112.

FTC v. Zuccarini (2002), 2002 U.S. Dist. LEXIS 13324. (E.D. Pa.).

Fuji Film Co., In re (2006), Serial No. 75589709 (T.T.A.B. Dec. 19).

Fun-Damental Too Ltd. v. Gemmy Industries Corp. (1996), 111 F.3d 993 (2d Cir.).

Gateway Inc. v. Companion Products Inc. (2004), 384 F.3d 503 (8th Cir.).

Gator Corporation Software Trademark & Copyright Litigation, In re the (2003), 259 F. Supp. 2d. 1378 (Judicial Panel on Multidistrict Litigation).

General Electric Broadcasting, In re (1978), 199 U.S.P.Q. 560 (T.T.A.B.).

General Electric Co. v. Alumpa Coal Co. (1979), 205 U.S.P.Q. (BNA) 1036 (D. Mass.).

General Foods Corp. (1984), 103 F.T.C. 204.

General Motors Corp., In re (1977), 196 U.S.P.Q. 574 (T.T.A.B).

General Steel Corp. (2003), NAD Case #4095 (Sept. 29).

Genesee Brewing Co. v. Stroh Brewing Co. (1997), 24 F. 3d 137 (2d Cir.).

Georgetown Publishing House, Ltd., Inc. (1996), 122 F.T.C. 392.

Giant Carpet Stores of American Inc. v. Retail Kane Carpet, Inc., New Jersey Super Ct, Bergen Cty (11/19/1991) No. C–494–91E *reported in* 61 *Antitrust & Trade Regulation Reports* (BNA) 710 (Dec. 12, 1991).

Gillette Co. v. LA Labs. Ltd. Oy (2005), ECJ Case C–228/03, 2005 ETMR 67.

Gillette Co. v. Norelco Consumer Prods. Co. (1999), 69 F. Supp. 2d 246 (D. Mass.).

Gillette Company v. Wilkinson Sword, Inc. (1989), 1989 U.S. Dist. LEXIS 8276, 89 Civ. 3586 (KMW) (S.D.N.Y. July 6).

Gillette Company v. Wilkinson Sword, Inc. (1992), 1992 WL 30938, 89 Civ. 3586 (KMW) (S.D.N.Y. July 6).

Girl Scouts of U.S.A. v. Bantam Doubleday Dell Publishing Group (1993), 996 F.2d 1477 (2d Cir.).

Girl Scouts v. Personality Posters Manufacturing (1969), 304 F. Supp. 1228 (S.D.N.Y.).

Global World Media Corp. (1997), 1997 FTC LEXIS 314.

GMC v. Lanard Toys, Inc. (2007), 468 F.3d 405 (6th Cir.).

GNC Corp.: Triflex Prods. Mktg & Sales Practices Litigation (2015), 14–1724, 2015 U.S. App. LEXIS 10351 (4th Cir.).

Goodman v. FTC (1957), 244 F.2d 584 (9th Cir.).

Google France SARL v. Louis Vuitton Malletier SA (2010), 2010 ECJ EUR-Lex LEXIS 119 (Mar. 23).

Google, Inc. v. Am. Blind & Wallpaper Factory, Inc. (2007), 2007 U.S. Dist. LEXIS 32450 (N.D. Cal.).

Gorilla Glue Co. (2006), NAD #4486, May 3.

Government Employees Insurance Co. v. Google, Inc. (2005), 77 U.S.P.Q.2d 1841 (E.D. Va.).

Grand Rapids Furniture Co. v. Grand Rapids Furniture Co. (1942), 127 F.2d 245 (7th Cir.).

Huguin v. Land O' Lakes, Inc. (2016), No. 15-2815 (7th Cir.).

Hunt Masters, Inc. v. Landrey's Seafood Restaurant, Inc. (2001), 240 F.3d 251 (4th Cir.).

Hy-Cross Hatchery, Inc. v. Osborne (1962), 303 F.2d 947 (C.C.P.A.).

IDT Corp. (2005), NAD Case #4288 (Feb. 25).

ILC Peripherals Leasing Corp. v. IMB Corp. (1978), 458 F. Supp. 423 (N.D.Cal.), *aff'd sub nom., Memorex Corp. v. IBM Corp.* 636 F.2d 1188 (9th Cir. 1980), *cert. denied,* 452 U.S. 972 (1981).

Illinois Tool Works, Inc. v. Independent Ink, Inc. (2006), 126 S. Ct. 1281.

Image Technical Services, Inc. v. Eastman Kodak Co. (1997), 125 F.3d 1195 (9th Cir.).

Independent Service Orgs. Antitrust Litigation (2000), 203 F.3d 1322 (Fed. Cir.).

In-N-Out Burgers v. Chadders Restaurant (2007), Case No. 2:07–CV–394 TS, 2007 U.S. Dist. LEXIS 47732 (D. Utah).

Intel Corp. v. Advanced Micro Devices, Inc. (1991), 756 F.Supp. 1292 (N.D.Cal).

International Flavors & Fragrances, Inc., In re (1999), 183 F3d 1361 (Fed. Cir.).

Interstate Bakeries Corp. (2002), 2002 FTC LEXIS 20, FTC Docket No. C–4042, April 16.

Invicta Plastics (U.S.A.) Limited v. Mego Corporation (1981), 523 F. Supp. 619 (S.D.N.Y.).

ITT Continental Baking Co. (1973), 83 F.T.C. 865.

J & J Snack Foods Corp. v. McDonald's Corp. (1991), 932 F.2d 1460 (Fed. Cir.).

J.B. Williams Co. (1972), 81 F.T.C. 238.

J.G. Wentworth SSC Ltd. v. Settlement Funding LLC (2009), 2007 U.S. Dist. LEXIS 288 (E.D. Pa. Jan. 4).

Jack Wolfskin Ausrustung Fur Draussen GmbH & Co. KGAA v. New Millennium Sports, S.L.U., 797 F.3d 1363 (Fed. Cir. 2015).

Jacob Siegel Co. v. FTC (1946), 327 U.S. 608.

James v. Screen Gems, Inc. (1959), 174 Cal. App. 2d 640.

Jim Henson Prods. v. John T. Brady & Assocs. (1994), 867 F. Supp. 175 (S.D.N.Y.).

Joffe v. Acacia Mortgage Corp. (2005), 121 P.3d 831 (Ct. of App. Az. Div. 1, Depart. E).

Johnson & Johnson v. Carter Wallace, Inc. (1980), 631 F.2d 186 (2d Cir.).

Jordache Enterprises, Inc. v. Hogg Wyld, Limited (1987), 828 F.2d 1482–1491 (10th Cir.).

Joseph Mill Trading (1966), 70 F.T.C. 1064.

Juice Generation, Inc. v. GS Enterprises, LLC (2015), 2014–1853 (Fed. Cir. July 20).

Keebler Company v. Nabisco Brands, Inc. (1992), 1992 U.S. Dist. LEXIS 6826 (N.D. Ill.).

Kellogg Co. (1982), 99 F.T.C. 8.

Kellogg Co. v. National Biscuit Co. (1938), 305 U.S. 111.

King-Seeley Thermos Co v. Aladdin Industries (1963), 321 F.2d 577 (2d Cir.).

Kitchens of Sara Lee, Inc. v. Nifty Foods (1959), 266 F.2d 541 (2d Cir.).

Kmart Corp. (2001), NAD Case #3775 (June 4).

Kodize Process Corp. (1945), 40 F.T.C. 441.

KP Permanent Make-up, Inc. v. Lasting Impression I. Inc. (2004), 543 U.S. 111.

Kraft Foods, Inc. (1995), NAD Case #3201 (June 6).

Kraft Inc. v. FTC (1992), 970 F.2d 311, *cert. denied*, 61 U.S.L.W. 2091.

Kremen v. Cohen (2003), 337 F.3d 1024 (9th Cir.).

Kroger Co. (1981), 98 F.T.C. 639, *ordered modified,* 100 F.T.C. 573 (1982).

K-T Zoe Furniture, Inc., In re (1994), 16 F.3d 390 (Fed. Cir.).

L & F Products v. Proctor & Gamble Co. (1995), 45 F.3d 709 (2d. Cir.).

L.E. Waterman Co v. Modern Pen Co. (1914), 235 U.S. 88.

L.L. Bean, Inc. v. Drake Publishers, Inc. (1987), 811 F.2d 26–33 (1st Cir.), *cert. denied,* 483 U.S. 1013.

Lawrence Mfg. Co. v. Tennessee Mfg. Co. (1891), 138 U.S. 537.

Laws v. Song Music Entertainment, Inc. (2006), 448 F.3d 1134 (9th Cir.).

Leegin Creative Leather Prods., Inc. v. Psks, Inc. (2007), 2007 U.S. LEXIS 8668.

Leibovitz v. Paramount Pictures Corp. (1998), 137 F.3d 109 (2d Cir. N.Y.).

Lenscrafters, Inc. v. Vision World (1996), 943 F. Supp 1481 (D. Minn.).

LePage's Inc. v. 3M (2003), 324 F.3d 141(3d Cir.), *cert. denied,* 124 S. Ct. 2932 (2004).

Levi Strauss Co., Inc. v. Tesco PLC (2001), Case 415/99 ECR (Nov. 20), 8691.

Lombardo v. Doyle, Dane & Bernbach, Inc. (1977), 396 N.Y.S. 2d 661 (App. Div.).

Londontown Manufacturing Co. v Cable Raincoat Co. (1974), 371 F. Supp. 1114 (S.D.N.Y).

Louis Vuitton Malletier, S.A. v. Haute Diggity Dog, LLC (2007), No. 06–2267, 2007 U.S. App. LEXIS 26334 (4th Cir.).

Lugosi v. Universal Pictures (1979), 25 Cal. 3d 813.

Maidenform Inc. v. Bestform Foundations, Inc. (1969), 161 U.S.P.Q. 805 (T.T.A.B.).

Mangini v. R.J. Reynolds Tobacco Co. (1993), 22 Cal. App. 4th 628, *aff'd,* 7 Cal. 4th 1057 (1994).

Mangini v. R.J. Reynolds Tobacco Co. (1997), Settlement and Consolidation Agreement, available at https://industrydocuments.library.ucsf.edu/tobacco/docs/#id=fzlh0063, accessed 4 April 2016.

Manufacturing Research Corp. v. Greenlee Tool Co. (1982), 693 F.2d 1037 (11th Cir.).

Martin Luther King Ctr. for Social Change v. American Heritage Prods. (1983), 694 F.2d 674, 680 (11th Cir.).

Masson v. New Yorker Magazine, Inc. (1991), 501 U.S. 496.

Mastercard International Inc. v. Sprint Communication. Company (1994), 30 U.S.P.Q. 2d 1963 (S.D.N.Y.).

Mastercrafters Clock & Radio Co. v. Vacheron & Constantin-LeCoultre Watches, Ltd. (1955), 221 F.2d 464 (2d Cir.), *cert. denied*, 350 U.S. 832.

Masterfoods Ltd v. Controller of Patents, Designs and Trade Marks (2003) E.T.M.R. 84.

McDonald's Corp. v. Arche Technologies (1990), 17 U.S.P.Q. 2d 1557 (N.D. Cal.).

McDonald's Corp. v. Druck & Gerner DDS, P.C. (1993), 814 F. Supp. 1127 (N.D.N.Y.).

McDonald's Corp. v. John L. McClain (1995), 37 U.S.P.Q. 2d 1274 (T.T.A.B.).

McDonald's Corp. v. McBagels, Inc. (1986), 649 F. Supp. 1268 (S.D.N.Y.).

McDonald's Corp. v. McSweet, LLC, 112 U.S.P.Q.2d 1268 (T.T.A.B. 2014).

McDonald's Hamburgers Ltd. v. Burger King Ltd. (1985), [1986] FSR 45 (Chancery Div.), *aff'd*, 1987 FSR 112.

McFarland v. Miller (1994), 14 F.3d 912 (3d Cir.).

MCI Communications v. American Tel. & Tel. Co. (1983), 708 F.2d 1081 (7th Cir.), *cert. denied*, 464 U.S. 891.

McNeil Nutritionals, LLC v. Heartland Sweeteners LLC (2007), 511 F.3d 350 (3d Cir.), *injunction granted*, 566 F. Supp. 2d 378 (E.D. Pa. June 28, 2008).

McNeilab, Inc., v. Am. Home Prods. Corp. (1988), 848 F.2d 34 (2d Cir.).

McNeil-PPC v. Guardian Drug Company (1997), 984 F. Supp 1066–1074. (E.D. Mich.).

Mem Co. v. Yardley of London, Inc. (1981), 212 U.S.P.Q. 280 (S.D.N.Y.).

Menard, Inc. (2003), NAD Case #4017 (Feb. 24).

Menashe v. V. Secret Catalogue, Inc. (2005), 2005 U.S. Dist. LEXIS 38585 (S.D.N.Y).

Merck & Co. Inc. v. Mediplan Health Consulting, Inc. (2006), 425 F. Supp. 2d 402 (S.D.N.Y. 2006).

Meridian Rack & Pinion DBA buyautoparts.com, In re (2015), 114 U.S.P.Q.2d 1462 (T.T.A.B.).

Microsoft Corp., United States v. (1995), 159 F.R.D. 318 (D.D.C), *rev'd per curiam*, 56 F.3d 1448 (D.C. Cir.).

Microsoft Corp., United States v. (2001), 253 F.3d 34 (D.C. Cir. *en banc*).

Microstrategy Inc. v. Motorola, Inc. (2001), 245 F.3d 335 (4th Cir.).

Midler v. Ford Motor Co. (1988), 849 F.2d 460 (9th Cir.).

Miller Brewing Co. (1985), 226 U.S.P.Q. 666 (T.T.A.B.).

Miller Brewing Co. v. Carling O'Keefe Breweries Ltd. (1978), 452 F. Supp. 429 (W.D.N.Y.).

Miller Brewing Co. v. Falstaff Brewing Corp. (1981), 655 F.2d 5 (1st Cir.).

Miller Brewing Co. v. G. Heileman Brewing Co. (1977), 561 F.2d 75 (7th Cir.), *cert. denied*, 434 U.S. 1025 (1978).

Mobil Oil Corp. v. Mobile Mechanics, Inc. (1976), 192 U.S.P.Q. 744 (D.Conn.).

Mobil Oil Corp. v. Pegasus Petroleum Corp. (1987), 818 F.2d 254 (2d Cir.).

Morton-Norwich Prods. (1982), 213 U.S.P.Q 9 (CCPA).

Moseley v. V. Secret Catalogue, Inc. (2003), 537 U.S. 418.

Motorola, Inc. v. Griffiths Electronics, Inc. (1963), 317 F.2d 397 (C.C.P.A.).

Motschenbacher v. R.J. Reynolds Tob. Co. (1974), 498 F.2d 821 (9th Cir.).

Multi Time Machine, Inc. v. Amazon.com, Inc. (2015), Nos. 13–55575, D.C. No. 2:11–CV–09076–DDP–MAN (9th Cir.).

Multistate Legal Studies Inc. v. Harcourt Brace Jovanovich Legal and Professional Publications, Inc. (1995), 63 F.3d 1540 (10th Cir.), *cert. denied,* 116 S.Ct. 702 (1996).

Murphy Door Bed Co., Inc. v. Interior Sleep Systems, Inc. (1989), 874 F.2d 95 (2d Cir.).

Mutual of Omaha Insurance Company v. Novak (1987), 836 F.2d 397–402. (8th Cir.), *cert. denied,* 488 U.S. 933 (1988).

Myles Ltd.'s App., R 711/1999–3, [2003] ETMR 56.

Nabisco, Inc. v. PF Brands, Inc. (1999), 191 F.3d 208 (2d Cir.).

National Biscuit Co. v. Baker (1899), 95 F. 135 (C.C.N.Y).

National Football League Properties, Inc. v. Wichita Falls Sportswear, Inc. (1982), 532 F. Supp. 651 (W.D. Wash.).

National Hockey League v. Pepsi-Cola Canada Ltd (1992), 6 W.W.R. 216 (B.C.).

National Housewares, Inc. (1977), 90 F.T.C. 512.

National Patent Dev. Corp. (1986), 1 U.S.P.Q.2d 1921 (T.T.A.B.).

Native American Arts, Inc. v. Waldron Corp. (2005), 399 F.3d 871 (7th Cir.).

Nature's Way Prods., Inc. v. Nature-Pharma, Inc. (1990), 736 F. Supp. 245 (D. Utah).

NBTY, Inc. (2005), NAD Case #4370 (Aug. 1).

Nestle SA's Trade Mark Application (Have a Break) (2003), FSR 37 (High Court); [2004] FSR 2 (Court of Appeal) (2005) ETMR 96 (European Court of Justice).

New Kids on the Block v. News America Publishing, Inc. (1992), 971 F.2d 302–8. (9th Cir.).

Newcombe v. Adolf Coors, Co. (1998), 157 F.3D 686 (9th Cir.).

Nextel Communications Inc. (2004), NAD Case #4251 (Nov. 9).

NicSand, Inc. v. 3M Co. (2007), 507 F.3d 442 (6th Cir.).

Nike Corp. v. Just Did It Enterprises (1993), 6 F.3d 1225 (7th Cir.).

NitroLeisure Prods. LLC v. Acushnet Co. (2003), 341 F.3d 1356 (Fed. Cir.).

Nora Beverages, Inc. v. The Perrier Group of America, Inc. (2001), 269 F.3d 114. (2d Cir.).

Norm Thompson Outfitters, Inc. v. General Motors Corp. (1971), 448 F.2d 1293 (9th Cir.).

Northam Warren Corp. v. FTC (1932), 59 F.2d 196 (2d Cir.).

Novartis Consumer Health Inc. v. Johnson & Johnson-Merck Consumer Pharmaceuticals, Inc. (2002), 290 F.3d 578 (3d Cir.).

Novartis Corp. v. FTC (2000), 223 F.3d 783 (D.C. Cir.).

Novo Nordisk A/S v. Becton Dickinson & Co. (1998), 997 F. Supp. 470 (S.D.N.Y.).

N.V. Organon, In re (2006), 78 U.S.P.Q.2d 1301 (T.T.A.B.).

N.V. Organon (2006), Serial No. 76467774 (T.T.A.B., June 14).

O2 Holdings Ltd v. Hutchinson 3G Ltd. (2006), 2006 EWCA Civ. 1656.

O'Brien v. Pabst Sales (1941), 124 F.2d 167 (5th Cir.), *cert. denied*, 315 U.S. 823 (1942).

OHIM v. *Erpo Mobelwerk GmbH* (2004), Case C–64/02.

OHIM v. *Wm. Wrigley Jr. Company* (2003), ECR 1–12447.

Ohralick v. Ohio State Bar Ass'n (1978), 436 U.S. 447.

Oliveira a/k/a/ Gilberto v. Frito Lay, Inc. (2001), 251 F.3d 56 (2d Cir.).

Omega Environmental, Inc. v. Gilbarco, Inc. (1997), 127 F.3d 1157 (9th Cir.).

Onassis v. Christian Dior, Inc. (1984), 472 N.Y.S. 2d 254 (S.C.).

Oppedahl & Larson v. Advanced Concepts (1997), U.S. Dist. LEXIS 23105 (D. Colo.).

Oppedahl & Larson, LLP, In re (2004), 373 F.3d 1171 (Fed. Cir.).

Original Appalachian Artworks, Inc. v. Granada Electronics, Inc. (1987), 816 F.2d 68 (2d Cir.).

Owens Corning Fiberglass Corp., In re (1985), 774 F.2d 1116 (Fed. Cir.).

Palmer v. BRG of Georgia, Inc. (1990), 498 U.S. 46.

Panavision International v. Toeppen (1998), 141 F.3d 1316–25 (9th Cir.).

Parfums Christian Dior SA v. Evora BV (1997), Case C–337/95, 1997 EMTR 937.

Park 'N Fly, Inc. v. Dollar Park & Fly, Inc. (1985), 469 U.S. 189.

Pavesich v. New England Life Insurance Co. (1905), 122 Ga. 190.

Payless Drug Store Co. (1972), 82 F.T.C. 1473.

Pepsico, Inc. v. Grapette Co. (1969), 416 F.2d 285 (8th Cir.).

PepsiCo, Inc. v. Coca-Cola, Co. (2002), 315 F.3d 101 (2d Cir.).

Philip Morris, Inc. v. Allen Distributors, Inc. (1999), 48 F. Supp. 2d 231 (D. Mass. 2001).

Phillip Morris, Inc. v. RJR Tobacco Co. (1975), 188 U.S.P.Q. 289 (S.D.N.Y.).

Philip Morris, Inc. v. Star Tobacco Corp. (1995), 879 F. Supp. 379 (S.D.N.Y.).

Piazza's Seafood World, LLC v. Odom (2006), 448 F. 3d 744 (5th Cir.).

Pignons S.A. de Mecanique de Precision v. Polaroid Corp. (1981), 657 F.2d 482 (1st Cir.).

Pilates, Inc. v. Georgetown Bodyworks Deep Muscle Message Ctrs., Inc. (2001), 157 F. Supp. 2d 75 (D.D.C).

Pizza Hut, Inc. v. Papa John's Int'l Inc. (2000), 227 F.3d 489 (5th Cir.), *cert. denied*, 532 U.S. 920 (2001).

Plaskolite, Inc. (1983), 101 F.T.C. 344.

Plasticolor Molded Prods. v. Ford Motor Co. (1989), 713 F. Supp. 1329, 1335 (C.D. Cal.), *vacated by consent judgment*, 767 F. Supp. 1036 (C.D. Cal. 1991).

Playboy Enterprises, Inc. v. Calvin Designer Label (1997), 985 F. Supp. 1220 (N.D. Cal.).

Playboy Enterprises, Inc. v. Netscape Communications (1999), 55 F. Supp. 2d 1070–74 (C.D.Cal.), *aff'd*, 202 F.3d 278 (9th Cir.).

Playboy Enterprises, Inc. v. Welles (1998), 7 F. Supp. 2d 1098 (S.D. Ca. 1998), *aff'd mem.*, 162 F.3d 1169 (9th Cir.).

Polaroid Corp. v. Polaraid, Inc. (1963), 319 F.2d 830 (7th Cir. 1963).

Polyglycoat Corp. v. Environmental Chems. Co. (1980), 509 F. Supp. 36 (S.D.N.Y).

Potato Chip Institute v. General Mills, Inc. (1972), 461 F. 2d 1088 (8th Cir.).

Prestonettes, Inc. v. Coty (1924), 264 U.S. 359.

Priceline.com (2003), NAD Case Report No. 4073 (Aug. 4).

Princeton Vanguard LLC v. Frito-Lay Inc. (NEED YEAR), 786 F. 3d 960 (Fed. Cir.).

Procter & Gamble Company v OHIM (2002), Case C–383/99 P, E.T.M.R. 22 (ECJ).

Q-Tips, Inc. v. Johnson and Johnson (1953), 206 F.2d 144 (3d Cir.).

Quaker State Corp. (1995), NAD Case #3212 (July 1).

Qualitex Co. v. Jacobson Products Co., Inc. (1995), 514 U.S. 159.

Quality Inns International v. McDonald's Corp. (1988), 695 F. Supp. 198 (D.Md.).

Reader's Digest Association, United States v. (1981), 662 F.2d 955 (3d Cir.), *cert. denied*, 455 U.S. 908 (1982).

Reeves v. United Artists Corp. (1985), 765 F.2d 79 (6th Cir.).

Remington Products, Inc., In re (1987), 3 U.S.P.Q.2d 1714 (T.T.A.B.).

Rescuecom Corp. v. Google Inc. (2009), 562 F.3D 123 (2d. Cir.).

Retail Services Inc. v. Freebies Pub. (2004), 364 F.3d 535 (4th Cir.).

ReverseAuction.com (2000), Civ. No. 99–WM–783 (D. Colo. June 27).

Revlon Consumer Products Corporation v. Jennifer Leather Broadway, Inc. (1994), 858 F. Supp. 1268–82 (S.D.N.Y.), *aff'd without opinion*, 57 F.3d 1062 (2d Cir. 1995).

Ride the Ducks. L.L.C. v. Duck Boat Tours, Inc. (2005), 75 U.S.P.Q.2d 1269 (E.D. Pa.).

Ringling Bros.-Barnum & Bailey Combined Shows, Inc. v. B.E. Windows Corp. (1996), 969 F. Supp. 901 (S.D.N.Y.).

Ringling Bros.-Barnum & Bailey Combined Shows, Inc. v. Celozzi-Ettleson Chevrolet, Inc. (1988), 855 F.2d 480 (7th Cir.).

Ringling Bros.-Barnum & Bailey Combined Shows, Inc. v. Chandris American Lines, Inc. (1971), 321 F. Supp. 707 (S.D.N.Y.).

Ringling Bros.-Barnum & Bailey Combined Shows, Inc. v. Utah Div. of Travel Dev. (1999), 170 F.3d. 449 (4th Cir.).

Roberson v. Rochester Folding Box Co. (1902), 64 N.E. 4442 (N.Y.).

Roland Machine Co v. Dresser Industries, Inc. (1984), 749 F.2d 380 (7th Cir.).

Rothery Storage and Van Co. v. Atlas Van Lines (1986), 792 F.2d 210 (D.C. Cir.).

Roux Lab., Inc. v. Clairol, Inc. (1968), 157 U.S.P.Q. 391 (T.T.A.B.).

Royal Construction Co. (1967), 71 F.T.C. 762.

Rudolph Int'l, Inc. v. Realys, Inc. (2007), 482 F.3d 1195 (9th Cir.).

S.C. Johnson & Son, Inc. v. Clorox Co. (2001), 241 F.3d 232 (2d Cir.).

Sandra Hosiery Mills, In re (1967), 154 U.S.P.Q. 631 (T.T.A.B.).

Sands, Taylor & Wood Co. v. The Quaker Oats Co. (1992), 978 F.2d 947 (7th Cir).

Satterfield v. Simon & Schuster, Inc. (2009)

Savett v. Whirlpool (2012), 2012 U.S. Dist. LEXIS 124086 (N.D. Ohio).

Savin Corp. v. Savin Group (2004), 391 F.3d 439 (2d Cir), *cert. denied*, 126 S. Ct. 116 (2005).

Saxlehner v. Wagner (1910), 216 U.S. 375–380.

Schumann v. Loew's Inc. (1954), 135 N.Y.S.2d 361.

Schwan's IP, LLC v. Kraft Pizza Co. (2006), 460 F.3d 971 (8th Cir.).

Scott Fetzer Co. v. House of Vacuums, Inc. (2004), 381 F.3d 477 (5th Cir.).

Sears, Roebuck & Co. v. FTC (1982), 676 F.2d 385 (9th Cir.).

Shields v. Zuccarini (2001), 254 F.3d 476–84 (3d Cir.).

Shire U.S. Inc. v. Barr Labs, Inc. (2003), 329 F.3d 348 (3d Cir.).

Sieckmann v. Deutsches patent-und Markenamt (2002), Case C–273/00, 2003 E.T.M.R. 37.

Siemens AG v. CIPA Gesellschaft fur Visualisierung und Prozessautomatisierurng mbH (2006) (EJJ 1st Chamber—unreported) (C59/05).

Silhouette Int'l Schmied GmbH & Co.KG v. Hartlauer Handelsgesellschaft mbH (1998), Case 335/96 ECR (July) 4799.

Simmonds Upholstery Co. (1953), 49 F.T.C. 1508.

Sinatra v. Goodyear Tire & Rubber Co. (1970), 435 F.2d 711 (9th Cir.).

Sinkler v. Goldsmith (1985), 623 F. Supp. 727 (D.Ariz).

Slokevage, In re (2006), 78 U.S.P.Q.2d 1395 (Fed. Cir.).

Smith Kline & French Lab. v. Broder (1959), 125 U.S.P.Q. 299 (S.D.Tex).

Smith v. Chanel, Inc. (1968), 402 F.2d 562 (9th Cir.).

Smith v. M & B Sales and Manufacturing (1990), 13 U.S.P.Q. 2d 2002 (N.D. Cal.).

Sony Computer Entertainment America, Inc. v. Bleem, LLC (2000), 214 F.3d 1022 (9th Cir.).

Sorensen v. WD-40 Co. (2015), 115 U.S.P.Q.2d 1128 (7th Cir.).

Southco, Inc. v. Kanebridge Corp. (2000), 53 U.S.P.Q.2d 1490 (E.D. Pa.).

Starbucks Corp. v. Wolfe's Borough Coffee, Inc. (2013), 736 F.3d 198 (2d Cir.).

Stephano v. News Group Pub. Inc. (1984), 64 N.Y.2d 174.

Sterling Prods. Co. v. *Crest Mfg. Co.* (1970), 314 F. Supp. 204 (E.D. Mich.).

Stouffer Foods, Corp. (1994), 118 F.T.C. 746.

Sun Oil Co. (1974), 84 F.T.C. 247.

Sunmark, Inc. v. Ocean Spray Cranberries, Inc. (1995), 64 F.3d 1055 (7th Cir.).

Sunshine Makers, Inc. (1992), National Advertising Division Case Report dated March 16.

Surgicenters of America, Inc. v. Medical Dental Surgeries Co. (1979), 601 F.2d 1011 (9th Cir.).

Sykes Enterprises, Inc. v. *Office of Harmonization in the Internal Market* (2003) E.T.M.R. 57.

Sykes Laboratory, Inc. v. Kalvin (1985), 610 F. Supp. 849 (C.D. Cal.).

Taylor Building Corp. v. Benfield (2007), 2007 U.S. Dist. LEXIS 43667 (S.D. Ohio June 15).

Tea Board of India v. The Republic of Tea, Inc. (2006), 80 U.S.P.Q.2d 1881 (T.T.A.B.).

Tetra Pak v. Commission (1996), ECR I-05951.

Thaddeus Davids Co. v. Davids Man. Co. (1914), 233 U.S. 461.

The Eyeglass Factory (1997), NAD Case #3370 (March 1).

The Home Depot (2005), NAD Case #4342 (June 9).

The Home Depot, Inc. (1998), NAD Case #3485 (Sept. 1).

Thompson Medical Co., Inc. v. FTC (1986), 791 F.2d 189 (C.A.D.C.), *cert. denied*, 479 U.S. 1086 (1987).

Thomson v. Winchester (1837), 36 Mass. 214 (S. Ct.).

Tiffany & Co. v. Tiffany Productions, Inc. (1933), 188 N.E. 30 (N.Y.).

Timken Roller Bearing Co. v. United States (1951), 341 U.S. 593.

Tin Pan Apple, Inc. v. Miller Brewing Co. (1990), 737 F. Supp. 826 (S.D.N.Y).

Tommy Hilfiger Licensing, Inc. v. Nature Labs. LLC (2002), 221 F. Supp. 2d 410 (S.D.N.Y.).

Topco Associates, Inc., United States v. (1972), 405 U.S. 596.

Tops Markets, LLC (2004), NAD Case #4245 (Oct. 21).

Toshiba Europe GmbH v. Katun Germany GmbH (2002), 3 C.M.L.R. 7 (ECJ 5th Chamber)(C112/99).

Toyota Motor Sales USA, Inc. v. Tabari (2010), 610 F. 3d 1171 (9th Cir.).

Toys "R" Us v. Akkaoui (1996), 40 U.S.P.Q. 2d 1836 (N.D.Cal.).

Toys "R" Us v. Canarsie Kiddie Shop, Inc. (1983), 559 F. Supp. 1189 (E.D. N.Y.).

Toys "R" Us, Inc. v. Eli Abir (1999), 1999 WL 61817 (S.D.N.Y.).

Trade-Mark Cases (1879), 100 U.S. 82.

TrafFix Devices, Inc. v. Marketing Displays, Inc. (2004), 532 U.S. 23.

Triangle Publications v. Knight-Ridder Newspapers (1980), 626 F.2d 1171–76 (5th Cir.).

Two Pesos, Inc. v. Taco Cabana, Inc. (1992), 505 U.S. 763–773.

Ty, Inc. v. Perryman (2002), 306 F3d 509 (7th Cir.).

U-Haul International, Inc. v. WhenU.com (2003), 279 F.Supp.2d 723 (E.D. Va.).

U-Haul Int'l, Inc. v. Jartran, Inc. (1986), 793 F.2d 1034 (9th Cir.).

United States Jaycees v. Cedar Rapids Jaycees (1986), 794 F.2d 379 (8th Cir.).

United States Steel Corp. v. Vasco Metals Corp. (1968), 394 F.2d 1009 (C.C.P.A).

University of Georgia Athletic Ass'n v. Laite (1985), 756 F.2d 1535 (11th Cir.).

University of Pittsburgh v. Champion Products, Inc. (1982), 529 F. Supp. 464 (W.D. Wash.).

University of Pittsburgh v. Champion Products, Inc. (1983), 566 F. Supp. 711 (W.D. Pa.).

Van Bergen v. Minnesota (1995), 59 F.3d 1541 (8th Cir.).

Verizon Wireless (2004), NAD Case #4246 (Oct. 28).

Vidal Sassoon, Inc. v. Bristol-Myers Co. (1981), 661 F.2d 272 (2d Cir.).

Visa International Service Association's Application (1999), Decision of the First Board of Appeal of 15 July 1999, R 45/1999-1.

Visa U.S.A., Inc., United States v. (2003), 344 F.3d 229 (2d Cir.), *cert. denied*, 543 U.S. 811.

Volkswagen Aktiengesellschaft v. Church (1969), 411 F.2d 350 (9th Cir).

Volkswagen Aktiengesellschaft v. Uptown Motors (1995), 1995 U.S. Dist. LEXIS 13869 (S.D.N.Y.).

Volvo Trademark Holding AB v. Volvospares.com (2010), 703 F. Supp. 2d 563 (E.D. Va).

Volvo Trucks North America, Inc. v. Reeder-Simco GMC, Inc. (2006), 126 S. Ct. 860.

Waits v. Frito-Lay, Inc. (1992), 978 F.2d 1093 (9th Cir.).

Wakefern Food Corp., In re (1984), 222 U.S.P.Q. 76 (T.T.A.B. 1984).

Wall v. Rolls Royce of America, Inc. (1925), 4 F.2d 333 (3d Cir.).

Wallace v. IBM (2006), 467 F.3d 1104 (7th Cir.).

Wallace International Silversmiths, Inc. v. Godinger Silver Art Co., Inc. (1990), 916 F.2d 76 (2d Cir.), *cert. denied*, 499 U.S. 976 (1991).

Wal-Mart Stores, Inc. v. Samara Brothers, Inc. (2000), 529 U.S. 205.

Wal-Mart Stores, Inc. (1994), NARB Report #77 (April 20).

Wal-Mart v. American Drugs, et al. (1995), Supreme Court of Arkansas, No. E–92–1158, Antitrust & Trade Regulation Reporter, 68(Jan. 26), 109–119.

Warner v. Searle & Hereth Co. (1903), 191 U.S. 195.

Warner-Lambert Co. v. Breathasure, Inc. (2000), 204 F.3d 87 (3d Cir.).

Warner-Lambert Co. v. FTC (1977), 562 F.2d 749 (D.C. Cir.), *cert denied*, 435 U.S. 950 (1978).

Warner-Lambert Co. v. McCrory's Corp. (1989), 718 F. Supp. 389 (D.N.J.).

WCVB-TV v. Boston Athletic Association (1991), 926 F.2d 42 (1st Cir.).

Weight Watchers Int'l, Inc. v. Stouffer Corp. (1990), 744 F.Supp. 1259 (S.D.N.Y.).

Wells Fargo & Co. v. WhenU.com (2003), 2003 U.S. Dist. LEXIS 20756 (E.D. Mich.).

Wendt v. Host Int'l, Inc. (1999), 197 F.3d 1284 (9th Cir.).

Wendy's Int'l Inc. v. Big Bite Inc. (1983), 576 F. Supp. 816 (E.D. Ohio).

Westward Coach Mfg. Co. v. Ford Motor Co. (1968), 388 F.2d 627 (7th Cir.), *cert. denied*, 392 U.S. 927.

White v. Samsung Electronics of America (1992), 971 F.2d 1395 (9th Cir.), *rehearing en banc denied*, 989 F.2d 1512, *cert. denied*, 508 U.S. 951 (1993).

William R. Warner & Co. v. Eli Lilly & Co. (1924), 265 U.S. 526.

Winn-Dixie Stores, Inc. (1996), Report of NARB Panel #90 (Sept. 26).

Wonder Labs, Inc. v. Proctor & Gamble Co. (1990), 728 F. Supp. 1058 (S.D.N.Y.).

Wood v. Lady Duff-Gordon (1917), 118 N.E. 214.

World Wrestling Federation Entertainment, Inc. v. Big Dog Holdings, Inc. (2003), 280 F. Supp. 2d 413 (W.D. Pa.).

Yale Electric Corp. v. Robertson (1928), 26 F.2d 972 (2d Cir.).

Yankee Candle Company, Inc. v. Bridgewater Candle Company, LLC (2001), 259 F.3d 25 (1st Cir.).

Yellow Cab Co. of Sacramento v. Yellow Cab Co. of Elk Grove (2003), 266 F. Supp. 2d 1199 (E.D. Cal.).

YouGottaEat, Inc. v. Checkers Drive-In Restaurants, Inc. (2003), 81 Fed. Appx. 392 (2d Cir.).

Zacchini v. Scripps-Howard Broadcasting Co. (1977), 433 U.S. 562.

Zatarain's Inc. v. Oak Grove Smokehouse, Inc. (1983), 698 F.2d 786 (5th Cir. 1983).

Zeran v. America Online (1997), 129 F.3d 327 (4th Cir.).

Index